IN AND AGAINST DEVELOPMENT
VOLUME 2

Critical Reconstructions of Political Economy, Volume 6

Studies in Critical Social Sciences Book Series

Haymarket Books is proud to be working with Brill Academic Publishers (www.brill.nl) to republish the *Studies in Critical Social Sciences* book series in paperback editions. This peer-reviewed book series offers insights into our current reality by exploring the content and consequences of power relationships under capitalism, and by considering the spaces of opposition and resistance to these changes that have been defining our new age. Our full catalog of *SCSS* volumes can be viewed at https://www.haymarketbooks .org/series_collections/4-studies-in-critical-social-sciences.

IN AND AGAINST DEVELOPMENT

VOLUME 2

The World Bank behind the Looking Glass

CRITICAL RECONSTRUCTIONS OF POLITICAL ECONOMY
VOLUME 6

BEN FINE

Haymarket Books
Chicago, IL

First published in 2025 by Brill Academic Publishers, The Netherlands
© 2025 Koninklijke Brill NV, Leiden, The Netherlands

Published in paperback in 2026 by
Haymarket Books
P.O. Box 180165
Chicago, IL 60618
773-583-7884
www.haymarketbooks.org

ISBN: 979-8-88890-790-0

Distributed to the trade in the US through Consortium Book Sales and
Distribution (www.cbsd.com) and internationally through Ingram Publisher
Services International (www.ingramcontent.com).

This book was published with the generous support of Lannan Foundation,
Wallace Action Fund, and the Marguerite Casey Foundation.

Special discounts are available for bulk purchases by organizations and
institutions. Please call 773-583-7884 or email info@haymarketbooks.org for more
information.

Cover design by Jamie Kerry and Ragina Johnson.

Printed in the United States.

Library of Congress Cataloging-in-Publication data is available.

Contents

Preface

This is the second of two Volumes on development economics (and studies) and the sixth in the Series on the *Critical Reconstructions of Political Economy*. The previous Volume was primarily devoted to critically interpreting what has happened to development economics in terms of economics imperialism, alongside the offering of alternatives from political economy whilst drawing upon what were traditional approaches to development before its capture by contemporary mainstream economics. This Volume focuses more specifically upon the major role of the World Bank, as Knowledge Bank, in reflecting and leading the charge in these changes. It also offers analytical and policy alternatives. As most will appreciate, the book's subtitle references Alice in Wonderland, something I first deployed critically in entering the world of social capital (Fine, 2008 and 2010b) – it's a dream that is not and cannot come true. Across its scholarship, ideology and policy in practice, the World Bank creates a world vision that surely leads us to imagine how they access their magic mushrooms. I hope to have provided some sort of answer in terms of the fantastic connections to the material and intellectual terrains involved, and traverse the highs (leave most everything to the market) and lows (TINA) of developmental optimism and pessimism.

Previous prefaces have laid out the rationale for this series and what it has involved. Suffice it here, once more, to thank co-authors and all others who have positively contributed to my endeavours. But one new point, prevailing across all Volumes, that I have previously taken to be understood by readers without needed to be commented upon. Occasionally, I do supplement original texts with an extra reference or footnote (over and above amending by using a different version than the one published and correcting errors or improving the text for meaning however fully). That I have done so should be obvious enough in context, not least, as is usually the case, as what is involved is reference to events or other publications that occur after the published piece itself. This is at most token assistance to the reader with fuller retrospectives confined to Preambles and introductory Chapters.

Locating Development Economics

My engagement, through more or less formal invitation from the ANC from the mid-1980s, with economic policymaking for a post-apartheid South Africa, and my subsequent move to SOAS in 1992, catapulted me into the world of development. The results of my scholarly endeavours for South Africa will primarily be covered in a subsequent Volume (or Volumes considering how the first intended volume in the series became three, and the one on development has become two). Inevitably, in the worlds of research, teaching and policy (and their intersections), I came up against the World Bank (WB, and, to a lesser extent, the International Monetary Fund, IMF, as well as the two together, see below). At the time, the Washington Consensus was in full flow and the Post-Washington Consensus was not yet on the horizon. Even so the lingering influence of Keynesianism/modernisation/welfarism and the old/ classical development economics (and, correspondingly, what I term the Pre-Washington Consensus) remained significant, alongside a wide range of political economies of development for which dependency, and combined and uneven (under)development were prominent – amongst proponents and critics alike.

As a result, in the policy arena, as far as microeconomic aspects involved, it seemed to suffice to draw upon longstanding arguments in favour of interventionism and to set these against the hopelessly inadequate WB/IMF theoretical and empirical arguments for privatisation and free trade, quite apart from the other elements of the Washington Consensus. Privatisation is addressed in Chapter 2, and trade in Chapters 5 and 6 of the previous Volume (Fine, 2025a). It might be expected that the macroeconomics of development could be handled in much the same way, counterposing Keynesianism favourably to monetarism. But I had long been wary of the distinction between micro and macro (when and how does the one become the other without descending into some sort of General Equilibrium) and, especially, of extrapolating the macro theory, inspired however appropriately by the conditions of developed countries, to the entirely different contexts of developing countries.[1] So, in major part

---

1   I was rudely reminded of this at a conference in Ouagadougou, organised jointly by ECOWAS and the WB, and to which I was issued an invitation to speak as an act of dissent, and at which one after another of recently WB funded and trained African PhDs offered a paper each on the non-accelerating rate of inflation of unemployment (NAIRU) for their home countries,

motivated by teaching purposes (macro in development context at SOAS), I decided to explore the WB/IMF macro theory in fine detail, especially around the structural adjustment and stabilisation policies associated with them.[2]

The results are stunning in and of themselves and, equally, for not having been brought out by others, despite a very powerful and successful set of empirical critiques of Washington Consensus policies on the basis of their failed performance and in harming those already impoverished by lack of development. Initially, stabilisation was based upon the so-called Polak model, something that reigned sufficiently long that it could celebrate its fortieth anniversary (Polak, 1998). What I showed is that the simple form of the model could be solved for its equilibrium. I came to the inescapable conclusion (it's in the simple algebra, stupid) that an economy settles on, or moves around, an equilibrium determined by how much it needed to pay for imports – end of story.[3]

For me, this raised a series of issues. First, what has equilibrium got to do with development, irrespective of how well or badly it is modelled? Development is about at the very least changing from one equilibrium to another or, at a deeper level, changing the supposed equilibrium faster than you move towards it. Or, at the deepest level, acknowledging development is not about equilibrium at all and should not be conceived as such – it is about fundamental, even revolutionary, economic and social change.

Second, given this (a big ask), why are the ability to pay for imports and propensity to import taken as given rather than taken as the problems to be addressed through import substitution, export promotion, tariffs, targeting domestic production for domestic needs, etc. In other words, on its own terms, development should be about targeting the exogenously fixed parameters in the model, not accepting them as determining an equilibrium that precludes development.

Third, why was there this (implicit) focus on the ability to pay for imports. The parenthesis is appropriate. In any case, and especially in the wake of my

---

based on the data alone and without any reference to the nature of their economies (usually single-product export-based).

2   What follows on the Polak model and its afters can be found covered across Fine (2006a) and Fine and Hailu (2003). Although drafted some years apart, a similar precis is to be found in Fine (2025c).

3   More precisely, output is given by A/m where A is money available to spend on imports, and m is propensity to import. This is a bit like a simple Keynesian multiplier only on propensity to import, as opposed to save, as dampening output (potential).

scrutiny of the Polak model, I would hammer home to my students that,[4] if you have a model, the very first thing you do is to solve it for its equilibrium. This is because it tells you what, around which with stability or instability, the model outcome is organised. It is standard procedure for any mainstream model and modeller.[5] It is even commonplace to transform variables into their deviation from equilibrium (which becomes the origin, as it were, in graphical terms) to simplify presentations. The Polak presentations simply ignored this analytical norm. Instead, they just moved the model forward a couple of periods to see what would happen in the short run. Perversely, a few periods of adjustment might not reflect all future, or long-term movements even in the right direction let alone quantitatively (algebraically speaking).

Fourth, or more a corollary of the third consideration, the purpose and focus in use of the Polak model by the IMF was twofold. On the one hand, it was purely and simply to manage short-run balance of payments crises arising out of excessive imports. On the other hand, if a little technical, the Polak model is purely a monetary model of nominal income – it does not distinguish outcomes in terms of whether there are changes in prices or goods. This meant that something was needed to 'close' the model, to distinguish output from price changes. And the way this was done was through IMF missions to the country every few years, with the designated role of assessing what output potential there might be so that policy could be geared to target this without excessive price increase and, as mentioned, balance of payments problems. In other words, the mission had complete discretion to come up with whatever outcome it chose, focusing on whatever 'real resources' it deemed to be available as well as provision of its own loans, with conditionalities attached. This confirms the previous analytical observations that the model excludes the main business – what determines output, and how do we target it to be developmental, and the concern is entirely short run and in no way developmental.

Before moving forward to consider developments with and beyond the (simple, initial) Polak model, I first dwell upon the (developing) insights that my close scrutiny of the Polak model offered me about IMF (and WB) analyses. These have tended to be confirmed, and continued to inform, my critiques of

---

4 I used to say – it was the second such – have it tattooed on your forehead, so you never forget. The first was the properties of Cobb-Douglas, just to save derivations in exams for which there would be no credit (at graduate level) just taking up space and time in answers.

5 And not just in economics but in any mathematical modelling, especially in a context of a unique equilibrium, as tended to be the case with the simple Polak models. Otherwise, in any case, the model has to focus on potential dynamics both to, and between, equilibria, and which are stable or not.

the IMF and WB to a greater or lesser extent. First, and present(ed) here in extreme form, the analysis is useless and entirely unfit for purpose (other than of whatever those are of those who are putting the analysis forward). This is not a judgement formed purely out of the criteria of myself as a mad lefty but on the basis of the mainstream economics from which the Polak model derives. Second, specifically, and as cannot be emphasised too strongly, the model does not contain within it any prospect of development. It is entirely concerned with the short run and not the long run. And all the considerations associated with development are either absent or taken as exogenous parameters. Third, and as yet unmentioned, I was astonished to find that these relatively simple and devastating criticisms had not been discovered and pronounced by any-one else, neither from the mainstream nor even heterodoxy (for which criti-cism was extensive but focused upon the impact of stabilisation in practice for good reason as will become clear). The lack of interest from the mainstream was confirmed at a later date, in light of a set of my criticisms of the later, more complex Polak-type models (see below). It was reflected in the enormous difficulty I had in getting my results published, devastating though they were and of some significance. I remember, in particular, a referee's report along the lines of, yes, the author has shown that these models are entirely inade-quate. I suggest the author instead should set about modelling with different assumptions, so reject. Fourth, then, Polak of no use for policy, with all the action elsewhere (in the missions), begging the purpose of even modelling in a different way instead. So, I was entirely correct but the point of the exercise, that this was what the IMF/WB were doing across scholarship and policy, and the relationship between the two, seemed to be entirely lost.

In other words, there seemed to be a cordon sanitaire around even main-stream criticism of the IMF/WB, an issue I take up again later in terms of the thicket of other protective devices in place, beyond the syndrome that this is so useless we have to discard it altogether and start again as if it did not exist (but it does and it is the IMF/WB). Last, though, my confrontation with the Polak model brought to light, and into question, the nature of the relationship between scholarship, such as the Polak model, and policy in practice. My con-clusion was, and remains, that they are not independent of one another but nor are they necessarily aligned. Indeed, they can even be inconsistent with one another. After all, all the policy action is in the mission assessments, and these can be manipulated to suit whatever the outcomes and impact of sta-bilisation analysis via Polak. It also became clear to me that the dissonances between scholarship and policy in practice also incorporated ideology – in case of Polak, is this monetarist or not with heavy flavours of monetarist/ neoliberal ideology within the stances adopted by the IMF/WB but with some flexibility in allowing output to vary according to the levels of imports deriving from monetary flows (rather than all going into price increases or outflows of capital). More generally, and across stabilisation and other issues, the positions of the IMF, and especially the WB, across scholarship, ideology and policy in practice can be complex, shifting, inconsistent and variable across time, place and issue (especially given the promotional activities of the IMF and WB other than through scholarship and policy leverage).

So much for the simple Polak model. In the early 1970s, it was revised, or augmented, to incorporate fuller interactions with monetary variables such as the rate of interest, demand for money other than for transactions, and international capital flows. I approached the new model with the same critical, mainstream devices as I had done for the old, with some similar conclusions. There is a short-run equilibrium, and corresponding adjustment, around a long-run equilibrium. So this is not about development and all the action is in the exogenously give parameters. Without explicitly acknowledging the long-run equilibrium, immediate short-run movements (until next mission) may give a false indication of what is going on. What also emerged is that the new analysis was none other than the classic Keynesian IS/LM/BP model. In other words, fit development into the standard model applied to developed countries. It should be added that capital flows, rather than trade balance, had become increasingly acknowledged as sources of instability (alongside capacity to pay for imports), so these needed to be incorporated. This suggests the pace of change and changing content of the scholarship are less responsive, if at all, to analytical inadequacies if these are even recognised or acknowledged, than to the contingencies of the moment.

By the late 1980s, the approach had moved forward again, albeit at a snail's pace. The rationale was to incorporate growth (a token acknowledgement of development) in what was termed the marriage model. The marriage involved three overlapping elements: it combined what had been previously separate models of the WB and the IMF; the WB model had been 'real' without money or prices, and the long run without the short run, whereas the IMF was essentially the other way around in both respects, so bringing the two together offered model closure; more seriously, it reflected that the WB and the IMF had to get their policy worlds together and coordinate with one another rather than offering funds, or not, for policy and for consistent purposes.

I took the marriage model to pieces. It is unimaginably awful and, correspondingly, unfit for purpose. As constructed technically, it did not even allow for growth in the long term – once again solving the model for its equilibrium properties was overlooked. This was because world demand for exports was not allowed to increase over time. As a result, an export-dependent economy was constrained by demand for its products unless it progressively reduced its prices to zero. Strangely, some growth was allowed through the allocation of exogenously given productivity increase to the domestic economy.[6] However, this was a lump sum per period with a relative decline to zero contribution to growth over time with growth itself. As before, alongside almost every other assumption made, whether by accident or by design, the potential for growth was whittled away over (model) time. Nor was this noticed since the same procedure as before was adopted of running the model for a few periods rather than solving for the long run, (asymptotically) zero growth outcome.

The marriage model was, then, based on ridiculous assumptions, as if a wedding ceremony could foresee the future of a marriage. What I did do is to correct the model so that it could at least generate steady state growth, as is standard mainstream practice. Basically, you could grow if everything always remained in the same proportions, with international balance across all variables or if a country's growing balance of trade deficit (surplus) was compensated for by the interest accrued (paid) on the ownership of a growing stock of foreign capital (debt). Neither of these can be considered realistic. In addition, even though it became complicated algebraically, I managed to unravel the stability properties of the model. Essentially, any equilibrium was extremely unstable (a saddle point) suggesting the need for intervention to prevent volatility. So, why not add in further interventions for targeting development itself – where does adjustment to equilibrium end (no development) and adjustment of equilibrium (development) begin.

But this was beginning to push the analysis beyond parody, although Polak himself disowned the marriage model on the reasonable grounds that his own should have remained a bachelor, only suitable for analyses involving short-run adjustment – begging the question, already raised, of what then did it have to do with development. Be that as it may, the marriage came and went, possibly having contributed to the purpose of integrating WB and IMF analyses in impoverished analysis, inevitably removed from policy practice (mission). With the passage of another decade, and entry into the new millennium, the WB/IMF took on poverty and development with Poverty Reduction Strategy Papers (PRSPs), with a fanfare around country ownership of the modelling. The first basic model was truly remarkable for having a single labour market and full employment – greater poverty derived from shifting terms of trade to the disadvantage of consumption. Yet, the two single most important sources

---

6   More generally, the model was based on the simple Harrod-Domar growth model, first developed within the 1930s, with little or no account of subsequent theoretical developments even from the mainstream.

of poverty are unemployment and low wages each of which was precluded by the model. Oh dear.

This is as far as I got with the macro of stabilisation, after which contributions across the IMF/WB became more fragmented and topic-specific, with the aim of adjusting within countries to instability, and moving through preventing such instability to containing its contagion to other countries, not least as these issues intensified with increasing financialisation. Ultimately, immediately before the Global Financial Crisis, the general opinion across the mainstream, as voiced by Blanchard (2008) is that "The state of macro is good". As soon as joining the IMF as its Chief Economist, his view changed, Blanchard et al. (2010), pinpointing sins of omission of such startling simplicity that it beggars belief that they were confessed and perpetrators did not look for some dark place in which to hide themselves – we took insufficient account of fiscal policy, targets other than inflation, policy instruments other than the rate of interest, and considered that finance was merely a microeconomic matter, and our corresponding policy tools guaranteed continuing stability, assigning crises to the dustbin of history. Unlike Liz Truss, whose length of tenure as British Prime Minister has been compared to the shelf-life of a lettuce in light of her disastrous policies and the economic rationale for them, the IMF and the WB seem to get away with it indefinitely. Confess and move on or, more exactly, more of the same, differently presented and/or tweaked for circumstances.[7]

Even by the time of the marriage model, around the turn of the millennium, other things were already going on in my confrontation with the WB in both scale and scope. First and foremost was the shift from the Washington to the Post-Washington Consensus, pioneered in the late nineties by Joe Stiglitz, Chief Economist at the WB. At the time, it was perceived as a major, even revolutionary change at and from the WB, with state interventionism not rejected but open to be adopted on a piecemeal basis, and a much more even-handed response to stabilisation in terms of sustaining demand as opposed to imposing austerity. As chance would have it, I had already offered a much broader critical take on Stiglitz's market imperfection approach to economics, saw it as part and parcel of the mainstream in almost every respect other than that markets may not work perfectly, but conceded, and even promoted, the view that it was revolutionary. This was less as a result of its shift in economic analysis from perfectly to imperfectly working markets and more as a consequence of its implications for extending economic analysis from the economic to the

---

7 Most tellingly, I would argue that the much-heralded revolution in thinking, with the contemplation of introducing capital controls in principle (very little practice), had much more to do with fears of financial contagion than dramatic change in outlook.

social sciences and its subject matter more generally. In other words, the colonisation by economics of the other social sciences and of the non-economic, or, as I termed it, economics imperialism, was on a roll. And, with Stiglitz at the WB, it was inevitable that economics imperialism would apply to development with the WB taking a leading role.

I first pointed to economics imperialism as a revolution within and from mainstream economics in Fine (1997b); its first application to development, targeting Stiglitz, came soon after (Fine, 1999a). Subsequent contributions on economics imperialism are covered in the first three Volumes of this Series, with the fifth heavily featuring development economics/studies as economics imperialism. Further, my obsessive critical attention to social capital from the mid-1990s onwards added a new dimension to my confrontations with the WB (see Fine 2001, 2010b and, most recently, 2023). It became heavily adopted and promoted by the WB from the late 1990s in ways that confirmed, reflected and promoted hypotheses around economics imperialism, its relationship to development and the nature of WB economics.

As already indicated, these issues in relation to social capital are covered in great detail elsewhere. Here I will confine myself to the less substantive academic aspects of developments around social capital at the WB to reveal the nature of its scholarship. Soon, after my assault upon social capital at the WB, I received a sympathetic email from a relatively high level researcher informing me that three things would happen: my criticisms would never be addressed; I would be asked to go easy as the WB was changing and those behind the changes needed support not criticism; and I would be offered a job in order to internalise dissent.

Primarily, these forecasts were observed in the breach. I was never offered a job. But my criticisms were answered, on the basis of needing to promote change internally, if only in retrospect after the WB was abandoning social capital with its job having been claimed to have been done. Basically, I was told that all of my criticisms were valid but social capital had been strategically deployed to civilise the hegemonic and numerically dominant economists within the WB into taking the social and the social sciences seriously. And this project had proved entirely successful. In other words, I inhabited some ivory tower of academic purity whereas there was a World (Bank) out (or in) there needing to be changed by whatever means available, even intellectual dishonesty.[8]

---

8 See previous references for coverage of my post-diluvian debate with the WB social capitalists and, most recently, Bebbington and Foo (2024), for one of my protagonist's lingering affection for social capital.

Unsurprisingly, I beg to differ, not only in retrospect but as expressed at the time that these machinations were being implemented. Far from civilising WB economists, social capital offered them the option of reducing the social to the economic and a conduit for them to do the same for whatever other social variable they cared to incorporate. Further, whilst the economists needed civilising in relation to their relations with the social sciences and the social, they needed even more to be civilised in relation to their economics. Indeed, whilst Stiglitz's tenure at the WB as Chief Economist allowed social capital to prosper, once he sought to turn his market imperfections economics into policy practice, he was shown the door, forced to resign. Meanwhile, in the policy arena, WB support to adjusting countries was rapidly shifting from budgetary support to support for the private sector wing of the WB for the purposes of promoting private as opposed to state provision. On all of this, our civilising, if strategising, angels were simply silent.

Taken together, these developments in, and contributions from, my own thinking heavily reinforced the previously observed take on the WB as inconsistently combining scholarship, ideology and policy in practice although this does not mean they are disconnected from one another. The shifting position on privatisation offered another example – once all the easy to privatise had been achieved, poor results were beginning to emerge with corresponding resistances, and state funding for private sector to provide offered a further option, with a pecking order for what should be privatised with energy and telecoms at the top, water at the bottom and transport somewhere in between (Bayliss and Fine, eds, 2008). Situated at SOAS I also took a leading role with others in putting forward collective critiques of WB scholarship and policy-making across whatever topics that critics could be persuaded to cover in light of their expertise. It began with the Post-Washington Consensus as such (Fine et al. eds, 2001). The whole exercise though was repeated almost a decade later with (Bayliss et al. eds, 2011). This volume was prompted by the appearance of the Deaton Report (Deaton et al. 2006) commissioned by the WB itself. It had offered a generally devastating critique of World Bank research for its low quality, for its lack of engagement with non-WB research, and for being self-serving of WB postures (as well as for the careers of researchers who supported them).

The assessments from the Deaton Report were all the more telling for remaining confined to mainstream framings and for tempering criticism in order to nudge some change.[9] Our volume took Deaton as critical point of departure

---

9   I was acquainted with Angus Deaton, subsequently a Nobel Prize Winner, because I had commented extensively on his joint authored, classic econometrics text (Deaton and Muellbauer 1980), John Muellbauer having been a colleague at Birkbeck in the 1970s/1980s. In a personal

both in introducing alternatives from political economy and situating WB research/scholarship in the broader context of WB ideology and policymaking as well what was happening in the global economy alongside developments within and across development economics and studies more generally.

Unfortunately, the Deaton Report and, more tellingly, its recommendations for improving WB research have been more observed in the breach, even neglect as far as if the Report had never been commissioned. This is itself par for the course as the WB's (and the IMF's) own internal auditing departments are often highly critical of operations but are simply ignored as at most a minor and temporary inconvenience. They seem to serve the function of legitimising the organisations simply because they do exist and irrespective of what they do or say if no doubt the WB's own preference is for them to report favourably on operations, whether in scholarly or policy domains.

Criticism from without is another matter. In my continuing work, with others, the goal has always been to situate the scholarship of the WB in the broader context of its shifting relationships to ideology, policy and what is happening in the world. Although not entirely a bad starting point, the idea that the WB is simply an instrument of US imperialism, justifying and purveying neoliberal policies has only limited, and even, misleading purchase. Now, in retrospect, it is possible to offer a more nuanced picture of the evolving nature of WB research, and its contemporary features, drawing upon the analysis already presented in the previous Volume (number 5 in the Series) on development economics/studies more generally.

There I located development economics/studies in the context of economics imperialism. As a result, four phases of development economics disciplines were identified in one-to-one correspondence to those of economics imperialism. For the latter these are: the phase prior to the emergence of economics imperialism; the old economics imperialism drawing upon the social as if perfectly working markets (associated most closely with Gary Becker); the new economics imperialism and the social as reaction to market imperfections (with leading light, Joe Stiglitz, at least for the economics); and the newer economics imperialism of today in which economists feel free to suspend their traditional analyses (around supply and demand, individual optimisation, etc),

---

communication, Deaton confirmed that criticism within his Report had been muted from his own perspective in the vain attempt to be more effective with the WB paymasters. See also Deaton (2009b). He has since moved onto other (bigger and better) issues such as critique of RCT (Deaton and Cartwright, 2018; and Bédécarrats et al. eds, 2020 more generally) and seeking to pinpoint and explain the unprecedented decline in longevity of (white, working class) Americans not least due to drug dependence (Case and Deaton, 2020).

if not their traditional mathematical and statistical methods, and incorporate any social variable that takes their fancy. As indicated, there are corresponding phases for development economics, even if arriving on the scene with greater or lesser lag: modernisation and what is now known as the classic or old development economics; the new development economics in tune with Becker's old economics imperialism (and pioneered, most notably, by Anne Krueger at the WB); what I call the newer development economics, linked through Stiglitz to the Post-Washington Consensus; and the mish mash of what I now term the newest development economics in which it is free to roam over whatever it likes with a corresponding mish mash of conceptualisations even if grounded in or around mainstream economics (with the WB's temporary but energetic promotion of social capital a leading example).[10]

As is already apparent, the position of the WB in these developments around economics imperialism takes a leap forward with the Washington Consensus. It has the effect of posing development in terms of the relative role of state and market. With the Post-Washington Consensus, and beyond, the WB has arguably strengthened its powers over agenda setting not least because of the projection of itself as the Knowledge Bank that it has established through its research (including weight of own personnel and commissioned work), publications, active engagement with research and educational funding, revolving doors between itself and academia, consultancies, and targeting of mainstream journals and so on.[11] The Post-Washington Consensus sees development in terms of correcting market imperfections and creating the institutions for doing so, and to harmonise the workings of state and market (and civil society) rather than trading them off against one another. At the same time, the scope of what the WB covers has increased prodigiously not so much infringing upon the traditional terrains of development studies but also incorporating them into its agenda setting, with much understandable dissent from

---

10   For what appears to be a similar periodisation on the basis of Women in Development (WID) (and tensions across scholarship, ideology and policy in practice), for which a close scrutiny of the resonances with economics imperialism might be rewarding, see Bazbauers and Madkour (2024, p. 181), "Unsurprisingly, the evidence reveals that gender-focused investments are not a core business for the MDBs, despite a considerable expansion in gender policies and strategies throughout the 2000s and 2010s, with what little commitments approved emerging primarily in the retroliberal WID era. While this does constitute a degree of progress, the concern here is that the greatest expansion in gender-focused interventions has been during a period of considerable conceptual narrowing".

11   For the provision of education itself (as opposed to within economics alone), see Menashy and Read (2016) for how the WB exercises dominance by neoclassical economists from the North in making education policy discourse around private provision.

within the constituent discipline(s) in view of its differences with mainstream economics in methodologies, methods, theories and conceptualisations.

There is, then, much that is welcome from across development studies in its critique of the various phases of economics imperialism and its application to development economics/studies, not least as the political economy of development sustains a hold across the discipline. However, despite this, and without having examined it in detail myself other than casually, the dull weight of the WB's presence and the resources it commands with it, almost inevitably not only increasingly sets the agenda of development studies but shifts it towards the positions of the WB with dissent even serving to legitimise.[12] One reason for this, already highlighted through the account of stabilisation above, is that the weaknesses of WB research are so wide and deep that it discourages serious scholars even to engage – something I experienced in my campaign against social capital.[13] There is also the less honourable motive of keeping your options open for WB scholarships, grants, consultancies and employment.

But across my earlier Volumes on economics imperialism, I also pinpoint what I term a watershed in the prominence of economics imperialism across scholarship. With the old economics imperialism, associated with neoliberalism in its own first phase of shock therapy and leave everything to the market, its proponents were absolutely open and proud around what they were doing – reducing social science to their own reduced version of economics. As a result, there was a corresponding critical reaction against them from both (market imperfection and Keynesian as opposed to monetarist) economists and social scientists. With, however, the emergence of the new economics imperialism, with its own critique of the old, explicit reference to economics

---

12　For a post-pandemic assessment, for example, see Wiegratz et al. (2023), for whom, in light of the aid and research industry, "In the UK, with the increased marketization of higher education since the 1990s, academic departments have been set in competition with one another to access sources of revenue. This is the case in terms of publications, reputation, students, research and, increasingly, consultancy grants. The increased emphasis on grants with a global outlook has put UK-based development studies departments and centres in an advantageous position in comparison to other disciplines. Traditionally home to interdisciplinary scholars committed to globally oriented research, development studies departments have been well placed to compete for and secure grants funded by the UK government and Foreign, Commonwealth and Development Office, such as the Global Challenges Research Fund. Thus, development studies departments – though often working closely with one another – are incentivized to present themselves as being ahead of the curve or leading the latest academic trend".

13　I would ask leading figures who readily agreed with me to speak out but they tended to respond it was too stupid and insufficiently interesting to engage their attention and energies.

imperialism has eroded even as its incidence has expanded prodigiously. When it is acknowledged, it tends to be along the lines of economics is being reformed by incorporating ideas from the social sciences (oh so familiar to me from the earlier discussion of social capital at the WB).

In short, the critique of economics imperialism and its application to development has been extensive from positions adopted from within political economy and development studies. I suspect this has had the effect of reducing the depth of impact of these criticisms and the momentum with which they are engaged across a wider scope of analyses. Look, you are pointing to the same thing in different contexts without realising it. Let's fit the pieces together.

And context is a lot if not everything. As previously emphasised, WB scholarship dovetails with its ideology and its policy in practice (and, on occasion, I put the three together with value added as world vision), and these have a complex and shifting relationship across one another by time, place and issue. Each is also informed by developments within contemporary capitalism for which, apart from the post-war boom, three phases are identified for neoliberalism; shock therapy, Third Wayism and the overt interventionism across state, finance and industry as currently. These three phases of neoliberalism correspond to the new, newer and newest development economics (and old, new and newer economics imperialism, respectively). Underpinning them all is how globalisation, neoliberalisation and financialisation are engaged in economic and social restructuring within and across countries.

This is a drastic summary of extensive analyses to be found in the Chapters that follow, the previous Volume, and a multitude of other publications on the nature of neoliberalism and how it is (mis)understood (Fine et al. 2016a; Bayliss et al. 2024). This Volume begins with five chapters that are explicitly addressed at criticism of WB interventions. Chapter 2 concerns WB support for private capital (or, more exactly, making economies favourable for it), taking in privatisation along the way. Chapter 3 is an explicit confrontation at an early stage with the new economics imperialism and the newer development economics, locating them in relation to both social capital and (its relationship to) the Post-Washington Consensus. Chapters 4 and 5 offer critical responses to two of the WB's flagship World Development Reports, one on the new economic geography, the other on behavioural economics and 'nudge'. Each is framed by reference to economics imperialism but the later one necessarily gets a handle on the newest development economics and the "suspension" of its core principles. Chapter 6 takes the opportunity to dissect Justin Lin's attempts, as a post-Stiglitz WB Chief Economist, to launch a new structural economics (and corresponding framework for industrial policy) which proves to be as riddled with contradictions as it is ambitious in academic and policy persuasion (each of which failed miserably). Lin's, like so much of WB scholarship after serving purpose, is dust-binned with Stiglitz the exception that proves the rule as a result of having become a public intellectual but whose impact in practice and in policy remains strikingly limited (Fridell, 2011).

The last two chapters depart from critique of the WB for a more constructive approach to putting forward alternative policy proposals. What they have in common is that each was commission by a UN organisation. Unevenly within and across such agencies is to be found considerable dissent with WB/IMF policymaking. With considerably less resources across the board than their WB/IMF rivals, and subject to political and/or funding restrictions if too effective or prominent in their endeavours, these organisations cannot command anywhere near the same level of policy leverage.[14] In a sense, this can be liberating as proposals can be put forward for polemical purposes, secure in the knowledge they will never be implemented.[15] There is a battle for ideas. Chapter 7 has a go at industrial policy (for UNCTAD) and Chapter 8 at social policy (for UNRISD). Each, as a background paper for others to deploy, is also liberated from constraints of length, allowing the subject matter covered to range over wide terrains.

In the introduction to the last Volume, I report that an edited volume on the World Bank was about to appear. I close this Chapter with a select review of its contributions for reasons that will be given within it.

Postamble: Locating the World Bank

I am very conscious that this Volume is primarily focused upon the scholarship of the World Bank, and the alternatives to it. Even so, the analysis is mindful of a broader framing around the connects or disconnects across the scholarship, ideology and policy practice of the World Bank as well as the broader material, intellectual and ideological environment in which it has operated. Hence, the setting out of the nature of neoliberalism, its three phases, as well as those of the Washington Consensus, (as such and pre, post and post-post). These sit alongside the old/classic, new, newer and newest development economics

---

14   In contributing and debating policy drafts for ECOWAS, the Economic Community of West African States, great care had to be exercised around human (women's) rights and policies to achieve them given the political sensitivities involved.

15   I had a similar experience at the Greater London Council in the mid-1980s, given its being due for abolition by Mrs. Thatcher.

(across which the World Bank has played an increasing role) corresponding to phases of economics imperialism (ex ante, old, new and newer).

As mentioned in the previous Volume on development economics (and studies) as economic imperialism (Fine, 2025a), whilst it was being prepared *The Elgar Companion to the World Bank* was about to be published to which I had contributed (Bayliss and Fine, 2024; Vetterlein and Schmidtke, eds, 2024). This has allowed me sneakily to access all the other contributions in proof and to use them to seek some degree of remedy to the one-sided focus on scholarship in this, my own, Volume on and around the WB. To a large degree, I was disappointed for two reasons. On the one hand, reasonably from its own perspective if far from prominently paraded, the Companion is primarily concerned with the World Bank as an international organisation, with corresponding framings around international organisation theory and its concerns. Good, bad or indifferent, the latter is only of passing interest to me especially given, on the other hand, that it leads in general to much more consideration of how things are done as opposed to the substance of what is done and, in particular, with a correspondingly extremely limited coverage of the economics and policies in practice of the World Bank.[16]

At least, we do learn something of the Bank's history, its origins in reconstruction of the developed economies after the second world war, the movement towards addressing developing countries by the 1970s, and the Bank's initial emphasis upon infrastructure and the ethos of being a bank, with bankers not economists to the fore. Whilst there are occasional (references to) case studies to make particular points, coverage of the continuing business of the Bank is notably thin.[17] Nonetheless, consulting the Companion proved a worthwhile exercise although I am mindful that, by reading its contributions through my own framing (briefly summarised above), I inevitably find them as (implicitly) confirming and/or conforming to my approach or simply wrong or irrelevant. Some simple illustrative examples are:

> The tensions across scholarship, ideology and policy in practice, how Weaver (2024, p. 107) seeks, "to explain two enduring puzzles: the underlying causes of the persistent 'disconnect' between the talk and action of the World Bank and the reasons why Bank hypocrisy is so persistent and hard to uproot, even after it is revealed and threatens organizational

---

16   Apart from our own contribution, the major exception is Selwyn and Leyden (2024) which addresses labour markets in light of Global Value Chains.

17   For an outstanding overview of the Bank's policies and discourses, see Toussaint (2023) and consult the ongoing Bretton Woods Project, https://www.brettonwoodsproject.org.

support and external legitimacy". This complements reference to "'strategic ignorance' and 'organized hypocrisy' – to better understand the workings of US hegemony in the Bank", Eitinger and Wade (2024, p. 118);

The expanding domains of the Bank across scholarship, ideology and policy in practice, not least with mission creep or is that better described as mission gallop, engaging ever more with private finance, SDGs, and the environment, health and gender to the fore as global public goods (Heldt and Dörfler, 2024), in part to compete and cooperate with newly emerging multilateral development banks, not least with Chinese support

RUDYAK, 2024; and ZACCARIA, 2024

And the newer economics imperialism as newest development economics, not only through the USA as 'principal agent' (see below) but also the environment as in headings, "REVISING MARKET INCENTIVES TO INTERNALIZE ENVIRONMENTAL EXTERNALITIES", and "FACILITATING COOPERATION IN THE MANAGEMENT OF GLOBAL PUBLIC GOODS" (Schonberger, p. 376 and p. 377, respectively) although my favourite is the critical description of WB housing as "mortgaging development"

CLEGG, 2024

A good starting point for what the World Bank does, and why, is the contribution from a mainstream economist who has the nerve and necessity to state baldly what everyone else, with a modicum of critical edge, is thinking (alongside legions of activists and representatives of the South, governmental or otherwise). For Stone (2024, pp. 81/82), in deploying a principal-agent model with a game to be played between the various players:

A wide range of actors are available to potentially influence the World Bank. This brief review of the recent empirical literature suggests that the strongest evidence supports the influence of two competing principals, the US president and the US Congress. While there is some evidence of influence by other countries, especially developed countries, but also developing countries that appoint EDs [Executive Directors], this evidence is much weaker and less systematic than evidence of US influence. No other country figures as prominently as the United States, and the only legislative body that appears to influence World Bank policy is the US Congress. There is evidence that NGOs have influenced major reform initiatives and that MNCs lobby effectively for preferential treatment, but the channels for these forms of influence run through the US Congress.

Furthermore, the fundamental incentive for the US executive to meddle in World Bank lending appears to arise through conflict with Congress, because this meddling occurs when power is divided in Washington so that the president faces a Congress controlled by the opposing party.

So, the main message is the US rules OK, and there are not many that can dis-agree with that given how the Bank is set up (in terms of US control through effective veto, financial contributions and voting rights, which remain contro-versial and unresolved).[18]

Unresolved is the operative word when it comes to the World Bank; it has problems that will not go away.[19] One is the absence of human rights and eth-ics (Hitchcock, 2024; and McNeill, 2024). As Sarfaty (2024, p. 383) puts it:

Established on 1 July 1944, the World Bank has become the largest lender to developing countries, lending over $20 billion per year. Its mission is poverty reduction, which it primarily carries out through its develop-ment lending. While the institution has adopted a number of social and environmental policies and works on issues as diverse as judicial reform, health, and infrastructure, it has not adopted any overarching opera-tional policy on human rights.

This is indicative of an inability to justify what it does ethically and in terms of its mission.

Then, there is accountability – to whom and how or, more exactly, how to avoid. As Gasbarri (2024, p. 63) puts it:

On the one hand, law serves the purposes of the organization by main-taining the fiction of a functional organization not involved with politics,

---

18   I do recall a conference on the World Bank, at which I presented a paper on social capital (Fine, 2002c), held at Northwestern University. There were three well-dressed attendees sitting together, apart from everyone else, and whom no one knew. Conspiracies reigned until it was found that they were acting on behalf of the US Office of Management and Budget, keen to gather criticisms of the World Bank in assessing whether funds were being wisely spent. Note that many of the points made in this postamble are well illus-trated by my work on social capital (Fine, 2001, 2010b and, most recently, 2023).

19   But in a way that must be the envy of other international organisations, as Gasbarri (2024, pp. 70/71) observes, "The evolution of the role of the World Bank from postwar recon-struction to an agent of globalization stands out among international organizations suf-fering from lack of funding and backlashes against multilateralism", with all of their issues of politics, ethics, human rights and accountability.

and, on the other hand, it provides the rationale for developing competences and for limiting accountability.

Indeed, p. 71:

> The establishment of the institutional panel [as late as 1993] and the enjoyment of immunities at the domestic level led to the internalization of accountability mechanisms, setting up internal standards in the absence of an external control over the activity of the organization.

And, from the penultimate quote, there is reference to the irresolvable contradiction between what the World Bank does and its oft-referenced requirement to be apolitical. As Gasbarri (2024, p. 70) neatly puts it, "Since its foundation, the World Bank profited from an approach to law and legal studies as a means to transform political decisions into [the false appearance of] technical issues". And, as Bhargava (2024, p. 362) reports:[20]

> Politics permeates the ecosystem of corruption and governance ... Facing this reality, the World Bank managers have to tread very carefully and be always cognizant of the fact that the World Bank charter prevents it from political considerations and activities in its work. It was almost 45 years after its founding that the Bank found a legally acceptable framework to address governance issues in its work and another five years to begin addressing corruption issues.

But, arguably, far more significant in this regard has been the predominance of economists and an economics that believes in the illusion of the possibility of development policy without politics, a discipline better equipped to pursue technicism – no wonder Hitchcock (2024, p. 52) reports that:

> The majority of employees in the Bank however are economists, development economists and policy analysts, some 12,500 of the 18,046 current World Bank employees ... (World Bank August 2022 data). At their height in year 1996, World Bank staff anthropologists numbered 250.

---

20   Bear in mind that Chapters 28–31 of *The Companion* are authored by World Bank "practitioners", Guggenheim, Plummer, Bhargava and Schonberger (see above on latter).

It is a moot point whether the presence of those from other disciplines, or even more rounded economists, plays more of a role in easing the delusion of absence of politics in delivering predetermined policies as opposed to allowing some, select participation in formulating them.

Squaring the circles around the irresolvable involves a number of processes. In terms of 'participation', the select review of Fox (2024, p. 138) suggests "Over the longer term, their most ambitious power-shifting elements were either reversed (Mexico, Brazil, Ecuador), watered down (Indonesia) or contained (Colombia)". Do partnerships allow for dissent or for it to be outflanked, controlled or even incorporated (Kramarz and Wilkinson, 2024). From a practitioner, we are offered all of the buzz and fuzz (Cornwall and Eade, eds, 2010) of 'civic engagement', including participation, people-centric, good governance, empowerment, poverty reduction, accountability, voice, service delivery, engagement, demand-side actors, and social contract all within a single paragraph (Plummer, 2024, p. 345):

> Although the Bank shift toward a people-centric development paradigm (Guggenheim [2024], Chapter 28 in this volume) was well underway, James Wolfensohn, during his leadership, established the institutional mandate to work directly on participation from a governance perspective. In 2000, empowerment was introduced as an element of poverty reduction; and in 2004, a focus on voice and accountability emerged as a critical aspect of service delivery. By 2007, the governance and anti-corruption strategy (Bhargava [2024], Chapter 30 in this volume) included the engagement of demand-side actors as a core principle. The leadership of Robert Zoellick and the development of the 'social contract' approach strengthened this focus on citizen participation as a critical aspect of governance in the context of the Arab Spring, bringing with it the rhetoric of 'demand for good governance'. Although these initiatives were interspersed with periods of leadership ambivalence towards citizen engagement, the Bank furthered people-centric approaches through a range of operations and expanded public sector management under a broader umbrella of governance that included citizen voice and accountability.

But the sting is soon to be found in the tail, brutally revealed behind the buzz and fuzz, p. 353, second emphasis mine:

> Substantively, in the current climate, it is critical to ensure that strategic alignment and mutual reinforcement of *other priority reforms* is given

> precedence, *such that citizen engagement efforts are synergized with immediate and urgent Bank priorities.*

Your priorities are ours as long as they are ours, with much affinity to country 'possession' of structural adjustment and stabilisation policies of the World Bank (and IMF) as long as they are what the latter would have done if they possessed without the pretences of country ownership, participation, etc.

In short, the World Bank is always in the process of promise of improvement against what are generally recognised to be dark, inner institutional constraints, or those from without whether it be the US or the forces of the global economy and order. We are far from perfect but we do the best we can – without engaging with whether whatever is achieved serves to consolidate what is not or deemed to be unachievable. This is beautifully expressed by Guggenheim (2024, pp. 340–41) as an apologetic but enthusiastic practitioner, and worth quoting at length (in justifying the Bank's community development initiatives and his own role within it for the Kecamatan Development Program, KDP):

> The 1997 East Asia crisis and the sudden fall of the Suharto government in Indonesia was an epistemological shock to senior Bank policy-makers, particularly following the appointment of a tough reformer like James Wolfensohn to the Bank's presidency. What had been a major country's development success story had suddenly turned into mass protests, accusations of Bank complicity, and genuine fears of breakup and poverty. With so much of the development infrastructure lying in ruins, KDP got a chance that it almost certainly would not have had five years previously. However, it is also important to note that nothing in KDP actually threatens the core operations of either the Bank or government. In that sense the critics are right. KDP builds small infrastructure for poor people; it does not address the problems of unequal accumulation, political capture by entrenched elites, or the ongoing and unsustainable consumption of Indonesia's natural resources. But delivering large volumes of basic infrastructure to millions of people who never had it before is nothing to sneeze at, either. The idea that all projects (and project officers) are so constrained by structure and context that there is no alternative to doing more of the same is simply not true. Getting community development accepted into the World Bank took a lot of work. It required investing in serious field analysis; molding ethnography into the vocabulary that the Bank and government can assimilate; assembling a diverse and committed project team; and building alliances across the institution. In terms of the general themes of this volume, development bureaucracies

such as the World Bank are certainly constrained by political economy, but there is more relative autonomy for individual action than is often acknowledged.

Fair enough but only justifiable if what is achieved is sustainable and builds momentum for more, something that is not ignored, pp. 341–42:

> The large number of people who worked on KDP understood from the beginning that changing the way that Indonesia approached development was a small part of a much bigger social change. Indonesia's democratic transition is still being written, and even now we do not know for sure whether it will succeed or whether the authoritarian elitism of the past will return. The social analysis that created KDP has provided a way for development to engage people not just as individual beneficiaries, but as social and political beings whose institutions, priorities, values, and voices mattered. In today's world, when trust in government, in institutions, and in democracy itself are at record lows amidst record high standards of wealth and consumption, these lessons are not just historical relics to be studied in graduate classrooms, but guides for the development ideas of the future.

But what of the development ideas of the present which the World Bank, as Knowledge Bank, studiously ignores? The issues are neatly captured by Vetterlein (2024, p. 293):

> On the one hand, we can see that the Bank has responded to reform calls. On the other hand, some of these policy changes can be interpreted as fending off responsibility claims. Initially, when development was defined as a lack of modernization, the Bank acknowledged its responsibility to provide financial resources as well as knowledge and skills and to manage development progress in the developing world. When poverty was not reduced as expected according to modernization theory, development became a matter of policy adjustment during the 1990s, that is setting the right conditions for poor people to participate in economic activities. Thus, getting out of poverty became the responsibility of each individual. When this theory with its economic modeling and policy planning also did not achieve the outcome anticipated, the notion of holistic development shifted responsibilities again. With ownership, participation and partnership, states are now part of creating their own development strategy, which in turn makes them responsible for their

own developmental outcomes. Differently put, we could observe a shift from external to internal (i.e., country) responsibility with the move to the PRSP. Finally, the latest change is twofold. On the one hand diffusing responsibility across different actors ... might lead to responsibility gaps ... in which either no responsible actor can be identified or no one feels obliged to assume responsibility. On the other hand, explaining persisting poverty with risks such as financial crises or natural catastrophes disposes of responsibility altogether, or locates it to higher forces, that the Bank, or any other actor for that matter, cannot control. Both developments might lead to ... organized irresponsibility, that is situations in which it is not possible any longer to clearly attribute responsibility to specific actors.

In short, whilst everyone has a criticism of the World Bank until its funds, partnership, blessing or employment (as staff or consultant) are in the offing, its location remains one that both reflects underlying determinants and, in major measure, helps to reproduce them. That this is a complex set of processes, involving how US interests are formed, represented and contested within the Bank, its internal machinations, and across those with which it engages across all constituencies from clients to critics, is undeniable. But, at the end of the day, whoever pays the piper calls the tune, whatever the level of social constructivism and discursive engagement. Vetterlein and Park (2024, pp. 103–104) see the virtues:

> in adding critical discourse analysis to the tool box ... (extending) the list of explanatory factors beyond the geopolitical interests of the most powerful member states to organizational variables such as design, mandate, incentive structures, and particularly also to the individual level of staff. How do staff interpret specific political challenges, where do they get their education from that influences such interpretations, and what other practices are at work ... that shapes their responses to policy problems.

Unfortunately, as far as the World Bank is concerned, the more you scratch the 'softer', discursive levers, the more you find it is the economy and the economists, stupid, who veil and pursue the hard politics, with correspondingly limited flexibility over what is done and what is said, given these principal determinants.

Beyond *Bureaucrats in Business*: A Critical Review of the World Bank Approach to Privatisation and Public Sector Reform

Postscript as Personal Preamble

Although published in 1998, the piece that follows was certainly drafted long before, and shortly after the publication in 1995 of its object of critique.[1] As a result, there is no hint of reference to economics imperialism nor of its new, market-imperfections form associated with the Post-Washington Consensus, for which my own first publications appeared in Fine (1997b and 1999a), respectively.

Nonetheless, these aspects are immanent as well as imminent. For analytically, there is heavy reliance upon what I had called the (mainstream) synthesis around privatisation that I had first raised, and criticised as an application of market imperfection economics (Fine 1990a and b). It arose out of assessment of the Thatcher privatisation programme, dubbed Britain's most successful export, and the synthesis (other than in name) itself became commonplace across university examinations with setting of questions along the lines of which is better, state or private ownership. The answer was expected to be, it does not matter. What does matter supposedly are the conditions of competition and regulation. And, policy-wise, (lack of) competition is to be dealt with by appropriate competition policy, and natural monopolies by appropriate regulation. Given all of this, it would make no difference what form ownership takes since it merely determines who receives the normal profits of the (artificially) competitive and regulated sector.

Analytically, my critique of the synthesis ran to a dozen or so points, mainly pointing to omissions. The most telling of these is that the synthesis comes to the conclusion that ownership as such does not matter (as opposed to competition and regulation) because it is based upon an approach that has no concept of each of ownership as such (other than claim to residual income) nor of the state (other than as a more or less well-intended and well-informed agent).

---

[1] It is also testimony to thirty years of collaboration with Kate Bayliss, from critique of privatisation to promoting (progressive) systems of provision, and more.

So, of necessity, with such shallow understandings of both ownership and the state, it is hardly surprising that they are rendered irrelevant.

Otherwise, as is again covered in this Chapter, the synthesis has a very narrow conception of industrial policy and the reasons for it, at the levels of the firm, the sector and the economy as a whole. This is addressed in more detail in later Chapters in this Volume. But there is a sense in which the World Bank's position, as represented in this piece and more generally at the time, is not guilty of these two omissions – of treating ownership and the state as insignificant and industrial policy in narrow terms (although the latter is so essentially). Sorry to say, this is not because it benefits from greater scholarly and analytical depth. Quite the contrary. For the World Bank, the state really does matter because it is bad and should be minimised in deference to the market. This is so whatever the state does (beyond some loosely defined minimum of guaranteeing the market as if this were or could be independent of how markets function) and, correspondingly, there is no need to define industrial policy because, whatever it is, it is bad.

In other words, the World Bank is gung ho for privatisation and had been for a decade or more. Its arguments in favour inevitably rejected the synthesis because it had to suggest that ownership does matter. But it had little, or no, analytical justification for this stance, especially against the mainstream. Accordingly, it rejected the synthesis (suggesting economists can come up with all sorts of ideas against privatisation but they should not be taken seriously) and relied both ideologically and policy-wise on promoting privatisation – just do it.

But, then, it faced a problem which its publication *Bureaucrats in Business* seeks to address. If privatisation is so great, why is it not being adopted, and with considerable enthusiasm and success? The latter is dealt with, as so often in World Bank research, by poor empirical research whose inadequacies, errors and omissions always seem to have the far from random consequence (why not errors for and against rather than always for) of supporting its propositions. In addition, a relatively new general argument is introduced in the specific context of privatisation although it also achieved heavy presence in structural adjustment and stabilisation policymaking as a whole. It is that there is nothing wrong with the policies at all in the sense that they have failed. Rather, it is that they have not been adopted, not adopted properly, or not adopted in the right circumstances and preconditions. This is to move heavily, if not completely, to the position either that the policies are unquestionable or that they are vacuous (if all the factors that prevent the policies from working were removed, they would work).

Significantly, this small step – do as we say or you will fail and if you fail you did not do what we said – had two further implications. As discussed in passing in the piece, the first is that the World Bank began to push up against the limits of its responsibilities – for the failure to implement or to create favourable conditions for implementation are taken to be, at least in part, political. So you need to change the politics to change and make successful the policies. How do you do this, or can you, without transgressing the required boundaries of not interfering in the politics of countries that are to be the recipients of aid when that aid can be made, at least implicitly, conditional on having the right (i.e. correct) politics. Indeed, it is more appropriate to see the World Bank's interventions, whether ideologically, in scholarship or in policy in practice, as profoundly political rather than being capable of being apolitical. Then, it becomes a matter of what politics and, hopefully, openness and debate over them. In short, aid and advice do not come without politics attached.

The second implication of addressing what are the conditions under which our advice is properly followed is that it opens up, alongside other initiatives, the analytical and policy arena of World Bank interventions. If its policies are to succeed, it has to have an interest in not only politics, but also institutions and, as is explicit, the so-called *Bureaucrats*. Or, put in other terms, it needs to range beyond identifying and supporting the right policies to embrace the issues of who has power and how is it implemented, and in whose interests. This differs from the first implication in extending the range and scope of the Bank's potential scholarship and ideology (and range of policy in deciding what institutions and corresponding interest groups to support). In short, there are avenues opened up for economics imperialism for the World Bank by its stance of seeking to understand the failure of its policies in terms of failure of their adoption. Given the antipathy to the state, it gave rise, for example, to the meteoric rise and promotion of social capital within the Bank as it sought non-state, civil society solutions to its implementation problems.[2]

In short, *Bureaucrats in Business* is an ideal illustration of the World Bank's appropriation and promotion of the new development economics (and, as such, the first phase of economics imperialism) albeit with its own specific features like other applications. In particular, in promoting a mix of scholarship, ideology and policy in practice (and world vision uncomfortably and inconsistently accommodating all three), it is marked by a total abandonment of (mainstream) scholarship to promote its ideological and policy nostrums.

---

2 See Fine (1999a) and on social capital at the World Bank, Fine (2001 and 2010b) and most recently, Fine (2023).

This is hardly surprising as the mainstream synthesis sought to handle market imperfections, defined in terms of absence of competition (to be addressed by competition policy) and increasing returns to scale (associated with "natural" monopolies) which market perfection economics would prefer to downplay if not overlook altogether (with a predilection to see them as being caused or worsened by the role of the state and its interventionism).

Subsequent developments, however, proved even more remarkable, as laid out in detail in Bayliss and Fine (eds) (2008) with case studies for electricity and water from Africa and references to the relevant literature. In the early noughties, the World Bank, more or less for the first time if subsequently remaining rare, admitted it had made a mistake over privatisation. It had been too ideologically committed to privatisation, and there remained a case for state ownership to continue in certain, admittedly rare, circumstances. Its analytical rationale for this change was to adopt the synthesis it had previously summarily dismissed as academic as opposed to practical and worldly. Nonetheless, a more than lingering commitment remained for privatisation, especially for those state enterprises readily open to profitable sale and operations. Indeed, a ranking for privatisation was made, topped by telecommunications, followed by energy, transport and water, in terms of priority for renewed attempts at privatisation.

What brought about this change of heart? Was it the embracing of the Post-Washington Consensus even if with some delay, and some shift in policy, as well as in scholarship and ideology, towards the synthesis? The answer is essentially no for the following reasons. First, much privatisation had already been achieved, it had experienced mixed results, with some disasters especially around water leading to renationalisations. Adopting a stance of further privatisations without alternatives might well have been resisted and given rise to the exclusion of the World Bank from policy influence. Second, and related if more important, was the policy shift within the World Bank itself, towards promoting its private sector financing wing as a more important use of aid and loans as opposed to general budgetary support. So, the private sector was to be promoted to provide public provision even if privatisation as such was not the means by which it was to be implemented. In other words, a change in circumstances and in policy is what was involved with ideology and scholarship shifting to suit rather than informing. As is apparent, this marked a shift from the new to the newer development economics, and from the first to the second phase of neoliberalism, as laid out in Chapter 1, even if with the usual inclination towards the market as opposed to the state. It also paved the way for the subsequent shift to the newest development economics and the third phase of neoliberalism, with all social and economic variables and policy issues to be placed on the agenda. In a nutshell, so well does the market work relative to the state, that, when the market fails, the state's resources (and aid and policy) should be directed at supporting the market to provide what have previously been its own preserve across economic and social provisioning.

This is already to begin to look back from where we are now as opposed to looking forward to how we got there. The glaring absence in this account is financialisation and how privatisation (and commercialisation more generally) has both been promoted and motivated by it as is readily apparent from the lead taken in developed countries let alone elsewhere. Surprisingly, or not, the nostrums around the superiority of the private sector and its imperatives have strengthened despite the extreme dysfunctions suffered by the (global) financial sector and economy more generally. I am mindful of having written long ago on the role of multinational corporations and nationalisation, with a key issue being whether they should be nationalised with or without compensation (Fine and Harris, 1985). This is no longer on the agenda and discussion of (re)nationalisation tends to be confined to those enterprises or provisioning that have overtly failed across multiple criteria of performance.

Nonetheless, privatisation hopes spring eternal, not least from those associated with the World Bank. In a retrospective, a long-time associate of the World Bank essentially looks back upon its privatisation efforts benignly (Nellis, 2021). Subject to a little more qualification than had been expressed at the time, the position adopted is pretty much as described previously with one of the most striking aspects being the claims of success in empirical term, of necessity in seizing the moments to privatise against opposition, and lessons to be learned from the positive experience of China and the negative ones from eastern Europe. What is otherwise striking is the total absence of any sort of systemic analysis (other than as context, for example in the east European shock therapy), let alone the performance of the private sector other than as comparator for the public. It is as if financialisation does not exist, that the Global Financial Crisis never happened (other than to give rise to temporary bail-outs and renationalisations), that there are no environmental crises, and privatised health provision has nothing to do with handling the pandemic. There is little or no wider discussion of industrial policy irrespective of the form taken by ownership. Last, but by no means least, there is a welcome reference to dissenting voices but these are mostly on the friendly side of fire. More significantly, in line with longstanding World Bank "scholarly" practice, works cited are heavily confined. Of the fifty or so references, ten or more are to the author's own work (enough even to make me blush), almost as many to that of the World Bank, and many of the rest spin-offs or the like from the Bank, as is the author's affiliation with the Center for Global Development, one of those 'independent' Washington research institutes. Unsurprisingly, there is no reference to the magnificent PSIRU, Public Services International Research Unit.[3]

I close on a personal note. As previously footnoted, this is the first piece jointly published with Kate Bayliss, paving the way for a longstanding and rewarding collaboration, more step by step accidental than by long-term design. We have since worked together continually, on privatisation and public sector alternatives, on the poverty of World Bank scholarship more generally, and, more recently, in developing the system of provision approach and, most recently, its application to public sector provisioning and the environment.[4] As chance would have it, just after completing the Chapter and looking for files for the next, I found a file of a short debate between John Nellis and ourselves, the existence of which I had forgotten. Our rejoinder to his critique of our book (Bayliss and Fine, eds, 2008) is reproduced here as an Appendix.

1   Introduction[5]

Although privatisation has been adopted in many developing countries, implementation in Africa remains relatively sluggish and, it seemed in the late 1980s, its popularity was waning (Fontaine and Geronimi, 1995). Recently, however, the pressure to privatise seems to have gathered strength with international donors and developing country governments, with both pushing for an increase in the pace of privatisation, although the approach now is a little more pragmatic. This renewed enthusiasm is manifested in the 1995 report *Bureaucrats in Business* (hereafter referred to as the Report) issued by the World Bank (1995), hereafter referred to as the Bank.

The Report was the subject of a recent 'Policy Arena' in this Journal.[6] This Chapter contributes to the critical literature, highlighting that many relevant

---

3   For longstanding and continuing analyses of the failings of privatisation, and growing resistances and alternatives, see publications on its website, https://www.gre.ac.uk/research/psiru.

4   See Bayliss and Fine (2020, 2021a and b, 2022 and 2024), Bayliss et al. (2018), Bayliss and Fine (eds) (2008) and Bayliss et al. (eds) (2011 and 2018), and six working papers with FESSUD, on financialisation and well-being, available at https://fessud.org/working-papers/, with FESSUD covered more generally in Fine et al. (2024) with other long-term collaborators, Mary Robertson and Alfredo Saad-Filho, quite apart from Kate.

5   Originally published as Bayliss and Fine (1998). Thanks to two anonymous referees for comments.

6   See *Journal of International Development*, vol 9, no 6, pp. 843–897. Some papers are of particular relevance here. Chang and Singh (1997) explore the fact that private enterprises also have bureaucracies and raise a number of analytical and empirical points. Jalilian and Weiss (1997) find, using the data from the Report, no evidence to support the Report's central

factors are omitted from the Bank's approach, the neglect of which accounts, in part, for the fact that the Report fails to stand up to close scrutiny. The Report is shown to have many of the deficiencies that have marked the Bank's earlier assessment work – an analytical framework based on state versus market with bias in favour of the latter, limited scope of variables and factors, selective use and misinterpretation of evidence, self-fulfilling techniques for inferring pre-ferred conclusions, etc. Whilst an analytical step backwards compared to the *East Asian Miracle* (World Bank, 1993), which is more accommodating to the state if it is market-conforming, there is a push towards stronger political, as opposed to economic, conditionality to encourage proponents of privatisation.

The following section provides a brief critical review of the privatisation lit-erature. This is followed by an outline of the Report. These serve as background to the critical assessment of the Report. A brief final section contains some clos-ing observations.

2   Privatisation Theory: The New Synthesis

The theoretical framework underlying the approach adopted by the World Bank in this Report has its origins in the New Institutional Economics (NIE) and New Political Economy (NPE).[7] It has been argued that the theory of privatisation has given rise to a new synthesis incorporating strands from NIE and NPE and from the neo-Austrian school (Fine, 1990a and b).[8]

This synthesis has been shown to suffer from a number of analytical weak-nesses, which are summarised briefly below. The literature is marked by its circumstantial origins with a narrow analytical framework deriving more from fashions within economic theory than the genuine problems posed by privatisation.[9] There is little understanding of long-term impacts. The litera-ture is often based on a false dichotomy between the state and market with an undue bias, in theory and evidence, towards the role of the market and private

---

hypothesis, i.e. that countries with large state sectors have a lower than average economic performance. Cook (1997) questions the theoretical and empirical basis of the Report and explores the inconsistencies in the Bank's approach to public enterprise reform.

7   See Shirley (1997, p. 856) for some of the theoretical influences behind the Report.

8   For standard treatments of the literature, see Vickers and Yarrow (1988) and Yarrow and Jasinski (eds) (1996) for a four-volume collection of articles. See also Cook and Kirkpatrick (eds) (1988 and 1995).

9   As in the new institutional economics (see Harriss et al. 1995 for example).

capital.[10] The conclusions drawn have been over-generalised and are insensitive to the range of economic and political factors involved, as well as the way in which they interact with one another. There is a tendency to suffer from the panacea syndrome – the notion that privatisation will itself generate or enhance the appropriate economic and political circumstances required for it to be successful. Alternatives for public sector reform and for developing the capacity for 'good governance' are ignored.[11] The impact of the constant pressure for privatisation, or at least to be market-like, on the motivation and ethos of the public sector has been neglected.[12] The framework is too narrow in its treatment of industrial policy. The significance of the historical, social, economic and political context of privatisation is not adequately considered – privatisation has generally led to a further consolidation of economic power, with an increased concentration of corporate ownership even where there has been the aim of spreading share ownership.[13] The literature neglects the demanding nature of regulation (Fine, 1997c). The incidence of privatisation shows no systematic relation to economic and political variables,[14] although pressure from donors does seem to have been significant.[15]

Whether privatisation occurs and how successful it is depends upon a complex range of economic and political pre-conditions. Consequently, international donors have become less enthusiastic about the immediate prospects for privatisation and seem to advise a more cautious approach. Whilst this apparent shift in policy stance would seem to be in recognition of the weaknesses of the earlier single-minded focus upon privatisation, the analytical and policy framework being employed remains remarkably unchanged and uncritical.[16] Further, such a policy has, as its counterpart, an implication that donor

---

10   See Haque (1996), Grosh and Mukandala (eds) (1994), and Fine and Stoneman (1996). See also Vogel (1996) who demonstrates that liberalisation (in the sense of more market competition) is associated with re- and not with de-regulation. Further, such liberalisation and re-regulation are articulated in country- and sector-specific ways. The hypothesis that state actors, rather than politically organised interest groups, are primarily responsible for initiating liberalisation is more open to question.

11   See Haque (1996), Kumssa (1996) and Baer (1996).

12   See Haque (1996).

13   See Adam et al. (1992).

14   See Jalilian and Weiss (1997) who use data from this Bank Report to conclude that there is no support for the hypothesis that countries with large state sectors have a poorer than average economic performance.

15   See Ramamurti (1992).

16   See Kumssa (1996) and Hemming and Unnithan (1996).

aid in support of good governance will be on terms that promote the interests and position of those who favour and stand to gain most from privatisation.[17]

Broadly, then, pressure to privatise comes from:

- an unfounded belief in the superiority of the private over the public sector and of the amorphous market over the state;
- a neglect of the pre-conditions required for privatisation to be successfully managed or simple faith that those conditions will be induced by virtue of embarking upon a privatisation programme; and
- neglect of the broader social, political and economic environment in which privatisation is located.

Paradoxically, the World Bank seems to have reached similar conclusions despite its pro-market stance. For, it would appear from the Report that the Bank is dissatisfied with the extent to which privatisation has taken place and with the results where it has. This poor performance is attributed to the influence of political factors. However, the Report's analysis remains seriously flawed.

3   Bureaucrats in Business: Context and Outline

This Report follows three earlier reports, The *East Asian Miracle* (hereafter referred to as the *Miracle*), *Adjustment in Africa* and *Averting the Old Age Crisis* which are seen by the World Bank as part of a series of which *Bureaucrats in Business* is the fourth that "bring to a broad audience the results of World Bank research on policy issues", according to the cover of the latest publication. Without commenting on the third, the first two of these previous volumes, which are centrally concerned with economic policy, have been shown to be sorely inadequate.[18]

Much of this Report's content and conclusions come from its own data and analysis. The Report examines the experience of state-owned enterprise (SOE) reform in a sample of 12 countries: Chile, China, Czech Republic, Egypt, Ghana, India, Republic of Korea, Mexico, Philippines, Poland, Senegal and Turkey.

The Report looks at the performance of SOEs in these countries in terms of financial performance, productivity and the savings-investment deficit, pp. 57–64. Three countries consistently performed well (Mexico, Chile and

---

17   See Kumssa (1996).

18   See special section in *World Development*, vol 24, no 4, 1994, Fine and Stoneman (1996), Wade (1996) and Mosley et al. (1995) for devastating critical discussion of these World Bank Reports and the thinking and methods that have informed them.

Korea). The Report then analyses the reform process to determine how success and failure are related to policy makers' reliance on what they call "the five components of state-owned enterprise reform", p. 67. These are: the extent of divestiture; the intensity of competition; the hardness of budgets; the extent of financial sector reform; and the institutional arrangements between government and enterprises. The chapter concludes that these five elements are closely related to each other, with the countries which had the best performing SOE sectors, undertaking the most comprehensive approach to reform, pp. 67–96.

The Report then considers the nature of contractual arrangements where the government continues to have ultimate control over an enterprise. Three types of arrangement are considered – performance contracts, management contracts and regulation. These are assessed in terms of their impact on profitability and productivity, which operate via the "three incentive factors – information, rewards and penalties, and commitment", p. 109. On this basis, performance contracts were not deemed successful. Management and regulatory contracts performed better.

Having putatively demonstrated the benefits to be achieved from SOE reform, the Report questions why so little effort at implementation has taken place. Factors other than economic efficiency must be at work and these are explored in Chapter 4: "The Politics of SOE Reform". The proposition is that, in order for reform to succeed, it must be *politically desirable, politically feasible* and *credible*. This hypothesis is tested using data from the sample countries with various proxies to account for the above three variables. The finding is "that the three conditions of reform readiness ... consistently explain the reform outcomes for our entire sample", p. 177. The subsequent chapter provides details on what to do once these political conditions are established (and what to do when they are not) in the form of a decision tree offering a step by step guide for overcoming the obstacles to enterprise reform and divestiture, p. 232.

The Report closes, in its short final chapter, with implications for international financial assistance. It recommends that donors make a distinction between committed and uncommitted countries systematically on the basis of the three indicators of reform readiness.

4   A Critique

The Report falls into the pattern of those that came before although it is less researched and less substantive than the *Miracle*. It occupies a peculiar position relative to the *Miracle* which it follows by more than a year in publication. In terms of its analytical, empirical and policy position, it represents a considerable step backwards. For, unlike the earlier report, it has once again narrowed the terrain of discussion around industrial policy towards quite narrow parameters. It fails to consider (dynamic) economies of scale and scope and the creation rather than the use of comparative advantage. Reference to selective finance and subsidies and the like is all from a perspective that primarily emphasises their negative consequences. At least the *Miracle* recognised the positive – even the essential – role to be played by industrial policy beyond the provision of infrastructure, although it tends to be interpreted as what the market would have done if it had been perfect.[19] On the other hand, this Report goes beyond the *Miracle* and most if not all previous reports by the extent to which it implicitly points towards donor agencies, presumably including itself, exerting an indirect influence on countries' political outcomes and processes. The Bank's analytical framework falls fully within that of the privatisation synthesis, and the problems outlined in the second section, above, all apply here. Where the approach of the Bank differs slightly from that of the broader mainstream as theory is in its focus on the bureaucratic nature of state intervention rather than on the micro-level, incentive-based details, which preoccupy much of the synthesis. The Bank's neglect of the role played by bureaucracy in the private, as well as the public, sector has already been documented (Chang and Singh, 1997).

The Report constructs its understanding in terms of a simple dichotomy, and hence conflict, between the state and the market, creating a narrow analytical, empirical and policy framework within which all aspects of public and private sector activity are located. The evidence inevitably points to the desirability of as much privatisation as possible or as much reliance upon market forces as possible where state-ownership is maintained. As a result, a number of analytical weaknesses emerge, in particular:

1. Within this framework the Report takes an ideologically favourable stance towards the market, thereby overlooking or reinterpreting evidence that favours state economic intervention. Even contrary evidence is used to support the pro-market stance. In other words, the evidence will rarely, if ever contradict the predetermined analytical and policy positions. This is very much in conformity with the *Miracle* where, for

---

19 The *Miracle* also argues that the market-conforming policies of East Asia cannot be replicated in other countries. According to Busumtwi-Sam (1996), this stance is contradicted in a confidential World Bank report on Ghana which suggests that it follow the East Asian model of economic development.

example, state intervention is perceived, when successful, to have been market conforming. To ensure that the evidence fits the framework, many obvious questions and implications arising from the analysis are not adequately explored.

2.   The use of evidence is selective, biased and tied to much stronger conclusions than are warranted even if the evidence itself could be considered satisfactory.

3.   The Report takes a very narrow view of what constitutes industrial policy tending to interpret it alone in terms of whether there are price distortions or not. Therefore the conclusions reached from the study are inappropriately applied to a vast range of varying circumstances.

These points are explored further below, although it is acknowledged that there is considerable overlap between the broad headings.

4.1   *Narrow Analytical Framework*

The broad conclusions of the Report are as follows. Privatisation is in most cases desirable and, where it is not, regulations of state-owned or private enterprises are more desirable the closer they come to the market in the form that they assume. This raises the issue of why more privatisations have not taken place and why they have not always been successful when they have occurred – there is dissatisfaction with the extent of privatisation, especially in low-income countries where, according to the Report, the benefits are liable to be particularly great. Of course, one obvious conclusion to investigate from this evidence is that privatisation has not occurred so much because it is undesirable and that it has often been unsuccessful because it has been forced through when it should not have been; and this is especially so for low-income countries where, at an early stage of development, state ownership might be essential. The desirability of privatisation is never in question.

To some extent the Report accepts that privatisation might have been unsuccessfully adopted as a policy but only if done so prematurely. It even suggests that the World Bank has itself been guilty in this respect by promoting premature privatisations ("well-intentioned outsiders, including the World Bank, have sometimes attempted to prod developing countries that are not ready for reform into acting", p. 231) although the Report is notably short of details of this (where and when) and of self-criticism in examining how this could have come about. Nor is there any examination of what follows logically from this admission of premature privatisation – that they might be reversed or that there may be private capitals that should be taken into public ownership; better a bad privatisation or private sector than to encourage state ownership!

What the Report argues in order to explain limited privatisation and less than perfect success in privatisations is that the three desired conditions for reform have not been met. This framework raises a number of obvious questions which are not adequately explored in the Report.

First, the *political desirability* of the policy needs to be established. In other words, there has to be government support for the policy. It is argued that this is liable to come about either through a shift in political regime (change of power bloc by whatever means) or through an existing crisis that shifts the perceived balance of costs and benefits for an existing regime. Although it is not a step taken in the Report, it follows that a shift in regime or even the engineering or threat of an economic crisis might be desirable in order to attain the longer term goals of more and more successful privatisation. This represents a considerable departure from the earlier World Bank approach which warned that public enterprise reform in periods of crisis was not usually sustainable (Cook, 1997, p. 893).

Second, there is the need for the privatisations to be *politically feasible*. This implies that those who lose by the policies have to be defeated or compensated if they have the power to obstruct them. The Report hastens to observe that it does not necessarily see this as less of a problem in an authoritarian regime especially in conjunction with desirability and credibility (on which see next) but does seem to regard favourably the link between feasibility and authoritarianism.[20]

Third, government reform has to be *credible*. Other agents have to be confident that policy intentions will actually be carried out. This implies the creation of a reputation for honouring commitments and the presence of domestic and international restraints on policy reversals.[21]

The triplet of political desirability, political feasibility and credibility provide more or less for an analytical and empirical guarantee that whatever outcomes or evidence might present themselves, they will conform to the previously developed hypotheses. If privatisation does not occur or is unsuccessful, it can be readily interpreted as having lacked desirability, feasibility

---

20   Thus, World Bank (1995, p. 191), "whether a country has a more or less authoritarian form of government is therefore a strong indicator of feasibility". See Busumtwi-Sam (1996) for a discussion, in the context of Ghana, of the irrelevance of authoritarianism versus democracy as a starting point for addressing the performance of the state. For similar, more general conclusions, see Haggard and Kaufman (eds) (1992) and Haggard and Webb (1993).

21   The notion of credibility has its origins in part in game theory, where agents have to be assured that those with whom they bargain, including the state, will keep to their word.

or credibility. These three factors provide a descriptive framework into which either success or failure almost inevitably sit comfortably. This is the case, despite the fact that the framework is not entirely devoid of causal content. For example, the feasibility factor is empirically operationalised for statistical purposes by measures of overstaffing which is intended to provide an indicator of the strength of opposition to reform, p. 191.

This Report goes further than its predecessors with the final short chapter where it recommends that international financial assistance should be organised around the achievement of privatisation, providing support according to whether the criteria for desirability, feasibility and credibility are met. In other words, support for public sector reform and for privatisation should be tailored to take account of performance in all three areas. Again it is but a short step to see this as an implicit form of political conditionality, the latter being quite extensive in terms of regime or power bloc shift appeasing those who are both powerful and liable to lose by the privatisation process and giving high priority to both domestic and foreign interests in pre-empting policy reversals (thereby tying the hands of future governments).

The Report also goes beyond those earlier in its recognition of the fact that the market does not always work best, arguing that privatisation (and more general support for reform of state enterprises) ought to wait upon other reforms or changes in political conditions. Put another way, this is an argument for sequencing in which privatisation needs to be delayed until other economic and political conditions have been met. This raises the issue of what should be done in the meantime. The answer is a step back into orthodoxy once again with emphasis on policies that are conducive to the growth of, and dependence upon, market forces. Until privatisation can proceed, it is essential to adopt policies that correspond to orthodox stabilisation and structural adjustment, p. 237. This solution is accepted uncritically despite the record of poor outcomes, whatever the claims of *Adjustment in Africa* to the contrary. There is an inherent contradiction here as it is likely that the countries which are not ready for reform are low-income countries, and yet these are the very countries which the Report says have most to gain from reform.

4.2   *Selective Use of Evidence and Bias in Interpretation*

The Report presents limited evidence in support of the superior performance of the private sector and, as is habitual in its publications in general, overlooks the literature that questions this conclusion. Page 37 provides details of empirical literature, "that deals with the issue of private versus public efficiency". The citations are selective and biased (see Cook 1997, who identifies some relevant omitted studies, and also Chang and Singh, 1997). The study by Galal et al.

(1992) is cited a number of times in the Report as evidence of the beneficial effects of privatisation of monopolies, despite the fact that the authors of this study specifically warn against extrapolating their findings to very poor countries or the former socialist countries.[22]

A number of points need to be made here. First, quite apart from the difficulties in devising and making appropriate measures of performance between public and private enterprises, the criteria employed generally favour the private sector since the public sector may be subject to other conditions of operation. Second, there is a sense in which the sample is biased since those private sector enterprises that fail will be excluded from the sampling. Third it is forgotten that privatisation often arises out of the creation of enterprises through state inspired initiatives that would not have occurred under private enterprise, and which may be abandoned by the private sector in less favourable circumstances

The fact is that the empirical evidence to date of significant difference between public and private enterprise performance is extremely weak. Sometimes one is superior, sometimes the other even by the criteria of the private sector itself.[23] What is much more important is that the difference in performance between enterprises of one country as opposed to another is far more significant than the difference of ownership within countries. It is what private and public share in common within a country that needs to be examined carefully. Even if the performance of public and private enterprises were equalised (up) within countries, this would raise economic performance very little compared to the differences of performance from one country to the next.

This conclusion would seem to be borne out by evidence from the Report, which finds that the same countries (South Korea, Chile and Mexico) consistently achieve the best results. The focus upon differences in ownership rather than common conditions of operation is a major weakness of this Report both analytically and in policy proposals, discussed further below.

The selection of indicators of strength of SOE reform ensures that the procedure yields the desired results, when in fact the causality could work the other way. Suppose that enterprise performance is independent of the features

---

22   "Caution must be exercised in extrapolating our results to very poor countries which lack some of the institutions and markets our [middle-income] sample possess. The same caution applies to the former socialist countries which ... almost completely lack private sector institutions and the kind of market mechanisms taken for granted in mixed economies. In both instances divestiture outcomes may differ from those found here", Galal et al. (1992, p. 563).

23   See Rowthorn and Chang (1992) and Chang and Singh (1993) for example.

listed (divestiture, competition, hard budgets, financial sector reform and relationship with government). Suppose also that there is considerable pressure
for privatisation from domestic as well as international agencies. Successful
state sector reform could be the engine of market-led policies – it is easier
to divest more fully if your enterprises are successful. Similarly, you can bear
competition in product markets, impose hard budget constraints, draw upon
and sustain financial sector reform and arrange for greater independence from
government.

This alternative perspective can be used to interpret the apparently anomalous finding that the countries that divested the most tended to improve
(remaining) SOE performance the most, p. 58. The Report, somewhat weakly,
attempts to account for this result using the market-focused framework discussed above:

i)   "By reducing the size of the state owned enterprise sector, they may have
      been able to concentrate scarce managerial skills on those that remain,
      thus improving their performance", p. 70; and

ii)   "Further, former SOEs that have been privatised may have induced
      greater competitive pressure on remaining SOEs", p. 70.

Both explanations are inadequate as the first implies a substantial increase in
availability of state resources once an enterprise is sold. This is not usually the
case and in fact the divestiture process itself can use up significant amounts of
"scarce managerial skills". The second is unlikely as competition is not expected
to be significantly affected due to the limited weight of privatisation and what
is liable to be an extremely narrow overlap between the markets served by the
private and the continuing public sector.

This reasoning in the Report implies that privatisation can, in itself, generate an improvement in the performance of SOEs. However, a closer look at the
data (in the Report's Table 2.2, p. 69, not reproduced here) raises further questions. Of the three "good performers" only two carried out significant divestiture. South Korea actually did very little, thus invalidating the blanket claim
that "successful reformers divested more", p. 69. The Report attempts to get
round this by pointing out that South Korea already had a small state sector.
Why then did Turkey, which apparently had a smaller state sector and carried
out greater privatisation than Korea, remain a "poor performer"? There are further caveats to account for this. The fact is that these results do not lend themselves to the conclusions drawn.

The Report fails to explore that the so-called 'good performers' already had
a strong state sector before reform or divestiture took place. They are also the
countries with the most developed financial sectors, p. 89. They are also middle-
income countries. A much more obvious explanation of the 'anomalous'

finding is that there are similar factors or policies that have enhanced the performance of the public, financial and private sectors, independent of privatisation as such.

Similar concerns can be raised when it comes to the contractual options put forward for enterprises remaining in the public domain. The possible arrangements identified are performance contracts, management contracts and regulation. Subject to capacity to implement, these are favoured in reverse order of listing on the basis of another triplet of putative causal factors: first, informational considerations (which are seen somewhat strangely as being enhanced exclusively by competition rather than for example by auditing even of the type that the Bank is itself engaged upon in this Report); second, the use of rewards and penalties to provide appropriate incentives; and, third, commitment to ensure that contracts are properly formulated and monitored by government or independent agency.

The desired analytical and empirical results can be interpreted as almost inevitably corresponding to the descriptive framework and the causal associations could easily function in the opposite direction. The critique of performance contracts, for example, is quite detailed but more in the vein of their inadequate specification and implementation than their unsuitability per se.

This evidence presented provides no clear proof of the superiority of one system over another. Conclusions are reached on the basis of very small samples using measures which clearly favour market-based arrangements – it cannot be a surprise that the introduction of performance contracts, where state ownership is retained, does not bring about an increase in profitability. Yet these results are used to support the adoption of management contracts and regulation rather than performance contracts. Further, there is a questionable logic in the reasoning put forward to account for this conclusion. For example, the discussion on information asymmetry under the performance contract arrangement describes a low-paid government official who is at a disadvantage dealing with the enterprise representative of much higher status, p. 121. Surely this is equally if not more pertinent to the issue of regulation of a private sector monopoly. However, the discussion on information asymmetry with regard to regulation contracts focuses on competition, pp. 156–58, which is bizarre when it is the absence of competition which provides the need for regulation.

One might be tempted to think that the conclusions have more to do with the ideological standpoint than the evidence. Not surprisingly, performance contracts, which are the least market-oriented of the arrangements under discussion, are the least favoured.

It seems that much of the analysis falls into varieties of ad hocery which is simply designed to support pre-determined conclusions. The treatment of

China is superficial and biased. Take, for example, the discussion of China's Township and Village Enterprises (TVES). TVES are widely acknowledged to be the engine of growth in China and they are, according to this Report, publicly owned. However, they are classified as non-state, not on the basis of ownership but because of the way they are managed – they are locally run, face hard budget constraints, have greater autonomy with fewer social obligations and operate under greater competition, Box 2.4, p. 74. Surely this is a case of adverse selection when well-run publicly owned enterprises are not classified as SOES largely because of the way they are run. Rather than going through hoops to fit such enterprise organisations into the public/private dichotomy, would it not be more useful to see what can be learned from the success of TVES?[24]

Also we are treated to the observation that there is a cross-country correlation between greater deficits on the public enterprise account and the overall fiscal deficit – leading to the conclusion that state-ownership is bad for public finance. However, such a correlation is more or less automatic given that the one deficit is a part of the other!

4.3   *Narrow View of What Constitutes Industrial Policy Leading to Over-Generalisation of Conclusions*

Private and public ownership and forms of competition and regulation are just a part (and not necessarily the most important part) of industrial policy. One consequence of the Report's approach is that its policy proposals are generalised without sensitivity either to the specifics of the country concerned – its level of development, its position in the world economy, its internal economic and political dynamic, etc – nor to the specifics of the sectors involved. This leads to over-generalisation both in terms of the policy framework adopted and in the empirical evidence employed. This is evident in the decision tree, Figure 1, reproduced here.

Are we really to believe that this is adequate for decision making irrespective of the sector concerned and irrespective of the country, region or level of development?[25] This is not a matter of detail, which is thin within the figure, but whether the same species of tree is appropriate in all circumstances. This is especially important in view of the narrow experience upon which the Report

---

24   See Chang and Singh (1997, p. 872) for a detailed critique of the treatment of the SOE sector in China.

25   For a much more complicated "tree" with far more hoops to leap before embarking upon privatisation, see Rodinelli and Iacono (1996). Despite the latter's sympathy for privatisation, the preconditions they infer as necessary for privatisation would tend to preclude any taking place in practice!

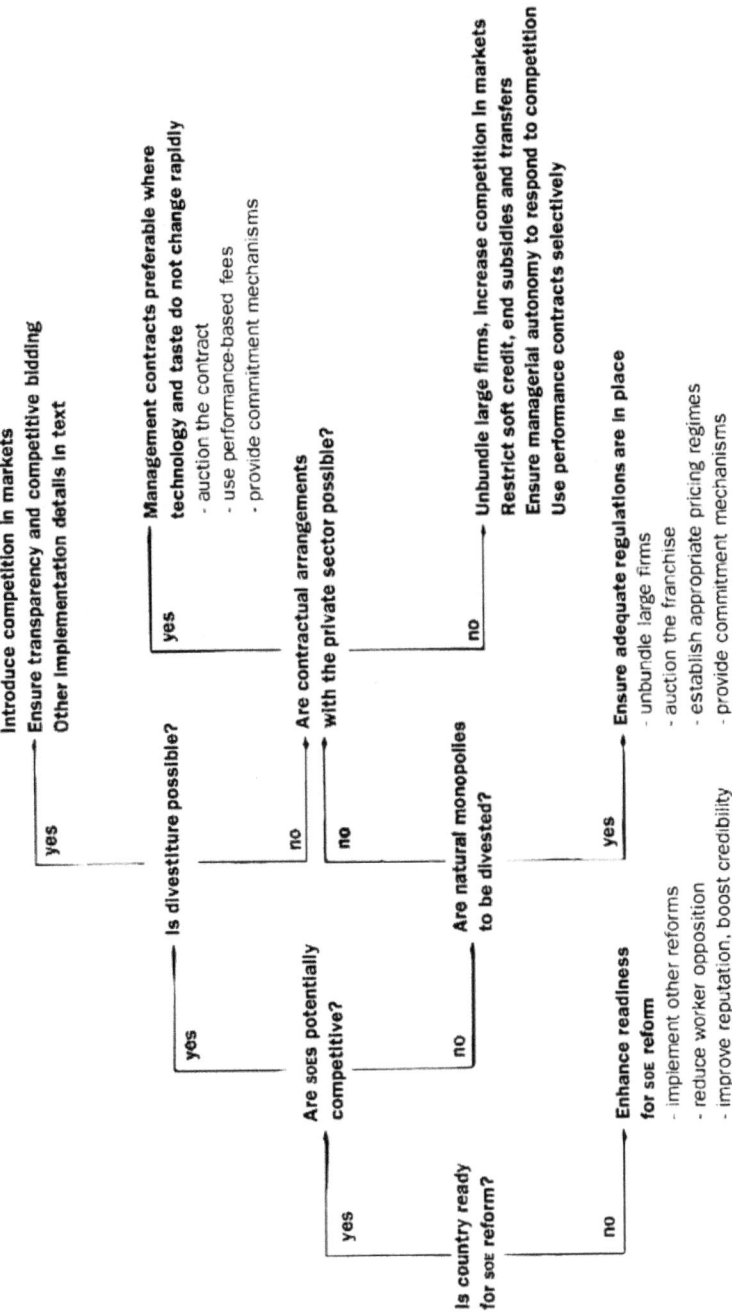

FIGURE 1   A decision tree for State-Owned enterprise reform

draws (a limited review of twelve diverse countries) irrespective of how well it does so.[26]

The privatisations that have occurred so far in developing countries are primarily in Latin America, Asia and Eastern Europe (World Bank, 1995, Table 1.1, p. 27) and are concentrated in primary, industry and infrastructure sectors (World Bank, 1995, Table 1.2, p. 28). Since 1988, the value of infrastructural privatisations in developing countries has been totally dominated by telecommunications (60 percent) and, to a lesser extent, power which accounts for a further 27 percent with gas distribution accounting for a further 10 percent, p. 151. Can we extrapolate from these examples? The answer is surely in the negative. Taking for example the telecommunications industry, this has unique features which do not prevail in other sectors of the economy. These include the (prospective) scale of the market and existing state of the network, the linkages upstream and downstream with other activity such as electronic and electrical goods manufacture and data processing, the availability of skilled labour and the need to engage in joint ventures and negotiate with powerful multinational corporations.

Such considerations significantly do not figure in the decision tree nor in the analysis in the Report at all. Their incidence will be different, and they will interact differently from one country to the next and from one sector to the next. Accordingly, in general, the Report is not suitable as a guide to policy – indeed, it is a contribution only in the negative sense of precluding the sort of policy frameworks and policies themselves that might be most apposite. For, far from starting from a dogmatic position favouring the market, in the context of reform of public sector enterprise, it is more appropriate to make a sector-specific and country-specific industrial policy. This should take into

---

26   In addition is notable that the decision tree floats entirely free from World Bank objectives such as promoting the supported economy and, thereby, directly or indirectly addressing, poverty. As an ex post addendum, a touch of (empirical) realism is significant in this context. On the basis of a large (270 cases) data base of infrastructure privatisations for sub-Saharan Africa, Foch (2013, p. 349) reports that, "A first result is that foreign and G10 firms benefit more from infrastructure privatisation when it is supported by the WB than when it is not. But the most striking result is that the WB provides greater support to privatisation in the sub-sectors of infrastructure that benefit the most to G10 firms". I first came across this paper through communication with the author, and then reviewed it most positively but unsuccessfully for a leading development journal (as opposed to transport economics!). The article was originally entitled "Why Does the World Bank Support Infrastructure Privatization in Sub-Saharan Africa", to which an exceptionally clear answer is provided. As we see, the renamed article did appear, but in tracking it down, I seem to have found that the author went from dissenting PhD student to employee of the OECD and then the World Bank (incorporating dissent?, see Postamble to Chapter 1).

account economies of scale and scope, technological requirements etc. Then, on this basis, although the sequencing between policy formulation and forms of implementation need not be so rigidly separated, decisions can be made concerning the most appropriate form of state economic intervention including ownership decisions, in order to pursue the strategy formulated.

It can even be argued that this is the way in which policy is in fact implemented even if in favour of special interests and not always as consciously as laid out here and with as wide a scope of factors taken into account. Further, the successful late developers can be interpreted as having consciously employed such a policy process in conjunction with specific development goals. By contrast, not only is such a targeted framework eschewed in this Report in favour of a generalised reliance upon the market as far as political conditions allow, it even sets aside scope for the formulations and use of industrial policy where privatisation is recommended however appropriately. For one policy recommendation is to devote as few resources as possible to public enterprises targeted for privatisation in view of the limited extent to which such resources are liable to be well-spent and to accrue a return in the sale price. The only exceptions made are for smoothing the privatisation process itself through capital write-offs and redundancy payments to reduce overstaffing. In short, nothing could illustrate better the extent to which the Report is ideologically wedded to a general belief in the superiority of the market and the futility of the state deploying an industrial policy even where this is to function through prospective privatised enterprises.

5   Concluding Remarks

For almost two decades, debate over industrial policy for developing countries has been dominated by the agenda set by the World Bank and the IMF. This has pitched the state against the market with the Washington Consensus heavily favouring the latter and breaking with an earlier traditional dependence upon industrialisation led or heavily influenced by the state sector. More recently, longstanding theoretical and empirical criticism of the Washington Consensus has, in conjunction with other factors, such as the increasing importance of Japan as an international donor, begun to have an effect particularly in the light of the experience of the East Asian NICs for which state economic intervention has been shown to have been both necessary and highly effective.[27]

---

27   See Wade (1996).

But old ideas die hard – and unevenly. If there is a sea-change swelling up against the Washington Consensus it still remains far over the horizon. This is evident in the 1996 World Development Report (World Bank, 1996) which advises transition countries on how to become fully-fledged market economies by adopting the standard package of liberalisation and stabilisation policies. Further, despite the apparently moderate tone and stance towards the state of the 1997 World Development Report (World Bank, 1997a), the message is even more radical in so far as states are urged not to operate in areas where they do not have the capability.[28]

If the fields of development economics and development studies are to embark upon a new agenda it is imperative that it is not set by those responsible for the old agenda. The fundamental framework within which privatisation, for example, has been debated by the bureaucrats in the Bank is unacceptable and would remain so even if it were modified to be more state-friendly in principle rather than market-friendly by dogma.

Appendix:[29] Debating the Provision of Basic Utilities in Sub-Saharan Africa: A Response to Nellis

Both delight and surprise are prompted by John Nellis' One Pager #31,[30] a rejoinder to the Bayliss and McKinley IPC Policy Research Brief #3 on "Privatising Basic Utilities in Sub-Saharan Africa".[31] The Brief reports on the book edited by Kate Bayliss and Ben Fine, *Privatization and Alternative Public Sector Reform in Sub-Saharan Africa: Delivering on Electricity and Water* (Basingstoke: Palgrave MacMillan).

The book inevitably goes beyond material covered in the Brief. It offers a swingeing and detailed critique of World Bank thinking and policy on privatisation, including a heavy dose of scepticism about the Bank's current *mea culpa*: "we were wrong; we privatised too much too soon and without

---

28   According to *Bureaucrats in Business*, if the conditions for reform are not clement, governments are encouraged to focus on the macroeconomic climate. The latest advice from the Bank, however, is for these states (for they are likely to be the same countries) to match their role to their capability, signalling a reduction in the significance of the public sector and increased reliance on the private sector.

29   As in the main article, co-authored with Kate Bayliss, then described as an independent consultant, Brighton, United Kingdom. Now available at https://www.ipc-undp.org/sites /default/files/pub/en/IPCOnePager32.pdf It was first posted on April Fool's Day, 2007.

30   https://www.ipc-undp.org/pub/IPCOnePager31.pdf.

31   Now available at https://www.ipcig.org/pub/IPCPolicyResearchBrief3.pdf.

preconditions in place". The Bank has partly come to its senses because, despite ample support for privatisation and exaggerated promises for its performance, it has performed miserably in sub-Saharan Africa.

The time is indeed ripe for a thorough 'rethink', which would involve giving the public sector a fair crack at the helm. Appearances to the contrary, this is not what the World Bank nor Nellis is proposing. Their priority is to continue supporting the private sector whilst exhorting the state to build up capacity – but primarily to support private-sector, not public-sector, provision of utilities. The easiest privatisations are over; privatisation is now evidently floundering. So the state must work even harder, they argue, to make it a success. No assessment is given of what might be achieved by devoting the same resources and commitment to public sector provision. And this stance continues despite the admission, confirmed by Nellis, that the provision of electricity and water in sub-Saharan Africa will remain mostly the responsibility of the state.

Such is the context for Nellis' rejoinder. For twenty years his position on privatisation has reflected, even informed, that of the World Bank – starting with cautious endorsement of privatisation, followed by a full-scale embrace and, finally and most recently, culminating in implicit acceptance of its failings. His current five-point acceptance of our diagnosis is welcome. Delivering basic utilities in sub-Saharan Africa is no easy task. But the privatisation experiment has made it worse, by eroding state capacity or preventing it from being expanded.

Like the World Bank, Nellis is no longer committed dogmatically to a 'one size fits all' privatisation model. As mentioned, the priority of the new model is to get the state to support the private sector rather than simply leaving it to its own devices. This is apparent in his closing sentence: "So, in a nutshell, the solution is not to eschew private investment, but rather to find mechanisms to make it more politically acceptable, more socially responsible and more mutually beneficial".

To be fair, whilst accepting our diagnoses, Nellis does tax us on three points. The first is that we 'overestimate' state capacity in sub-Saharan Africa. He offers no evidence for this assertion, most likely because no estimate has been made. Our point is that the privatisation experiment has clearly over-estimated the capacity of the private sector. More importantly, Nellis accepts that public service provision will be predominant into the foreseeable future and, by implication, that it will have to be the focus of efforts at reform and capacity building – irrespective of its current failings.

Nellis reasonably questions how this might be done. This is a positive step over presuming that it cannot. He correctly anticipates that we address this crucial point in our book, putting forward the 'public sector system of provision' approach (PSSoP). This does not start from (private) market *versus* (public) state provision but from the specificities of each country and sector, in terms of practice and potential. For this approach, presumptions about under- or over-estimation of state capacity are beside the point: public service delivery must be addressed and evaluated as an option.

The second point relates to Nellis' assertion that we under-estimate the need for private capital to fill the huge investment gap in Africa. But private capital has already failed to fill the gap. This is why the new Bank model encourages ever increasing efforts by the state (as well as consumers) to absorb higher levels of risk to satisfy the guarantees now demanded by private investors. Crucially, private capital comes at a price, and one that is not necessarily cheaper than public finance. We are not precluding the participation of private capital, but we situate it within the economic and social functioning of a country as a whole and try seriously to weigh alternative forms of public and private financing of provision.

Nellis' third point relates to his positive example of the Athi Water Services Commission, billed as a hybrid of private management and public ownership (a project which was undertaken, not coincidentally, against donor advice). We give other examples of such initiatives in our book. Some work, some do not. This project, by Nellis' own account, is far from ideal. Most critically, it fails to address the lack of investment finance. What is significant, though, is that Nellis still assumes that private sector management can work but public sector management cannot. Such presumptions became self-fulfilling during the era of privatisation when the capacity for public service provision was systematically undermined.

So, in a nutshell and as a counterpoint to Nellis, our solution is "not to eschew *public investment*, but rather to find mechanisms to make it more politically acceptable, more socially responsible and more mutually beneficial".[32]

---

32 As is apparent, this is a direct quote from the last sentence of Nellis' one-pager, only "private" has been replaced by "public".

The Developmental State Is Dead – Long Live Social Capital?

Postscript as Personal Preamble

This is the first paper that I published explicitly focusing on the relationship between economics imperialism and the study of development. In date of publication, it follows by a couple of years my first contribution on economics imperialism more generally (Fine, 1997b). As such, it is marked by immaturity for at least two main reasons. First, and especially at the time of drafting, the Post-Washington Consensus and its impact on the World Bank's scholarship and broader discourses had yet to take hold fully and so it was impossible to do anything more than speculate over the depth, breadth and nature of the changes taking place at the Bank, alongside the shifting and influential reasons for them. Second, my own engagement with the world of economics imperialism was heavily influenced and triggered by the simultaneous and overlapping rise of both the Post-Washington Consensus and social capital (for which it became, for the Bank, the 'missing link' in explaining and promoting development).

In addition, opposition to the World Bank's Washington Consensus, acknowledged if dismissively in its report on East Asia, in major part drew upon what I have termed the developmental state paradigm. The result was, in this piece, to bring together social capital, the Post-Washington Consensus and economics imperialism as part and parcel of a discursive and policy strategy for outflanking the role of the developmental state, with social capital to serve to sideline or substitute for the roles it might play.

I have to confess, more than willingly, that my speculation proved incorrect. Social capital did experience a meteoric rise at the Bank before being precipitously abandoned in the early noughties. It did play a major role in allowing Bank economists to incorporate the social into its otherwise more purely economistic treatments. But the prominence of the developmental state paradigm was not sustained sufficiently for social capital to need to serve as a surrogate, let alone for it to do so.

Nonetheless, the World Bank's social capitalists, as I am wont to call them, saw themselves as civilising the Bank's hegemonic economists into taking the social and the social sciences seriously, considered that it was worth sacrificing scholarly standards to do so, and that they had succeeded and could move onto other major issues such as empowerment. I have suggested otherwise, not least that the economists took social capital as a godsend for incorporating the social on their own (imperialistic terms), equally allowing them to leave their impoverished economics unexamined, and supporting the extensive incorporation of social policy and more into the Bank's analyses, discourses and policymaking and, most important of all, conditionalities. Meanwhile, the change in direction inspired by the Post-Washington Consensus, which created the space for social capital to prosper, otherwise made little impact on policy in practice (other than its extension to more areas), as symbolised by Stiglitz's removal from the Bank once he sought to impact upon policy as opposed to offering legitimisation for it.

This is all documented elsewhere, although fully covered in the references now attached to this Chapter.[1] Suffice it to hope that what might now be thought to be an inappropriately extensive discussion of social capital in what follows does at least indicate the thin to thick end of the wedge that it temporarily provided and that this has far more extensively facilitated the Bank to incorporate the social on the terms of market imperfection economics into its scholarship, ideology and policymaking. Social capital is dead, long live (development) economics imperialism, not least as development studies more generally has come within its orbit.

1   Introduction[2]

For those following the development literature, there surely can no longer be any doubt that some sort of intellectual and ideological upheaval is taking place within the World Bank. The signs have been there for some time, not least in the process leading from the *East Asian Miracle* (World Bank, 1993) through to the production of the World Development Report for 1997 (and draft, at time

---

1 See especially discussion of, and debate between, Bebbington (2004) and Bebbington et al. (2004 and 2006) and Fine (2008, 2010b and 2023). For a later, more muted, defence of social capital (at the Bank), see Bebbington and Foo (2024).

2 Originally published as Fine (1999a). Thanks to Costas Lapavitsas, John Sender and an anonymous referee for comments on earlier drafts. This article arises out of a programme of research at SOAS to assess the shifting positions of the World Bank and the IMF, if especially the former. Note it was to lead, amongst many other publications, to Fine et al. (eds) (2001) and Bayliss et al. (eds) (2011), focusing critically on the Post-Washington Consensus and its subsequent research, respectively.

of writing, of that for 1998).[3] From anti-market, through market-conforming, to market-friendly, the state is now seen more positively if cautiously so. The analytical agenda is shifting from one based on a simple dichotomy between market and state as good and bad, respectively. Even more dramatically, the demise of the Washington Consensus has been marked by the increasingly aggressive campaign of the World Bank's Senior Vice-President and Head of Economic Research, Joe Stiglitz. In early 1998, he made a speech heavily criticising the Washington Consensus and, more positively, proposing the alternative of a Post-Washington Consensus (Stiglitz, 1998a).[4] Essentially, this acknowledges the prevalence of market imperfections and provides a rationale for micro and macro interventions on this basis.

In short, even before the old Consensus has been decently buried, the pretender to its throne is already grabbing at the crown in a palace revolution. However welcome the demise of the old Consensus might be to those who have opposed it for almost two decades, the question of succession needs to be contested. Nor is it simply a matter of posing alternatives to the new Consensus but whether it should be allowed to dominate the development agenda – as did its predecessor by posing state versus market.

Section 1 of this Chapter provides an outline of the economic analysis that supports the new Consensus. It leads to consideration in Section 2 of its counterpart in non-economic analysis and the rise to prominence of the notion of social capital. Section 3 suggests that these new initiatives together hold out the prospect of an even stronger stranglehold over the development debate than was held by the Washington Consensus. The concluding remarks call for a revival of political economy based on rigorous conceptualisation of class and capital. Otherwise, both in analysis and in policy making, a pale version of Keynesian/welfarism/modernisation will prevail on the basis of correcting micro-imperfections in economic and non-economic relations.

---

3 See special issue of the *IDS Bulletin* for April, 1998, for a critical assessment of the World Development Report for 1997 on the state. The WDR for 1998 was on knowledge.

4 For a more tempered statement of his position in the context of the East Asian crisis, see Stiglitz (1998b). Nonetheless, possibly referring to the previous Consensus, p. 26, "In any case, only an ideologue would claim that *but for their system of close government and business cooperation* they would have grown even faster". For evidence of the rapid spread and ambition of the Post-Washington Consensus, consider the soon to be published report on Latin America, entitled *Beyond the Washington Consensus: Institutions Matter* and also the interview with Grzegorz Kolodko in the June, 1998, edition of *Transition*, the World Bank's house journal on eastern Europe.

2   The Microeconomic Foundations

The intellectual origins of the new Consensus are readily identified. They arise out of the micro-foundations of macroeconomics or the new Keynesian economics.[5] Essentially, the motivating idea is very old – that market imperfections justify state intervention to rectify them. The new twist, however, is to broaden the scope of what constitutes market imperfections. These are now organised around informational imperfections and asymmetries of various sorts, including the presence of transaction costs, so that market outcomes depend upon who has what information before, during and after the economy's passages in and out of exchange.

Stiglitz has been extremely active for almost two decades in this line of research, especially focusing on markets for finance.[6] But, even though financial markets are an obvious area of application, given the respective roles and knowledges of borrowers and lenders, other markets are equally susceptible to the new micro-foundations. Akerlof's pioneering contribution concerned the 'market for lemons' or second-hand cars, and the labour market is also prominent as an application – as is any market involving coordination failure, and monitoring of any sort including adverse selection and moral hazard.[7] When information is imperfect, even in equilibrium, markets may not operate at efficient levels, they may not clear (by bringing supply and demand into equality), and they may even fail to exist altogether.

It is crucial, however, to set these developments at the forefront of economics within a broader setting. Three aspects are significant. First, as is apparent from use of the term the micro-foundations of macroeconomics (as opposed to the alternative term, the new Keynesian macroeconomics), relatively simple ideas at the *microeconomic* level are being translated into models of how the *macroeconomy* functions. This is transparent in the use of representative individuals or agents in macroeconomics models whose aggregate behaviour is more or less successfully coordinated through the market. Market imperfections at the microeconomic level, whether of the old or newer sort, become extrapolated to the economy as a whole and can give rise to results with a Keynesian flavour.

---

5   For a fuller account, in the context of labour markets, see Fine (1998a, Chapter 2). See also Fine and Dimakou (2016).

6   His early contribution (Stiglitz and Weiss, 1981) is a classic. He has also been prominent in the new microeconomic approaches to rural institutions (as represented in Hoff et al. eds, 1993).

7   More generally, see Akerlof (1984). On labour markets, see Fine (1998a, Chapters 2 and 4).

Second, the new microeconomics has spawned, or at least has been associated with, a blossoming of other new endeavours. The list is impressive – the new growth theory, the new trade theory, the new institutional economics, the new household economics, the new political economy, and so on. What these all tend to have in common is the extension of microeconomic principles to areas that have previously been unexamined or taken as exogenous in the light of standard assumptions within economics. From where do productivity increase, comparative advantage, economic policy, family decisionmaking, and non-market institutions derive?

In the work of economists such as Gary Becker, and those that follow him, the answer is primarily provided in terms of simply universalising the so-called 'economic approach' based on utility maximisation to all areas of life, including those that are traditionally perceived as lying outside the domain of economics.[8] This has allowed for considerable advance into some of the areas concerned, most notably in the general, and now uncritical, acceptance of the notion of human capital. It is also apparent in the new household economics and the new political economy or any analysis incorporating simplistic notions of rent-seeking.

However, the new microeconomics has given rise to a most significant result as far as shifting the analytical boundaries of the scope of economic analysis is concerned. In what appears to be a squaring of the circle, it allows for the explanation of *social* structures and institutions even on the basis of *individual* optimisation. Faced with imperfect information, individuals can decide to create or engage in socially structured activity both within and between market and non-market forms of organisation. These forms become endogenous on a microeconomic basis, where previously they were taken as exogenous. Third, then, and most novel from an intellectual point of view, mainstream neoclassical economics now has the power to offer an explanation of the social, without taking it as exogenous as previously. Ultimately, though, it always has to take something as exogenous whether it be informational or initial conditions. Otherwise, individuals would have nothing over which to optimise.

---

8   See Becker (1996) and Tommasi and Ierulli (eds) (1995). A critical assessment of Becker's work in the light of some of the themes explored in this Chapter is provided by Fine (1995, 1997b and d and 1998c). Most recently, see Fine (2024a–c) for economics imperialism in its Becker and subsequent phases.

3   The Forward March of Social Capital

The significance of this last point will be taken up later. Before doing so, consider an equally rapid change that is evolving within and around World Bank thinking. It is the astonishing rise to prominence of the notion of 'social capital'. It has already made its way into the World Development Report for 1997 and, as Harriss and de Renzio (1997, p. 920) suggest:

> Since 1993 "social capital" has become one of the key terms, of development lexicon, adopted enthusiastically by international organizations, national governments and NGOs alike.

They cite uses ranging from that of the IDS at the University of Sussex as a theme for a research programme to the terms of reference of tenders for research on social policy formulated by the UK's Department for International Development, DfID. For the World Bank itself (World Bank, 1997b), even though its use only seems to date back to 1994, it is already being heralded as the 'missing link' in development. It figures prominently in the draft programme for the World Development Report for 2000 which has Poverty and Development as its theme.

It is important, then, to 'deconstruct' this conceptual wunderkind, a process that has already begun with a critical literature, including surveys such as Harriss and de Renzio (1997) and the even more comprehensive Woolcock (1998). The purpose here is to draw upon, and add to, these contributions in order to understand why the notion of social capital should be so conducive to World Bank thinking even as it is itself establishing a new agenda.[9]

Consider, first, problems surrounding the definition of social capital. It is usually distinguished from physical, financial and human capital, with these generally being interpreted from within neoclassical orthodoxy. Although it can require the use of economic resources, it has to be something over and above other types of capital but, as such, it seems to be able to be *anything* ranging over public goods, networks, culture, etc. The only proviso is that social capital should be attached to the economy in a functionally positive way for economic performance, especially growth. As Harriss and de Renzio (1997, p. 921) observe in quoting Narayan and Pritchett (1996, p. 2) in what is probably an understatement, "Social capital, while not all things to all people, is many

---

9   For social capital at the World Bank, see especially Fine (2001 and 2010b) and, most recently, Fine (2023) but also Fine (2001, 2002c, 2003b, 2004b and c, 2005a, 2006d, 2008 and 2011b) and Fine and Ortiz (2016).

things to many people". In a three-page footnote of references, Woolcock (1998, p. 193–96) identifies seven different fields of application for social capital – (dys)functional families, schooling, community life, work and organisation, democracy and governance, collective action, and intangible assets.

The ambiguity and scope attached to social capital, however, are strikingly illustrated by the attempts to trace back its intellectual origins, a task which testifies to the speed and depth with which the notion has already been established.[10] At one extreme, Hyden (1997) locates the concept within the different approaches to the relationship between the state and civil society as development proceeds, dating first explicit references to the mid-nineteenth century albeit in Italian. In this context, social capital is concerned with grand theory and systemic analysis from whatever perspective.

At the other extreme, the more recent and more influential origins of social capital are far more mundane. They derive from the work of James Coleman (1987, 1988 and 1990). He is professor of sociology at the University of Chicago and is the counterpart and practising intellectual partner to Gary Becker. He is fundamentally committed to methodological individualism, although this is tempered by reference to social networks and the like.[11] Coleman has inspired a range of empirical studies, mainly for the United States, that seek to demonstrate how individual attainment is affected by family or other aspects of the micro-social environment, readily interpreted as (individual possession of) social capital. Whether parents are separated, mothers work or not, families belong to particular ethnic or cultural communities, are new or long-established migrants, move frequently, communicate with their children, watch tv, and so on are the variables that make up positive or negative social capital. These factors are used to interrogate success at school or college, including drop-outs, and correlation with criminality, delinquency and political extremism.[12]

It cannot be over-emphasised how crude are such studies: speculate about a few causal relations and then seek to demonstrate their validity through a statistical exercise. There is a striking parallel with mainstream econometrics but with the absence of the latter's reliance upon some underlying formal

---

10   See Harriss and de Renzio (1997, p. 921) and Woolcock (1998) but especially Fine (2007a).

11   For a more detailed account, see Fine (1998b).

12   For a recent selection of such work, in order to give a feel for its scope, see Bianchi and Robinson (1997), Furstenberg and Hughes (1995), Hagan et al. (1995 and 1996), Meyerson (1994), Parcel and Menaghan (1994), Sanders and Nee (1996), Schneider et al. (1997), Smith et al. (1995), Teachman et al. (1996), Valenzuela and Dornbusch (1994), White and Kaufman (1997) and Zhou and Bankston (1994).

mathematical model. A further analogy applies where macro-data is substi-
tuted for micro-data as if there were representative individuals with crime
rates, for example, explained by levels of unemployment, mobility and marriage (MacMillan, 1995). Such studies have the explicit aim of leaping from the
individual to the social by the use of macro-structural indicators and statistics
to avoid both conceptual issues and the causal mechanisms and processes by
which the social is reproduced.

From a moment's reflection, it is apparent that such endeavours have nothing
new to contribute through appeal to social capital which merely serves as a convenient peg on which to hang collections of dull and mechanistic empiricism.
This is despite the unlimited scope of such studies in terms of variables that can
be included and hypotheses putatively tested. But the notion of social capital is
open to a richer qualitative interpretation which expands its compass even further, especially in the context of development. For Shetler (1995), as limited an
object as a Kiroba text of popular history forms social capital in Tanzania since
it depicts a constellation of networks and social relations that can inform and
sustain those who draw upon it. Putterman (1995), also addressing Tanzania,
seeks to generalise social capital as culture beyond a set of individual ties "to
encompass the repertoires of entire material cultures", p. 15. Indeed, "a society's
division of labour with respect to the holding of its overall cultural capital stock
can be regarded as a kind of collective memory algorithm".

Such cultural interpretations of social capital have affinities with the work
of Bourdieu which preceded by a decade or so the contributions of Coleman.[13]
Bourdieu is concerned to demonstrate how class distinctions are constructed,
created and reproduced by the inter-connections between the different
spheres of economic, political and cultural life. His approach involves deployment of various different types of social capital, such as the cultural and educational, the consideration of how these are converted into one another, and the
attachment of such capitals to individuals as well as to socioeconomic group-
ings. In short, the language and analogy of economic capital is embraced, and
Bourdieu has engaged in case studies based on surveys. Consequently, his work
has been referenced in support of other social capital studies.

Nonetheless, there is a major difference, even analytical barrier, between
Bourdieu and most of the subsequent literature.[14] Whilst critical of the excesses

---

13   See Fine (1998b) for a fuller critical account of Bourdieu's understanding of social capital
      and how it has been distortedly incorporated into more recent understandings.
14   For this reason, in an otherwise highly perceptive review, it is unfortunate that Harriss
      and de Renzio (1997) simply perceive Bourdieu's use of social capital as similar to that of
      followers.

of postmodernism, and of Baudrillard in particular, Bourdieu is acutely aware that social capital has to be constructed in terms of its content as meaning. In contrast, current use of the notion of social capital relies almost entirely upon distinction by extrapolation from physical notions of capital. Whilst explicitly seeking to generalise beyond the physical, to distinguish social from economic and even human capital, the conceptual framework primarily remains tied to an understanding of the social as the informational or other cultural externalities between individuals. Accordingly, a network of whatever sort, for example, is the favoured non-individualistic example of social capital – although this begs the question within this perspective of how a network is created and how and why individuals participate within it. The result is to generate an abstract theory of social capital which focuses on the logistics of networks, at greater or lesser levels of formality (as for Burt, 1992; Granovetter, 1985 and 1992; and Ostrom, 1994).[15]

Consequently, the next major stage in the evolution of social capital is in the passage from Coleman to Putnam (1993a and b and 1995). From a conceptual point of view, he has added very little, and his study of differential Italian economic development according to local politics is open to question.[16] Most important, though, is the spread of use of social capital to politics and the state. Whilst his more recent work has focused on the revitalisation of US social capital, to the point of self-parody in seeking more ten-pin bowling clubs (Putnam, 1995), the implications of his work for development have proved most attractive (Putnam, 1993b, p. 38):

> Social capital is coming to be seen as a vital ingredient in economic devel-
> opment around the world. Scores of studies of rural development have
> shown that a vigorous network of indigenous grassroots associations can

---

15 Note that Burt (1997) appeals to the emerging network analysis to consider the content of flows within the network relations. But, significantly, this would imply that the substance of the network would be conflated with discursive content within the network, as if the two were interchangeable. By analogy, it would be necessary to distinguish between a grid and what flows along it. Social capital, in effect, is caught between being grid alone and both grid and flow. This reveals the ambiguity of the network notion of social capital, since identical networks can function positively or negatively for economic or other performance according to what is communicated. See also later discussion of perverse social capital.

16 See discussion and references provided in Harriss and de Renzio (1997). Most important are questions of causation between economic development and civic society and of differential development *within* as well as between regions.

be as essential to growth as physical investment, appropriate technology, or (that nostrum of neoclassical economists) "getting prices right".

From one study of Italy (Putnam 1993a) in which the concept of social capital is only first introduced in a closing chapter, the floodgates are opened for that "vital ingredient" to explain "economic development around the world"!

In short, the notion of social capital is all-encompassing. As Woolcock (1998, p. 155) observes:

> It now assumes a wide variety of meanings and has been cited in a rapidly increasing number of social, political, and economic studies, but – as so often happens with promising new terms in social science – with limited critical attention being given to its intellectual history or its conceptual and ontological status. These indiscriminate applications of social and "other" capitals are part of what Baron and Hannan (1994, p. 1122–24) disparingly refer to as the recent emergence of a "plethora of capitals". Sociologists, they lament, "have begun referring to virtually every feature of life as a form of capital".

A second major feature, then, of social capital follows in that it is a totally chaotic concept, drawing its meanings from the more or less abstract studies or tidal waves of case studies on which it depends. This, in turn, has led to a critical literature along a number of lines which essentially reflect the imprecision with which the dual notions of "social" and "capital" have been used and combined. The social takes as its point of departure anything that is not reducible to individualistic exchange relations and, correspondingly, social capital is anything other than tangible assets. This immediately creates problems since it can never be clear where the capital ends and the social begins, once it is recognised that the impact of social capital depends upon its social context – unless any element of social capital is redefined holistically.

The point is illustrated by evidence of 'perverse' social capital. The term derives from the study by Rubio (1997) of Colombia where criminal activity is associated with strong networks.[17] The simplest economics, however, suffices to make the same point – as Adam Smith observed, producers meet and

---

17   See also Seron and Ferris (1995) who argue that men gain in professional occupations, over and above the networks in which they engage, because they enjoy the gendered social capital that requires that private lives are secondary and taken care of by others, presumed to be their wives. For a critique of Putnam from a perspective of the 'dark side' of social capital, see Putzel (1997).

require trust to operate a cartel.[18] There is not necessarily anything positive or pre-determined about the impact of social capital, until both its intrinsic and extrinsic content is examined. As Dezalay and Garth (1997) argue for the functioning of international law, large US law firms and law schools comprise legal and social capital (political connections) that lead to the Americanisation of laws to the advantage of US economic power.[19] The study by Beall (1997, p. 960) of waste collection services draws analogous conclusions:[20]

> Synergy across the public-private divide ... between representatives of communities and governments were seen to reinforce and cement relationships founded on patronage and clientelism rather than to foster more inclusive forms of civic engagement ... As with Bangalore so in Faisalabad, power relations and existing structures of inequality have to be understood because in both cases, investment in social capital in waste proved to be a solid investment, but for some far more than others.

This example illustrates that the chaotic and incoherent content of social capital as a concept does not, however, lead it to be without systematic content and influence. A third feature of the literature is that it tends to neglect power and conflict (no doubt reflecting the putative Pareto improvements that can be made with social capital), and to proceed from the micro to the macro (in conformity with its individualistic origins). It also spawns popularisation, as with Putnam but also Fukuyama (1995 and 1996), for whom trust begins where history ends![21]

---

18   Note also that the idea that the gaps between dense networks are a source of profitability, as opposed to networks themselves, is implicit in Hilferding's concept of finance capital.

19   On the other hand, note that Arnold and Kay (1995) suggest that large law firms embody social capital since they are more liable to be self-monitoring in establishing legal and ethical standards.

20   See also Fox (1997). Stone (1995) draws similar conclusions for social capital concerning problems of definition and causation in commenting upon the account by Hinrich (1995) of inequality and redistribution in health provision in Germany.

21   To give him credit, Fukuyama does have the capacity to capture the intellectual mood, even if in the crudest forms (Fukuyama, 1996, p. 13), "Over the past generation, economic thought has been dominated by neoclassical or free market economists, associated with names like Milton Friedman, Gary Becker, and George Stigler. The rise of the neoclassical perspective constitutes a vast improvement from earlier decades in this century, when Marxists and Keynesians held sway. We can think of neoclassical economics as being, say, eighty percent correct: it has uncovered important truths about the nature of money and markets because its fundamental model of rational, self-interested human behavior is correct about eighty percent of the time. But there is a missing twenty percent of human behavior about which neoclassical economics can give only a poor account. As Adam

These features of social capital – as catch-all, ambiguous if not incoherent, and yet analytically selective – have, paradoxically, been the source of a vibrant research programme around it rather than a cause of its demise. On the one hand, theory has sought to construct a range of intermediate concepts within which to accommodate the analytical and empirical anomalies that inevitably arise – from networks and trust to structural holes,[22] and from notions that social capital is free to its being slow to create and quick to dissipate.[23] By the same token, initial lines of causation posited from social capital to social outcomes can be reversed and refined. On the other hand, social capital can be taken for granted conceptually and incorporated into an ever-expanding collection of case studies or statistical exercises. These two different ways of proceeding feed upon one another, creating a web of eclecticism in which the notion of social capital floats freely from one meaning to another with little attention to conceptual depth or rigour.[24] As Woolcock (1998, p. 159) proposes:[25]

Smith well understood, economic life is deeply embedded in social life, and it cannot be understood apart from the customs, morals, and habits of the society in which it occurs. In short, it cannot be divorced from culture". For a critique of Fukuyama along the lines that it is the rule of law rather than custom that is important, see Fellmeth (1996) who concludes, on the discovery that political culture matters to economic behavior, p. 169, "Fukuyama has merely rediscovered the wheel, although he has used it as an impediment rather than a mode of transport".

22   See Fedderke et al. (1998) who also emphasise that the ambiguities attached to social capital have their counterpart in the difficulties of operationalising the factors concerned empirically. Nonetheless, empirical studies proceed apace (as in Knack and Keefer, 1997, for example).

23   See Wilson (1997) for whom social capital is free, invisible but real, involving stakeholder participation, professional protocol, social learning, collaboration, trust, solutions to tragedies of the commons, collective responsibilities, etc. For Walker et al. (1997, p. 111), "social capital is a means of enforcing norms of behavior ... and thus acts as a constraint as well as a resource"!

24   Most notable is the way that combinations of Bourdieu, Coleman, Putnam, Granovetter, Burt and, increasingly, Fukuyama, are referenced for authority. See Nichols (1996), for example, for the idea that Russia lacks trust. See also Kolankiewicz (1996) for appeal to Bourdieu and Putnam to explain who will become the new capitalists in eastern Europe. Pahl (1996) prefers to emphasise access to property than to social capital. For various examples of the rounding up together of the founders of social capital, see, for example, Meyerson (1994) and Pieterse (1997) as well as Harriss and de Renzio (1997) and Woolcock (1998).

25   Yet, despite his initial criticisms, Woolcock became charmed by social capital (or the rewards of being seduced), and one of its leading proponents at the World Bank. See Fine (2008) and Preamble for the extreme apologetics involved.

Where do these criticisms of the idea of social capital … leave us? Short of dismissing the term altogether, one possible resolution of these concerns may be that there are different types, levels or dimensions of social capital, different performance outcomes associated with different combinations of these dimensions, and different sets of conditions that support or weaken favorable combinations. Unraveling and resolving these issues requires a more dynamic than static understanding of social capital; it invites a more detailed examination of the intellectual history of social capital, and the search for lessons from empirical research that embrace a range of many such dimensions, levels, or conditions.

4   Neither Washington nor Post-Washington Consensus

It seems, then, that what has already happened with social capital as an organising concept is set to gather pace and momentum especially, if not exclusively, in development studies. For it is prospectively nothing other than the rewriting of social theory with some degree of economic content. But the question is why? In part, the answer is to be found in the shifting stance of the World Bank. The proposal for a Post-Washington (economic) Consensus from Stiglitz has social capital as its exact social and political counterpart. It builds up from the micro to the macro from notions of civil, as opposed to market, imperfections and with the potential for non-market improvements with impact upon the market.

It is one thing, however, to argue in principle that the economic analysis attached to the Post-Washington Consensus and the notions of social capital are mutually compatible. It is another to establish in practice that they are driving one another and are being integrated to form a new synthesis. At most, given early days, such a synthesis can only be suggested to be prospective. Stiglitz, for example, does not appear to use the term himself. However, this reflects the following factors that are of more general relevance.[26]

First, he does not need to do so. The new micro-foundations, on which he has built his reputation and with which he is attacking the old neoliberal Consensus, have been around for at least two decades. The notion of market imperfections suffices as a proxy for social capital within the economist's

---

26   Stiglitz remained relatively aloof from social capital, at least until long after he had departed the World Bank, even if also simultaneously managing to jump the post-diluvian micro-credit bandwagon, Haldar and Stiglitz (2016), long after it had already lost its sheen (Fine, 2023).

vocabulary. Second, as an economist, Stiglitz has preferred to recognise the importance of the non-economic in the form of institutions, customs, etc but without incorporating these as variables within his own analysis. Third, economists tend to rely upon extremely formal mathematical models for which the vague notion of social capital is unhelpful. Rather than use the term, economists are liable to refer to its microeconomic specifics, as in infrastructure, networks, transparency, trust, monitoring, etc.[27] Whether economists use the term, and whether they are happy with it, is less relevant than the way in which their new microeconomic understanding of market imperfections is being incorporated into the economic understanding of non-economists.

Nonetheless, Stiglitz comes as close to using the notion of social capital as his intellectual history allows. In the paper following his appointment to the World Bank, he asserts (Stiglitz, 1997, p. 19):

> Today, we recognize that development is more than the accretion of physical capital and even more than the accretion of human capital. It includes closing the knowledge gap between rich and poor economies. And it includes other transformations, such as those that result in lower population growth rates and changes in economic organization.

However, irrespective of his personal stance, taken together, the new Consensus and social capital offer the World Bank the analytical opportunity to resolve what has been a glaring contradiction between its ideology and practice. Given the previous stance in favour of state minimalism, even if serving as a veil for considerable discretionary intervention in practice, there has been a problem in addressing what role the state should play given its continuing importance. You cannot argue that the state should do nothing but also fail to debate what the state should do. The World Bank has been disarmed by its own ideology. Now, rather than becoming genuinely more state-friendly, it is more appropriately interpreted as seeking to be more influential than before over what the state does – both in depth and scope.[28]

This new agenda explains why Putnam, for example, should prove to be so popular with the World Bank. Consider Putnam (1993b, p. 42):

---

27   See the treatment by Konrad (1995), for example, of infrastructure as social capital. An older generation provides it for the younger, not out of altruism, but as an intertemporal optimising exercise in view of the later higher taxes it can take from the next generation's higher earnings for use as social security transfers to itself.

28   For a clear and perceptive account, see Hildyard (1998).

> *Social capital is not a substitute for effective public policy but rather a*
> *prerequisite for it and, in part, a consequence of it. Social capital ... works*
> *through and within states and markets, not in place of them ...* The social
> capital approach promises to uncover new ways of combining social
> infrastructure with public policies that work, and, in turn, of using wise
> public policies to revitalize America's stock of social capital.

And what is good enough for the United State is good enough for the rest of
the world. In short, as it is being deployed, social capital allows the World Bank
to broaden its agenda whilst retaining continuity with most of its practices
and prejudices which include the benign neglect of macro-relations of power,
preference for favoured NGOs and grassroots movements, and decentralised
initiatives.[29]

The rapid rise to prominence of social capital has also had, as will be seen
shortly, two crucial analytical effects. Initially, observe, as Wade (1996) has
shown and is common knowledge, the shifting position of the World Bank has
very little to do with consideration, let alone acceptance, of the overwhelming
weight of scholarship that has long been turned critically upon its analytical
posturing and the impact of its policies in practice. Nor is it a response to the
new micro-foundations orthodoxy, for Stiglitz and others have been active in
this area for two decades. Rather, the increasing significance of Japan as donor,
foreign investor and self-reflective case study has rendered the old Consensus
increasingly unacceptable.[30]

Broadly, the criticisms that have been ignored by the old Consensus have
been formulated, at times explicitly, around the notion of the case and conditions conducive for a developmental state. This is hardly surprising since
to counter the old Consensus on its own terms is to posit the potential for a
developmental state as opposed to relying as far as possible upon the supposedly free market. For the role of the state to be addressed more positively by
the new Consensus, the issue arises of how it is to relate to the developmental
state literature.

First, then, the notion of social capital has provided the World Bank with
the analytical capacity to propose its new agenda without having had to come
to terms in any serious or substantive way with the critical literature of the old
Consensus, especially that around the developmental state. And, one suspects,

---

29   See Brown and Ashman (1996) for a selection of case studies tied to the notion of social
      capital.
30   See also Gyohten (1997) but especially the relevant articles collected in Ohno and Ohno
      (eds) (1998).

the new Consensus will be mild in reassessing the past practices of the old and how they were rationalised by those who will, presumably, continue to provide the rationale for the new agenda in the future. Whatever its merits, the literature on the developmental state will be ignored, as in the past, in pushing forward an agenda based on social capital and the need to enhance the market and relieve market imperfections.

Indeed, the way in which this is being done already has remarkable parallels with the way in which the developmental state literature did itself develop. As Fine and Stoneman (1996) and Fine and Rustomjee (1996) suggest, there have been two broad approaches to the developmental state, denoted as the "economic" and the "political" schools. One identifies, for example from market imperfections, the case for state intervention without addressing why the state might have the capacity or the will to undertake the necessary policies. The other considers the (political) conditions under which the state is capable of, or induced to, undertake appropriate interventions without identifying what these are. The integration of these two schools has been quite limited but each has prospered by a widening circle of empirical case studies undermining more abstract theory and leading it to be refined by a proliferation of ideal-types – most notable in the different theories of the sources of comparative advantage for the economic school and also the proliferating models of developmental or non-developmental states for the political school.

Corresponding to the economic school approach to the developmental state is the new micro-foundations of market imperfections. As Stiglitz emphasises repeatedly, such informationally-based imperfections can rationalise state intervention. Yet, this depends upon applying a dramatic reductionism to the rationale for state intervention to a micro-level, around a single informational motif in sharp contrast to the wealth of the theoretical and empirical factors that make up the economic school within the developmental state literature.

Social capital, following on hard upon the new microeconomics, is the corresponding counterpart to the political school within the developmental state literature. It is about how the non-economic, or non-market, makes the economic work or work better. Again, a reductionism is involved, although it is less drastic than for the economic school, as it allows for notions such as custom, trust, culture, networks, etc. Where it does correspond more closely with the new economic approach is in its capacity to set aside the broader methodological and theoretical agenda to be found within the critical developmental state literature emanating from the political school.

Second, then, the notion of social capital allows the new Consensus to be selective in where and how it addresses the role of non-economic factors in economic performance. In this light, social capital has had the analytical effect not only of perpetuating neglect of the critical contribution of the developmental state literature, it also allows for that literature and its proponents to be incorporated on the terms set by the new Consensus. As Harris and de Renzio (1997, p. 921) ask:

> Does the fact that it means so many different things reflect the fact that it is an idea which serves as a convenient peg for different agendas?

The answer is in the affirmative in that it opens up an agenda for those who opposed the old Consensus; but there is an admission price in terms of accepting the social as based on micro-foundations and capital as based on market or non-market imperfections. Notably absent will be a political economy based on class and power, and capital interpreted as a social relation rather than as a non-physical, atomised resource. In short, where the developmental state literature previously stood as a critique of the old Consensus, it can now either be overlooked or be repackaged as new in terms of a much less radical content attached to market imperfections and social capital.

The prospect, then, is for the developmental state literature from the political school to be re-digested within a social capital framework, just as the new micro-foundations of macroeconomics have demonstrated the potential to incorporate much radical political economy based on institutions and macroeconomic structures. Consider, for example, the response to social capital of one of the leading proponents of the developmental state within political science. In a special section in *World Development* on social capital and the role of the state in the public/private sector divide, there is a remarkable and acknowledged synergy between the political and the sociological involved in networks and embeddedness (Evans, 1996a, p. 1033):[31]

> By labelling such norms and networks "social capital" contemporary theorists ... project primary ties as potentially valuable economic assets ... The language echoes Granovetter's classic work on the embeddedness of market relations.

In this way, the politics of bringing the state back in and the theory of the developmental state have become tied to the notion of social capital and rendered more amenable to the tacit postulates of the mainstream economic theory associated with the Post-Washington Consensus. Of course, the location

---

31   Granovetter is a sociologist who has inspired the notion of social capital as networks.

of such capital within the discipline of political science can lead to a more sophisticated account of, and focus upon, conflict which is perceived otherwise to be overlooked in addressing problems of collective action across the public/private divide – as Evans (1996b, p. 1127) unremarkably deduces in summarising the analytical conclusions of a number of case studies:

> If a community is riven by conflicting interests, the nature and meaning of social capital becomes more complicated.

The inevitable implication from this conclusion is that if conflict undermines the notion of social capital, then why not take conflict and its theoretical underpinnings as starting point rather than social capital which is rendered both ambiguous and redundant. To proceed otherwise is to deploy social capital as a generalised proxy for the developmental state in ways such that conflict and its analytical prerequisites can be secondary, muffled or even be brought out.

5   Concluding Remarks

Elsewhere, I have argued that conceptual initiatives around social capital are part and parcel of a more general, possibly revolutionary, shift taking place not so much within as around economics in its relationship with other social sciences.[32] Economics is colonising other disciplines through universalising its methods, including those new microfoundations that now explain the social on the basis of the individual. The response from other social sciences has been mixed in depth and content. The promotion of social capital in the context of the Post-Washington Consensus is an example drawn from development studies. It promises to create economists out of social scientists who know no economics, just as it has been given life by economists as social scientists who know no social science. Even those Marxists most committed to base-superstructure models would be embarrassed by the reductionism of the economic approach to social science. By the same token, those wedded to some notion of autonomy, should shrink from the absence of the economic in many of the ways in which social capital is being deployed across the social sciences. For those genuinely committed to political economy, both the opportunity and the obligation have arisen to develop alternatives to, and to oppose,

---

32   See Fine (1997b, 1998b, 1998c and 1999b).

social capital and the new Consensus before they dominate the development agenda as did the old Consensus before them.

These observations are strikingly illustrated by the opposing conclusions drawn by two recent surveys of the social capital literature. This is despite each of them making very similar critical commentary on the ambiguity and inconsistency of the notion. For Woolcock (1998, p. 188):

> Social capital provides sociologists in particular with a fruitful conceptual and policy device by which to get beyond exhausted modernization and world-systems theories ... In social capital, historians, political scientists, anthropologists, economists, sociologists, and policy makers ... may once again be able to find a common language ... that disciplinary provincialisms have largely suppressed over the last one-hundred-and-fifty years ... Theoretical claims and policy recommendations made on the basis of the incremental accumulation of evidence constitute the surest and most responsible agenda for future research.

Harriss and de Renzio (1997, p. 919) are considerably less sanguine:

> Policy arguments which pose civil society against the state, or which rest on the view that rich endowment in "social capital" is a precondition for "good government", are almost certainly misconceived.

They seem to seek a critical rethinking of social capital in which the traditional concerns of more radical social and economic theory are incorporated – whether it be conflict, class, globalisation or whatever.

In each of these surveys, despite its acknowledged conceptual weaknesses, social capital is accepted as a potential source for new research, although Woolcock is more upbeat in case of greater refinement in concrete details and Harriss and de Renzio for the incorporation of a radical content that could easily be omitted. As already suggested, the outcome is most likely to be a reworking of the developmental state debate, only on an analytical terrain that is less conducive to opponents of the new Washington Consensus, even though some advance is made, as intended, over the old. For the notion of social capital is fundamentally misconceived, especially in the context and sources from which it has evolved. For to deconstruct in the crudest way, term by term in reverse order, "capital" has been defined negatively – by what it is not. It is not tangible, such as physical endowments or human capital. Rather, it is anything connecting individuals that contributes to the economy on the basis of their individual endowments of non-social capital. By the same token, the "social" is the set of relations, market or non-market, that connects these individuals with a greater or lesser degree of imperfection. With these notions of social and capital, their genuine counterparts within political economy or within social theory – economic structures and tendencies, on the one hand, and power, stratification, conflict, on the other – can only be incorporated in bastardised or hopelessly eclectic forms.

It is imperative, then, that as and when the World Bank and the development agenda become potentially more progressive, that "capital" and the "social" be appropriately constructed on the basis of systematic understandings. As Marx and Marxists, for example, have long insisted, economic "capital" is not a thing in the first place but is already social, global, exploitative, and embedded, to coin a phrase, in broader relations of which the state forms a part. The social can only be added to capital if it has been illegitimately excluded in the first place. Such elementary insights need to be the starting point for developmental dissent to whatever Consensus the World Bank peddles.

Flattening Economic Geography: Locating the World Development Report for 2009

Postscript as Personal Preamble

This is the first of two chapters, each of which offers a critical response to World Development Reports. In the next Chapter, the target is the WDR for 2015, and its introduction has a brief comment on the WDRs as a whole (Fine et al. 2016b). Its topic is behavioural economics and 'nudge'. This Chapter covers the WDR for 2009 and the new economic geography (NEG). I am unsure why I targeted some WDRs and not others. Some topics would have been more or less outside my areas of expertise. It may have had more to do with some combination of levels of critical despair and of not being otherwise engaged. I have always been disturbed and disappointed at the extent to which the WDRs have escaped ruthless criticism although it has been far from absent if tending to be confined to a small group of dedicated scholars and organisations and whatever is the topic for one year to the next.

Nonetheless, the WDR on NEG offers an exemplary case of economics imperialism in general, and of its application to development economics/studies, in particular. In part, this is reflected in the presence of idiosyncratic features marked by the topic as such, how it has evolved within non-economic disciplines, and how these have received and responded to the designs of economics imperialism. Significantly, economic geography has long embraced the social (and the spatial) which has led to a reaction against the deterministic approaches (more in line with regional science) associated with economics (imperialism). It has also been heavily influenced both by postmodernism and Marxist approaches, with David Harvey and Doreen Massey to the fore for the latter and still highly influential. As a result, NEG has been embraced by some within economic geography but firmly rejected by others (as both wrong and reinvention of a previously discarded wheel). In this respect, there are affinities with the split engineered between economic and social history as a result of the cliometrics revolution (Fine, 2024c).

In addition, whilst NEG has its technical origins in market imperfection economics, these are different from those attached to informational imperfections, most strongly associated with Stiglitz. Indeed, NEG's origins are most strongly underpinned by that supposed instance of market imperfection, increasing returns to scale. As these must be absent for much of economic theory to work (at least in narrowly conceived conditions of competition), this is why they are designated as an imperfection (although the world would not get on very well without them). And, just as increasing returns displace informational asymmetries, so Paul Krugman displaces Joe Stiglitz as pioneer.[1] Moreover, NEG gets worked together with, or draws upon the same factors as, new trade theory and new growth theory.[2]

Apart, implicitly, from the notions that I dub Boxonomics and the XY syndrome (see below), given when it was written this Chapter only hints at the third phase of economics imperialism. It is fully critically embraced in the next Chapter.

1   Introduction[3]

The focus of the World Bank's, World Development Report for 2009, entitled *Reshaping Economic Geography* and shortened here to WDR09, offers an opportunity to assess the state of play of the so-called new economic geography (NEG) on which the Report heavily if not exclusively draws. But, to put it bluntly for maximum effect, WDR09 is not a serious work of scholarship other than on its own narrow terms. Yet it does need to be taken seriously. In this critique, I seek to locate its contribution in the context of the evolution of an economics imperialism (EI) that has incorporated both the NEG, see Section 2, and the new(er) development economics, Section 3. This allows much of the content of WDR09 to be fixed in terms of its substantive content, although it also allows for some flexibility, Section 4. The final section remarks upon the extraordinary absence of both climate and finance from the Report and concludes by seeking a renewal of political economy and geography as a means to address the specific with the systemic.

---

1   I have always been curious about the relationship between Stiglitz and Krugman, each Nobel Laureates, each on the progressive side of mainstream economics and its policies, and each leading figures in market imperfections economics and economics imperialism even if with one emphasising asymmetric information and the other increasing returns. In most respects, possibly the media aside, Stiglitz is earlier and more prominent than Krugman. But there would appear to be a remarkable lack of engagement between the two despite so much in common, including purpose and energy.

2   See, for example, Fine (1996 and 2000, 2003a and 2006b, respectively).

3   First appearing as Fine (2010a). Thanks, especially to Stefan Ouma, for indispensable comments and suggestions on a first draft, leading to a more rounded and tempered outcome.

2   NEG as EI

From the perspective of those working within the discipline of (economic or human, and even I suspect, physical) geography, the WDR09 is extraordinarily limited in the theory, concepts, methods and the corresponding literatures upon which it draws. This is so much so that the suspicion must be that this is not a deliberate choice on the part of its authors but an almost unimaginable display of ignorance and lack of scholarly integrity as far as commitment to relevant literature is concerned. The academic economist is much more likely to look into a well-established technical toolbox based on orthodoxy than other treatments of the topic at hand that tend to be dismissed as lacking rigour or science for any departure from a (formal/mathematical) deductive method. For, as observed of the Report (Maringanti et al. 2009, p. 47):

> Only six citations are to geography journals, in a 25-page bibliography; five are authored by card-carrying economists and the sixth was published 40 years ago. Of the 250 or so individuals thanked for their contributions, comments, guidance and support at the end of the Report from all over the world, two are geographers (as far as we know).

Of course, such neglect is not only true of the WDR09 itself but also of the new field of new economic geography upon which it draws as will be only too familiar to critical economic geographers. Critiques of NEG are devastating and almost as longstanding as the field itself, pointing especially to lack of originality and knowledge of literature and of consideration of the social (re) construction of space itself in any meaningful sense (Martin, 1999) and (Fine and Milonakis, 2009), and a cascade of corresponding absences as has been remarked upon already by reviews of the WDR09 by geographers (Bryceson et al. 2009; Rigg et al. 2009; Scott, 2009; Harvey, 2009; and Maringanti et al. 2009).[4]

There are those in a much better position than me to make these criticisms, and they should be made again and again, tedious and unrewarding though the task may be, both in order to defend economic geography against the designs of the NEG and to highlight and promote richer and more soundly-based alternatives. Otherwise, of course, the NEG will simply prosper as it has

---

4   All of these offer useful critical and wide-ranging insights on the WDR09 from the perspective of geographers, so the intent here in part is less to do this than to provide the same from the perspective, not entirely different, of political economy (whilst bringing out and unduly emphasising differences with the geographers).

already done so by virtue of the dull compulsion of its proponents' untiring and well-rewarded efforts. What I would emphasise in addition is that the *narrowness* of the NEG from the perspective of geography looks entirely different from the perspective of (mainstream) economics where the presumption is that an unduly confined discipline is *broadening* both its explanatory content and scope of application. In this respect, the encroachment, to put it mildly, of economics onto geography is far from unique as the same process has been involved across the other social sciences although, it is to be emphasised, the incidence, depth and content of such initiatives are differentiated by discipline and topic for a range of reasons around both supply and demand for them, to deploy the vernacular.

In other words, how does the emergence of NEG relate to what has been termed 'economics imperialism', the colonisation of the other social sciences by economics. This is a matter both of substance and chronology, as is evident from the *historical logic* of economics imperialism (Fine and Milonakis, 2009). For EI derives from the now standard microeconomic principles (axiomatic deduction from optimising behaviour around utility and production functions) that were first adopted and then developed and refined following the marginalist revolution within economics of the 1870s. By the 1950s, the inner logical development of the principles had reached fruition with the formal results around supply and demand derived from individual optimisation, and the aggregation of corresponding rational economic behaviour over all individuals, in conditions of perfect markets, to allow for general equilibrium. From this point on, these microeconomic principles became more or less sacrosanct and the mark of an increasingly exclusive, professionalised and Americanised discipline, especially in the wake of what has been dubbed the formalist revolution of the 1950s, led by Paul Samuelson.

Paradoxically, though, the triumph of these principles logically could only be achieved in the first instance at two great, closely related costs. On the one hand, to obtain them required what is best described as an implosion around the core principles, discarding methods, concepts, factors, even realism, to obtain the required results so that utility becomes reduced to a logic of choice from given preferences over given goods, and so on, the taking of the historical and the social out of economics. On the other hand, until the 1950s, such endeavours were perceived, even within the discipline of economics itself, as at most filling out one small part of individual economic behaviour as opposed to addressing the role of more rounded individuals *and*, in addition, systemic analysis. Significantly, in the thirties, what is now dubbed the old institutional economics, founded and most closely associated with Thorstein Veblen, was as prominent as today's mainstream in the United States. And, of course,

Keynesianism emerged as a response to the Great Depression with the fledgling microeconomics scarcely capable of addressing its systemic concerns either analytically or in policy terms (how to sustain full employment through manipulation of effective demand).

In short, the *historical* place of microeconomics within the discipline immediately after the second world war was for it to be both subordinate to macroeconomics and for it to be more or less confined, however sufficiently from a more critical point of view, to supply and demand within the market. However, the *logic* of the principles, once established, was one of *universal* application as utility maximisation and its corresponding technical apparatus are without historical or social specificity (other than by critical reference to the environment of the intellectual origins that spawned it). This historical logic has given rise to a tension in the scope of application of microeconomic principles, one with a distinct and paradoxical chronology in outcome. As already indicated, prior to the formalist revolution of the 1950s, the principles imploded in content and application in order to be able to be established. But, once established, subject to favourable inner and outer conditions, that excluded content could be broached once more, albeit in the reduced form compatible with the core principles, in an explosion of application both within the discipline and across the social sciences more generally.[5]

As a result, EI first began to take serious hold from the 1950s onwards in a first phase in which the non-economic was treated as if equivalent to a market. In retrospect, Gary Becker took the lead, across a number of applications of which human capital is the most prominent, but it also included public choice theory and the new economic history pioneered by Douglass North. Despite these successes, the appeal and scope of EI remained limited, primarily because of the limited success within the discipline of microeconomics itself as Keynesianism and various more rounded, empirically-based elements of applied economics continued to hold sway. This all changed with the collapse of the post-war boom, the triumph of neoliberalism and the emergence of a particularly virulent and extreme attachment to methodological individualism and hype-rationality, the New Classical Economics, in which markets are perceived to work perfectly and the state is ineffective at the macroeconomic level and distorting at the microeconomic level. As put in Lucas (1987, p. 108), "the term 'macroeconomic' will simply disappear from use and the modifier 'micro' will be superfluous". We are even served up with real business cycle

---

5   See Fine (2007c) for the hypothesis that more account was taken of the assumptions involved in taking the historical and social out of economics in the passage from marginalist to formalist revolution than in bringing them back in again through economics imperialism.

theory in which fluctuations in the economy are either due to random shocks and/or to the rhythm of voluntary unemployment as workers tend only to choose to be in the labour market when productivity increase is faster.

The impact of such developments within the discipline, apart from supporting neoliberalism ideologically, was to consolidate the technical apparatus associated with its peculiar form of methodological individualism, to reduce macro to micro (the systemic to the individual), and to pose opposition to these extremes in terms of explaining why markets might work imperfectly despite optimising behaviour. Within economics, this soon gave rise to a new microeconomics, in a reaction against the New Classical Economics, of emphasising market imperfections in general (although these were far from new as such), with the idea of imperfect information as the novelty in explaining why markets might be efficient, not clear, or fail to emerge at all in some cases. In addition, emphasis could be placed on externalities and increasing returns to scale as market imperfections requiring property rights and account of transaction costs and institutions as a means to handle them. The result was not only to reconstruct a version of Keynesianism based on micro-foundations and to reinvigorate the piecemeal case for state intervention (to improve static efficiency). In addition, the way was opened for a new phase of EI, and one much more palatable in varying degrees to the other social sciences. For, instead of treating the non-economic as if equivalent to a market, it could be understood as the response to market imperfections. So, economists could now proudly announce that institutions, history, customs, culture, even apparently non-rational behaviour, matter despite what they might have said in the past, as they represent the rational, individualistically-based but possibly collectively-evolved, responses to so-called market imperfections.

The result was to open up or to renew fields within economics and EI. There has been a proliferation, literally, of 'new' fields – such as the new growth theory, new labour economics, new welfare economics, new financial economics, new economic sociology and, of course, new development economics and new economic geography.[6] Some of these might better be termed 'newer', as they

---

6 Some wish to exclude the new economic sociology (NES) from the menu of economics imperialism, seeing it, from Granovetter onwards, as a critique from sociology of the limited assumptions and methods of economics. My own view, though, is that the new economic sociology is a mixed bag including, at one extreme, more wide-ranging and deeper criticisms than offered by Granovetter (around collectivities and meanings of networks for example) *and, at the other,* a reductionism of the sociological to the economic. This is indicative of the different forms, directions and impacts of economics imperialism across disciplines and topics. For the NES, there is a mixed amalgam at the boundaries of the two disciplines although

depart from the 'new' in emphasising market imperfections as opposed to as if perfect market accounts of the non-economic.[7]

I will discuss development economics subsequently but where does this drastically abbreviated account locate the NEG? What is striking is its relative absence within the first phase of EI. This is not to say that questions of uneven (spatial) development were unaddressed at the time from a variety of perspectives – as in the old development economics, see below, and the work of Gunnar Myrdal in particular, and the more or less radical versions of regional science, such as Perroux (1950) and gravity-like models for location theory. In addition, economic geography itself was otherwise embarking upon a trajectory that has been totally incompatible with EI, not least in the two influences of postmodernism (across the social sciences as a whole) and Marxism (especially strong within geography) that came to the fore from the 1980s onwards (Barnes, 2001 for an informative account). In short, for the new economic geography to emerge in strength, it was necessary for EI to have moved to the second phase of EI, and for both neoliberal and postmodernist discourse to have waned, as began to occur, at least in the intellectual arena (most notably with the rise of 'globalisation' studies) from the 1990s onwards.[8]

Given these more conducive conditions, NEG took off, and it did so in two different mirror image variants with corresponding common features. One, now closely associated with Paul Krugman and his collaborators, and possibly more influential with (economic) geographers in search of deterministic theory, essentially obliterates geographical difference (in physical terms) so that it can be (re)constructed out of the distribution of economic activity whose location as opposed to patterns are more or less accidental, and determined by first-mover (dis)advantages. As opposed to this 'technicist' approach, as I will term it, is the 'physicalist' approach, closely (and previously) associated with Jeffrey Sachs for example, in which the specificity of place in terms of (dis)advantage (proximity to coast for transport, climate, prevalence of disease, etc) is all-important. The differences between the technicist and the physicalist approaches are not simply theoretical in terms of source of prime causal factor but also a matter of method, with the technicist primarily providing abstract, deductive models of equilibria with uneven outcomes, and

---

not leading, as (Hodgson, 2008) would suggest, to an evaporation of the separate disciplinary contents.

7 Ultimately, the newest form of economics imperialism is to wed the new and newer to supplementary behavioural assumptions to those of economic rationality.

8 For the dual retreat of social science from the extremes of neoliberalism and postmodernism, see Fine and Milonakis (2009).

the physicalists relying less on theory, other than as a backdrop, and running regressions of economic performance against varieties of (physical) geographical determinants.

It is essential to emphasise, though, that both approaches substantively depart from mainstream orthodoxy in economics in the most minimal of ways, simply drawing upon increasing returns to scale as a rationale for uneven spatial distribution of economic activity. Even here, it is necessary to import arbitrarily prominent assumptions that seem both trivial and yet mountain-moving. The imperfectly competitive consequences of increasing returns to scale are attached, in the technicist approach, to quality differences in products that are craved by consumers as a device to explain intra-industry international trade. As often, this is driven by the analytical requirements necessary to be able to deduce desired mathematical results as opposed to any serious consideration of the diversity of quality in consumer products and how they relate to consumer culture and commercial success. More generally, there is an isomorphic mapping between the two branches of the new economic geography and the new growth theory. For the latter, there is a theoretical branch which turns speculative or casually identified microeconomic market imperfections into increasing returns and endogenous growth (the more we invest and produce the more we increase productivity as opposed to given growth rates of old growth theory). And there is an empirical branch, Barro-type regressions, which run multiple regressions of hundreds of variables to determine the sources of growth. Significantly, new growth theory and the new economic geography both emerged and flourished at the same time, from the mid-1980s. As a simultaneous reflection of EI, no economic and social variable was safe from theoretical and empirical (and policy)[9] designs of an exploding orthodoxy.[10] Nonetheless, both strands of NEG, in light of their respective origins in speculative abstract theory as opposed to physical geography, respectively,

[9]   New growth theory offered a growth- (and hence poverty-) elasticity for every economic and social policy variable, see (Devarajan et al. 2002) in the context of the World Bank's Poverty Reduction Strategy Papers, PRSPs, and (Fine, 2006a) for a critique.

[10]   For my critique of new growth theory, see (Fine, 2000, 2003 and 2006b). Significantly, whilst still heavily present within economic orthodoxy, the theoretical and empirical gloss that it once commanded has now lessened. More sophisticated growth econometrics, for example, has shown Barro-type regressions to have been fundamentally flawed in method, incapable of providing definitive results, and (readily overlooked) the empirics themselves are inconsistent with the theory (growth is not steady, for example, as is required by equilibrium growth paths). See especially Rodriguez (2006), Islam (2003) and Durlauf et al. (2004) but also, for a laugh from their titles, Sala-i-Martin (1997) as opposed to Hendry and Krolzig (2004).

tended to eschew social variables variously gathered under the rubric of institutions and the new institutional economics around which a critique could be
launched especially against the physicalist approach.[11]

Here, though a further point should be emphasised from within economics
(over and above those that derive from a more considered understanding of
space itself that is not flattened out to exclude social relations and meanings).
This is that NEG proceeds on the basis of the methodology, method and techniques of mainstream economics by which the implosion of content allowing
it to be established is more or less entirely, but not totally, preserved (what
economists pride themselves on in terms of theoretical parsimony). This is not
simply a matter of the absence of the historical and the social (the institutional
as orthodox critics from within would have it) and even more rounded individuals in anything other than an ideal sense, but the erasure of the state, class,
conflict, power, politics, ideology and so on. This gives rise to merely mechani-
cal modelling on a simplified axiomatic deductive basis, driven by the explicit
or implicit assumption of increasing returns to scale and the consequences for
equally reduced, narrowly interpreted physicalist outcomes. There are no cities, rivers, seas, mountains, etc in the NEG, other than to define ideal locations
for economic activity, as with circular cities (with concentric roads) for example, or as the means to define transport and transaction costs and land values,
and so on for regression purposes.[12]

Related to this is a factor that primarily goes unnoticed other than by a few,
careful and disregarded critics not least because economics as a discipline

---

11   The institutionalist critique is especially associated with Daron Acemoglu and his colleagues. See Acemoglu et al. (2001) – and see the response by McArthur and Sachs (2001)
which is revealing in its abstract in setting the nature and scope of the debate, "Acemoglu,
Johnson and Robinson ... suggest weak institutions, but not physical geography and cor-
relates like disease burden, explain current variation in levels of economic development
across former colonies. Using similar data and expanding the sample of countries ana-
lyzed, our regression analysis shows that both institutions and geographically-related
variables such as malaria incidence or life expectancy at birth are strongly linked to gross
national product per capita. We argue that the evidence presented in Acemoglu, Johnson
and Robinson is likely limited by the inherently small sample of ex-colonies and the limited geographic dispersion of those countries".

12   On a personal note, I first started studying economics in 1971, and, because I had a degree
in mathematics I was immediately introduced into the closed workshop of the handful of
mathematical economists at the University of Oxford, including Mirrlees, Stern and Dixit
(my tutor). I still recall the discussion of the square city where transport was held at rest
for half the time by traffic lights to prevent accidents at crossroads. I remember simply
suggesting that drivers might seek to optimise by seeking to turn just before the lights.
I was ignored possibly in light of the difficulties in optimising on this basis.

plays scant attention to its own history and, paradoxically, lays claims to scientific rigour, inner coherence and logic whilst always sacrificing them in deference to its core microeconomic principles. For, the ability to bring back in increasing returns to scale to a technical apparatus that studiously excluded them to obtain its core results is, not surprisingly, fraught with dangers for that technical apparatus. One of its leading exponents has put this extremely well (Arrow, 2000, p. 173):[13]

> The steady history of competitive equilibrium theory and the contrasting history of increasing returns theory are themselves conditions on the coherence of one theory and the lack of it in the other ... Increasing returns arguments have been applied fruitfully ... but one has to start again each time. In particular, what should be the core of any economic theory, a theory of value, is still not yet well defined.

In other words, in the presence of increasing returns, we have no theory of price, how the market grinds out supply and demand through the market mechanism. Significantly, in much NEG, the market is erased altogether leaving no mechanism for more or less efficient allocation of production to more or less arbitrary locations. Where is the market itself that ought to occupy pride of place in any economics, let alone one that praises its allocative role? How are prices formed when productivity is changing even as they are being formed.[14] What comes first, the places or the prices, and so on. These problems could be avoided in the absence of increasing returns, since the economy is essentially timeless and without scale and can, therefore, be situated wherever, as thick or thin as you like. In other words, NEG only addresses one problem – its own version of spatial development – by erasing another, and more fundamental, value theory.[15]

Of course, exactly the same observation applies to the new growth theory that, as indicated, is essentially NEG with more factors arbitrarily thrown in – as is even implicitly acknowledged by orthodoxy itself (Schmutzler, 1999). Growth takes place without the market and without prices, because of

---

13   See Mirowski (2007) for highlighting Arrow's dual role of both progressing and promoting mainstream economics and exposing its limitations on its own terms.

14   Note Smith and Marx are the only prominent economists to address this problem, how are values formed as technology is changing (Fine, 1982; and Milonakis and Fine, 2009).

15   The same is even true of 'rationality' assumptions which come into question with increasing returns to scale because of the need to act strategically in relation to the preferences, actions and beliefs of others.

increasing returns or other factors such as health, education, spillovers, and so on to include a hundred or more variables. As suggested, these are omitted rather than included within (theoretical models for) NEG. And this is necessarily so for analytical reasons, and not just because of mathematical intractability. Once we start to incorporate other variables, the whole edifice becomes indeterminate, not least the role of the state in any of its increasing returns appropriating policies given the extraordinary advantages of being a first comer.[16] As is observed of themselves in accepting the first Alonso prize (Fujita and Krugman, 2004, p. 142):

> Put one thing on top of another, and it all starts to look too complicated to convey any insights. But provided one is willing to make some silly but convenient assumptions ... things need not be so bad.

The issue is, though, convenient, bad and silly for whom?

For, we are sternly told that the apparently unambiguous case for state intervention to accrue economies of scale has to be set against the inclination of policymakers to abuse their power in pursuit of self-interest. But this reinforces the point that such issues have to be taken into account as much as those of increasing returns, agglomeration, transport costs, and so on. And, of course, even accepting that NEG establishes spatially differentiated outcomes, there is a bit more to this than the virtues or vices of policymakers. We are, after all, addressing the history of the world, its formation of nation-states, internal and external wars, imperialism, slavery, and so on. For NEG, these tend to be retrofitted with the result that the history serves the theory rather than vice-versa in its representation or, more usual and important, its absence.

Accordingly, for WDR09, history is a teleology displaying the triumph of Nobel economists such as Lucas on new growth theory, variously distributed across the document, and for the British industrial revolution, p. 204:

> With more secure individual property rights to land, English cities grew rapidly. Indeed, England may have been the first to industrialize because it introduced such rights before other European countries. The Nobel prize–winning economist Douglass North uses this to spotlight what land institutions can do for long-run growth and development. The 'enclosure' movement made individual private property rights possible.

---

16 Is it accidental that the developmental gains associated with (urban) development do not figure in NEG?

Starting around 1500 open commons were fenced, hedged, or otherwise closed off and deeded or titled to individuals. By 1545 around 40 percent of England's surface area belonged to private individuals. The Enclosure Act of 1604 fostered the conversion of open commons into private plots, which continued until the early twentieth century. Most researchers agree that enclosures in England increased agricultural productivity, which released labor from the land, and provided the food surplus to support the rapidly increasing urban population. This allowed England to become, for a time, the 'workshop of the world'.

No less breathtakingly simple and, essentially ahistorical for what it leaves out of account, is the astonishing suggestion of "Spatial inefficiency and the downfall of the Soviet Union", pp. 90–91 and background note (Treyvish, 2008). And we thought it might have something to do with the Cold War or other internal or external factors.

Not surprisingly, then, within the WDR09, there is a heavy erasure of historical time and physical space, only introduced as more critical economists are wont to remark, in order that everything does not take place simultaneously in the same location.[17] Where time and space are used it is for own narrow convenience. There is, for example, no world economy other than for trading and migration for given nation-states upon which a more or less arbitrarily detailed teleology is imposed. Development is first and foremost industrialisation and urbanisation to accrue economies of scale, inevitably leading to growing (homogenised) inequality (so-called divergence) with rural and other areas that can ultimately benefit from compensating social policies and migration to ameliorate inequality (convergence). Crucial here, and simply overlooked is, to deploy the vernacular, the continuing impact of first-mover advantages within and between nation-states and the correspondingly remarkable end or lack of history for those that have realised the teleology both for themselves and for their impact upon those lagging behind (this is otherwise known as strategic interests or how did our oil get under their sand). And, of course, such an idealised teleology leaves unaddressed the question of when, by when and why not already for those who have yet to realise its benefits. Is it seconds or

---

17   "While Joan Robinson quoted [Henri] Bergson as saying that 'time is a device to stop everything from happening at once', the late Dharma Kumar suggested that 'space is a device to stop everything happening in Cambridge'", http://www-users.cs.york.ac.uk /susan/cyc/q/quotes.htm.

millennia over which these processes play themselves out,[18] an issue of some relevance to the billions of the world's population who have not embarked upon the journey to the promised land even if they are making their way to the most convenient and overcrowded cities.

In short, why, then, do some factors get taken into account, such as economies of scale and product variety, as opposed to others? As remarked, on the one hand, they reflect the mildest of breaks with continuing core methods. On the other hand, it is simply a matter of extending these on the basis of purely speculative reason. Consider Romer, the pioneer of new growth theory, who explicitly reveals his working methods to Snowdon and Vane (2005, p. 686):

> Schumpeter coined some wonderful phrases like 'creative destruction' but I did not read any of Schumpeter's work when I was creating my model ... I really worked that model out from a clean sheet of paper. To be honest, the times when I have gone to try to read Schumpeter I have found it tough going. It is really hard to tell what guys like Schumpeter are talking about [*laughter*].

And Krugman is similar in some respects. The model is the thing, manipulated as necessary to tease out outcomes to correspond to stylised facts (core-periphery patterns of development, for example) or novel results for orthodoxy,[19] pushing the consequences of deduction beyond reasonable limits given what is absented from consideration (not least the role of the state and policy, see above, let alone the exercise of political power at the global level). Is it unfair to point to the theory of interstellar trade (Krugman, 1978), when goods travel at the speed of light and so arrive at a different time for those travelling as opposed to observing them (raising questions of what interest to charge

---

18   There is some reference via Lucas to the idea that it might take decades, WDR09, p. 161, "Even in the rapidly growing economies of the post-colonial world, the passage from a 90 percent agricultural economy to one that is 90 percent urban is a matter of decades".

19   Note that economics imperialism has also had the effect of appropriating heterodox economics, as in the hagiographic Elmslie (2010, p. 12), citing Krugman for various topics in development, "The 1980s and 1990s saw many cases of mainstream economic theory crowding out heterodox theory by using the everexpanding standard set of tools to better understand issues long part of heterodox theory ... Thus, Krugman can be held at least partly responsible for the identity crisis that has plagued heterodox economics for the past 30 years, as orthodox theory came to dominate many traditionally heterodox areas of research". Whether there is such an identity crisis is a moot point and, if so, it is the intolerance of the orthodoxy more than its expansion into heterodoxy that is responsible. See (Lee, 2012).

over the period of transit)? As he says himself, excusing the spoof, "This paper, then, is a serious analysis of a ridiculous subject, which is of course the opposite of what is usual in economics", p. 2. But the same might be said of NEG![20]

3   From Pre- to Post-Washington Consensus

Because of its universalism, one of the striking, endearing even, features of NEG is that it ranges over the fortunes of single industrial districts to the spatial history of the world, with Krugman for example happily and casually adopting the language of core-periphery without any apparent awareness of its roots in dependency and world systems theory or earlier uses in regional planning such as Friedmann (1966). By the same token, the same principles apply to development as they do to space. Consequently, new (and newer) development economics shares analytical principles with NEG as well as subject matter to a large degree, see below. Nonetheless, the two do have different histories by virtue of origins and trajectories.

Development economics first emerges as an acknowledged field immediately after the second world war as a response to decolonisation and competing influences at a global level from the USA and the USSR. For reasons already laid out for the division between macro and micro, the latter was considered totally inappropriate for understanding the systemic issue of development. Instead, orthodoxy was dominated by empirically and historically grounded analyses, more attuned to the old institutional economics, giving rise to what has subsequently been dubbed the old or classic development economics, with notions of modernisation to the fore in the sense of the need for developing countries to emulate the social and historical processes identified with the emergence of western capitalism. Empirical and inductive measures were to the fore in seeking regularities in the nature and processes of development.

Significantly, and to some extent ironically, economic history in the United States tended to be located within economics departments, as a result of the earlier strength of the old institutional economics, and was a teaching requirement. By contrast, development studies as a discipline was located in a

---

20   Note that Vromen (2009) categorises Krugman's interstellar piece as funny economics, a joke, as opposed to economics for fun in which he places the intentionally serious freakonomics. But he also demonstrates that the distinction between the two cannot always be maintained. He also rejects the notion of economics imperialism on empirical grounds or, at least for lack of evidence, but seems blissfully unaware of NEG, new development economics, new economic history, etc. See Fine (2024b, Chapter 8).

fragmented fashion across other disciplines. Accordingly, in the first phase of economics imperialism, such economic history was immediately subject to an assault from mainstream economics in the form of the new economic history or cliometrics. As its leading pioneer as economist was to put it, mainstream economics should be used to address historical problems irrespective of any realism (North, 1963).[21] On the other hand, (the old) development economics remained relatively untouched and alternative political economy approaches prospered within the discipline, across other disciplines and in newly-founded development studies departments around the world, removed from economics as such (Fine, 2009a, for a fuller account).

This all changed with the collapse of the post-war boom, the rise of neoliberalism and the emergence of the new development economics as a form of economics imperialism of the first phase albeit delayed. This soon co-existed with, and was superseded by, a newer development economics characteristic of the second phase of economics imperialism. For this (lack of) development is seen as a consequence of the way in which institutions, etc, respond to market imperfections. Within economics, the old development economics was increasingly marginalised (if surviving to a greater or lesser degree within development studies) and development economics became subordinate to the application of universal principles, see Corbridge (2007) on 'monoeconomics' in development studies. As pioneering neoliberal Chief Economist at the World Bank, and a major proponent of the new development economics, puts it in the first issue of the *World Bank Research Observer* (Krueger, 1986, p. 62):

> Once it is recognised that individuals respond to incentives, and that 'market failure' is the result of inappropriate incentives rather than non-responsiveness, the separateness of development economics as a field largely disappears.

Whilst the newer development economics is probably less extreme in its dismissal of its subject matter as a separate field, it shares this stance other than in allowing for endogenously generated market imperfections.

Significantly, of course, as Chief Economist, Krueger played a prominent role at the World Bank in the early 1980s in clearing out the old development economists and replacing them with the new, and the corresponding promotion of what has become known as the Washington Consensus. This involved

---

21   For critique of North, see (Fine and Milonakis, 2003) and (Milonakis and Fine, 2007). See also Fine (2024c).

departure from what can now be termed the Pre-Washington Consensus at the Bank for which, corresponding to the old development economics, an extensive role for the state was accepted in terms of the modernisation associated with Keynesianism, welfarism, industrialisation, provision of economic and social infrastructure, and so on. The structural adjustment and stabilisation policies associated with the Washington Consensus have been heavily debated, and criticised, as has the subsequent Post-Washington Consensus inspired from 1997 onwards by market imperfections World Bank Chief Economist, Joe Stiglitz. The new Consensus is deeply rooted in the newer development economics, and offers a piecemeal understanding of development and policy in terms of the incidence of, and remedies to, specific market and institutional imperfections.

The trajectory from Pre- to Post-Washington Consensus is not then unilinear as is evident in the relative stances taken on the role of the state – going from extensive, especially for infrastructure, to minimal before currently occupying an intermediate position. On the other hand, other aspects of the Bank's role have moved continually in the same direction. One is to have been increasingly wedded to mainstream economics. Second is to have expanded scope of interest both across the economy and from the economy to the social. Third, understanding and specifying the nature of development has become subordinate to policymaking. Fourth has been the Bank's increasing projection and, ultimately designation, of itself as a Knowledge Bank in which it occupies a central position in developmental thinking, policy and advocacy even by way of those offering critical departure. Fifth has been the increasing incorporation of development studies along all of these lines. Sixth, both the Washington Consensus and the Post-Washington Consensus, in contrast to the Pre-, have no concept of development as such as opposed to a means, paradoxically, to achieve it, reliance upon the market or its piecemeal correction, respectively.

But the situation is even more complex than this in that the Bank's positions are constituted out of the three components of ideology (rhetoric or advocacy), scholarship, and policy in practice. As emphasised in (Fine, 2001 and 2010b), especially in the context of social capital as a developmental buzzword at the World Bank, the relationship within each of these across topics is not consistent, or even coherent, and the same is even more so across these elements. This is not to say that each element is independent of the other, only that the relationship between them is variegated and shifting across time and topic. Thus, in general terms, policy under the Washington Consensus was heavily *interventionist* under the ideology of non-intervention, with the promotion of private capital being paramount, especially of finance. Further, under the nominally more state-friendly Post-Washington Consensus, the policies or conditionalities associated with the Washington Consensus have, in practice, both tightened and been extended to a wider range of interventions (Van Waeyenberge, 2009), and see below on health and education. As it were, whereas the Washington Consensus allowed for discretionary intervention under the rhetoric of promoting free markets, the Post-Washington Consensus does the same on a wider terrain on the basis of correcting the market. Further, the shift from the one to the other corresponds to a broader shift between two phases of neoliberalism – a shock phase in promoting private and international capital, especially finance, followed by one of extensive intervention to sustain the process and temper its worst effects (from privatisation to public-private partnerships, for example, and more attention to the dysfunctional consequences of adjustment) to allow for safety nets, MDGs and PRSPs.

As is apparent, then, one conduit for economics imperialism has been through the deployment of differently denominated types of capital. This most immediately allows the corresponding factors to be incorporated into the mainstream's pre-existing technical apparatus. Human capital is an early and enduring example but there has been a 'plethora' of capitals, each associated with some aspect of economic or social functioning, with natural and environmental capital familiar to geographers. Ultimately, over the past twenty years, with the World Bank having taken a lead in its promotion in general and in development studies in particular, social capital has come to the fore even if its origins are not from within economics. It essentially fills out the entire gamut of resources and functioning that cannot be reduced to narrowly economic and/or individual alone. For social capital in particular, but much more generally, there is an extraordinary fetishism involved in separating the economic from the non-economic, and attaching them, respectively, to capitals that are not or are, social, respectively, with a heavily physicalist interpretation of as much of these capitals as possible (to fit, to put it crudely, into a production function).

There is, however, another route through which economics fills out the non-economic (as it has itself defined the shifting boundaries between the two as amenable to its technical and conceptual apparatus). This is to seize upon one or more generic concept that can serve as proxy for whatever has not yet been covered. Again an early example is provided by 'institutions', and it endures across the various phases of economics imperialism in the form of the new and the newer institutional economics, also serving as an inspirational factor for the new and newer economic history (especially through Douglass North). Such conceptualisations have been analytically underpinned by marginal deviations from purest forms of market functioning as with the introduction of transaction costs, imperfect information, definition of property rights, externalities and, most notably for NEG, increasing returns to scale.

Significantly, of course, the latter alone serves Krugman in foisting upon us not only NEG but also new(er) trade theory and, if to a lesser extent on his own account, the newer development economics. And it is important to recognise that his stellar rise derives primarily from his exploitation of increasing returns to scale across his chosen areas of application. This puts him in one camp of contemporary economics and economics imperialism, which also includes the new growth theory, as opposed to the other camp which is more likely to emphasise the market imperfections arising out of imperfect information as with Akerlof, Spence and Stiglitz, Nobel Prize Winners as such in 2001.[22] For the latter, emphasis tends to be upon static inefficiencies that can be corrected now, whereas the IRS/NGT approach is focused upon outcomes over time. Whilst both rely upon highly idealised, simplified and universalised models of the economy, the IRS/NGT also tends to be more ambitious in its empirical, that is econometric, work (although this does not tend to be spawned by the theorists themselves). In particular, whilst for mathematical tractability it is necessary only to include only a few variables within models, these are used (quite illegitimately) to throw as many variables as desired into statistical work (as many as 150 for example in the NGT in estimating the sources of growth).

4   Fixing the WDR09

Against this extensive background, how are we to interpret the WDR09? As already indicated, reviews from geographers have assessed it as a work of scholarship and, with exceptions, have found it to be understandably drastically wanting. But this approach to the WDR09 is itself mistaken. It is not and should not be considered a work of scholarship. Significantly, for example, there does not seem to be a single review within an economics journal and, I suspect, that this is typical if not so extreme of previous WDRs. Further, if not for the first time, as usefully revealed by the Deaton Report (Deaton et al. 2006) in an evaluation of World Bank research from 1998 to 2005 by mainstream economists from within the perspectives of mainstream economics, such research is revealed to be heavily influenced by the imperatives of

---

22   There appears to be analytical and possibly personal rivalry between those mainstream
      economists who rely upon increasing returns as opposed to market as informational
      imperfections even if they agree over the need to see markets as working imperfectly, the
      Stiglitz/Krugman syndrome?

advocacy as opposed to quality and intellectual integrity.[23] This is not to say that the WDR09 is uninformed and uninfluenced by scholarship, only that it is not scholarship itself without myself setting about defining what this means precisely. I have struggled to find an appropriate analogy for this. It is as if the World Bank decided to focus the next WDR on crime (not too far off the mark given it is on Conflict, Security and Development for 2011), and asked Quentin Tarantino to make a feature film on the issue. His account has no attachment to crime as such, only to other select and genre media representations of crime. Much the same is true of the WDR09's use and even manufacture (for use) of scholarship (through its background papers).

There are two techniques worth highlighting in this Kill Bill scholarship. One is what I call boxonomics. It involves the showcasing of select evidence and case studies to support the arguments (the industrial revolution, the collapse of the Soviet Union and the success of the United States, see below). Often these are not without interest but they never stand up to close scrutiny on either theoretical or empirical terms nor to generalisation to other case studies. The other is what I call the XY syndrome. This takes two separate issues, complex enough on their own, such as growth and inequality, and brings them together. Magically, despite their individual complexities, simple relations can be drawn by bringing the two together. Is migration (especially urbanisation) good for growth or not, and similarly for regional integration. To be fair, especially in the background papers to this WDR09, something more akin to an XYZ ... syndrome is involved, and results reported are more qualified in part in deference to presence or not of other factors, and use of more sophisticated econometric methods than the simplest of XY regressions.

But what are we to make of the conclusion from a complex statistical exercise correcting for labour market characteristics, from a Background Report (Clemens et al. 2008) that suggests, "a marginal wage increase of at least $10,000 pa for next worker allowed to move from a developing country to US". The implication that the WDR09 would wish to draw is that, ceteris paribus, migration is the best policy for poverty reduction (and might be thought to

---

23   For a critical assessment of World Bank research, taking the Deaton Report as critical starting point, see Bayliss et al. (eds) (2011). Note that spirited defence by Buckley (2009) of the WDR09 by reference to the Deaton Report is wide of the mark as revealed in Deaton's subsequent work, free of the constraints and restraints of his role in chairing the evaluation (and venting the frustration in its being totally ignored), and his personal communications with myself. See, for example, the uncompromising suggestion (Yusuf, 2009, pp. 113–4) that, "the development expertise that is the centre of the World Bank's mission may not exist in useful form or, at the least, needs to be fundamentally rethought and restricted".

dominate any of the gains to be made from the heavily promoted freedom of movement of goods). Yet, whilst interesting and suggestive, this exercise tells us absolutely nothing about how labour markets work to generate these wage differentials and, so, what the impact of interventions would be.[24] Do we really believe, other than as tautology, that removing all constraints on the mobility of labour would lead to equitable outcomes in labour markets, even if $10,000 currently measures, however accurately, the weight of their presence for the marginal worker?

Boxonomics and the XY syndrome are widely used by the World Bank to marry scholarship and advocacy. More specifically for the scholarly influences on this WDR09, first, in taking the NEG/Krugman route of economics imperialism, the analytical framework deployed is both to draw upon increasing returns to scale and to attach these to a broader but still limited set of universal (ahistorical and asocial) principles by which to explain everything. There are, for example, deployed the three Ds of distance, density and division, complemented by the three Is of institutions, infrastructure and incentives. These are supplemented by circular causation, neighbourhood and spillover effects, agglomeration, specialisation, transport and transaction costs, and so on.

Second, by virtue both of the subject matter and the shift from Washington to Post-Washington Consensus, there are, admittedly faint, legitimising hints of restoring the old development economics.[25] The Report begins with Kuznets, p. 33, makes reference to Adam Smith not for virtues of the market but for the significance of the division of labour, and emphasis is placed upon the virtues of unbalanced growth (and necessity for growing inequality to achieve development prior to the spread of the benefits). Here, it is important to recognise how impoverished is the restoration of the old, deriving as it does from a simple technical exercise (the microeconomic implications of increasing returns to scale extended both to world economic history and development policy), complemented by a particular version of the history of (development) economics itself whereby precursors were correct but incapable of representing their ideas in acceptable mathematical forms (as opposed to accepting the limitations of such microeconomics relative to more rounded inductive and

---

24   As Deaton (2009a, p. 14) has argued, "The general lesson here is once again the ultimate futility of trying to avoid thinking about how and why things work; if we do not do so, we are left with undifferentiated heterogeneity that is likely to prevent consistent estimation of any parameter of interest".

25   Does this help to explain that nostalgia for the old development economics is now condoned, see Yusuf (2009).

systemic methods).[26] However, this flavour of the old development economics within the new(er) is heavily trumped by the absence of reference to other scholarly work on the subject of increasing returns in the passage from Adam Smith to Dixit and Stiglitz (1977) (for which increasing returns allow for imperfect competition).[27]

Third, much heavier than the restoration of the old development economics is that of the Pre-Washington Consensus, again if in diluted form, but through an apparently unwitting appeal to modernisation, acknowledged if incorrectly by Maringanti et al. (2009, p. 46) as a revival of the much more refined and wide-ranging Rostow and stages of economic growth. What is remarkable, possibly inadvertent especially in relation to critical literature on modernisation, is the extent to which the model of development arising out of NEG is imposed both upon the history of the now developed economies and the future path of those presumed to be in the process of developing. It is not simply that this WDR09 unusually devotes so much of its text to developed countries but these, and especially the United States, are taken as the model to be emulated. A particularly rosy picture is painted of the path of inequality in the USA with its previously unbalanced and unequal growth now evened out by low transport costs, spread of the benefits of development, and internal migration. There seems to be little awareness of current controversies over public health provision let alone the unprecedented rise in income inequality over the past thirty years, reversing the previous trend and witnessing the share of income of the top 1% of earners rising from under 10% to over 20%. Race, gender and other divisions simply do not arise.

Fourth, the WDR09 is also selective in its treatment of (international) trade. On the one hand, increasing returns to scale and imperfect competition allow for international intra-industry trade to be explained as opposed to the specialisation associated with orthodox trade theory and comparative advantage. On the other hand, the consequence of this is to provide the inescapable rationale

---

26   This sort of view was initiated by (Krugman, 1994a) and is too readily accepted (Harvey, 2009, p. 1276) for example. For the quality of the scholarship that informs Krugman's account of the "the rise and fall of development economics", see his opening, "This is not exactly a paper about Albert Hirschman. In the first place, I am unqualified to write such a paper. My acquaintance with Hirschman's works is very limited. In essence, the Hirschman I know is the author of *The Strategy of Economic Development* and little else. So I am in no position to write about his larger vision".

27   On neglect of such literature, see Rigg et al. (2009, p. 130), Harvey (2009, p. 1275) and, more generally, as Scott (2009, p. 584) puts it, "the neglect of geographers' work in the Report is all of a piece with a very much more troubling and pervasive form of intellectual provincialism".

for protection to promote national, infant-industry champions. This is simply overlooked for the virtues of allowing the market to decide what (urban) development should take place where, with the state at most facilitating and supporting the choices rather than making them. For, on the international arena, "market potential is a powerful driver of increases in income per capita and average wages ... results show that in 2003, bringing the market potential of the Congo Democratic Republic to the one of Thailand is predicted to increase its GDP per capita by a factor of around 24", from background paper (Mayer, 2008, p. 20). And, within the nation, "New noncapital cities that seem to succeed are those where the purpose and location are chosen over time by markets and in cases in which the government hastens the pace of growth by coordinating investments in infrastructure, housing, and general governance. For these reasons, cities and towns should be seen as market agents that, just like firms and farms, serve market needs", WDR09, p. 145. What is remarkably absent, rather than absented as in case of the state as source of success, are firms themselves as opposed to the market as agent of judicious locational choice. Despite the attention to intra-industry international trade, and the breaches with specialisation, comparative advantage and orthodox trade theory, there is no mention at all of the extent to which the vast majority of decisive trade, especially in manufacturing, takes place within the confines of individual firms through their internationally organised multi-nationally located affiliates. In short, it is not the market that decides at all but General Electric and the like, ably assisted no doubt by government.

Fifth, as indicated, the various elements that go into making up the new economic geography, let alone the ideology, scholarship and policy in practice of the Bank's treatment, are far from coherent and consistent in their combination. By the same token, this allows for some innovation and idiosyncrasy in the outcome. This is especially so in relation to both the prominence of, and the stances adopted on, migration (as well as the variety in layering of policies for different levels of government from local through to international regional). In other words, essentially a strong rejection of the thesis of what might be summed up as urban bias is unable to have been anticipated, as well as the corresponding propositions that development requires unbalanced growth around urban areas through migration that should be permitted in order that more balanced growth (and equality) can be achieved subsequently through spread of the benefits.[28]

---

28   The striking mix of the ad hoc with populism is also characteristic of the treatment of agriculture (Oya, 2011).

Sixth, then, this suggests that it is mistaken to take a rigidly deterministic interpretation of the WDRo9 or World Bank research, etc, more generally. It cannot simply be reduced to the imperatives of a particular set of more or less (neoliberal) ideologies, theories or policy imperatives. In other words, in cruder terms, the WDRo9 is not to be seen as a conspiracy to convey and foist preconceived conclusions upon a more or less receptive audience. This reflects neither the nature nor the process of producing the WDRo9 (with the added advantage of such flexibility in content legitimising a sense of openness). Nonetheless, as should be heavily emphasised, the space for breach from institutionalised requirements is both amorphous, if unevenly so, and tightly constrained. This is evidenced by the controversies that have surrounded dissident research within the Bank, including the prominent resignation over production of the WDR itself for 2001.[29] What is crucial for the Bank, if putting it in conspiratorial terms, is that its research, etc, should legitimise its policies in practice either by supporting them directly or by placing a veil over them.

In this respect, the WDRo9 is totally complicit in its support for the 'market', that is private capital, and the facilitating role of the state. Amazingly, the filling out of space (location of cities, for example) is treated as a market mechanism just like the filling out of economic activity, best left to the self-discovery of those involved since, to repeat the extraordinary fetishism, "towns and cities should be seen as market agents ... just like firms and farms", p. 145. This does, though, have to be seen in the context of the current phase of neoliberalism, one in which the state is explicitly required to support the private sector rather than simply being replaced by it. Bear in mind, for example, that critics of the Bank's over-homogenising of the nature, causes and consequences of urban migration (first unbalanced step in development, the divergence before the convergence) have suggested that, in Africa, it reflects a greater degree of movement to access public services. The Bank is ready for this, anticipating with its own support, that 60% of growth in future health provision will derive

---

29   Rigg et al. (2009, p. 131) suggest that the WDRo9 "reflects the extent to which relatively orthodox economists are once more in absolute ascendance inside the Bank following a decade of internal debate about development, perhaps best reflected in the furore over the 2000/2001 WDR, which led to the resignation of the team's Director, Ravi Kanbur". As argued elsewhere, especially in the context of social capital, this is a total and self-serving misreading of the loss of ascendancy of the World Bank's economists in the period highlighted (Fine, 2008 and 2010b). There was no such loss but it did allow for the economists to range more widely and freely and create the illusion, for some, of their loss rather than their greater reach of hegemony!

from the private sector (IFC, 2009).[30] Essentially, privatisation never appears within the WDR09, an implicit recognition that it has both already been accomplished as far as possible and that the private sector now needs the state to intervene discreetly and discretely to reconstruct the spaces within which hordes of migrant labour can be exploited.

5   From Finance to Climate by Way of Conclusion

Reference to privatisation (and development by way of public ownership that often made it possible) is by no means the only notable absence from the WDR09. To put it bluntly, it is not only as if the current financial crisis does not exist, the same is more or less true of finance itself. There is an embarrassing exception in light of recent events, p. 206:

> When a country's financial system is more developed and mature, the public sector can encourage a secondary mortgage market, develop financial innovations, and expand the securitization of mortgages. Occupant-owned housing, usually a household's largest single asset by far, is important in wealth creation, social security, and politics. People who own their house or have secure tenure have a larger stake in their community and thus are more likely to lobby for less crime, stronger governance, and better local environmental conditions.

But the implicit Panglossian view of subprime apart, there is much more to this than the simple neglect of the relationship between finance and development and their influence upon economic geography.[31]

For finance itself poses an extraordinary challenge to the NEG even if, no doubt, it is sufficiently inventive to meet it on its own terms by the dual appeal to declining transaction costs, on the one hand, and the benefits of agglomeration, on the other.[32] Needless to say, there is total neglect of the continuing

---

30   See also "Private Schools Urged to Acquire Capital Finance", https://www.newvision.co.ug /news/1231150/private-schools-urged-acquire-capital-finance.

31   Consider, for example, the role of finance in South(ern) African development – even without which the universal propositions of the WDR09 do not begin to gain any purchase on the appropriate questions let alone appropriate answers concerning the nature of racialised patterns of development (Fine, 2009f for recent considerations).

32   Note that the absence of finance within NEG is itself in part a reflection of the previously observed tendency to absent markets (and value theory) in deference to the logic of (physical) increasing returns.

geography of finance literature (and debate about whether location remains relevant or not,[33] it certainly does!) let alone any sense of the increasingly systemically inefficient role of finance in the era of financialisation, as most dramatically revealed by the current crisis. How do we explain that three times as many financial assets are needed to service one unit of GDP than thirty years ago, and the continuing concentration of financial power in specific locations, especially the United States (and the reserve role of the dollar) despite its deficits and minimal interest rates. And what are and have been the implications of this for the location of economic activity? A stunning silence is the only answer as finance is reduced to money and money to a neutral veil that is neither seen nor heard. If combined and uneven development is to be explained over the period encompassing both the East Asian NICs' miracles and the more general neoliberal aftermath, it must surely address the end of the Cold War, the nature of US hegemony, the role of the nation-state in the new world order, the transformations in labour markets (not least in China) and the nature and incidence of new technologies. Each of these takes at most a secondary role within the technicist and physicalist approaches within the NEG.

And neglect of finance, just as it uncomfortably, prominently, and dysfunctionally occupies the world stage, is complemented by an almost absolute absence of the environment, remarkable for an account of economic geography. No doubt, this might be excused by acknowledging that this serves as the topic of the next WDR for 2010 (World Bank, 2009b). Even so, one might have expected the word climate to have appeared more times in the context of the 'natural' environment than for the inevitably and heavily promoted (private) *business* climate. Apart from pointing to the "negative externalities of transport" as congestion, emissions and pollutions, pp. 190–2, the WDR09's analysis is confined to the boxonomics in support of the proposition that "Climate change calls for a different urban form, not slower urbanization", p. 211.[34] It concludes that Atlanta should build more stations for its metro so that it is used as much as in Barcelona. There is, of course, a total absence of systemic and global analysis – how do we know that such measures do not merely create the space for more pollution to continue as is integral to cap and trade and offsets (Lohman and Sexton, 2010 for a brief account) – with more than a whiff of fiddling whilst Rome burns.

---

33   For recent contributions in light of the crisis, see special issue of the *Cambridge Journal of Regions, Economy and Society*, vol 2, no 2, 2009.

34   Note that the World Bank accommodates the apocalyptic vision of climate change of Swyngedouw (2009 and 2010a and b) by projecting the calm of business as usual.

But the World Bank is no Nero, and is fiddling or, more exactly, orchestrating to deal in carbon trading (at over 10% commission) and to occupy the off-set finance for developing countries for environmental measures that may or may not accrue. That this should be viewed with dismay by developing countries and activists is hardly surprising. It is a recipe for continuing largesse towards the developed world's polluting and the thick end of a wedge already in place in applying conditionalities to Bank finance – quite apart from the dirty business as usual as the Bank prepares to make its biggest ever energy loan in Africa to underpin dirty coal-fired power stations in South Africa (Hallowes, 2009).

Effective absence, then, of finance and the environment from the WDR09's NEG is par for the course alongside those absences that have been previously highlighted above and in geographical critiques. Of course, the latter's understandable response has been to deplore the absence of geographers and the geographical in the round, the square and most other shapes. I would, however, both in relation to the WDR09's NEG and World Bank 'research' more generally, put this differently. What is wrong, at least in the first instance, is not the economist's impoverished geography but their impoverished economics. This has to be addressed, both logically and strategically, before its geography can be put right although it is a task upon which geographers can and must engage if, in part, by way of dialogue with their own political economy. The marriage between geography and political economy is essential for an offspring that draws upon and locates both the systemic and the specific. As progeny of NEG, the WDR09 is barren and does neither.

Nudging or Fudging: The World Development Report 2015

Postscript as Personal Preamble

By the time this second critique of a World Development Report was being drafted, I was already well into the mature stage of my understanding of economics imperialism, and its application to development, specifying their third phases of the newer economics imperialism and the newest development economics, respectively, in which core mainstream principles are suspended to whatever degree whilst being supplemented by whatever appeals and takes hold. In this case, rather than the new economic geography as in the previous Chapter, it is behavioural economics in general and the use of randomised control trials in particular. Subsequently, leading proponents of RCT within (development) economics, Abhijit Banerjee, Esther Duflo, and Michael Kremer were amply rewarded with the Nobel Prize in Economics for 2019 no doubt promoted by and promoting their contributions (and others) on behalf of the World Bank. Never mind that Angus Deaton, also a Nobel Laureate and erstwhile critic of WB research, has offered correspondingly devastating reservations over the use of RCTs, especially for their lack of specifying and empirically grounding the pathways between causes and effects.[1]

In light of my attention to RCTs, behavioural economics and their relationships both to development economics/studies and (the third phase of) economics imperialism, I attempted to set up an IIPPE (iippe.org) Working Group on the topic. I failed but there do remain continuing critiques, if primarily as a minority sport (see especially Bédécarrats et al. eds, 2020).

1   Introduction

In 1978, the World Bank published its first World Development Report (WDR) at the instigation of its then President, Robert McNamara.[2] This launched a series

---

1   See especially, Deaton (2010a and b and 2020) and Deaton and Cartwright (2018).
2   Originally co-authored with Deborah Johnston, Ana Santos and Elisa Van Waeyenberge (Fine et al. 2016b).

that was rapidly to attain a large circulation worldwide. It reflected McNamara's attempt to transform the Bank into a development institution with an explicitly intellectual leadership role. Each year the Report focuses on a different topic. This allows the Bank to explore more systematically what it considers to be the core issues in development. The Reports do not seek to break new ground but serve as a vehicle through which Bank member governments can be mobilised around a particular understanding of development (Yusuf, 2009, p. 17).[3] The WDRs provide us with "an extraordinary window" on the way the Bank understands the discipline and practices of development economics.[4] They lend an opportunity to assess the way in which the Bank exercises its knowledge role and of the implications this has across the discipline.[5]

The latest WDR (World Bank, 2015), entitled *Mind, Society and Behaviour*, draws on behavioural economics and seeks to redesign development policy on the basis of "an expanded understanding of human behaviour", p. 13. The Report focuses on how individual decisions can be managed for better outcomes, but overlooks the need for consideration of underlying structural features. This Chapter offers a critical assessment of the Report across four dimensions. The first section situates the Report within the broader and evolving knowledge role of the Bank. This bears on how the Bank understands its role in the production and dissemination of knowledge, even applying its latest insights into the behaviour of its own staff.

The next section locates the Report in the context of the evolution of economics as a discipline and how this informs the Bank's development economics. The substance of WDR 2015 is shown to be a result of the promotion of a particular (economic) understanding of development into which behavioural economics, and the policy of 'nudge', easily fits.[6] The Report is shown to constitute a leading example of the latest phase of economics imperialism applied to development. Instead of expanding the domain of application of economic theory through the application of utility-maximising principles in a variety of

---

3 Shahid Yusuf was himself the Director of the 1999/2000 WDR.
4 See the World Bank website, no longer available but, as for other such citations, the reader can readily search out new sites on the WDR: http://econ.worldbank.org/WBSITE/EXTER NAL/EXTDEC/EXTRESEARCH/EXTWDRS/0,contentMDK:20227703~pagePK:478093~piPK: 477627~theSitePK:477624,00.html See also World Bank (1998).
5 See Bayliss et al. (eds) (2011) for a collection of essays dissecting the Bank's research across a range of topics.
6 *Nudge* is the title of Thaler and Sunstein's (2008) bestselling book, having become the verb that synthesises the behavioural economics approach to policy making.

domains, economics (imperialism) now expands and consolidates its scope through appending behavioural economics' view of human action.[7]

The Report is then assessed for its take on behavioural economics itself. It is argued that its is a narrow view, both from within the behavioural sciences and in the associated understanding of the social determinants of individual behaviour. Finally, the significance of the promotion of such behavioural economics is considered in practice through an examination of its use in health interventions, with a particular interest in those seeking to affect HIV/AIDS prevalence.

The Chapter concludes that the incursion of behavioural economics into development policy is indicative of the World Bank's avoidance of tackling fundamental problems. It moves its actions further away from a tradition based on the identification of the structural problems that trap countries in impoverished development, offering the alternative of minor tinkling with extant structures. This is not particularly surprising. It resonates with previous paradigmatic shifts in development policy and is equally in tandem with developments within economics itself. What is new is that the obstacles to development and poverty alleviation are now deemed to reside in deficient decision making and that the remedies to tackle poverty consist of 'nudges', i.e. minor changes to context that make it easier for the poor to choose better options.[8]

2   WDR 2015 and the Knowledge Bank

The WDR constitutes the most important flagship report produced by the economics research department of the Bank (Development Economics Group, DEC). It offers a useful lens for a critical appraisal of the Bank's knowledge role, providing insights into the way in which the Bank's production and dissemination of development expertise underpins its intellectual and political influence. A few years ago, on the occasion of the thirtieth volume within the series, the 2015 Nobel prize winner, Angus Deaton offered a strongly negative

---

7   See Fine and Milonakis (2009) and Mäki (2009) on the concept of economics imperialism. See also Fine (2024a-c).

8   In this respect, the Report compares unfavourably with its predecessors, which at least focused on the major issues of agriculture, gender, jobs, the environment, etc. See (no longer available): http://econ.worldbank.org/WBSITE/EXTERNAL/EXTDEC/EXTRESEA RCH/EXTWDRS/0,contentMDK:20227703~pagePK:478093~piPK:477627~theSitePK:477 624,00.html.

appraisal of the Reports and what they reveal regarding the Bank's intellectual role.[9] In a short piece, entitled "World Development Report at 30: A Birthday Tribute or Funeral Elegy", Deaton (2009b, p. 113) wonders whether the WDR has turned from a star "to a red dwarf or even a black hole". He continues, "the development expertise that is at the centre of the World Bank's mission may not exist in useful form, or at the least, needs to be fundamentally rethought and restricted". This raises a set of issues regarding the WDR and the Bank as a putative, self-designated "Knowledge Bank".

Before exploring these in more detail, however, attention should be drawn to the way in which the WDR is funded. Originally covered by the Bank's own research budget, the WDRs are now co-financed through Trust Funds.[10] Trust Funds are provided to the Bank by specific donors which, in return, can exert a significant degree of control over the deployment of these funds.[11] The WDR 2015 itself was funded through substantial donor contributions, including by the UK's official aid agency DfID, the Department for International Development (World Bank Group, 2014, p. 30). Against that backdrop, the Report then emerges not solely as a reflection of what the Bank sees as pertinent to development, but also as an attempt on the part of the British and other governments to increase the influence of behavioural economics over policy.

Indeed, on casual evidence, there seems to be something of an increasingly revolving, if not open, door between the worlds of scholarship, politics and self-interest. Behavioural economics is no exception. Since the UK's DfID has partly funded the WDR, it may come as no surprise that the current UK Government has set up its own "behavioural insight team", popularly known as the "nudge unit". It is headed by David Halpern, and it has been privatised (a first for a government think tank), with its staff taking a third of the shares themselves partially in order to be able to be paid more flexibly. It is being housed in the

---

9   The earlier Deaton Report (Deaton et al. 2006) offered strong criticism of the Bank's scholarly role but failed to put any serious dent into the Bank's stature within, or influence over, the field of development economics (and studies). See Bayliss et al. (eds) (2011) for a comprehensive review.

10   The costs of producing a WDR have increased dramatically, from US\$3,613,000 (of which US\$1,188,000 came through Trust Funds) for WDR 2002 to US\$8,427,000 (of which US\$2,232,000 was provided through Trust Funds) for WDR 2010 (World Bank, 2011, p. 55).

11   Research programmes within the Bank that have been financed through Trust Funds include the Poverty Dynamics and Public Service Delivery Trust Fund, the Global Public Goods Trust Fund, the Investment Climate and Trade and Integration Trust Fund (World Bank Group, 2014).

charity Nesta, an innovation foundation headed by Geoff Mulgan.[12] The benefit to all concerned will accrue through government and other contracts, not least, no doubt, from the World Bank itself as it promotes nudge consultancy.[13]

Returning to the specific issue of the WDR and the Bank's exercise of its scholarly role, several questions arise. First, what is the development expertise or intellectual stature lodged with the DEC which the WDR seeks to showcase? To illustrate the stature of the Bank's research enterprise, consider its scale. For nearly a decade, the resources of the Bank's economics research department have largely exceeded those available to any university department or research institute working on development.[14] Since 1995, Bank researchers have published over 15,000 scholarly books and articles, and the Bank has led a vast expansion of development data (World Bank, 2012a, p. 2). Between 2009 and 2011 alone, Bank staff and consultants produced over 3,000 publications,

---

12   Mulgan is currently Professor of Collective Intelligence, Public Policy and Social Innovation at University College, London. He was knighted in 2020. On a personal note, I had a bitter dispute with him in 1984 at the Greater London Council (under Ken Livingstone and soon to be abolished) over whether public libraries should make charges for users (to ensure, in his view, that they met popular needs) but lost (in principle if of little significance in practice given abolition on the horizon) with very little success in garnishing support from those responsible for the cultural industries (including both Robin Murray and a disinterested Paul Gilroy). I debated Halpern both at the Runnymede Trust (Fine, 2005a) and on the BBC's "Thinking Allowed" following the publication of my book (Fine, 2010b) and previously available at http://www.bbc.co.uk/iplayer/cons ole/b00ss2q6.

13   Note that both Halpern and Mulgan seem to have moved seamlessly from being researchers in Tony Blair's Cabinets, with Mulgan heading overall research and Halpern, amongst other things, heading the unit for promoting social capital. Strikingly, social capital was itself heavily promoted by the Bank from the mid-1990s before being precipitously abandoned at the beginning of the millennium. Whilst the Bank's own take on social capital studiously ignored its role in promoting the elite, rich and powerful, it is possibly germane that the Institute for Government, for which Halpern served as Founding Director twixt serving Labour and Tory governments, has been primarily funded by the Gatsby Charitable Foundation, whose chief donor (of £1 billion or so) is former Labour Cabinet Minister, Lord Sainsbury. In this light, it is unsurprising that behavioural economics should be deployed as a vehicle for promoting particular postures irrespective of its suitability for such and the scholarly standards involved. Social capital also seamlessly morphed into Prime Minister David Cameron's Big Society, with both Halpern and Mulgan on board with leading roles.

14   The budget of the Bank's research department has been hovering around US$50 million annually for the last few years (World Bank, 2012a, p. 113). This can be compared, for instance, to the budget for research and grants of the UK's Overseas Development Institute (ODI), which stood at £25 ($35) million in 2014; see, now unable to access due to block, http://www.odi.org/sites/odi.org.uk/files/odi-assets/publications-opinion-files /9774.pdf.

including over 200 books, 1,300 scholarly articles in peer-reviewed journals and 1,000 policy research working papers, p. 3. The Bank's working papers form the second most downloaded series via the search engine Research Papers in Economics (RePEc), behind the NBER Working Paper series, p. 4. In the words of Stern and Ferreira (1997, p. 524), the Bank cannot be seen as "just one of a number of fairly equal actors in the world of development economics".

Second, how has the Bank traditionally understood its own intellectual role as practised through its WDR series? The Bank sees four objectives for its research programme: to generate knowledge that is a global public good and serves the development community; to guide the Bank's corporate strategies, policy advice, lending operations and technical assistance; to support specific Bank operations; and, finally, to assist in developing research capacity in Bank member countries (World Bank, 2012a, p. 1). For the Bank, its knowledge role then resembles that of a "clearing house for knowledge about development", "disseminator of development knowledge and policy lessons"; its knowledge provides an "international public good", and the Bank operates as an "honest knowledge broker" (Stone and Wright, 2007, p. 14; and see also Wolfensohn, 1996). The Bank's research exercise is bestowed with neutral and professional qualities, with this image reinforced by the assumed technical and apolitical character of economics, the discipline dominating its research (Benjamin, 2007; and Swedberg, 1986). Clearly, the Bank's own account of its knowledge role is prone to misgivings. The Bank's knowledge exercise is not a neutral, politically impartial nor confined to (indisputable) technical enterprise, but needs to be understood within its political, economic and disciplinary contexts. There exists a large body of critical commentary on the Bank's knowledge role drawing explicit attention to a set of governance features (see Broad, 2006; and Wade, 2002), as well as to the role of economics as the Bank's foremost scholarly discipline (Fine, 2001).

Third, how is this taken forward in WDR 2015? In a chapter dealing with the "biases" of development professionals including its own (World Bank, 2015, Chapter. 10), WDR 2015 puts forward proposals to make development organisations, like the Bank, more effective. This would entail that, "development practitioners become more aware of their own biases and that organizations implement procedures to mitigate their effects", p. 5. This sounds promising, but how is it understood? Development professionals are seen as influenced by their own mental models, which may be inappropriate for understanding the context within which project beneficiaries operate. The reasons for this inadequacy are manifold, but the Report highlights the "disciplinary, cultural and ideological priors" that govern the engagement of development professionals with development problems. Yet, these "priors" are entirely understood in terms of personal attributes of the individual, rather than being seen as attached to the culture of a discipline, collectively created and enforced through a host of processes, including university education, publication strategies, awarding of research funding, etc., or as related to the institutional context and the particular policy imperatives that this, and other strategic factors and influences, may imply.

Sense-making in the WDR is reduced to an individualised, isolated process, even if the individuals are projected to "think socially" as well as being potentially caught in particular "mental frames". The latter are not located in the realm of disciplinary and intellectual contexts (World Bank economics) but derive entirely from the professional's characteristics as an individual (like any other), rather than as an economist or social scientist, reproducing a disciplinary order governed by particular canons, or as affected by particular institutional dynamics relating to the Bank's shareholder realities, the origins of its funds and the particular policy agendas and biases that these imply. So, if "social" or "mental" models are brought into the analysis, this "recognition" remains devoid of any reflection upon the specificities attached to the individual reproducing him/herself within a specific disciplinary culture and institution. There are no implications attached to the practice of economics, nor to the resonance of particular trends within economics, or to the location of the professional within the World Bank. Bank development professionals are not seen to make mistakes because of the use of particular, generally inappropriate, analytical categories, the selective use of evidence, the promotion of findings in support of particular policy imperatives, etc.

Essentially, the Bank's professionals are deemed to make mistakes merely because they are not the poor people for whom they prescribe policies (and hence do not share their mental models). This is all a far cry from Broad's (2006) account of the soft laws governing Bank scholarly activities or from the evaluation of Deaton et al. (2006), each of which highlights that Bank research tends to favour particular policy practices.[15]

3   Situating the Turn to Behavioural Economics at the Bank

The evolution of the World Bank's economics can be tracked through a number of overlapping and sequenced trajectories (see Bayliss et al. 2011; Fine,

---

15   But see Van Waeyenberge and Fine (2011, pp. 35–6) on how the underlying reasons for these biases remain ill-explored in the Deaton Report.

2002a, 2009a; Fine and Milonakis, 2009; and Milonakis and Fine, 2009). Most obvious has been that of mainstream economics, which has evolved along several opposing divides. Foremost, at least initially in the post-war period, was that between (Keynesian) macroeconomics and a subordinate but prominent microeconomics. This left separate space for a variety of applied and empirical fields (such as development economics). Other social sciences remained more or less untouched by economics as a consequence of a relatively rigid interdisciplinary division of labour.[16]

These conditions around scholarship dovetailed with the separate trajectories of context and corresponding policy imperatives. For the restricted scope of macroeconomics and microeconomics allowed the old or classic development economics, and a corresponding development studies, to prosper, drawing upon economic and social history and other social sciences and inductive methods. Within the Bank, this took the form of looking for empirical regularities in the development process and for models of, and policies for, modernisation that served Cold War purposes, ultimately leading intellectually to the longstanding part played by Hollis Chenery as Chief Economist at the Bank, serving from 1972 to 1982.[17]

The end of the post-war boom in the 1970s signalled not only the monetarist counter-revolution spearheaded by Milton Friedman but even more virulent forms of laissez-faire macroeconomics and microeconomics, with increasing subordination of macroeconomics to microeconomics. The University of Chicago took the lead in consolidating the influence of various strands of neoliberal thinking. Further, the independent fields of applied and empirical economics (such as public, regional, industrial and development economics) were increasingly incorporated into microeconomics. Moreover, under the banner of perfectly working markets, and perfectly rational individuals, the nature and role of the state was reduced to total ineffectiveness other than to allow for inefficient distortion. With a short lag, the new development economics emerged in the early 1980s, denying that development required separate principles, focusing on the microeconomics of corruption and rent-seeking and otherwise leading towards markets working perfectly if not subject to state intervention (see Krueger, 1986).

---

16   'Economics imperialism', however, had deep roots in the 1950s with the emergence in particular of cliometrics, public choice theory and human capital theory. This 'old' form of economics imperialism was pioneered by Gary Becker and reduced the non-market to a more or less perfectly working market (Fine and Milonakis, 2009).

17   In 1982, he and others of his ilk were cleared out by Anne Krueger in paving the scholarly conduit for the Washington Consensus.

At the Bank, the Washington Consensus shaped scholarship, ideology and policy in practice, with loose and at times inconsistent relations of these to one another. For scholarship, in particular, the Bank began to define the field of development economics almost to the point of appropriating it; not least in setting the agenda of state versus market. Further, for policy, from earlier preoccupations with providing funding for 'hard' infrastructure, through 'softer' concerns for poverty alleviation, the Bank began its journey to what has now become a self-appointed responsibility for all aspects of economic and social policy (social security, pensions, labour markets, health, education, etc.), while having recourse to an ever-narrower set of intellectual and policy tools to address them. And, for ideology, neoliberal mantras coincide with substantial, wide-ranging and continuing interventions to promote the 'market'.

Such expansion in scope of World Bank activity across scholarship, ideology and policy in practice was accelerated rather than diminished by the launch of the Post-Washington Consensus in the late 1990s, and what might be termed the 'newer' development economics. It unavoidably aligned with the new phase of economics imperialism associated with imperfectly working markets due to asymmetric information, in which economic and social structures, institutions, customs, habits, culture, are explained as the rational, and possibly collective, responses to imperfectly working markets.[18] Significantly, this retained both the optimising individual and the predominance of microeconomic principles as the basis for macroeconomics and macro phenomena more generally.

By treating non-market institutions as responses to market imperfections, this new phase of economics imperialism extended the reach of economics over the other social sciences and over development economics itself. Microeconomic principles had become so well-established that it became second nature to combine them with other disciplinary resources from across the social sciences. Ironically, this included variables or approaches that had been explicitly excluded from the purview of economics when these core principles were established in the first place.[19] In addition, this process of "suspension" (see Fine, 2011c) – taking core principles as uncritical point of departure; they are both there and not there at the same time – has been accompanied by a parallel process of simply adopting the methodology and formal techniques of

---

18   Krugman's alternative draws upon increasing returns to scale as opposed to asymmetric information. It has been much less prominent in scale and scope but has inspired new international trade theory and the new economic geography, with the WDR for 2009 dedicated to the latter; see Fine (2010a) for a critique.

19   Fixed preferences and motivation are examples.

economics. Statistical investigation has become especially prodigious within economics, with at most the loosest of attachments to theory. The result is the emergence of *The Economics of Almost Everything* (Frank, 2007).[20] Within the field of development what might be termed the newest development economics has emerged, the most prominent illustration being randomised control trials (RCT). RCT reduces policy making to a mere technical problem with the aid of expert knowledge and opinion (Prince, 2012); it relocates the study of development from the field to the laboratory whilst consolidating the shift in focus of analysis from major transformation to individual psychology and behaviour.

This sets the scene for the WDR's focus on behavioural economics, an approach strengthened by the global crisis; if (financial) markets did not work perfectly, individuals must be, in some sense, at fault and/or misled. The application of behavioural economics recipes to the developing world, however, is not new. Two renowned advocates of the behavioural approach to development, Banerjee and Duflo (2011, p. 269), had already advanced arguments for this shift. First, they note that the poor in developing countries and their counterparts in the developed world are equally prone to cognitive limitations and self-control problems, and thus similar policy prescriptions apply. Second, behavioural economics lessons are argued to be even more relevant in the developing world as individuals in these societies can rely neither on properly functioning markets nor on a protective welfare state. The behavioural approach to development is seen as even more pertinent as "the poor bear responsibility for too many aspects of their lives, being far more vulnerable to cognitive and self-control biases". Finally, behaviourally-inspired approaches that involve minor tinkering with the context of choice have the additional advantage of being perceived as cost-effective. This is clearly a feature of the behavioural approach to development welcomed by WDR 2015, "The behavioral perspective on decision making suggests that seemingly minor and low-cost policy changes may have a large impact on the achievement of development goals and the reduction of poverty" (World Bank, 2015, p. 38).

The behavioural approach to development thus represents yet another paradigmatic shift further away from the older tradition focused on the structures that trap poor countries and poor people. It instead adopts a micro-level approach devoted to the management of choice within a given set of socioeconomic constraints, reinforcing the structures that might have generated the problems in the first place. In the developing world, with underdeveloped markets and weak or non-existent welfare systems, the possibilities for the

---

20   Or 'Freakonomics' (Levitt and Dubner, 2005).

behavioural approach appear overwhelming. Indeed, the more meagre the prospects for the advancement of market forces and the narrower the scope for government intervention, the more attractive an individualistic approach to development based on improving individual choices becomes.

4   The WDR Approach to Behavioural Economics

4.1   *The WDR's Mental Model*

The WDR 2015, while showcasing behavioural economics and promoting behaviourally-inspired development policy, still adopts neoclassical economics as its preferred mental model. Indeed, the neoclassical model is pervasive throughout the WDR. Consider the Report's stated goal, "to inspire and guide researchers and practitioners who can help advance a new set of development approaches based on a fuller consideration of psychological and social influences" (World Bank, 2015, p. 2); most significantly, though, the text then proceeds with the immediate disclaimer that "the new tools based on this full consideration of human factors do not displace existing policy approaches based on affecting self-interested personal incentives; rather, they complement and enhance them", p. 3.

This literally echoes the way behavioural economics' positions itself towards neoclassical economics. Camerer and Loewenstein (2004, p. 3), two leading practitioners in the field, highlight how, "at the core of behavioural economics is the conviction that increasing the realism of the psychological underpinnings of economic analysis will improve the field of economics on its own terms – generating theoretical insights, making better predictions of field phenomena, and suggesting better policy". They also emphasise that the consideration of psychological factors is complementary to neoclassical economics since the relevance of human psychology to economics does not imply "a wholesale rejection of the neoclassical approach to economics based on utility maximization, equilibrium, and efficiency".

The WDR's reliance on behavioural economics as 'neoclassical plus' is evident in its policy approach as it focuses on "how humans think (the processes of mind) and how history and context shape thinking (the influence of society) [and how this] can improve the design and implementation of development policies and interventions that target human choice and action (behaviour)" (World Bank, 2015, p. 2). The emphasis on the processes of the mind draws on the seminal work of Kahneman and Tversky (1979) and Tversky and Kahneman (1974 and 1981) and on heuristics and biases, later reframed as the automatic system of judgement and choice as opposed to the deliberative system (Kahneman, 2003). The interest in the influence of society is inspired by the game-theoretical strand of behavioural economics, which incorporates in the individual utility function the agent's concern for the welfare of others (i.e. his/her social preferences in addition to the agent's concern for his/her own welfare) in the study of strategic and cooperative problems of social interaction (e.g. Camerer, 2003). Yet, attention to automatic systems of judgement and choice implies a revision of the rationality assumption of neoclassical economics and, together with the game-theoretical strand, undermines the assumptions of self-interested behaviour and exogenous preferences. While both research strands then apparently challenge the neoclassical economics model of human action, these challenges are limited if not deceptive. For once context and interdependence come into play, these ought to be addressed as socially-determined not individual attributes.

To the contrary, the appeal of behavioural economics arises both from its continuities with, and its departures from, neoclassical economics (Davis, 2008; and Fine, 2002a). If, on the one hand, behavioural economics incorporates more realistic psychology in economic theorising, making it more palatable to policy makers, on the other hand, it generally conforms to economics' preferred methods (i.e. individualism and formalism) and pro-market stance (Davis, 2008; Santos, 2011; and Santos and Rodrigues, 2014). Like other attempts at incorporating insights from other social sciences (Fine and Milonakis, 2009), those from psychology that are deployed in the behavioural economics approach are filtered through their compatibility with neoclassical economics' technical apparatus, resulting in a lack of genuine engagement with other behavioural sciences (see also Bazerman and Malhotra, 2012; Berg and Gigerenzer, 2010; Davis, 2013; and Sent, 2004).[21]

Automatic thinking, central to the WDR's take on behavioural economics, is deemed to simplify decisions, using associations and belief systems that compensate for missing information and facilitate decision making. Automatic thinking is thus fast, effortless and associative, but is presumed sometimes to lead to large and systematic mistakes. These stem either from errors in information processing (bounded rationality) or a mismatch between intentions and actions (bounded will power), i.e. failure in carrying out previously deliberated courses of action. Automatic thinking contrasts with deliberative thinking, which neoclassical economics characterises as decisions made on the basis of unbiased, effortful and reflective calculations of all possible outcomes

---

21   This is crucial in rejecting the hypothesis of reverse imperialism between economics and the other social sciences. See Fine (2024b).

from alternative choices. The dual system of thinking is taken to expand the standard economic model, allowing for the consideration of outcomes that deviate from those that would result from the deliberative system.

On this account, that individuals rely on automatic thinking has significant implications for understanding development and for designing policies to tackle poverty, which seek to make it simpler and easier for individuals to choose courses of actions consistent with their desired outcomes and best interests. This requires paying close attention to the "choice architectures" underlying all institutionally-mediated interactions (Thaler and Sunstein, 2008), assisting individuals in their decision making by framing choices, "adjusting what information is provided, and the format in which it is provided", p. 6. But such proposals, inspired by the heuristics and biases branch of behavioural economics research, still work with(in) the neoclassical framework approach, focusing on the problems posed by deviations to its rationality assumption, targeting solutions that make people behave more rationally despite themselves. In this sense, behaviour in practice is akin to a (market) imperfection to be corrected as far as possible towards perfect rationality.

The strand of behavioural research that has been inspired by game theory draws attention to so-called social preferences, i.e. people's aversion to inequality, tendency to abide by social norms, and reciprocal or altruistic behaviours (e.g. Camerer and Fehr, 2004). Again, consideration of these aspects of human sociality is contrasted with the autonomous, self-regarding assumption of neoclassical economic theory. The policy implication is that a sole focus on external material incentives like prices is insufficient, and policy makers need to resort to 'social incentives', mobilising social expectations, social recognition, patterns of cooperation, care of in-group members, and social norms in order to identify and implement new kinds of intervention.

This provides another indication of the intricate complementarity between neoclassical and behavioural economics. The former is taken to apply to situations in which market exchanges are considered adequate and efficient, and where individual actions stem from people's deliberative systems. The latter applies to situations in which forms of exchange based on trust and reciprocity are required and effective, and where individual actions have other-regarding considerations and the like. However, the functional articulation between market and non-market spheres, which neoclassical and behavioural economics promote, takes the idealised 'liberal societies' of the developed world as their implicit contextual framing. The two spheres are considered complementary by both neoclassical and behavioural economists (Santos and Rodrigues, 2014). The ultimate goal for policy then is to cultivate, through an appropriate institutional mix, the right combination of self-interest and other-regarding considerations. In response, individuals would learn to be, simultaneously, "habitual social exchangers" and "vigorous traders", meaning that markets could coexist with the social foundations on which they ultimately rely.

4.2   Behavioural Economics and Development: The Conquest of Another Frontier?

The behavioural approach then offers an exemplary illustration of the application of the newer phase of economics imperialism to development, highlighted by the 'optimising individual plus something else' approach. Most significantly, "(t)he new approaches do not replace standard economics" (World Bank, 2015, p. 4). Instead, it is supplemented by a range of ways of behaving, "automatically" instead of "deliberatively", as well as determinants of behaviour, "thinking socially", depending on what others think, and "thinking with mental models", p. 3. Such is the privileging of the economic, which remains inconsistent with the non-economic – an insight unwittingly highlighted by the Report which acknowledges that "'Economic man' is a fiction, not a reality", p. 25.

Why this fiction should prevail at all is left unresolved. For "[p]olicies that assume that rational decision making will always prevail can go astray in many contexts … Updating the standard assumptions about human decision making is essential". The WDR sees this as a new insight, for "[t]hirty years ago, people might reasonably have viewed the findings of behavioral economics as a few anomalies", p. 28/29. Yet it seems to have long prevailed, given that, "[t]he idea that people have two systems of thinking is not new and has been anticipated in the work of many psychologists and philosophers over the centuries", p. 27. By the same token, "[e]veryone knows that economic incentives can influence behavior. What is less commonly recognized is that social incentives can also exert a powerful effect on behavior", p. 43. In short, the WDR is caught between claiming the commonsense of not relying upon rationality (whilst privileging rationality), and ignoring the failure to have gone beyond rationality until recently.

Even so, the enrichment of rationality is extremely limited and conforms to reliance upon universal notions of human behaviour in forms that are characteristic of (economic) rationality itself. Continual reference is made to the economic and the non-economic, the automatic and the deliberative, the intuitive and the reflective, the social and the mental, the framing, the anchoring and the loss aversion, the effortless and the effortful, emotion and cognition, instrumental and intrinsic reciprocity, and so on. Significant here, from the smallest act of altruism to grand narratives of historical change, are the mental models that individuals adopt, for "[h]istorians attribute the rise of the modern world to a change in the mental model of how the universe works", p. 72.

Despite reference to the social nature or determinants of behaviour, these are totally decontextualised, implicitly reflecting asocial, ahistorical and universal notions of human, as individual, behaviour. Consequently, even as universals, there is no reference to power, conflict, class, gender, race, etc. in and of themselves, let alone as the raw materials for understanding the systemic origins of (non-rational) behaviour.[22] Indeed, we are informed that, "both poor people and people who are not poor are affected in the same fundamental way by certain cognitive, psychological, and social constraints on decision making", p. 81.[23] At most, appeal is made to the eponymous institutions, cultures and customs that underpin irrational behaviour. The acknowledgement of such influences naturally opens the space to use them for policy purposes and "gives policy makers new tools for promoting development and provides new understandings for why policies based on standard economic assumptions can fail", p. 72. The inevitable major conundrum for the WDR is, though, whether it is necessary to strengthen irrational behaviour in an imperfect world or reduce it to make it perfect. Thus, "[p]redicting exactly when these social relationships can help or hinder progress is still an open question and thus requires careful testing of program design", p. 90.[24]

Such decontextualisation of behaviour has two striking effects in the WDR. One is to allow a free range over examples of behaviours without regard to context, since all behaviour conforms to universally prescribed notions of human nature. The result is an extraordinary enfeeblement of the WDR, for there is an unusually wide appeal to illustrations that lack relevance for issues of development or are not drawn from development at all. For example, the WDR commends the use of stickers placed in minibuses in Kenya which reduced

---

22   Equally striking is the total absence of any reference to the global crisis and the role of finance and financiers within it.

23   As mentioned above, such behaviours are equally seen as characteristic of Bank operatives themselves, "Because policy makers are themselves subject to cognitive biases, they should search for and rely on sound evidence that their interventions have their intended effects, and allow the public to review and scrutinize their policies and interventions, especially those that aim to shape individual choice", p. 20.

24   Indeed, concluding the section on parenting and childhood, "More experimentation and testing are needed to tailor interventions to the situations that parents experience, harnessing insights from neurobiology and the behavioral sciences to understand and tackle the psychological and cultural barriers to effective parenting that arise from the contexts in which individuals live", p.108. For a critique of the newly emerged field of neuroeconomics, itself an exemplary illustration of the latest phase of economics, see Fine (2011c, Appendix 1).

the accident rate, p. 52–3, lockable metal boxes that increased investment in health products in a Kenyan project, p. 120, a water-saving campaign in a city in Colombia that featured the mayor and his wife taking a shower together, p. 176, posters of watchful eyes that boosted payment for milk at an open tea and coffee station in a university in England, p. 47, and a project that used stickers and moved bins and benches to reduce second-hand smoke in Copenhagen Airport, p. 194.

The other effect of decontextualisation follows from the reduced way in which the social and systemic have been constructed through the continuing commitment to a methodological individualism widened, minimally, beyond economic rationality.[25] This is most notable in the treatment of poverty; here, the role of behavioural economics is implicitly deployed as a means by which to encourage the poor to learn to live with the condition, possibly even to imagine escaping from it, without once discussing the structural causes of poverty that both make it inescapable in practice and condition the responses to it. Indeed, in a parody of economic rationality as optimisation subject to price and income constraints, the poor are seen as being both more behaviourally motivated and more behaviourally constrained, p. 81:

> First, poverty generates an intense focus on the present to the detriment of the future. When poor people must direct their mental resources toward dealing with the concerns of poverty – for example, paying off debts or keeping their children safe – they have less attention to devote to other important tasks that may be cognitively demanding, such as expending greater and more productive effort at work or making timely investments in education and health ... Second, poverty can also create poor frames through which people see opportunities. Poverty can blunt the capacity to aspire ... and to take advantage of the opportunities that do present themselves.
>
> Third, the environments of people living in poverty make additional cognitive demands. The absence of certain physical and social infrastructure that eases cognitive burdens in high-income contexts – like piped water, organized child care, and direct deposit and debit of earnings – encumbers those living in low-income settings with a number of day-to-day decisions that deplete mental resources even further.

---

25   Similar considerations apply to the neglect of the systemic sources of climate change, with an implicit presumption that this is driven by inappropriate individual (consumer) behaviour that can therefore be remedied behaviourally.

In short, the poor are offered a pathology of material *and* behavioural deprivation, which "in effect tax an individual's *bandwidth,* or mental resources. This
cognitive tax, in turn, can lead to economic decisions that perpetuate poverty",
emphasis in original.

The most obvious and immediate remedy might be to go to the source of the
problem – the material deprivation that intensifies individual and social dysfunction. Far from it, however, for it seems the goal is to rationalise intervention
to improve the choices made by the poor within their behaviour-determining
poverty (although, as will be seen, not always with their own benefit in mind
when it comes to working more and harder). This is the neoliberal nudge
dilemma; how to amend people's free will by steering their behaviour in their
own best interests. In this case, the WDR suggests, "[f]irst, shaping choices can
help people obtain their own goals", and "[s]econd, individuals' preferences and
immediate aims do not always advance their own interests", p. 20. Indeed:

> Still, it is not the case that when governments refrain from action, individ-
> uals freely and consistently make choices in their own best interest, unin-
> fluenced by anyone else. Any number of interested parties exploit people's
> tendency to think automatically, succumb to social pressure, and rely on
> mental models ... including moneylenders, advertisers, and elites of all
> types. In that context, governmental inaction does not necessarily leave
> space for individual freedom; rather, government inaction may amount to
> an indifference to the loss of freedom.

Whether governments should intervene to help people make decisions that
are in their own interests is a recurrent theme when discussing the policy
implications of behavioural economics, and one raised at the outset by Thaler
and Sunstein (2003, 2008), placing their nudge proposals within a libertarian
paternalistic approach to policy making. While they reject the assumption
that people always make choices in their best interest, justifying the grant-
ing to the policy maker the responsibility for organising the context in which
people make decisions (the paternalistic stance), they are keen to stress that
the policy maker must refrain from constraining the options of the individual (the libertarian stance). The difficulty of reconciling these two aims is, not
surprisingly, a subject of discussion.[26] Significantly, the WDR also engages in

---

26   See Sunstein (2014), as well as Goodwin (2012), Grüne-Yanoff (2012), Hausman and Welch
      (2010) and Sugden (2009) for a critique.

this discussion, and on these terms,[27] even if it adopts a forceful stance on the need for government action, "The standard justifications for government action in market economies are monopolies, externalities, public goods, asymmetric information, redistribution, and macroeconomic stabilization. This Report adds another *"Governments should act when inadequate engagement, situational framing, and social practices undermine agency and create or perpetuate poverty"* (World Bank, 2015, p. 203, emphasis added). Again, the discussion on the role of government reveals the WDR's mental model, taking neoclassical economics as the main theoretical and political reference. The market is retained as the default institution and non-market institutions are justified as offering rational solutions to market failures.

The limitations of this position are revealed in the illustrations deployed, with poor outcomes consistently blamed on the poor choices people make. Lack of self-control is seen as the fundamental cause of poor outcomes throughout the Report. We turn people away from choosing sugary foods (p. 36) but say nothing about the support offered to the production of sugar in a world in which the obese now outnumber the hungry. For exploitative credit markets, there is a presumption of poor decision making from lack of financial literacy (p. 122) as opposed to desperate attempts to deal with starvation and medical expenses. Despite the space given to experiments that improved people's financial information about payday loans, there is little reflection on the findings. In one experiment, individuals provided with better information about the true costs of payday loans (p. 32) were 11 per cent less likely to use a payday loan service in the subsequent four-month period. The Report ignores the meagre extent of the change – only 11 per cent – and the fact that many were just as likely to use payday loans even though they knew how punitive the costs would be. Similarly, the Report asserts "[l]ack of self-control is a leading explanation for lack of savings", p. 120, and argues for commitment-based savings plans, without looking at poverty and need. Most revealing of all is the section concerned with the workplace, where it is assumed that people simply need to work harder (p. 132–3) – although no justification is given for why this is to their benefit and why it is dysfunctionally irrational for them to be otherwise. Indeed, "there are many nonremunerative aspects of work that influence the effort that employees exert on the job", p. 139. Perhaps low pay and poor working conditions might be more pertinent than "intention–action divides and what their peers are doing".

---

27   The WDR closes with a section entitled, "Why should governments shape individual choices?" (World Bank, 2015, p. 202).

However, behavioural findings may support policy proposals that extend beyond the nudge approach (Dolan et al. 2010; and Oliver, 2013). For example, that human cognitive and emotional processes can be manipulated to serve the undesirable and inefficient interests of firms, moneylenders, banks and other interested parties may warrant regulations that impose limitations on their actions. Behavioural findings may, therefore, suggest a wider range of policies, such as regulatory measures and laws that aim to change or create new institutional conditions deemed conducive to human welfare. But moving beyond minor tinkering with the context of choice in development policy would entail profound institutional change, bearing, not least, on an institution like the World Bank. As the WDR reminds us, "achieving social change in a situation where mental models have been internalized may require influencing not only the cognitive decision making of particular individuals but also social practices and institutions", p. 12.

5   **From Behavioural Economics to World Bank Policy in Practice:
The Case of HIV-Related Cash Transfers**

The discussion so far may suggest that this WDR is mostly irrelevant. There is no substantive departure from the tenets of mainstream economics and the Report produces examples of behaviourally-aware policies that manage to be both mundane and ephemeral. Moreover, who would reject a policy approach that makes it easier for individuals to make better decisions? However, as innocuous as the Report appears in terms of policy, in practice it furthers a new trend in the design of development interventions which threatens to remove any commitment to the necessity for structural change as part of the development process. This has strong ethical as well as sustainability implications for development interventions. To illustrate the fundamental failures of an approach to development based on behavioural economics both in its limited understanding of poverty and its policy focus on individual choices, rational or otherwise (instead of engaging with underlying structural issues), we take a closer look at an example of health-related behavioural economics interventions, namely HIV-related cash transfers.

While behavioural economics policies in the WDR often appear as subtle nudges to the choice environment,[28] behavioural economics interventions in poor countries span a wide stage and take particularly intrusive forms. They

---

28   For example, health-related libertarian paternalism in the North might focus on the way that a change to the layout of school canteens can increase the uptake of fruit and

have generally involved cash incentives to take up health services or to affect behaviour in particular ways. Cash transfers are now used extensively, and rough estimates suggest that between 0.75 and 1 billion people in low- and middle-income countries currently receive non-contributory cash benefits (Barrientos and Niño-Zarazúa, 2010).[29]

However, it is necessary to distinguish between generic forms of cash transfers and those inspired by behavioural economics. On the one hand, standard cash transfer interventions aim to raise income of a particular group (targeted in terms of age or other characteristics) and, in their conditional form, they often require beneficiaries to use nutrition or health services. On the other hand, cash transfers inspired by behavioural economics do not aim to reduce poverty as such but to change specific incentives around health behaviour. Here, following behavioural economics, people are agents who ignore health messages because of the weight of social pressure or who are myopic and heavily discount the future benefits of health-seeking activity, while overly valuing their current pleasure. For example, myopic individuals will not choose to eat healthily because they focus on the immediate pleasure of unhealthy foods and remain oblivious to the future benefits of a balanced diet, or they may not complete a course of TB treatment, as they focus on the immediate costs of repeated hospital attendance, rather than on the ultimate result of such repeated visits.

A critical assessment of health interventions inspired by behavioural economics can be made on the basis of a closer examination of HIV-related policies. Within this context, individuals are seen as failing to take up HIV prevention messages by focusing on the immediate pleasure of unsafe sex while discounting the cost of acquiring HIV, either due to myopia or social norms. Thus, cash transfers become a way to affect the balance between short- and long-run benefits so that individuals become more likely to choose safe sex or abstinence (de Walque et al. 2012b, p. 2). The presumptions are, first, that incentives can increase the implicit price of unsafe sex (through the immanent loss of the cash reward); and, second, that even small regular payments may "'nudge' individuals to overcome inertia and extricate themselves from unduly risky sexual relationships". Third, de Walque et al. (2012a, p. 14) also suggest that cash incentives provide individuals with an excuse for deviating from social norms, allowing them to act in conformity with their true underlying

---

vegetables http://www.sciencedaily.com/releases/2013/02/130226172506.htm, no longer available.

29 For critical assessments of conditional cash transfers (CCTs), see Fine (2014), Lavinas (2013) and Saad-Filho (2015).

preferences for less risky behaviour. In essence, in such an approach, HIV epidemics are the result of sub-optimal decisions by individuals who (mistakenly) believe they are making, or are persuaded by social norms to deviate from, optimal decisions and who can be nudged into changing their choices (through cash transfers).

Let us examine the implications of these presumptions through a critical dissection of a set of existing programmes. Projects to change HIV risk behaviours have been implemented in Lesotho, Malawi and Tanzania, while others have begun in South Africa (Johnston, 2015). According to the designers of the Lesotho intervention, people engage in risky sexual behaviour despite high prevalence of HIV as they weigh the short-term benefits more highly than the long-term costs (Björkman-Nyqvist et al. 2013). De Walque et al. (2012a, p. 6) assert that the young people involved in the Tanzania RESPECT project "appear to understand their HIV risks and know how to behave to prevent transmission – yet they don't choose to act on that knowledge".

It should be noted that, in general, cash transfers to change health incentives typically operate with smaller cash outlays and more stringent forms of conditionality than standard cash transfer programmes. In standard cash transfer programmes, such as, for instance, the Kenyan Orphans and Vulnerable Children programmes, US$20 per month is given to "the main care giver" in each participating household (Handa et al. 2014). In contrast, in the Malawi rural incentive programme that sought to decrease HIV incidence rates, participants were allocated an amount of up to US$16 to be paid one year later if they maintained their HIV-free status (Kohler and Thornton, 2012). In the Tanzania RESPECT programme, participants were paid either around US$10 or US$20 per four-month testing round if they tested negative for four curable, sexually transmitted infections (STIs) (de Walque et al. 2012b). Finally, the Lesotho programme offered no guarantee of cash reward. If individuals tested negative for two easily treated STIs, they were eligible to participate in a lottery, with prizes of the equivalent of US$74 or US$147 per four-month testing round. In each round, four lottery winners were drawn (two men and two women) (Björkman-Nyqvist et al. 2013).

Projects inspired by behavioural economics also have more stringent conditionality embedded within them than general cash transfer programmes. Standard poverty-focused interventions may have no conditionality or might be conditional on school attendance. However, behavioural economics interventions tailor conditionality to incentivise behaviour change through higher frequency of rewards and use of external monitoring. De Walque et al. (2012a, p. 14) and Medlin and de Walque (2008, p. 5), for instance, argue that if people have high rates of discount (and thereby are at greater risk of acquiring HIV), they value quick payoffs; in such cases, awarding a reward after a long delay will tend to be ineffective. The programmes also often include frequent testing for STIs. In practice, however, HIV itself is not always used as a test indicator as it may be too insensitive to behaviour change and too expensive to run (Medlin and de Walque, 2008, p. 12–13; and de Walque et al. 2012a, p. 17–18).

Do projects inspired by behavioural economics produce their intended effects? In the Tanzania RESPECT study, with its two sizes of cash transfer, only the higher payment group had a statistically significant difference in the STI indicators compared to the control group at the end of twelve months (de Walque et al. 2012b). Moreover, the data on HIV showed no significant difference (de Walque et al. 2012b, p. 8), casting doubt on the link between the STI indicators and HIV risk. It was not clear whether the study encouraged a change in sexual behaviour or whether it was observing a change in the treatment sought for the curable indicator STIs. In the Lesotho project, two years after its initiation, HIV incidence was significantly lower among the study participants, especially for women and for those with the greatest potential lottery payout (Björkman-Nyqvist et al. 2013). However, in the Malawi Incentive Project, the authors were surprised to find that male recipients ended up with a greater HIV risk, possibly as extra cash made them more attractive sexual partners (Kohler and Thornton, 2012). In contrast, female recipients were less likely to report having had sex, leading the authors to conclude, rather myopically, that conditional cash transfers can be protective for women, p. 169.

It will be crucial to assess the longer-term impact of these programmes after they have come to an end. This is an area of limited information at the time of writing. In the Tanzanian RESPECT study, however, the impact on STI acquisition by women had disappeared two years after the end of the project (Heise et al. 2013, p. 4). Rigsby et al. (2000) studied the impact of a four-week cash transfer project on anti-retroviral drug adherence among a sample of US veterans. While the use of monetary reinforcement clearly helped treatment adherence during the project, adherence in the cash-transfer group had returned to near-baseline levels just eight weeks after its end.

Overall, then, these programmes have had mixed immediate results, and strong concerns remain regarding their long-run impacts (not least in the absence of attention to longer-term, structural determinants). Their design also raises ethical issues, specifically regarding whether inclusion and exclusion from health-focused interventions can be justified and whether the intrusion of interventions is outweighed by the benefits (Johnston, 2015). Through the design of projects that remove benefits to individuals (some of whom are children or young adults) when they become ill, challenging ethical precedents are set. Another ethical concern arises in the context of a programme that establishes lotteries with groups who are seen as having a poor ability to behave rationally let alone assess risk.

Finally, underlying these interventions is a narrow conceptualisation of ill-health as the result of poor choices by individuals. More specifically, behavioural economics does not recognise the role of systemic (rather than individual) factors in explaining poor health, which are diverse, specific to particular health conditions and often deeply political. When these are ignored, it is not surprising that cash transfer projects have complex and sometimes limited impacts. At the same time, they appear attractive to policy makers; the simplistic premise of these projects may offer short-cuts in dealing with polit-ically difficult questions of power, distribution and class. This is not to suggest that interventions inspired by behavioural economics are harmless; embedded within them are particular norms and values. By blaming individuals for their poor health, they cement stigma around the acquisition of illnesses like HIV. Further, by extending the commodification of health and welfare, they reduce the role of the state in guaranteeing health outcomes.[30]

6   Concluding Remarks

Using WDR 2015 as a lens through which to appraise the World Bank's shifting scholarly roles exposes a set of issues. First, while the Bank's arguments about its position as Knowledge Bank have previously been organised around the attributes of the discipline of economics, we now have forays into the behav-iour of development professionals, including Bank staff.

Second, across the Report, what seems like a contradiction between univer-sal notions of human behaviour and an emphasis on local context apparently dissolves once it is accepted that the latter is to be understood entirely in the service of the former, i.e. an interest in context emerges only to the extent that it allows a better understanding of the choice architecture facing individuals, rather than drawing attention to systemic or structural issues bearing on why poverty is reproduced.

Third, the inadequacies of the Bank's economics (in principle and practice) are obscured through reference to behaviour – itself understood in highly reductionist terms. This nudges us into doing the right thing, while simultane-ously steering safely away from structural issues bearing on worsening social

---

30   Arguably, the structural adjustment programmes of the 1980s exacerbated the HIV crisis in sub-Saharan African by crippling health systems, while the informalisation of labour markets has served to reduce employment-related health provision (O'Laughlin, 2013).

and economic outcomes across the world, except of course through the further deepening of labour market reforms, and the restructuring of public services to the profit of private enterprise. The more we nudge, the less we need to budge in the face of worsening inequalities and the continuing assault of finance on living standards and democratic accountability. Finally, WDR 2015 implies a dramatic reduction of what development is about (recall the Report's focus on stickers in cars, metal boxes in households, showers with partners, etc.). And, while the interventions this fosters in practice remain far removed from the mainstay of Bank activities, which have become increasingly organised around large public-private partnerships, they have proven popular in certain fields, including health, often with dubious impact and moral implications.

A Paradigm Shift that Never Will Be? Justin Lin's New Structural Economics

Postscript as Personal Preamble

Although written little more than a decade ago, the prompt to draft this Chapter, Justin Lin's venture into industrial policy, is already confined to the dustbin of history. Is this critique, then, merely academic, an exercise in the history of economic thought? Hopefully, the answer is no. First of all, history of thought is never only of academic interest as it gives us some insight into how we got where we are now and why, and so sheds light on the contemporary.

Second, the same applies to the history (of economic thought) at the World Bank. Lin is arguably the last, at the time of writing, Chief Economist at the WB who has been both prominent as an economist and in the position of Chief Economist itself. Unlike his predecessors in these two respects, Joe Stiglitz who launched the Post-Washington Consensus, and Anne Krueger with the Washington Consensus for a time, Lin's New Structural Economics made a little splash at the time without any lasting ripples (as the question mark in our title anticipates).

Third, then, why is Lin the dog that did not bark. As indicated by Wade (2012), he simply did not have sufficient support and weight in the Bank. But his exercise does shed light on the nature of the Bank's scholarship more generally, not least its complex and shifting relationship to ideology and policy in practice, its lack of quality even by the standards of the mainstream, and the capacity to command attention and direction in the short run when more fundamental rethinks are potentially on the agenda.

This is important not least as it has been generally acknowledged that (new) industrial policy is back on the agenda under the third phase of neoliberalism in which the state is actively and overtly engaged in promoting financialisation through use of its resources and its policy powers in engaging with both finance and industry (Bayliss et al. 2024, and the next two Chapters). In other words, in a corresponding third phase of economics imperialism, mainstream economics is bringing back in industrial policy and varieties of reasons for it and forms that it might take. What stands out, however, is how confined are these rethinks and renewals of industrial policy, so much so that they might even be considered to be driven by the motivation to contain rather than promote, however consciously. How do we place limits on state interventionism through positively confining it to a limited extension of industrial policy and an image of it as a dramatic change from the past neglect under what is, incorrectly, presumed to have been the passing of neoliberalism. The single most important symbols of this syndrome are the neglect, if not absence, of state ownership as a key policy instrument (as opposed to a last resort when all else, including private sector initiatives fail) and what is often an extraordinarily limited notion of development and the role of industry within it.

The latter is most evident in Lin, not least with his New Structural Economics focusing on structure as a mere shift in composition of output, a dual reduction of development to structure and of structure to output composition. In these respects, though, of allowing for industrial policy in order to contain it, Lin is far less ambitious in scope of analysis and interventionism than others, and this might be another reason why he has not been picked up and run with outside the WB, to complement general antipathy to a stance of interventionism within the WB (as we can always intervene as we choose when the situation demands it, without creating a scholarly wedge for interventionism of systematic and more extensive scope).

Undoubtedly, Dani Rodrik has been to the fore in deploying and justifying neoclassical economics as the way in which to conceive industrial policy. That the two go together in his work is vital. I justify industrial policy because I am a neoclassical economist and see it as the only appropriate economics, as long as an appropriate model is chosen for circumstances. This is apparent in the title of one of his books and at least he cares to address the issue (something rare within mainstream economics), *One Economics, Many Recipes*.

But that care is itself careless. Consider a later contribution playing to the same tune, *Economics Rules: the Rights and Wrongs of the Dismal Science*, in which he offers as the fourth of his ten commandments for economists that, "unrealistic assumptions are ok; unrealistic *critical* assumptions [his italics] are not ok" (Rodrik, 2015, p. 213). As a statement of methodology, this is simply bizarre. Even so, a model is determined by its bundle of assumptions so it is impossible to determine which is critical and which is not except in combination (although you can make judicious choices across them but by what criteria). Similar doubts or, at least, controversies arise out of what we judge to be realistic or unrealistic. It must be suspected that what is going on is that irrespective of any discussion in depth of what is critical and what is not, and what is realistic and what is not (let alone any discussion of many other long-established issues on methodology), the goal is to confine analysis to a toolbox of assumptions and methods drawn from mainstream economics, with scant regard for those derived from heterodox economics or social science more generally.[1]

I have criticised Rodrik and his collaborators for their past work in a South African context (Fine, 2009b and c) and also more generally in Chapters 7 and 8 in passing (for which much emphasis was placed by them on facilitating an economic environment in which self-discovery by private entrepreneurs is the gold touch for development as if, in their own metaphor, facilitating monkeys swinging through the jungle in search of bananas – if lucky enough to find the jungle has not been converted to maize, soya, palm or the like). But it is worth briefly bringing out some of the features of one of Rodrik's most recent works and its relationship to the remarks already made (Juhász, Lane and Rodrik, 2023).

First is to recognise that industrial policy is back on the agenda, p. 2:

> There are few economic policies that generate more kneejerk opposition from economists than industrial policy. This has not stopped governments from making abundant use of it, even when they seem ideologically hostile to it. The salience of industrial policy has risen greatly in recent years, as governments have increasingly engaged in self-conscious industrial policies as they address a variety of problems – the green transition, resilience of supply chains, the challenge of good jobs, and geopolitical competition with China.

Second is to push behind favouring (more and better) industrial policy, p. 3:

> Interestingly, the most recent vintage of papers, paying serious attention to identification and observability difficulties, produces results that are much more favorable to industrial policy. These papers tend to find that industrial policy has typically shifted resources in the desired direction, often producing large long-term effects in the structure of economic activity.

Third is to place great emphasis upon the empirical evidence, something that is welcome although how we interpret the evidence needs to finesse both theory

---

1   It is particularly disturbing that, in seeking to persuade their fellow mainstream environmental economists to become more realistic rather than remaining attached to traditional assumptions and methods that, in the *Journal of Economic Methodology*, Stern et al. (2022, p. 185) should positively cite and approve the quotation above from Rodrik on critical assumptions and realism (but not critical realism).

and context (with the latter tending to be reduced to institutions although there is always a need to rely upon the other or the excluded factors when the theory and the evidence do not match), p. 3:

> A new generation of work on ... industrial transformation is beginning to paint a more nuanced picture. This work, often using disaggregated data, pays careful attention to the diversity of policies in question and the structure of linkages and production networks. It shows that certain types of industrial policy were powerful in driving structural change in countries such as Japan, South Korea, and China. But it also suggests that it is very difficult to derive broad generalizations for other countries and time periods from this experience without taking institutional differences in consideration.

Fourth is to define industrial policy in very broad terms (is anything excluded?) but, paradoxically in an entirely reduced way, and bearing in mind, "Industrial policies can take various forms but always create incentives for private-sector actors", p. 4:

> We define industrial policies as those government policies that explicitly target the transformation of the structure of economic activity in pursuit of some public goal.

Fifth, the rationale for industrial policy is well-established within mainstream economics and is, once again, both broad and reduced, p. 4

> There is no shortage of well-grounded economic rationales for industrial policies. We can summarize those under three broad headings: externalities, co-ordination (or agglomeration) failures, and public input provision.

Sixth, the issue then is not to justify industrial policy but to learn what it should be and how to make it work successfully. And here, the two main obstacles are reduced to informational imperfections and corruption (Washington Consensus is reborn!), p. 6:

> the theoretical case for industrial policy is broad and strong. The controversy over industrial policy revolves not around these rationales – which are generally well accepted among economists – but around two practical

objections. One of these objections is about information shortcomings, the other about political capture.

Indeed, p. 6:

> Industrial policy is not that different from many other domains of policy where there exist clear theoretical justifications for government intervention, but evidence on what works is not that clearcut. One can list education policy (human capital externalities), health policy (moral hazard, adverse selection), social insurance and safety nets (incomplete risk markets, behavioral factors), infrastructure policy (natural monopoly), and stabilization policy (Keynesian "rigidities"). In all these areas, it is recognized that the market-failure arguments for intervention can be exploited by powerful insiders and overwhelmed by informational asymmetries. Similarly, the efficacy of different remedies remains contested, despite rich empirical literatures in each domain. But policy discussions in these areas typically focus not on whether the government should do it, but on how. The debates revolve around what works and under what conditions.

Leaving aside whether industrial is not that different from other domains of policy (or indistinguishable given how industrial policy is defined in terms of deliberate shift of economic activity but not health, education, infrastructure, etc?), the economic analysis and its reduction to market imperfections and the like, is necessarily drawn into the wider considerations of the non-economic as proxied by political capture, institutions, context, for which for all the more or less interesting and useful empirical evidence on what works or does not, no ready answers can be given. Instead, the implicit thrust of the policy advice is to target the largest market failures or those with the biggest impact. In response, it might be suggested who would do otherwise (target the smallest with the least?), and the biggest with biggest impact are lack of development, and the globe's (and advanced countries') record on environment, financial stability, inequality and poverty suggests prospects are bleak given failures of those who are already developed.

1   Introduction

As the term of office of Justin Lin, the latest World Bank's Chief Economist, drew to a close, the Bank published a collection of his scholarly contributions in a volume entitled *New Structural Economics. A Framework for Rethinking Development and Policy* (Lin, 2012a).[2] During his tenure at the Bank, Lin had used nearly every public appearance as an opportunity to promote his "New Structural Economics" (NSE).[3] This included what appeared at times to be bold statements regarding the need for industrial policy, particularly in low-income countries. As Lin returned to Beijing University, from which he had been seconded during his tenure as Chief Economist, he hoped that he had "planted the seeds" to "re-open the discussion of industrial policy in the coming years".[4] Given his prominence, Lin's attempt at redefining development economics in general and, presumably as its Chief Economist, to whatever degree, on behalf of the Bank itself, requires scrutiny. This is probably even more so given that Lin's emphasis on industrial policy was projected from within the Bank, which had previously sounded its death knell, most emblematically through its *East Asian Miracle Report* (World Bank, 1993).

In previous work, we have emphasised that activity in and around the World Bank can be understood in terms of a complex, diverse and shifting set of combinations of scholarship, ideology and policy in practice (Fine, 2001; and Bayliss et al. eds, 2011, for example). The exact nature of relationships across this troika is not necessarily one of consistency, nor of detachment, and how they are formed and evolve is different across time, place and issue. This frame will be applied to the attempt by Justin Lin to redefine development economics. Lin (2012a) brings together his work to date in this regard. The volume reproduces previously published articles, together with some commentaries by some more or less friendly critics. And whilst these contributions primarily derive from the time that Lin has been at the World Bank, the NSE derives from Lin's previous work on economic development and transition, undertaken while at the China Centre for Economic Research, University of Beijing, and several papers produced during that period are also included.

In terms of ideology, Lin's posture can be seen from two conflicting perspectives. On the one hand, he is no neoliberal and positively insists upon an interventionist role for the state. This has meant that his contributions have

---

2   Originally appearing as Fine and Van Waeyenberge (2013a), the longer version of Fine and Van Waeyenberge (2013b). Note the slight change in title.

3   No less prolific since departing office, Lin has already published a further volume, publicity for which describes him as the "architect of China's economic reform", online if no longer available http://www.odi.org.uk/events/3023-developing-economies-grow?utm_source =newsletter&utm_medium=email&utm_campaign=20121220.

4   http://blogs.worldbank.org/psd/from-old-taboo-to-new-consensus-industrial-policy-and -competitive-industries-pt-1.

been greeted with considerable if qualified welcome by erstwhile critics of the Bank, including those contributing to the volume. However, in the wake of the global crisis, and at least the potential loss of legitimacy of putatively relying upon free markets, Lin's commitment to a positive role for the state is as minimal or circumscribed as it is solid. As we will see, Lin is merely seeking for the state to support the private sector in pursuit of 'comparative advantage', with a correspondingly limited role and scope for industrial policy. So, on the other hand, it is possible to see Lin not so much as positively championing the cause of state intervention as holding it in abeyance against demands for more radical measures in reaction to the lost legitimacy of neoliberalism in which industrial policy, in particular, has been held to be an anathema.

To some degree, however, the association of neoliberalism with free markets is misleading as it has never been non-interventionist. As argued elsewhere (Fine, 2012c), neoliberalism in general, and the Washington Consensus in particular, have involved heavy intervention, essentially to promote the interests of private capital in general and finance in particular, even if within a rhetoric of favouring supposedly free market forces. Moreover, the Post-Washington Consensus (PWC) can be understood as reflecting the same goals in a second phase of neoliberalism, following its first shock phase. It rationalises a broader scope of interventions in the scholarly and rhetorical literature by reference to the need to correct market and institutional imperfections on a piecemeal basis and as a reaction against the previous Consensus. For policies in practice, though, on a broad brush, the PWC has, if anything, hardened on, not departed from, those associated with the Washington Consensus (Van Waeyenberge, 2009).

How then does Lin situate himself in relation to the Washington Consensus and PWC? First, he sees himself as presenting a new structural (development) economics on the scale of influence of the Washington Consensus and old structural economics of his predecessors but also as an improvement upon them. For Lin (2012a, p. 5), his NSE is an attempt to set out a third wave of development thinking, advancing a "neoclassical approach to study the determinants and dynamics of economic structure". In parallel with software, Lin refers to his contribution as Mark 3.0.[5] Second, Lin makes no mention of the PWC. This is odd given that the PWC was launched from within the Bank by his much-celebrated predecessor (and future Nobel Laureate). Yet, while of other Chief Economists only Stiglitz has claimed to redefine the field,[6] explicitly

---

5 He replies to comments from others, including Ha-Joon Chang, Anne Krueger, Dani Rodrik and Joe Stiglitz under the heading, "Rejoinder: Development Thinking 3.0: The Road Ahead", p. 66.

6 Although this was clearly Krueger's intention, see Krueger (1986, p. 62).

substantively, Lin has much less to offer than Stiglitz.[7] Lin's is a heavily reduced market and institutional imperfections economics, with little regard for the depth and breadth (of literature) that is attached to this paradigm that itself exploded out of the idea of the economy (and society more generally) as a market of second hand cars and the corresponding non-market responses to it.[8] Instead, central to Lin's whole analytical edifice is the notion of comparative advantage, a notion that can only have any legitimacy (i.e. none) in a world of perfect competition, see below. Not surprisingly, then, it makes sense for Lin to tread carefully around market imperfections for their more pervasive presence would potentially warrant more pervasive state intervention than he would wish for. This is less so of comparative advantage since it invites, but does not compel, the goal of achieving it through support of, rather than by, the state.

Through his NSE, Lin can then be seen as allegedly seeking to revive an analytical interest in structural and dynamic features of development (with a focus on industrial upgrading), in order to circumscribe the (industrial) policy realm. This is done by anchoring his analytical propositions in a very narrow (and inconsistent) set of neoclassical propositions centrally organised around the concepts of comparative advantage and factor endowments. This analytical stance, however, does not preclude support for a host of policy interventions, which, while ill-fitting with the projected analytical scheme, arise out of ad hoc acknowledgments of specific empirical realities. Further, such inconsistencies, or what we typify below as manifestations of a 'suspended' use of neoclassical economics, appear against the backdrop of a striking absence of any substantive theory of the state itself.

This paper uses Lin's contribution as a lens through which to reflect more broadly on development economics, development studies and development policy, and the role of the Bank across this spectrum. It proceeds as follows. Section 2 provides an elaborate critique of the core analytical propositions that

---

7   Arguably, Krueger made the greatest impact through facilitating the new development economics for which Stiglitz at most took market imperfections as critical point of departure.

8   For critical account of the PWC as an outcome of the 'newer development economics' in these terms, see Fine et al. (eds) (2001), Jomo and Fine (eds) (2006) and Bayliss et al. (eds) (2011). On the broader thrust of the new economics imperialism on which it depends, see Fine and Milonakis (2009). Note, Lin's studied disregard for the PWC is revealed by the index entry in his book which reads "Stiglitz, Joseph E., 56, 58, 59, 66, 67, 72–75, 78, 290, 313n17", but all but the last two of these are made by Stiglitz himself in his included commentary. Perhaps this neglect of his work and paradigm induced the diplomatic Stiglitz, as a sort of Bank Chief Economist in exile, to allow his own contribution to meander off on a scarcely relevant tangent around the issue of the "learning society".

constitute the NSE. This includes a critical engagement with its central notion of comparative advantage, and an assessment of how structural change, the role of the state, and finance are understood. Section 3 considers the implications of the NSE for research and policies both at the Bank and beyond. It describes an odd disconnection between Lin's scholarly ambitions and the policy implications that could be drawn from them versus those policies emanating from the Bank in practice. Further, it takes a critical look at Lin's projections for the Bank as a Knowledge Bank. Section 4 concludes by drawing out the broader implications of our critique.

2   From Comparative Advantage to Development: Lin and the NSE

In the NSE, the starting point of the analysis is an economy's endowments (of capital, labour and natural resources). These are assumed given at any point in, but changeable over, time. Factor endowments for countries at early stages of development are typically characterised by a relative scarcity of capital and relative abundance of labour and/or natural resources. Being given, endowments do not arise as the result of historical trajectories and do not need situating within a broader context of international and domestic political, financial and commercial realities. The analysis suggests that these given endowments imply a particular comparative advantage in different types of production activities. Developing industry, or determining the structure of production activities, following this comparative advantage provides the most competitive or optimal path for a country and produces the largest economic surplus and fastest capital accumulation. Capital accumulation implies the upgrading of the factor endowment structure and leads to changes in industrial structure, in line with a new or "latent", see below, comparative advantage. For a country's comparative advantage to be revealed to the private sector, the main stimulus in industrial upgrading, relative factor prices, must fully reflect scarcities. This necessitates "effective", p. 100, competition in factor markets. Government is to play an active, "facilitating" role in assisting the private sector in structuring productive activity according to comparative advantage by coordinating investments for industrial upgrading and diversification and compensating for externalities generated by first movers in the growth process, apart from engaging in its more traditional infrastructure-improving role, p. 5. For Lin (2012a, pp. 69–70), this all holds the key to industrial and developmental success:

> It is therefore imperative for a facilitating state in a developing country to identify and select new industries that are consistent with comparative

advantage, use its limited resources to improve infrastructure for a limited number of carefully selected industries, provide adequate incentives for first movers, and coordinate private firms' related investments in those industries so that clusters can be formed successfully and quickly. Whether the government plays the identification and facilitation role may explain why some developing countries can grow at 8 percent or more for several decades while most others fail to have a similar performance.

The framework proposed by Lin is then three-pronged, p. 101. It is centrally organised around the concept of comparative advantage; it relies on the market as optimal resource allocation mechanism; and it charts a role for a "facilitating" state in the process of industrial upgrading.

Critical for Lin, then, is the notion of comparative advantage, sitting at the core of his NSE.[9] Yet, despite its significance, it is simply taken for granted as a valid concept. It is as if Ricardo's first use of the notion can be seamlessly extended to the problems of development through the application of neoclassical economics to which Lin is overtly and uncritically committed more generally.[10] For David Ricardo, Portugal can produce both wine and cloth more cheaply than England but has a comparative or relative advantage in the production of wine (a token concession to reality). It makes sense for each country to specialise and trade in the product for which it has a comparative advantage, and this will be brought about by free trade.

---

9   Comparative advantage appears no less than 467 times in Lin (2012a), warranting half a page as an index entry.

10   For Lin, p. 137, "neoclassical economics is simply a useful tool in all this, not a constraint. It is flexible enough to model the externalities, dynamics, and co-ordination failures that give the government a role to play, while also providing the metrics to judge whether government is supporting industries that take the economy too far from its areas of comparative advantage". It is worth emphasising how much such an approach is broadly acceptable to those opposed to neoliberal orthodoxy. For Rodrik, for example, implicitly responds, "He wants to marry structuralism with neoclassical economic reasoning, and I applaud this idea too. So he has two cheers from me. I withhold my third cheer so I can quibble with some of what he writes", p. 53. This is hardly surprising given Rodrik's own stance that for, "*social* phenomena" neoclassical economics offers "*the only sensible way* of thinking about them". Chang is more circumspect and explicitly disagrees, p. 138, "Justin emphasises that neoclassical economics is flexible enough to allow us to deal with all the complex issues arising during the development process. I think it is not enough". However, he has previously conceded, pp. 133/4, "I think that, deep down, Justin and I actually agree ... Once Justin frees himself from the shackles of neoclassical economics, our debate will be more like two carpenters having a friendly disagreement over what kind of hinges and door handles to use for a new cabinet that they are building together, on whose basic design they agree".

Now there are huge problems with Ricardo's theory on its own terms – including consistency with his labour theory of value, his theory of money, and why England is not simply eliminated as a producer by virtue of its absolute disadvantages. These problems are not resolved but are compounded by incorporation into the neoclassical framework.[11] For this, comparative advantage is taken back one step to the so-called factor endowments (at least capital and labour, and possibly natural resources of various types) upon which production depends. Not surprisingly, your comparative advantage for a product is liable to depend upon your comparative endowments for producing it and whether its production is skewed, comparatively, towards depending upon use of the factors in which you are (relatively) well-endowed. Here, there is a huge analytical shift from the optimising *individual* to *national* endowments (with the nation as optimising individual as staging post in standard representations of elementary trade theory through Edgeworth box diagrams). This thoughtless slippage between levels of analysis is endemic within mainstream economics, not least with intra-national distribution set aside when considering national endowments, but conflicts in, and pursuit of, self-interest brought to the fore whenever rent-seeking, corruption and state capture are to be emphasised as obstacles to proper use of endowments, comparative advantage and the virtuous market.

Even setting these considerations aside, let us just list some of the assumptions that are necessary for the concept of comparative advantage to be legitimate, to be measurable and for it to be the basis for policy formulation.[12] First, there can be at most two sectors in the economy[13] (and only two countries as

---

11   As Reinert (2012, p. 6) puts it, "Economics *de facto* returned to the 'colonial' postulates of David Ricardo: that the international economy could and ought to be based on nations bartering labour hours: What a nation produced – industrial high-technology or subsistence agriculture – did not matter".

12   These are adopted from the parallel problem of under what circumstances the notion of effective rate of protection is legitimate, see Deraniyagala and Fine (2001 and 2006).

13   With an import and an export, this implies an absence of non-traded goods, not least whatever government itself does. The following is ironic, to say the least, and false (given that Barro-type regressions address more than a hundred variables), with two pots calling the single kettle black, p. 169, "In the growth literature, structural change has not received as much attention as technological change because of the use of a one-sector model, which is incapable of handling issues related to structural change, in the standard growth accounting and regression research". Note that, like many others including critics of the new growth theory, Lin accepts that the old growth theory predicts conditional convergence, p. 87. This is a purely ex post ideological construct of the new growth theory since old growth theory made no such predictions, believing that cross-country analysis was inappropriate (since the determinants of technical change and productivity increase

well).[14] Second, these must not be subject to what is termed factor reversals in international trade (in which the composition of the use of inputs or the demand for goods changes disproportionately with differences in the distribution of income or demand).[15] Third, there must be full employment. Fourth, there must be no increasing returns to scale and scope. Fifth, there must be no externalities. Sixth, there must be no factor mobility. Seventh, there must be perfect competition. Eighth, there must be no technological change, as opposed to change in technique to higher, or lower, capital-labour ratios.[16]

In other words, the notion of comparative advantage is useless whether conceptually, empirically or policy-wise, and especially all of these in combination, although this has not prevented it from being a workhorse of sorts in theoretical scholarship and empirical and policy application. It should be emphasised that these considerations arise from *within* the apparatus of neoclassical economics itself, not by virtue of some external critique. As a result, like many other, if not most, neoclassical economists, Lin ignores its deductive implications when they are inconvenient.[17] But it gets much worse than this, again in conformity with common practice within the mainstream. For then Lin proceeds to deploy the illegitimate concept of comparative advantage to bring back in the very factors that render it illegitimate if only on a self-serving, selective and relatively narrow basis. The narrowness arises out of strong commitment to a world of almost-perfectly working markets, creating theoretical legitimacy for a role, if confined, for the state. Indeed, the term "market imperfection" only appears twice, throughout the volume, and one of these is in a commentary by Stiglitz, see below.

---

were to be excluded, taken as country-specific and exogenous to the theory, not reduced to free flow of resources and technology or not).

14   Otherwise comparative advantage can change depending upon distribution of preference patterns across countries just as for factor reversals, see next point.

15   Thus, if income increasingly goes to a country that is both relatively rich in labour and whose preferences shift from capital-intensive to labour-intensive products as income rises, then comparative advantage will also shift as it will import capital-intensive goods at low levels of income and labour-intensive at high.

16   See Singh (2011) for a critique of Lin for his failure to get to grips with the deficiencies of the World Bank case for openness even if rejecting the absolute antipathy to industrial policy.

17   The classic examples of this are the Cambridge Critique of Capital Theory (undermining the use of one-sector production functions), the theory of the second best for policymaking (undermining the rationale for shift towards market forces if not making them completely perfect), and the presumption of the existence of a unique, stable and efficient general equilibrium (for which any number of restrictive assumptions are necessary).

The first bringing back in is to allow for government to affect, or to accrue potential, comparative advantage through its institutional/infrastructural support. Apart from adding a sector of the economy, and non-tradables at that, this implies at the very least that comparative advantage is jointly determined by factor endowments and government, and there is no reason why one should take priority over the other. In effect, government/institutions are an unnatural factor endowment to be traded indirectly through (latent) comparative advantage just like other factor endowments. It bears repeating, and possibly clarifying for Lin himself, that for him development is simply an appropriate choice of optimal change in, and use of, factor endowments (including balance of state and market) as development proceeds without regard to the restrictive assumptions on which this depends even with the deep attachment to neoclassical economics (and not least, no more than two sectors, of which one is institutions).

The second bringing back in is for comparative advantage to change over time with changing factor endowments (as capital is accumulated). But comparative advantage is unambiguously a product of comparative statics, of given endowments, preferences and technologies. Third, and more specific, is to allow, for example, for the role of foreign direct investment (internationally mobile capital) and for the nature of the financial sector (the only mention of market imperfections) to make a difference.

As a result of these bringing back ins, identification of comparative advantage, of necessity, departs from any foundation within neoclassical economics other than through guilt by association. So, how is comparative advantage to be identified? The answer is through a lurch away from theory to more or less casual empirical conformity to the developmental paths taken by those with higher per capita income. The telling point here is that we do not need any theory at all to do this however much the exercise might have been motivated by comparative advantage. More or less arbitrarily, we pick comparators with similar factor endowments who are a number of years or income per capita ahead of us, and we furnish institutions/infrastructure to emulate them.

Such a procedure is already in place in Lin's (2003) much earlier work,[18] reproduced in this volume. It is presented in terms of a choice between policy that targets being either comparative advantage following, CAF, or comparative advantage defying, CAD. The history of, and prospects for, developmental success (failure) is presented in terms of being CAF (CAD). Leaving aside the history for the moment, even such simple nostrums are riddled with the

---

18   And are developed at length in Lin's (2009) Marshall Lectures.

ambiguities and inconsistencies on which they are based, and are exposed as such once Lin's account is projected onto the grander stage of World Bank development economics mark 3.

For, if comparative advantage does not stand independently on its own two feet, how do we decipher the difference between following and defying it? Too heavy intervention, or support, to follow is surely tantamount to defying. This has been brought out in subsequent debate with Lin if in the context of refining and not defying rather than following the notion of comparative advantage. For Lin is neatly boxed in between those who are more and less interventionist than him albeit on the basis of acceptance of arguments around comparative advantage. For the former, the dichotomy is made between picking and creating winners, and they are more inclined to go for both rather than be confined to merely (infrastructurally) picking winners. Indeed, on the face of it, providing infrastructural and institutional support in picking winners is surely more or less indistinguishable from creating them, depending upon what is meant by picking and creating and where the line is drawn between them – finance, skills, research and development, transport, etc, all both pick and create winners.

Or is the option only to pick or create losers as is emphasised by the old, Washington Consensus guard who, to parody, are convinced that all policy is potentially rent picking and creating (or seeking to use the terminology in vogue) whether CAD or CAF.[19] In this light, Lin situates himself between the devil and the deep blue sea across those who deploy the notion of comparative advantage. Either, at one extreme, we proceed as if the conditions hold for comparative advantage to be defined and pursued by free markets or, at the other extreme, we acknowledge that such conditions do not prevail but we continue both to use comparative advantage as legitimate and target it for intervention in light of these conditions (that undermine it) to pick or create it – getting the prices wrong in Alice Amsden's famous phrase (although there is much more and much more important to it than this).

As indicated, Lin's stance of essentially balancing angels on pins is already available a decade ago. Support the provision or even provide the pin but leave the market to provide the angels as long as some other country ahead has angels on a pin but is liable to move on to a laser beam as balance point with development. Even then it was immodestly offered as holding the key to understanding why developing countries had failed to converge on the developed, with too much CAD (misguided pursuit of industrialisation through

---

19   See Krueger in the Lin volume.

pursuit of too capital-intensive production, too early) and not enough CAF in the past. As such, it might be thought to have had limited impact at least until Lin became Chief Economist at the Bank. Then, with little or no refinement or development of the analytical postures already in place, and by virtue of his position as nominal head of the Knowledge Bank, Lin has sought to project his flawed CAD/CAF framework across the entire field of development economics.

How he does so is of revealing significance. First, the CAD/CAF framework is itself more or less abandoned, possibly because of the ambiguities previously highlighted. Instead, we are offered a shift in terminology to *latent* comparative advantage, the comparative advantage in the making, worthy of limited state support, and following those a decade or so ahead on the path to development. Of course, substituting a change of terminology does not resolve the issue of flawed concept. But, remarkably, CAD/CAF more or less disappears from Lin's later accounts, confined to debate with Chang over Lin's more recent work (Lin and Chang, 2009, reproduced in the volume). And, as Fine (2012c) suggests, to interpret successful industrialisation as the correct pursuit of such latent comparative advantage is to border on the tautological. Indeed, this is the only conclusion that can be drawn from Lin's defence of everything from Posco to Nokia as indicative of the triumph of appropriately supported latent comparative advantage.[20]

Significantly, then, even as late as 2009 in his first presentation of "the new structural economics", Lin has yet to use the notion of latent comparative advantage. But he has, transparently, wedded himself to structural economics and his own version of it as the second, and most important, string in his bow of ambition. Once again, it is salient to point out that such appeal to structure is a relatively new tune in his repertoire, at least as far as its scope of ambition is concerned. In the earlier work, structure refers more or less exclusively to factor endowments, prices, capital-labour intensities and the composition of output. But with the new structural economics, we are suddenly projected into the world of structural *transformation*. With one exception, the third string treated next, it is easier to see what this is not than what it is. For Lin

---

20 See debate with Chang, and as discussed in Wade (2011) who suggests, p. 235, "The underlying argument seems to be that we know that Japan and Korea succeeded in the given industries, therefore those industries must have been within their existing comparative advantage. It smacks of tautology". There is also a revealing account by Lin in response to Stiglitz of Swiss industry and why its watches conform to the new structural economics, conveniently overlooking its rather differently seized latent comparative advantage for nuclear power, p. 73/4. But no doubt the latent thread between these sectors can be cleverly constructed.

rejects the old development economics and other versions of structuralism, without displaying much by way of knowledge of them, either methodologically or substantively (see below), and he equally sets aside Rostow's stages of economic growth for dividing development into discrete stages. Instead, his structuralism merely appears to be a continuous shift in the composition of production in the directions dictated by latent comparative advantage. Thus, contra Rostow, emphasis added, p. 26:[21]

> For the new structural economics, economic development from a low level to a high level is a *continuous* spectrum, not a mechanical series of five distinguished levels.

Thus, the new structural economics is little more than comparative advantage today supplemented by support for new comparative advantage tomorrow.

Third, though, whilst we have already indicated that the whole comparative advantage enterprise as target remains shrouded in ambiguity if not flaws, much the same applies to how it is to be achieved. The main instrument is the market but Lin's much lauded novelty, so it is supposed, is to allow for some sort of role for the non-market and for the state in particular, see below. However, on any sort of close examination, the catalytic role of the state in promoting latent comparative advantage (or CAF, not CAD, in earlier work) is, like the Cheshire Cat, peculiarly benign and elusive. In the earlier work in this vein, now packaged into two separate parts, perversely under the title of "Development Strategy, Institutions, and Economic Performance", there is a notable absence of substantive reference to institutions at all. For the more recent material, what we are offered is a general, if passing, appeal to the New Institutional Economics, and the work of Douglass North in particular. Essentially, Lin provides no theory of the state at all. Rather, the state is a sort of deus ex machina, much like the old welfare economics (if with a potential negative alter ego in deference to the Washington Consensus), and merely serves to resolve, or not, the problems that he has himself created by his analytical

---

21   To be fair, Lin continually refers to continuous technological upgrading and the like as characteristic of development. But, it should be added, this is less invention than accruing the benefits of latecomers in following latent comparative advantage, and so "exploit the latecomer advantages by developing matured industries in dynamically growing, more advanced countries with endowment structures similar to theirs. By following carefully selected lead countries, latecomers can emulate the leader-follower, flying-geese pattern that has served well all successful economies since the 18th century", p. 226. See below for the flying geese syndrome.

schema, together with all of its ambiguities and flaws. Thus, the state must provide the supportive conditions for latent comparative advantage, without descending into inappropriate rent-seeking through overextending itself across the margins of supporting, picking and creating winners. Much the same is true of his approach to institutions in general and infrastructure more specifically. Indeed, it is not clear whether he has any substantive distinction across the *state* (and *government*), *institutions* and *infrastructure* (and finance, see below) since each plays the same role, or not, as complement to the market in bringing about structural transformation through a continuous sequence of what was previously latent comparative advantage for others (ahead in the race) but currently latent for itself. As already suggested, irrespective of the merits of this analysis, it is purely arbitrary to deploy it as pertaining at any particular point along the continuum from neoliberalism to a (diluted) developmental statism, see below for the latter. And with the state, etc, subject to an effective reduction to the status of a factor endowment, it is hardly surprising that it should be stripped of any serious analytical or historical analysis (other than through econometrics).[22]

In short, then, where you situate yourself along the putative market-state dichotomy once accepting it, and picking/creating comparative advantage as analytical framework, is purely an ideological matter. Neoclassical theory as such cannot offer resolution even on its own terms since it has no determinate answer other than by appeal to circumstances (and a more or less broad scope of acknowledgement of deviation from perfect markets).[23] As a result, Lin's position is, in a sense, peculiarly logical because it both fails to recognise the indeterminacy of neoclassical economics *and* the corresponding implications for indeterminacy of (successful) developmental paths (otherwise, he could not deterministically advise to follow ten-year latent comparative advantage).

---

22   Inevitably, a striking example of this is to overlook entirely the whole 'institutional' history of colonisation, plunder, slavery, etc., as examples of latent comparative advantage violently grasped and supported.

23   The classic example here is offered by Krugman much of whose body of work rests on increasing returns to scale for which the logic to intervene to benefit is inescapable. As Hay (2012, p. 471) neatly puts it of Krugman, "Significantly, he concedes that 'there is more to life and even to international trade than comparative advantage' ... and that under certain specific conditions (perhaps even those pertaining in the above example) the case for protection and certainly intervention is a good one. Yet what he gives with the one hand he takes away with the other. For, despite conceding a place for strategic intervention within a positive sum theory of trade, he goes on to argue that such a case for selective protection should not be made publicly – since our 'mercantilist' political elites (who are either too stupid, too intransigent or both) will take it as an excuse for the kind of universal protectionism to which he sees them as inexorably drawn". See also p. 466, fn 1.

However, two logically flawed postures (or indeterminacies) that are consistent with one another do not make a right (or determinacy). Lin does interpret all successful development as the result of latent comparative advantage just as his opponents see it as picking and/or creating (or facilitating) comparative advantage with the potential at least for a little more developmental and institutional variation.[24]

Nonetheless, the inclination for Lin to situate himself closer to the market-conforming, for him CAF, extreme for whatever ideological reasons carries the additional (dis)advantage of being able to avoid a number of troublesome factors. For, in particular, in the wake of the global crisis that may, paradoxically, have prompted him to project his CAF/CAD frame as a new structural economics to fill the demand for something different, notably absent from his considerations is the role of finance. As previously suggested, "there is no discussion of substance of public ownership, of the global crisis, of finance, of the global and systemic more generally, and even or especially of the developmental state", Fine (2012c, p. 65). Whilst understandable given origins with the World Bank such absences are surely inexcusable in a text purporting to offer a new development economics.

Or, at least this was more or less true of the publications that immediately preceded and which continue mainly to fill out the text of his volume. Possibly, though, Lin felt it necessary once putting his volume together, not to push the issue of finance completely under the carpet if he were to retain any credibility, and the volume does include a specific treatment of finance arising out of the most recent of research at the Bank.[25] His, and his colleagues, efforts though are, however, more revealing than remedying. Essentially, Lin's treatment of finance draws heavily on, rather than contributing further to, his new structural economics in the sense that finance and the financial literature is simply recast through its prism both analytically and, correspondingly, terminologically. For financial systems are a special case of (optimal) institutions and can

---

24   Weiss (2011, p. 4) neatly sums up the differences, and closeness, between Lin and Chang (2009), "The difference in approach to economic distance underlies the debate on industrial policy between Lind (sic) and Chang ... When Lin writes of a facilitating state that supports activities with a comparative advantage and Chang of a more interventionist state that funds technological upgrading, they are, in effect, discussing different strategies towards distance, with Lin advocating a move to closer and Chang to more distant product lines to those in which an economy is currently specialized."

25   The section of the book entitled, "Financial Structure and Economic Development", is reported as co-authored with Lixin Colin Xu from a paper presented to the Sixteenth World Congress of the International Economic Association in Beijing, July, 2011. See also Lin et al. (2009), listed as 2011 in the book.

be (re)formulated as such once the general analytical framework has been put in place. Thus, the analytical starting point remains initial physical endowments, corresponding (latent) comparative advantage, and a pre-determined catch-up path of (industrial) development. As an institution and a structure, what form should finance ideally take (and what form has it taken) for success? An answer is provided initially by distinguishing between market-based and bank-based financial systems, one relying more upon the stock market and the other more upon banks as sources of finance for investment, respectively. Each system is seen to have its own advantages and disadvantages. The market system is deemed to be better for handling access to large-scale, risky funding whereas the bank-based is better for small-scale, secure investments drawing on local knowledge for viability of loans. Further, the dichotomy between the two systems is reinforced in terms of their respective suitability for labour-intensive, catch-up industrialisation as opposed to frontier innovation with high, if risky, capital requirements.

On this basis, the conclusion is drawn that the "optimal" financial system evolves from bank-based to market-based during the course of development. As a result, development is accompanied by a shifting financial structure (more market and less bank) associated with financial "deepening". It is claimed that the empirical evidence, ranging from the casual to the econometric,[26] is supportive of this account, with financial deepening accompanying development of countries, firms and poverty alleviation.[27] Particularly notable from the

---

26   We do not address the reliability of the econometric studies as such but would observe the self-serving role these play, as emphasised by Deaton et al. (2006) and Bayliss et al. (eds) (2011). Note the conclusions, though, based on a sample of developed and emerging economies, from Cecchetti and Kharroubi (2012, p. 15), "In this paper, we study the complex real effects of financial development and come to two important conclusions. First, both the size and growth of a country's financial system can be a drag on productivity growth. That is, there comes a point where further enlargement of the financial system can reduce real growth. And, because the financial sector competes with the rest of the economy for resources, financial booms are not, in general, growth-enhancing. Second, using sectoral data, we examine the distributional nature of this effect and find that credit booms harm what we normally think of as the engines for growth: those that are more R&D-intensive. This evidence, together with recent experience during the financial crisis, leads us to conclude that there is a pressing need to reassess the relationship of finance and real growth in modern economic systems. More finance is definitely not always better". See also footnote below.

27   In a sort of background paper for the book (Lin et al. 2009), there is demonstrated an astonishing mix of arrogance, simplicity and sheer historical invention, as economic and financial history is relegated to a footnote of the most grandiose proportions and which is worth quoting in full, reference to Madison only omitted, p. 21, "Our hypothesis provides a new explanation for differences in financial structure between the Japan-Germany model

policy point of view is the rejection of the neoliberal dogma concerning perfectly working financial markets (and the irrelevance of asset structure underpinning industrial finance) and the need even to constrain rather than promote a market system from emerging prematurely, p. 277. Of course, it is not only in less developed countries that the market system has given rise to excessive and inappropriate forms of finance, and corresponding crises, see below!

Thus, deviation of financial systems from optimum correspondence to latent comparative advantage can be the result of 'politics' and, in particular, undue zeal to leapfrog to an inappropriately advanced financial system. By the same token, politics may seek to promote unduly large capital-intensive projects through state-controlled banks (at expense of locally-financed SMEs) or to fund favoured coalitions through state directed finance. Once again, the presumption is that the state must play some, if minimal, role in charting the financial system along the trajectory of latent comparative advantage, and in tune with what this is at a particular point in time in terms of scale of finance and need for risk-taking innovation.

This represents a departure from Gerschenkron who is merely observed in passing by Lin to suggest that,[28] "banks are more important than markets in the early stage of economic development when the institutional environment cannot support market activities effectively", p 265. But, for Gerschenkron who initiated discussion of the forms taken by finance in late development, the role of the state is imperative (as it has been for China despite Lin's remarkable

---

and the U.S.-U.K. model. It is well documented that the bank was more prominent in Japan and Germany whereas the financial market was more prominent in U.S and U.K. From Industrial Revolution to the beginning of the 20th century, U.K. had been the most advanced country in the world. The United States has replaced the U.K. to be the most advanced country in the world since WWI. The leading industries and technologies in the U.K. and then in the United States have been at the world technology frontier. Therefore, financial markets which can mobilize huge amount of capital and diversify technological innovation risk and product innovation risk have been very active in the two countries' financial system. Germany and Japan were on a catching up progress until 1980s, measured by their per capita ... The leading industries and technologies in Japan and Germany were thus inside the world technology frontier before the 1980s. So firms in these two countries assumed less risk than their counterparts in the United States and the United Kingdom. Therefore, banks played a more important role in Japan and Germany than in the U.S. and the U.K. Naturally, as the Japanese and German economies develop, their leading industries and technologies are increasingly closer to the world technology frontier. Correspondingly, financial markets are more and more important in Japan and Germany as well, thus their financial structure is becoming more similar to that of the U.S. and U.K."

28   Inevitably, elsewhere, Lin appeals to Gerschenkron (1962) as supporting the idea of late-comer catch-up of latent comparative advantage.

claim to the contrary).[29] Also overlooked by Lin is the more recent literature on market- versus bank-based systems that derives from market imperfection economics, with the unreferenced Stiglitz one of the leading and continuing proponents. This literature, however, reached its zenith in the mid-1990s and has, subsequently, more or less totally disappeared.[30] This is so for two reasons. First, just on empirical grounds, across the varieties of financial markets and how they have functioned, the distinction between market- and bank-based systems has become increasingly difficult to sustain. Second, relatedly, the apparent superiority of the bank-based system (of Japan and Germany) for dealing with long-run investment and informational asymmetries between lenders and borrowers, has been increasingly subject to erosion as globalised financialisation has taken hold. If bank-based was so good, why has it eroded?

Interestingly, the demise of this approach to finance is inadvertently marked by Lin through a bimodal chronological distribution of references in his chapter on finance with but one reference between 2002 and 2011 and yet plenty of references both before and after this decade-long divide. As the two sets of literature deployed are primarily drawn from the World Bank, this may in part reflect a renewal of interest in finance on its part following the global crisis, and a need to distance itself from pure neoliberal, efficient market, stances. Consequently, the analytical substance has gone through a far from subtle change with the market- versus bank-based structural dichotomy for financial systems displaced by a focus on financial deepening – involving various continuous measures of financial activity (for example, private credit relative to GDP). With this shift to financial deepening – and the notion that it can optimally follow the yet to be invented *latent* comparative advantage – there is no reason to rely upon reference to the earlier paradigm of market- versus bank-based systems at all.

Further, the reliance on financial deepening in broad terms, and that this rather than the composition of those assets as such as finance disproportionately expands with the market system, allows for two significant oversights. First is to reduce the role of the financial system to the mobilisation and allocation of investment (to support latent comparative advantage or not) because this is what it is supposed to do within his theoretical frame (and, indeed, of the efficient market hypothesis and what might be termed the inefficient market

---

29   We cannot address here Lin's simplistic and self-serving account of China's economic transformation.

30   We leave aside the issue of the success of banking systems resting less on the resolution of inner informational asymmetries and more on outer certainties concerning the role of the state in finance, macroeconomic and industrial policy, see Fine (1997a).

hypothesis for deviation from such optimal functioning). Consequently, deviation from optimality is only addressed as support to the wrong levels and/or composition of real investment in productive activity. This is entirely to overlook the composition of assets in reality, and those particularly associated with contemporary shifts in financial deepening (and from bank- to market-based systems), namely the proliferation and expansion of assets associated with speculation and 'financialisation' more broadly. We are talking speculation here. It plays no part in Lin at all.

Second, more specifically, the idea that financial deepening corresponds to a stage of development in which capital-intensive, high-tech, high-skills, innovative, large-scale *production* is to the fore begins to look partial, if not sick, in the light of the current crisis and continuing recession. Particularly ironic is the suggestion that premature financial deepening has prompted crises in less developed countries just at the point in time when excessive 'deepening' has prompted such a global outcome with origins in US subprime markets. In short, Lin's account of financial structure in economic development is remarkable for its dual neglect of finance itself (and its role in self-serving speculation) and for the sorts of crisis with which such finance is associated, with recent events even unable to induce a broader take on the nature of finance.[31]

This, in part, reflects a continuing commitment to a narrow neoclassical economics with the systemic nature of finance being incapable of being addressed for which comparison with Stiglitz is telling. For the latter at least, the contemporary failure of the financial system rests neither on his favoured terrain of asymmetric information between borrowers and lenders nor, other than as reflection of something deeper, on the distorted developmental goals and self-interests of politicians in command of the state. Rather, for Stiglitz, the vested interests and ideology of finance have been at fault and explain why financial systems have been allowed to expand out of control despite the compelling logic, but ineffectiveness, of his own economic theory (and preference for bank-based over market-based financial systems), see Stiglitz (2002 and 2009) for example.

Analytically, that Stiglitz should *conclude* with vested interests as explanatory factor, rather than starting with them, is indicative not only of a difference with Lin but also of something that they share in common. This is to range

---

31   Significantly, the previously unquestioned positive relationship between financial development and economic performance is now being questioned, even from the IMF, albeit with arguments and motives that cannot be critically assessed here and which differ from Lin's (other than at most conceding a minimal role for state intervention). See Arcand et al. (2012).

over whatever explanatory factors they care to select irrespective of their roots within, and/or consistency with, the framework of the optimising individual. For Lin, this suspended use of neoclassical economics (it is there without being there) is most overt in case of his appeal to diagnostics. Unsurprisingly, for him, it is a matter in principle of identifying, ultimately by way of CAD/CAF along the way, latent comparative advantage corresponding to national factor endowments, and whether institutions correspond to their needs. A similarly named, and far more extensive, reliance upon diagnostics has been deployed by Rodrik and his Harvard colleagues,[32] with some emphasis on providing the infrastructural support for the self-discovery of comparative advantage by entrepreneurs (Hausmann and Rodrik, 2003), presumably only latent to the state in Lin's terms but not to the entrepreneurs themselves subject to appropriate state and endowment support. Other than for both as a marker for commitment to private capital, and a supportive if tightly constrained role for the state, it is notable how such analysis bears little or no reference to the optimising behaviour of entrepreneurs. This neatly dovetails with the parallel displacement from such optimising individuals to national factor endowments. This does not mean that anything can and will be deployed in diagnostics but what is selected is to some degree arbitrary and ad hoc albeit with no go areas, especially around the formation and evolution of class interests (see Fine, 2009b and c, in debate with the Harvard Group on South Africa, Hausmann and Andrews, 2009).

Significantly, Lin does provide a case study for Nigeria that illustrates these points of 'suspended' neoclassical economics,[33] and even takes them further by

---

32   See http://www.hks.harvard.edu/fs/drodrik/GrowthDiag.html It lists over thirty countries to which diagnostics have been applied to identify "binding constraints". Note that the title of Rodrik (2007), "One Economics, Many Recipes", innocently but almost exactly, captures the deployment of a suspended neoclassical economics.

33   There is also a set of commissioned industrial policy studies for Africa, see below. They are striking for emphasising scale economies as the driving force of productivity increase despite this being inconsistent with comparative advantage, latent or otherwise. For example, World Bank (2012b, p. 37) concludes, "In light manufacturing, in particular, a prerequisite for exporting today is having the capability to fulfill large orders competitively (price and quality) and quickly. Both require tapping into scale economies associated with labor-intensive, assembly-line production chains – that is, large firm operations. By definition, smaller firms cannot do this". Note these depend, then, upon both increasing returns to scale and heterogeneity of productivity of firms. These are associated, even within the mainstream, with the so-called new trade theory and the new, new trade theory, respectively, each of which is still attached to laissez-faire despite analytical thrust otherwise, but each of which is also entirely destructive of the notion of comparative advantage (based on factor endowments). Neither essentially is acknowledged by Lin's NSE.

suggesting that industrial policy needs to combine vertical (within sector) and horizontal (across sectors) considerations.[34] This is eminently sensible in principle but, in practice, involves the identification of where the market does not work well in a vertical context and whether and how the state might remedy such deficiencies – all indicative of a market-led, minimal-state inclination. It is also to draw upon a state versus market analytical dichotomy, with a relative absence of the global, systemic processes such as financialisation, evolving class and other interests that are formed and act through both state and market as latent comparative advantage, as it were, does or does not materialise. Elsewhere, such limitations have been critically addressed at length in the context of the developmental state paradigm, DSP (Fine et al. eds, 2013). They apply equally, if not more so, to Lin given that, like the DSP but without ever mentioning its contributions and significance, he also reduces development primarily to latecomer, catch-up industrialisation on the basis of methodological nationalism – that the nation, not the individual, is the unit of analysis and, in particular, its development is achievable for all if only appropriate policies are adopted independent of the role and policies of other nations let alone the world system as a whole, since each nation is on a ladder (or snake) to (or from) CAF (CAD) development.

Indeed, for Lin, other nations offer not so much competition and threat as opportunity (as with the theory of comparative advantage). In particular, he deploys an elementary, and flawed, flying geese approach, in which less developed countries can occupy the labour-intensive sectors being superseded by those countries ahead of them in the pecking order, with China seen as such a latent source of industrialisation for following nations. This is, however, to adopt far too linear a view of development in a world of global production networks,[35] and the position of China across them as it straddles both high and low-tech industries and the capacity to do so for the foreseeable future (Fine, 2011a). Thus, despite the constrained departure from the dogma of the Washington Consensus, Lin's orientation remains one of (latent, to coin a phrase) conformity to trade openness and for it to determine what to export as opposed to examining the potential for promoting domestic production to meet domestic needs, not least in what ought predominantly to be

---

34   See Fine (1997a) for this in context of South Africa, and Fine (2011a) for a more general and updated account.

35   As put by Whittaker et al. (2008, p. 13), "Global value chains embody three new dynamics; the fragmentation of value-added chains, the geographic dispersal of the fragments, and the functional integration, of work, firms and of entire industries across borders".

non-tradeables such as construction, energy, transport, health, education and other elements of economic and social welfare.

This is itself indicative of another remarkable absence in Lin's account but for the minor, implicit and misleading exceptions of claimed departure from the Washington Consensus and PWC (and premature financial deepening). It is the failure to consider the relationship between his own scholarship, not least as Chief Economist at the World (Knowledge) Bank, and its policies in practice, see below. Irrespective of whether his mild turn towards industrial policy is itself acceptable within the Bank, other than as offering some degree of scholarly, rhetorical and contested support to the softly-softly stance on extending state intervention, it is striking, if not surprising, that there should be no mention of how the Bank is responding to the crisis (and the role of its interventions alongside those of the IMF). And, in addition, the increasing shift of the Bank's resources to its private sector wing, the International Finance Corporation, IFC, in promoting Public-Private Partnerships for provision of economic and social infrastructure inevitably falls entirely outside his compass.[36]

In this respect, as with others, there is a significant contrast with Stiglitz given that his paradigm shift was deliberately designed to inform a major change in broad and detailed policymaking across the Washington institutions. What he achieved in practice is another matter, given his enforced departure from the Bank, but Pyrrhic victory with some degree of adoption of the PWC as scholarship and rhetoric, Consequently, for Lin, as for Stiglitz, the worlds of scholarship and policy at the Bank occupy parallel universes, although one does and one does not highlight this.

3   Lin and the Bank

Nevertheless, from within the NSE, Lin (2012a) offers a few preliminary insights on specific policies. This includes support for counter-cyclical fiscal policy, to be put in the service of infrastructure upgrading, p. 30. Further, the NSE supports the strategy of using revenues from commodities in resource-rich countries to invest in human, infrastructure and social capital to facilitate the diversification and upgrading of industry, rather than that these are channeled mainly into foreign reserve accumulation, p. 31. Monetary policy could be geared towards low interest rates to encourage investments in infrastructure,

---

36   See Bayliss and Fine (eds) (2008) and Bayliss et al. (eds) (2011).

rather than that interest rates are set solely with the purpose of price stability, p. 32. Monetary authorities should also deploy "temporary" interest rate subsidies and flexible credit allocation rules that target infrastructure projects that have been identified as binding constraints, p. 32. In the context of liberalisation of domestic finance and foreign trade, the NSE emphasises appropriate sequencing, p. 33. A differential policy environment is prescribed to regulate foreign direct investment compared to portfolio investment. This favours the former rather than the latter, p. 34. (Capital controls remain absent from the policy narrative.) Finally, the NSE highlights the importance of well-designed policy on "human capital" development, to include measures that foster skills to facilitate the upgrading of industries, p. 37.

In the context of industrial upgrading, the NSE seeks to go beyond the broad investment reforms traditionally promoted by the World Bank and draws attention to "specific, feasible, sharply focused, and low-cost policy interventions that can deliver a boost to output and productivity" (World Bank, 2012a, p. 41). Such an approach necessitates in-depth diagnosis of the constraints prevailing in specific sectors, undertaken through the Growth Identification and Facilitation Framework, and requires engagement with empirical realities of the processes and environments within which industrial activity takes place. The study entitled *Light Manufacturing in Africa* (World Bank, 2012b) typifies such an approach and is, according to Lin, the first research project based on the NSE, p. XIV.[37] Significantly, through its engagement with empirical realities, World Bank (2012b) documents features that are at odds both with the theoretical premises of the NSE and the broad policies traditionally promoted by the Bank. Instead, it presents a descriptive account of processes, structure and linkages across a set of manufacturing sectors for a set of countries and highlights a host of interventions that have led to successful output and productivity performance in other countries (China and Vietnam).[38] Policy measures are advocated on the basis of their success elsewhere rather than that they emerge from a set of theoretical propositions, drawn from the NSE or otherwise. An emphasis on scale prevails and advocated government policies include measures such as: "plug-and-play" factory shells, where the government incurs the

---

[37] See also http://web.worldbank.org/WBSITE/EXTERNAL/NEWS/0,contentMDK:23145 745~pagePK:34370~piPK:34424~theSitePK:4607,00.html.

[38] This includes a recognition that fast output and productivity increases in manufacturing can proceed "despite the presence of problematic institutional arrangements", p. 45. Drawing on the experience of China, it is recognised that protection of private property rights is not a necessary condition for manufacturing to thrive, nor is access to bank lending or formal financial markets.

fixed costs of utility-equipped factory shells which overcome firms' need for finance to construct factories; the provision of affordable residential housing for workers; affordable public transport for workers; provision of long-term credit by the government; and tax incentives.

While much of Bank rhetoric has traditionally been characterised by an undifferentiated celebration of small and medium enterprises as sites of development, World Bank (2012b) then offers a refreshing reminder of the realities of output and productivity growth in manufacturing, particularly by highlighting the necessity to tap into economies of scale. In the context of existing Bank research, the study distinguishes itself by a set of features. It deploys a mix of quantitative and qualitative methods and, through detailed studies at the subsector and product levels, it illustrates that: constraints in the manufacturing sector vary by country, sector and firm size; solutions to manufacturing problems cut across many sectors and require tackling issues in agriculture, education and infrastructure; and a focused approach with targeted interventions is necessary instead of the traditional approach of broad-based (macroeconomic or sectoral) reforms, p. 47. World Bank (2012b) is backed by "a panoply of comprehensive and detailed research materials", p. 39, and reflects a keen engagement with empirical processes and structures of manufacturing. One would hope that this kind of research endeavour, rather than Lin's theoretical insistence on understanding development trajectories on the basis of comparative advantage, could constitute his scholarly legacy at the Bank. However, no manufacturing or industry "hub" exists in the Bank's research department, nor is there a formal research work programme on manufacturing as a minimal legacy of the NSE.[39]

Moreover, the extent to which any of the above recommended policies, whether in the macroeconomic or industrial policy realm, will prevail across Bank policies is difficult to assess as policies vary, in practice, across countries and regions. The broad policy matrix deployed by the Bank to determine the amount of (concessional) resources allocated to its poorest clients

---

39   Email communication with lead author of World Bank (2012a). See also Wade (2012, p. 235), "Lin's arguments are an important new development in the industrial policy debate, especially because they come from the chief economist of an important norm-setting body, the World Bank. This is not to say that chief economist Lin and his ideas for strategic government intervention in industrialization have persuaded most World Bank economists. Lin himself says that less than 10% of World Bank economists are sympathetic to his arguments. My own field work in the Bank during the summer of 2010 revealed that many dismiss his arguments with the annoyance one might direct towards a fly. 'For every Korea there are 100 failures. Who would you put your money on?', declared one senior official".

has, however, remained unaffected by these propositions (Van Waeyenberge, 2011). This observation draws attention to a peculiar feature of Lin as Chief Economist of the Bank, see also above. Across his various contributions, Lin displays a curious lack of interest in the way in which his NSE may affect Bank policies. Although a disconnection between scholarship and policies in practice has often prevailed at the Bank, this was often despite attempts by Chief Economists to affect Bank policy directions. Lin's industrial policy recommendations, such as regarding the provision of infrastructure, the establishment of industrial parks or the use of direct credits are made, however, without reflecting on how the institution's lending policies and practices from within which he is advocating these policies may condition the scope for their implementation. This is particularly so given the shifts in lending, from the public to the private sector, that have occurred across the World Bank Group (Kwakkenbos, 2012; Van Waeyenberge et al. 2011), and the broader shifts in the international policy regime that have accompanied these, including the investment-related restrictions that prevail through membership of the World Trade Organisation or as a result of bilateral trade and investment agreements (Lall, 2004). The nature of the international financial institutions' response to the global economic and financial crises has, further, reinforced the prejudice against large government-funded policy initiatives, which stands out most clearly in the context of infrastructure.[40]

Lin's one-sided engagement from within the Bank, biased towards the ideational, transpires most blatantly from the nature of his proposition regarding a future role for the World Bank. In Lin and Rosenblatt (2012), such a role is understood entirely in 'knowledge' terms, with little interest in the Bank as a lending and policy-making institution. Indeed, the financing function of the World Bank Group is likely to become progressively smaller compared to net private capital flows, in line with developments prior to the global financial crisis. This echoes former Bank President Wolfensohn's formal celebration of the Bank as a Knowledge Bank in the latter half of the 1990s. It also reflected an awareness that the Bank's financial weight was on the decline. When international capital markets appeared over- rather than under-liquid, the Bank's knowledge and experience of development were cast as a justification for a continuing role for the institution (Gilbert et al. 1999). The Bank became identified as a source of 'global knowledge'. It would concentrate on becoming the world's premier development institution, forging a common agenda on major issues. Since the onset of the global economic and financial crisis, knowledge

40   See also Hildyard (2012).

remains at the centre of the Bank's mission, in keeping with Lin's vernacular bordering on unwitting self-parody: "Today more than ever, development knowledge helps to define the Bank's comparative advantage" (World Bank, 2010, p. 1).

The Bank exercises its knowledge function in a variety of ways. This includes the research undertaken in its research department, the Development Economics Vice-Presidency, as well as the much larger knowledge endeavour that takes place across its operational departments through Analytical and Advisory Activities, AAA. The latter, mainly but not exclusively through Economic and Sector Work (ESW), seeks to operationalise the general policy directions that emerge from the Bank's research department for specific country or sector contexts and are designed with the explicit intent of influencing client countries' policies.[41] Lin's support for the Bank as a Knowledge Bank suffers from the traditional shortcomings of those who have advocated such a role in the past. Bank knowledge is understood in neutral or benign terms as the Bank is portrayed as a disinterested "memory bank of best practices". The creation and dissemination of development knowledge by the Bank is presented as an international public good, the supply of which would be deficient without active support by the Bank. As argued elsewhere (Van Waeyenberge and Fine, 2011), such an account implies a dramatic disregard for the socio-historical, political and economic contexts within which knowledge, including Bank knowledge, is produced, as well as for the socio-political or economic functions knowledge may fulfil. A host of critical commentaries on Bank knowledge, nevertheless, abounds and has drawn attention to a set of features including: the shareholder realities of the Bank; its embedded relationship with financial markets; and the implications of the prevalence of economics as the Bank's 'high scholarly discipline' (Kapur et al. 1997a and b). These broad governance features have concrete implications such that research resonating with neoliberal ideology is privileged and dissonant discourse is neither encouraged nor promoted (Broad, 2006). Rather than resembling a neutral, politically impartial or technical enterprise, the Bank's knowledge exercise needs to be understood within its political, economic and disciplinary contexts.

Lin combines his support for the Bank as a Knowledge Bank with a plea for a "democratisation of development economics", p. 34, or the promotion of a "multi-polar exchange of knowledge", p. 45. By this he means the diversification of the Bank's staff pool to include a greater proportion of representatives

---

41   The Bank further offers a vast training programme through the World Bank Institute, sponsors a host of knowledge networks such as, for instance, the Global Development Network, and provides support for various economic research centres across the world.

from the developing world. Others have previously raised concerns regarding the homogenous nature of the academic profile of Bank staff, dominated by economists, and mainly the product of graduate economics departments of English-speaking but, especially, US universities.[42] Lin himself, however, although a Chinese national, is an economist by way of the University of Chicago and is staunchly committed to the neoclassical principles of rationality and choice (Lin, 2012b).[43] His plea for a greater proportion of developing country staff as researchers at the Bank then reflects a concern that Northern economists fail to appreciate the nature of the constraints within which decision makers in developing countries make choices, rather than that neoclassical economics itself may fail to provide a conducive framework within which economic problems of development or any other kind can be understood.[44] Indeed, Lin (2012b) provides a passionate plea for the further promulgation of neoclassical economics in the South, where the combination of the application of the "quintessential economic logic" of rationality and choice with an alleged better appreciation of the constraints under which decision makers (firms, individuals or governments) would contribute to the modernisation of countries and the advance of economics:[45]

---

42   There has been an increase in non-economist social scientists as research staff in the Bank, albeit outside its research department, but these non-economists employed within the Bank have tended to leave economic issues unchallenged, trying to peg their own concerns onto an otherwise undisturbed economic agenda (Fine, 2001; and Leiterlitz and Weaver, 2005).

43   Lin (2012b) is dedicated to Gary Becker, "who taught me the spirit of modern economic analysis". This might reasonably be thought to explain his commitment to understanding the economy in terms of (minimal to be corrected) deviations from perfectly working markets. For Becker is best known for applying the logic of neoclassical economics across any area of social life, where all human action, whether in the context of the family, crime, or addiction is understood solely in terms of rational optimisation under constraints, see Fine and Milonakis (2009). Unlike those such as Stiglitz and Rodrik, he does this on the basis of as if perfectly, as opposed to imperfectly, working markets whilst sharing in common the technical apparatus and architecture of neoclassical economics.

44   Lin's credentials as the first Chief Economist from the South have been widely paraded. The gossip is that his successor appointed from September 2012, Kaushik Basu, undertook an otherwise previously unexplained move back to India from Cornell in 2009 to take up a post, Chief Economic Advisor, in government for the first time. Wikipedia innocently reports that, "More recently, he has worked on aggregating infinite streams of returns, and the axiomatic structures, pertaining to inter-generational anonymity and different forms of the Pareto principle, that such aggregations can satisfy", http://en.wikipedia.org/wiki/Kaushik_Basu#cite_note-1.

45   There is a striking affinity here between the economics to be deployed and the ethos of good governance and country ownership of policy; indigenous participation (in economics) as long as it conforms with what the Bank would do anyway.

I firmly believe that as long as economists in developing countries command the basic research methods of modern economics and focus on their indigenous issues, they can contribute to the modernization of their countries and the advance of economies. However, to achieve this, they need to truly grasp the *benti* (the fundamental premise – that is, the rationality assumption) of modern economics and approach any phenomenon firmly with a *changwu* (without any preconceived theory) mindset.

Lin's emphasis on indigenisation reflects an unfortunate attempt to overcome a genuine concern regarding economists' failure to engage with empirical realities. This does not plague Northern economists more than Southern, but emerges out of economics' fraught accommodation of reality as a result of its highly deductive approach, where reality is brought in as an afterthought on the basis of econometric testing of particular a priori propositions. Lin tries to navigate this conundrum but mistakenly attributes the lack of explanatory power of mainstream theories of economic development to the geographical origins of their practitioners rather than to the limits imposed by their disciplinary method and scope. His attempt to overcome shortcomings of "Western" economics as a guide to understanding development is doomed to fail as his analysis remains staunchly committed to economics as a theory of choice based on the fundamental premise of rationality. Yet, Lin's discourse on indigenousness and neoclassical economics, not least as a result of the platform from where it was propagated, further contributes to the colonisation of development economics by neoclassical economics, to the detriment of a systemic and historically informed understanding of trajectories of development, situated within domestic and international relations, across political, economic, commercial and financial realms.[46]

It is, finally, a far cry from other indigenisation initiatives such as, for instance, the one launched by Mahmood Mamdani, Executive Director of the Makerere Institute for Social Research (MISR) through a new doctoral programme that seeks to produce researchers anchored in a tradition that historicises and contextualises phenomena, processes, and ideas. The programme at the MISR will seek "to combine a commitment to local knowledge production, rooted in relevant linguistic and disciplinary terms, with a critical and disciplined reflection on the globalisation of modern forms of knowledge and modern instruments

---

46   See Fine (2009a) on how development economics was captured by economics imperialism and on how economics increased its influence over development studies more generally.

of power" (Mamdani, 2011).[47] Interdisciplinarity sits at the heart of the programme, reflecting a recognition of the necessity to engage across politics,
political economy and history in order to advance an understanding of local
realities within global contexts and of the global from the vantage point of the
local. Mamdani's initiative constitutes a response to the urgent need within
the study of development to celebrate traditions that emphasise the historical and systemic, in counterpoint to the steady encroachment of neoclassical
principles and their narrow conception of the social or the economic. In addition, a broader and more comprehensive approach in the study of development would lead economic analysis beyond the flawed presumption implied
by a national framework such as advanced by Lin in which any country would
develop if only adopting the appropriate (latent comparative advantage) policies. Mamdani's plea also constitutes an attempt to offset the implications,
intended or otherwise, which the Knowledge Bank has had for knowledge generation in the South through its manifold knowledge initiatives (including ESW
or training provided through the World Bank Institute).[48] This has been compounded by the decline of the university as a centre of knowledge and learning
in much of the poorer parts of the South – itself often the result of World Bank
policies.[49] And, in contrast to Lin's agenda for the development of economics
in the South, Mamdani's initiative holds better prospects for the articulation of
progressive demands, where the (economic) ideational and policy realms have
become dominated by neoclassical ideas and their derived neoliberal propositions, not in the least as a result of the significant knowledge, policy and
lending roles performed by the Bank.

4   Conclusion

The chances are that Lin's programme for a new structural economics, unlike
those of Krueger and Stiglitz, will prove a paradigm shift that never took place.
Nonetheless, this does not mean that his attempt is of no significance since
it reflects developments in scholarship, rhetoric and policy in practice at the
Bank even if, for the latter, more by way of neglect. It is also liable to have some
influence on the evolution of development economics (and studies) by virtue

---

47   See also Mamdani on Stiglitz, http://pambazuka.org/en/category/features/83875.
48   Indeed, the development of Lin's career at the University of Peking was itself effected by a
      knowledge initiative of the Bank, when it provided a large proportion of the initial fund-
      ing for the China Centre for Economic Research of which Lin was the founding director.
49   See Samoff and Bidemi (2003) for an account in the context of Africa.

of its origins, and the weight these carry, if only reinforcing some trends and dispositions and weakening alternatives.

In short, it is worthwhile to unpick Lin on a broader canvas in the ways identified above. In summary, first, in the extreme form of lack of acknowledgement other than in passing of an alternative old structuralism, Lin's neoclassical economics finds no need for modification, let alone questioning in the wake of the crisis.

Second, though, this is not to suggest that Lin's, or others', neoclassical economics remains unchanging. It has to offer something 'new' whether by way of an air of scholarly originality or in response to the crisis. On the longer view, not least in the wake of the PWC, this has involved a renewal of market imperfection economics that has allowed for a second phase of economics imperialism including a corresponding second phase of the new or the newer development economics. Dovetailing with the PWC, this has provided a rationale for piecemeal, discretionary intervention across the market-state (and civil society) dichotomy ('trichotomy') as well as increasingly appropriating the broader subject matter of development studies to an extraordinary extent despite an equally extraordinarily narrow set of analytical principles.

Third, in principle, such analysis is derived from the axiomatic and individualistic deductivism of the mainstream. But, in practice, commitment to such crudely proclaimed logic, rigour or scientism is opportunistic in two different ways. On the one hand, those deductive results that are inconvenient for purpose are simply cast aside as if they did not exist. This is apparent, as argued at length, in Lin's unquestioning reliance on the notion of (latent) comparative advantage. On the other hand, so confident is the mainstream in its abused (and flawed and narrow) principles that it has increasingly and seamlessly wedded them to whatever other elements it chooses irrespective of mutual consistency across methodology, method and theory.

Such intellectual opportunism is as free-ranging as it is chaotic. It leads some to presume, particularly in light of broader deployment of individual motivation through behavioural economics, that the mainstream is in a process of disintegration from without or upon its frontiers.[50] We prefer the descriptor of suspension as the core principles are retained, at least as a background, but more usually as a core or norm from which other considerations can be viewed as a source of deviation to explain the otherwise inexplicable or what otherwise cannot be incorporated. This does mean that the course and content of

---

50   See Fine and Milonakis (2011).

the mainstream cannot be taken as given and read off from its principles or purer versions. Indeed, plus ça change, toujours la même chose.

This is especially, if not logically necessarily, so what has proven the mildest of intellectual and policy reactions to and against the current crisis in terms of the rationale and perceived scope for state interventionism. Whilst, as fully exposed here, this is to be expected of Lin and his stance of state minimalism in pursuit of a predetermined latent comparative advantage (and presented as some sort of paradigm shift to a new structural economics), what is possibly more surprising and disappointing is how readily such minor concessions have been warmly embraced, and engaged with, by erstwhile critical and heterodox development economists. Indeed, thirty years of creeping, even galloping, influence by the Bank over the fields of scholarship, rhetoric and policy in practice, have induced a corresponding loss of confidence in opponents previously in the vanguard, as most poignantly symbolised by the demise of the DSP to the status of a failed buzzword.[51] Significantly, with the, in some respects, peculiar exception of Wade,[52] the DSP might just as well not exist as far as both Lin *and* his more interventionist critics are concerned.[53] And, over a wider range of literature, there would appear to be the equivalent of a conspiracy to forge analytical principles, postures and their application allowing for the possibility of interventionism in principle but containing it in practice.

Unsurprisingly, such perspectives are strongly underpinned by international scholarship and organisations. Thus, whilst UNCTAD has long voiced its concerns over the role of finance in undermining potential for policies that underpin developmental goals, only now that circumstances might allow it a louder voice to a more influential audience, has its legitimacy in doing so been challenged.[54] Meanwhile, "diagnostics" blossom in order to enable the state to constrain itself to supporting the private sector. Weiss (2011), addressing

---

51   See Fine et al. (eds) (2013) for the developmental state as a 'failed buzzword'.

52   Wade (2010 and 2012) does appear to be committed to retaining the notion of the developmental state, in part to be able observe, like others before him, that there has been both extensive presence of industrial policy within the USA, and elsewhere, and the failure to acknowledge it as such. But, in his admittedly short response to Lin, the developmental state does not warrant a mention as opposed to the welcoming of acknowledgement of some role for industrial policy, as indicated by his title, "Why Justin Lin's Door-Opening Argument Matters for Development Economics" (Wade, 2011).

53   The term "developmental*" only appears six times in Lin's book, as: "developmental stages", p. 60; "developmental studies", p. 61; "developmentally oriented state", p. 119; "developmental banks", p. 154; in a reference, p. 178; and "developmental policy" in a cover puff provided by Stiglitz.

54   See Ghosh (2012) for an account.

industrial policy in the current century, is typical; in his abstract, he "makes a case for a pragmatic and limited approach to interventions as a means of stimulating industrialization in the context of current and future challenges facing newly industrializing countries". One of his concerns is that more interventionism is required where it is least likely to be successfully adopted, as echoed by Peres (2011) for Latin America. The ethos is one of cautious, piecemeal, context-specific intervention as far as industrial policy is concerned. And, by the same token, the UNRISD attempt to put the developmental welfare state, DWS, on the agenda is notable as an exception that fails to be adopted in theory let alone in practice. The point is not so much to see the DSP and DWS as uncritically acceptable as alternatives to the new almost universal pessimism over anything other than minimal state intervention. Rather it is to highlight the weaknesses of presence let alone influence of alternatives. This is the context within which to locate the broader role of the World Bank in scholarship, rhetoric and policy in practice, and as putative Knowledge Bank whose portfolio of intellectual assets is at the opposite extreme to the variety offered by the financialisation that it continues to support with such fervour and at such expense to development itself.

Locating the Developmental State and Industrial Policy after the Crisis

Postscript as Personal Preamble

This and the next Chapter are long enough without being further burdened by lengthy preambles.[1] But their contexts are important. For each of the Chapters, the personal and the contemporary situation are both significant. For the personal, this Chapter was marked by its having been commissioned by UNCTAD for one of its annual signature dishes, *The Least Developed Countries Report 2011*, with theme for that year of, *The Potential Role of South-South Cooperation for Inclusive and Sustainable Development.* The theme as such remains beyond my expertise but I was asked to address the issue in the context of the role of aid. So, following the detailed account of industrial policy, I did so with an ill-fitting final section that serves as a conclusion. I selectively reviewed literature and drew my own conclusions – the most prominent being that South-South cooperation tends to involve countries at different levels of development, correspondingly facing different issues and priorities, with progress tending to be focused upon the low hanging fruit with the lead being taken by the more developed of those cooperating.

Within the body of the text otherwise, another point of departure from any claim I might have for expertise is an extended discussion of China. As a developmental success by many, if by no means all, criteria, and hardly fitting into the mould of the East Asian NICs, China tends to be seen as an exception so that it can be casually set aside to avoid its offering lessons for others (with resonances to the World Bank's treatment of the East Asian NICs). Noticeably absent from the discussion is any reference to the road and belt initiative which has subsequently expanded and drawn close attention,[2] including from students researching its impact in Africa. Setting aside approaches that see all things Chinese as the cause of all things wrong in the world (economy), especially from a US perspective, conventional wisdom appears to run along

---

1   This paper originally appeared as Fine (2011a), and also included Social Policy in the title, reflecting the content. However, the sections on social policy were revised and updated to appear as part of Fine (2014) which itself appears here as Chapter 8.
2   See Calabrese et al. (2024) for a recent take on the belt.

the lines of China is far from being an innocent purveyor of aid but is less guilty than conventional western sources. Rather than viewing Chinese impact through the prism of good or bad for development, I suggest seeing its role and impact in terms of reflecting the economic and social conditions of recipients and, almost inevitably, consolidating them, especially in terms of class structures and corresponding dynamics.

At the time of writing, I seem to have been engaged in, or just be coming out of, a frenzy of research activity. Although continuing to the present day, my longstanding work on each of economics imperialism and social capital had already reached maturity.[3] They scarcely warrant a mention. Particularly notable is the discussion of the Post-Washington Consensus without reference to it as the newer development economics, nor to its successor, the newest development economics. On the other hand, heavy reference is made to financialisation as underpinning neoliberalism with, however, no reference to the latter's, partially prospective, third phase as opposed to the passage from Washington to Post-Washington Consensus as reflecting the two phases of neoliberalism to that point.

What is notably present is the opportunity taken to bring together longstanding and continuing work on the two topics that make up the two main sections of the Chapter, one on the developmental state and the other on industrial policy, each of these having been engaged, as will be apparent, as topics in their own right as well as in the context of South African post-apartheid economic policy. Subsequently, these two topics have experienced very different levels of prominence. The developmental state has been both reduced in conceptual content and neglected (Fine, 2025a, Chapter 7). Industrial policy has also been reduced but has become prominent across scholarship from varieties of perspectives (in my view, a reflection of the third phase of neoliberalism, Bayliss et al. 2024). The most interesting aspect of this new work is where it plays close attention to new technology since this raises issues of how what are generic issues (i.e. across sectors or what I dub horizontal) are integrated in practice and addressed in policy within particular sectors (the vertical).[4]

More important than any of these personal anecdotes for context is what was taken at the time to be the long shadow shed by the Global Financial Crisis

---

3   See Fine and Milonakis (2009), Milonakis and Fine (2009) and Fine (2024a–c and 2025a, the last for issues covered in this paragraph for development).

4   I have been conscious of these issues for a long time, not least because of my study of the British coal industry (and how 'new technology' would be introduced into mechanisation in the context of a state-owned monopoly) and also housing (with extreme fragmentation across processes of construction).

of 2008/9. For both heterodox economics, normally subject to the neglect and hostility of the mainstream, and for more progressive international and institutional policymakers, generally dominated by the World Bank and IMF, opportunities seem to have presented themselves to be promoted to varieties of audiences. Not only was mainstream economics in a mess – with a record of failing to allow for a crisis, and inability to explain and remedy it – so also were corresponding policymakers, with progressives seeking to reform the financial system and beyond. It seemed as if neoliberalism was dead, having fallen on the sword of its own excesses against interventionism that was then returning with a vengeance (admittedly to rescue finance in particular).

But I do recall being an invited speaker to a conference on "Social and Political Dimensions of the Global Crisis: Implications for Developing Countries", held by UNRISD in Geneva, 12–13 November, 2009. Mine was one of 24 papers selected competitively from 330 proposals, and the audience number was around one thousand. There was a buzz in the air, this was our moment and, as all knew, about to be published was *The Stiglitz Report: Reforming the International Monetary and Financial Systems in the Wake of the Global Crisis* (Stiglitz, 2010). I asked all and sundry one simple question – how long will our moment last, and my presumption was that it had already passed, and it had only lasted a few days.

Foreword

The breakdown of the Bretton Woods system, the last occasion on which global financial turbulence approached that currently being experienced, witnessed the rise of the postures of neoliberalism to an extreme and unprecedented extent, and in equally extreme and unprecedented forms, across each of scholarship, policy and ideology. Today, that bubble has burst together with the financial and economic system to which it has given rise. It is a time for bold and innovative thinking. Yet, even before recent events had exposed the fragility of the neoliberal era, and sent finance galloping to the state in a desperate attempt to save itself from itself, neoliberal hegemony had already been brought into question, not least in the wake of what has been the most limited progress in development and poverty alleviation under or through its auspices.

Such considerations raise the question of whether bold and innovative thinking, let alone corresponding policy perspectives, are on the agenda. Despite the crisis being of three- or four-years vintage, the unambiguous answer seems to be in the negative. Of course, neoliberalism was shaken by the crisis but it seems to have survived intact or even strengthened. Within economics itself, despite murmurings of discontent, there has been business as (un)usual with at most the concession that the wrong models were applied with insufficiently refined behavioural assumptions and account for material, or financial, realities. Otherwise, the methods and technical apparatuses and architectures associated with optimisation, efficiency and equilibrium are judged to be sound. Significantly, a recent google scholar search on "crisis in economics" offers only a few hundred entries, most dating back to the 1930s. By contrast, a similar search on sociology runs into thousands of entries although no one is blaming the sociologist, as opposed to the economists, for being responsible for, or complicit with, the crisis.

Of course, there has been some increase in the kudos and prominence of dissidents within economics, who had previously been marginalised to an extraordinary degree by the command of orthodoxy over the discipline. The putative Minsky moment has had its moment once more. But, in turning attention to those dissidents *within* orthodoxy (understood as practising with the methods and tools of the mainstream), it is striking how little they have reconsidered their approaches and, of much greater significance, how little they have influenced policy despite considerable popular prominence and profile.

Before, then, putting forward bolder alternatives, it is appropriate to question why both alternatives and alternative thinking have been so limited, not only over a long period but even in the more conducive conditions presented by the financial crisis that makes them so imperative. Of course, one part of an answer is to be found in the development of economics itself and of development economics in particular.[5] These do not, however, float entirely free from developments within the economy itself and, this leads to consideration of two paradoxes.

The first concerns the nature of the current crisis, particularly in relation to what economics orthodoxy used to refer to as the soundness of 'fundamentals'. The latter might be thought to refer to levels of deficits and the like but at a more fundamental level, the fundamental 'fundamentals' as it were related to underlying material conditions, the prospects for the global economy, have been extraordinarily strong both over the last thirty years of relatively slow growth compared to the post-war boom and into the current crisis. To be specific, what I have in mind, if simply listing and unduly overgeneralising for brevity: the capacity for productivity increase arising out of a huge diversity and range of application of new technologies; the decline in the strength and organisation of working class and progressive movements, especially across

---

5 See Fine (2009a, 2010b and g and 2012e).

trade unions, political parties and anti-imperial struggles; huge increases in the global labour force through migration, the Chinese road to capitalism, and increasing female labour market participation; high levels of advanced country cooperation under the hegemony of the USA not least with the collapse of the Soviet bloc; and the triumph of neoliberalism, not least in the form of containment of the social as well as the monetary wage.

In this light, the second paradox concerns the responses to the current global crisis. There can be little doubt that the neoliberal ideology of targeting minimal state intervention and leaving as much as possible, especially finance, to the free market has taken something of a battering. But the policy responses in practice have remained extraordinarily timid and limited in scope. If, for example, the state is making a comeback, it certainly is not along the lines experienced during the post-war boom when Keynesian macroeconomic policies were complemented by a whole, arguably more important, sheaf of interventionist policies around health, education, welfare and industrial and regional development. Rather, as symbolised by the notion of 'quantitative easing', the top priority is to restore the viability of the financial system. This is accompanied at most by weakening and token deference to re-regulation and clawing back of disproportionate rewards. Stimulus to effective demand has primarily been adopted in the mildest forms of Keynesianism through monetary policy whilst directed fiscal stimuli take a back seat (or are thrown off the transport altogether, as the deficits that have accompanied support to finance dictate austerity measures to cover interest payments to the very financial system that has created the problem and had, accordingly, to be rescued). This is all despite what is a unique characteristic of the current crisis, the common acceptance that it is in general in no way due to excessive wage demands or state expenditure to furnish a social wage. Nonetheless, the blameless in working and social conditions are being hit very hard and to an extent that would, or should, make even neoliberals or proponents of the Washington Consensus blush. If the Post-Washington Consensus is alive and well, as its supporters are no doubt aware, it is not in the world of policy.

How do we resolve these paradoxes? For the first, slowdown and crisis despite the most favourable fundamentals, I point to 'financialisation'. This is a new term, little more than a decade old, and it has yet to bed down in terms of what it is, what it does and how it is to be addressed theoretically. Perhaps, across these issues, it should remain controversial. I hope so as this would indicate significant attention to the defining economic character of the contemporary period so diverse is financialisation in content and so contested is monetary and financial theory – ranging from the nature and origins of money through to the efficient (or inefficient) market hypothesis and Minsky's moments. In brief, financialisation has involved: the phenomenal expansion of financial assets relative to real activity (by three times over the last thirty years); the proliferation of types of assets, from derivatives through to futures markets with a corresponding explosion of acronyms; the absolute and relative expansion of speculative as opposed to, or at the expense of, real investment; a shift in the balance of productive to financial imperatives within the private sector whether financial or not; increasing inequality in income arising out of weight of financial rewards; consumer-led booms based on credit; the penetration of finance into ever more areas of economic and social life such as pensions, education, health, and provision of economic and social infrastructure; the emergence of a neoliberal culture of reliance upon markets and private capital and corresponding anti-statism despite the extent to which the rewards to private finance have in part derived from state finance itself. Financialisation is also associated with the continued role of the US dollar as world money despite, at least in the current crisis, US deficits in trade, capital account, the fiscus, and consumer spending, and minimal rates of interest. I observe here, in passing and for future reference, that the policies adopted by the USA and some other developed countries have been exactly the opposite of those advised, or should that be imposed, on developing countries experiencing similar crises in the past. As Ha-Joon Chang has been at the forefront of arguing in the context of historical paths to development, those that have traversed it insist, "Do not do as we *did*, do as we say" to which should be added the nostrum, "Do not do as we *do*, do as we say".

However we define financialisation, its consequences have been: reductions in overall levels and efficacy of real investment as financial instruments and activities expand at its expense even if excessive investment does take place in particular sectors at particular times (as with the dotcom bubble of a decade ago); prioritising shareholder value, or financial worth, over other economic and social values; pushing of policies towards conservatism and commercialisation in all respects; extending influence of finance more broadly, both directly and indirectly, over economic *and* social policy; placing more aspects of economic and social life at the risk of volatility from financial instability; and, conversely, placing the economy and social life at risk of crisis from triggers within particular markets (as with the food and energy crises that preceded the financial crisis). Whilst, then, financialisation is a single word, it is attached to a wide variety of different forms and effects of finance with the USA and the UK to the fore. And, even if exposed in acute form by the crisis, its expansion over the last few decades has been at the expense of the real economy despite otherwise extraordinarily favourable 'fundamentals' as already remarked. It should also be emphasised that the forms, incidence and consequences of financialisation are highly uneven and diverse across and within national economies as sharply revealed by the current global crisis both within finance itself and more generally.[6]

Financialisation is also the key to resolving the second paradox, why the return of the state in the wake of the crisis should be so weak and narrowly confined. One reason has already been implicitly identified as a component part of the first paradox – the weakness of progressive movements that are more aligned to state intervention. In addition, though, also deriving from the first paradox, the last thirty years has witnessed the emergence, growth, strengthening and institutionalisation within governance and beyond of financial elites at domestic and international levels. As already observed, this implies not only particular sets of policies towards promoting private capital both directly, through privatisation for example, and indirectly through fiscal austerity, but also the transformation of the capacity to conceive and formulate alternative policy itself. I have, on a personal note, been associated with the Municipal Services Project, funded by the Canadian development agency, IDRC, http://www.municipalservices.org/ It has over some time been monitoring the effects of privatisation and commercialisation of basic services across the developing world. In its latest phase, it adopted the different stance of seeking out best practice alternatives underpinned by a more significant role for state provision. I am sorry to report that these are almost impossible to find and not because the state must or does perform worse than the private sector, as popular neoliberal rhetoric would suggest. Instead, it is apparent that developments over the past thirty years have tended both to squeeze out the presence of public sector alternatives where they do exist and also, and equally important, preclude them from emerging in the first place.[7]

Consequently, it is germane to pinpoint the relationship between financialisation and neoliberalism. It is no accident that the two should coincide with one another over the period of the last thirty years. This is certainly true at the ideological level as the imperative of freeing markets has been applied first and foremost to those pure markets associated with finance. But finance has also been associated with the emergence, strengthening and influence of financial elites at both national and international levels.

---

6   For example, see Akyüz (2011) for an extensive analysis of the consequences for capital flows to developing countries with some emphasis on increasing volatility both overall and in contagion effects from one market to another through synchronisation of commodity prices from impact of futures markets.

7   But see McDonald and Ruiters (eds) (2012) and the continuing research of the Municipal Services Project (MSP), https://www.municipalservicesproject.org.

As a result, I do not see financialisation as a simple associate of neoliberalism but as its defining or underlying aspect, with a reach that goes far beyond financial markets themselves. To make sense and even to defend this posture, two further points need to be made. The first is to highlight significant connections but also inconsistencies across the ideologies, the scholarship and policies in practice of neoliberalism (Fine et al. 2024). These have a shifting relationship to one another across time, place and topic. I have argued this at great length elsewhere, particularly in the context of development (Fine, 2001 and 2010b and g; Fine et al. eds, 2001; and Bayliss et al. eds, 2011). Crucial, for example, is that, despite its scholarship and rhetoric, neoliberalism has always been heavily associated with state intervention. This has, however, been intervention to promote private capital in general and finance in particular. The response to the current crisis is no exception in which the crisis within, and not of, neoliberalism has been associated with extraordinary measures of support to finance both in levels of finance and even in nationalisation of failing financial institutions. Indeed, so powerful has been finance's influence over policy in the wake of the crisis that it has jokingly been described as "socialism for the bankers" and as not a case of government Treasuries nationalising the banks but of the banks nationalising the Treasuries!

This is all indicative of a further feature of the relationship between financialisation and neoliberalism that, very roughly, the latter falls into two phases divided by the early 1990s.[8] The first phase is aptly characterised as shock therapy in which, most strikingly, first in Latin America and, subsequently, in the former Soviet bloc, the promotion of private capital proceeded without regard to the consequences. The second phase has been, if only in part, a reaction to the consequences of the first phase in terms of the dysfunctions created, not least in social welfare provision, but it is also more marked by explicit intervention by the state to sustain the processes of, and underpinning, financialisation. Once again, this is one way of perceiving responses to the crisis. And it is, for example, borne out by the shifting policy stances on privatisation.

It is hardly surprising, then, that the neoliberalism/financialisation dualism should tend to preclude alternative thinking and policy. As Mkandawire (2009, p. 45–6) perceptively observes:

> On the assumption that the appropriate structures to emerge will be dictated by market forces, the contemporary strategy of poverty reduction is usually silent on sectoral policies. The model that has dominated

---

8   See Fine et al. (2024) for discussion of what is now the third phase of neoliberalism.

economic policy during the past two decades has tended to treat any specific sectoral policies that are not axiomatically derived from the core model as 'distortions'. Up until recently, 'industrial policy', 'social policy' and 'labour market policies' were only acceptable if they involved self-negation and meant the extension of the reign of the market to these spheres.

In other words, and to some degree remarkably, proper consideration of such policies has been taken off the agenda or, when they do make it on, they have been considerably reduced in scope of content and application with this being equally true of those who offer opposition to pure reliance upon market forces. Both our material and intellectual worlds have been heavily constrained by financialisation, and positive prospects for development, and for the state's role upon it, depend upon insulating policy from financialisation so that economic and social reproduction is served by finance rather than the other way about.

Of course, as emphasised, financialisation is both multi-dimensional and uneven across and within each dimension across and within developed and developing worlds. Indeed, financialisation is generally least developed in LDCs and, to some degree, mercifully, this has allowed them to avoid the *direct* impact of contagion from the global spread of the financial crisis through financial markets themselves. But indirect effects have been significant in terms of loss of export markets with global recession and loss of migrant remittances, and there has been volatility and spikes in food and energy prices, with some gains from raw material prices where supply rather than demand has been on the short side.

In effect, the direct impact of financialisation on LDCs has as yet most probably been greatest where the influence of global (or external) factors have been most important rather than through domestic developments within financial systems. This involves externally imposed adjustment policies, and the corresponding liberalisation of capital movements, exposing economies to the risk of capital flight or destabilising inflows (now acknowledged as a risk by the IMF)[9] and the high cost of holding reserves to guard against such eventualities.

Otherwise, financialisation is more likely to have proceeded through the opening of domestic banking systems to foreign competition, again under the auspices of IFI conditionalities, promising much in terms of the mobilisation and allocation of finance for domestic investment. In practice, the evidence suggests totally different outcomes as foreign banks have targeted personal

---

9   See Blanchard et al. (2010).

banking of the wealthiest individuals as opposed to developmental finance. The liberalisation/deregulation model for developed countries now lies in tatters, but its impact upon developing countries has been equally significant not least across appropriate sequencing of both reform (prior availability of appropriate regulation and stability) and promotion of different types of developmental finance. As Van Waeyenberge et al. (2011, p. 21) summarise from the fuller account of dos Santos (2011), and the corresponding indefensible defence of IFI research in favour of foreign bank entry and banking liberalisation:

> Foreign bank entry then grew rapidly in Latin American and East European countries. The result was a major shift in the structure of lending away from domestic enterprises to individuals. Lending behaviour by foreign banks created vulnerabilities in host economies around the world.

Further, as Demir (2009, p. 314) claims for "the first empirical study that looks into the portfolio choice real sector firms in developing countries face between real and financial sector activities ... increasing availability and accessibility of alternative investment opportunities in financial markets when combined with domestic market rigidities and uncertainty can become instrumental in channelling real sector savings to short-term financial investments instead of long-term fixed capital formation and thus lead to deindustrialization in those economies". He concludes that as, "rather than investing in irreversible long-term fixed investment projects, firms may choose to invest in reversible short-term financial investments ... there is a need to reorganize the financial system in such a way that domestic (and foreign) savings are directed towards productive investments instead of financial ones", p. 322.

And, if we can take the step of reorganising the financial system, there remains the issue of the how greater availability of longer-term resources might be deployed. In this vein, in later sections, I bring industrial policy back onto the agenda as well as considerations of the developmental state. But, before doing so, I offer an account of new growth theory in part because of the light it does, or does not, shed on considerations of growth and development, and also in part because it illustrates the malaise that is characteristic of the new(er) development economics, how it differs from the old development economics, and how the strengths of the latter can be restored with regard to changed circumstances.

1   Introduction

It is now a quarter of a century since Romer (1986) drafted his classic and pioneering paper on new growth theory. He could not have anticipated the explosion of research that would follow, not least given the modesty of his own research methods. As he confesses in retrospect on whether he was influenced by Schumpeter's notion of creative destruction, Snowdon and Vane (2005, p. 686):[10]

> No, I can honestly say that it has not. Schumpeter coined some wonderful phrases like 'creative destruction' but I did not read any of Schumpeter's work when I was creating my model. As I said, I really worked that model out from a clean sheet of paper. To be honest, the times when I have gone to try to read Schumpeter I have found it tough going. It is really hard to tell what guys like Schumpeter are talking about [*laughter*].

Even if we reduce the issue of development to (endogenous) growth, contingent upon productivity increase, the resulting energy devoted to explaining it in theoretical and empirical terms has been astonishing. Hundreds of variables have been deployed and millions of regressions have been run.[11] They offered the promise of using the results for economic and social engineering – the first model underpinning Poverty Reduction Strategy Papers, suggested the use of growth-elasticities to trade off policy variables whether it be through choice of

---

10   Note that for Bronk (2010, pp. 106/7), "Very often what economic modelers do is to co-opt new metaphorical elements from a quite different discipline or modeling tradition, and apply them as a series of bolt-on amendments to their preferred existing theoretical framework. This is usually done in the name of remaining true to the central rationalist micro-foundations of neoclassical economics (with its assumptions that individuals rationally optimize, within given constraints, on the best information and probability forecasts available). An example of this is Endogenous Growth Theory, *which does attempt to build in Schumpeter's creative destruction*, but without dropping the modeling assumption that individuals and firms are rational, probability-calculating optimizers of consumption and profit". (Emphasis added). Note, this is an unduly positive interpretation of what Romer, and often what endogenous growth theory, does. First, on a minor point, probability is not prominent; second, and more substantive, there are many other influences on the theory, some with the loosest of micro-foundations and grounding in other disciplines or realism. As such Bronk is far too kind insofar as other influences are speculative and parasitical upon other contributions in this vein and do not even go so far as bolting on – more a stripping down, alongside ideal invention and subordination to technique and method as correctly suggested.

11   Literally, see Sala-i-Martin (1997) and, by way of parsimonious alternative at the other extreme, Hendry and Krolzig (2004).

the elimination of a black market in foreign exchange or the number of telephone lines per thousand head of population.[12]

Now, from similar exercises, especially in the consequences of financial liberalisation and the impact of trade openness, we should have been cautious about the intellectual, let alone the statistical, stability of banging out empirical results, whether on the basis of refined or elementary models. The outcome has been disappointing with a significant literature expressing doubts about the theoretical and empirical rationale of the exercise itself, that growth 'models' cannot be common across countries.[13] Yet, interestingly, so extensive has been the empirical work that it has given rise to the emergence of the subfield of growth econometrics, with corresponding survey articles.

What do we learn from these?[14] First as many as fifty or so growth theories are identified as well as three times as many variables (with corresponding opportunities for publication bias – towards finding positive or, at least, significant results – and data mining). Second, whilst most economies have grown over the past forty years, growth rates across countries have diverged to an unprecedented extent other than for all but the richest countries irrespective of initial conditions (casting doubt on convergence hypotheses). Third, growth across the globe has been poorer between 1980 and 2000 than in the previous two decades and with more dispersion of growth rates (although there have been 'take-offs' for China and India incorporating two-fifths of the world's population). Fourth, there have been convergence clubs of nations around growth rates, roughly coinciding with East and South-East Asia, South and Central America and Sub-Saharan Africa (in order of declining performance). Fifth, identifying the causes of take-offs and slumps in growth are of importance. Sixth, policy change and reform can be of significance as can be the more or less favourable response to more general 'shocks'. Seventh, there is a need for country-specific study focusing on historical and institutional context.

Stepping back from these lessons, we can draw three more general conclusions. The first is to reinforce the conclusion that models are liable to collapse the complexity and diversity of the growth experience, partly because of the nature of the beast itself and partly because of the nature of the models whether by virtue of necessity or by design in light of how theory and modelling

---

12   Remarkably, reported as -0.0153 and +0.0054, respectively, so precise are the parameters for policymaking. See Devarajan et al. (2002) and for critique on this and more, Fine (2006a).

13   See Kenny and Williams (2001), Fine (2000, 2003a and 2006b), Rodriguez (2006), Rodrik (2005a and b), Solow (2006) and Cesaratto (2009).

14   See especially Durlauf et al. (2004) and Islam (2003).

have evolved in practice. Second is to observe the inconsistency between the empirical results and the theories from which they derive, ones that are almost universally based upon a dynamic organised around steady state balanced growth. Third is the almost unwitting *revisiting* of the old development economics in the sense of seeking out empirical regularities and explanations and precedents for them, even if on the basis of considerably larger, later and more diverse data sets and more refined statistical techniques.

This is, however, to revisit not to reproduce and update the old development economics. It was bound by the inductively and historically derived experience of the developed countries, with emphasis upon the processes of industrialisation, urbanisation, agrarian and demographic transitions, and so on, with the expectation that similar patterns would be followed by developing countries as captured in the notion of modernisation. It also emerged during an entirely different intellectual and material climate.[15] The latter was dominated by the processes of decolonisation the context of the Cold War and, possibly the most influential contribution in this respect, is Walt Rostow's *Stages of Economic Growth: A Non-Communist Manifesto*. It carried a message to the world that could not be clearer in the wake of the launch of the Sputnik in 1957 and the perceived threat of Soviet economic and technological catch-up. Whilst Rostow's ideological credentials could not have been stronger in support of US hegemony, and his volume was to go through three editions and sell three hundred thousand copies, his own stance on economic history was not supportive of the single-minded theory and numbers characteristic of the then emerging cliometric (or new economic history) school.[16] His schema for development followed a stylised induction of stages of economic growth from the experience of the developed countries. Whilst in part relying on standard growth theory, for Rostow the ultimate causes of such growth are situated in a framework of modernisation, of breaking up of traditional societies and, correspondingly, of major shifts in political, cultural and social variables that are not reducible to the economic.

This is a consequence of the then established style of economic history to which Rostow adhered, but it also reflects his keen commitment to distance his approach from the 'economic reductionism' that he attaches to Marxism. Indeed, his book's last chapter is devoted to a critique of Marxism for its economic reductionism (making up 15% or so of the main body of the text). The (mis)representation of Marx should not be taken too seriously except as a

---

15   The following draws heavily on Fine (2012e).
16   See Fine (2024c).

fascinating ideological text, reflecting (lack of) scholarly values of the time, but the nature of his construct of Marxism is instructive (Rostow 1991, p. 149):

> The first and most fundamental difference between the two analyses lies in the view taken of human motivation. Marx's system is, like classical economics, a set of more or less sophisticated logical deductions from the notion of profit maximization.

Ironically, this is a better description of the 'economics imperialism' of the present day (Fine and Milonakis, 2009). Indeed, Rostow (1957, p. 510) stated his preference for interdisciplinarity, "because I was repelled by Marx's economic determinism". In contrast, "In the stages-of-growth sequence man is viewed as a more complex unit. He seeks, not merely economic advantage, but also power, leisure, adventure, continuity of experience and security; he is concerned with his family, the familiar values of his regional and national culture, and a bit of fun down at the local ... In short, net human behaviour is seen not as an act of maximization, but as an act of balancing alternative and often conflicting human objectives in the face of the range of choices men perceive to be open to them" (Rostow, 1991, p. 149).

In short, from its own perspective, Rostow provides a manifesto of sorts more against neoclassical economics than Marxism by seeking to retain the notion of a more rounded individual. His antipathy to the idea that history can be reduced to the optimising individual could not be plainer. For, "The theorist has generally been uneasy if not awkward if forced to work outside Marshallian short-period assumptions; the historian – like the human beings he writes about – cannot avoid working in a world of changing tastes and institutions, changing population, technology, and capacity" (Rostow, 1957, p. 514). Thus, the old development economics carved a place for itself, like much applied economics more generally, outside the domain of both microeconomics and macroeconomics. In part, this reflected an acceptance that development was to be construed as something more than the economic as traditionally conceived, with a corresponding deference to the limited applicability of depending exclusively on 'rationality' and needing to incorporate the insights and methods of the other social sciences to explain development fully.

Even if, as suggested by the account of new growth theory and for other reasons and applications too, the new development economics has warmed to some of the themes of the old, it does so by entirely different methods and theory. It is highly dependent upon deductive models, especially those derived from mainstream neoclassical economics, with little or no conscious reliance upon inductive and historical investigation as such, incorporating little historical and social specificity other possibly than to guide choice of model. For the Washington Consensus, universally acknowledged as an explicit rejection of the old development economics and its reliance upon the state as an instrument for achieving modernisation, the theoretical underpinnings are made explicit by Anne Krueger, Chief Economist at the World Bank between 1982 to 1986. In the first issue of the *World Bank Research Observer*, she asserts, "Once it is recognised that individuals respond to incentives, and that 'market failure' is the result of inappropriate incentives rather than non-responsiveness, the separateness of development economics as a field largely disappears" (Krueger, 1986, p. 62). Whilst the subsequent Post-Washington Consensus, PWC, has been more state-friendly and more reliant upon market imperfections in orientation, it is no less committed to the same methodology albeit with contingent eclecticism in relation to model choice. Dani Rodrik (2007, p. 3) whose *One Economics, Many Recipes*, emphasis added, could not be more explicit, emphasis added:

> At the core of neoclassical economics lies the following methodological predisposition: *social* phenomena can best be understood by considering them to be an aggregation of purposeful behavior by individuals – in their roles as consumer, producer, investor, politician, and so on – interacting with each other and acting under the constraints that their environment imposes. This I find to be not just a powerful discipline for organizing our thoughts on economic affairs, but *the only sensible way* of thinking about them.

Accordingly, it is possible to suggest the Washington Consensus and PWC have as much in common as they differ along the market versus state spectrum. Each adopts the same, extraordinarily reduced, method and underlying neoclassical principles; each, nonetheless, applies these across an ever-widening range of economic *and* social applications; and neither has a concept of development itself as opposed to a means to achieve it (reliance upon the market as opposed to piecemeal correction of market and institutional imperfections as and when these can be identified and remedied with positive outcome).[17]

---

17   The continuing emphasis on state as opposed to market, or the state as complementary support to the market, is stressed by Joe Stiglitz (2008, p. 2) on behalf of the 'left', new or otherwise, presumably a generic term for those in opposition to the Washington Consensus, "The left now understands markets and the role markets should and can play in the economy ... the new left is trying to make markets work".

As a result, the marriage of new development economics with some limited restoration of the old is an inappropriate mix by which to assess the record of the past and the prospects, and policies, for the future.[18] Nor is it sufficient simply to restore the old, contingent as it was upon its own context and the necessary inability to take account of changed circumstances as well as the decades of subsequent experience since it has gone into decline. How, then, to proceed? I do so by re-examining two core concerns that have paralleled rather than bridged the passage from what might be termed the Pre- to the Post-Washington Consensus. These are the developmental state and industrial policy.

2   Lessons from the Developmental State Paradigm

What is it that characterises a developmental state and what makes it so? Answers to these apparently simple questions are elusive. This is not just because of denial of the potential for, or desirability of, the developmental state in deference to the market as associated with the Washington Consensus. For nor does the Developmental State Paradigm (DSP) itself offer satisfactory responses. One reason for this is the tension between the *universal* applicability of the DSP (its analytical framework should apply everywhere, in principle, explaining as required both success and *failure*) and its often confinement in practice to examples of success.

This tension, and how it has itself been handled, is brought out by acknowledging that the DSP readily if roughly divides into two separate schools, as highlighted in successive surveys of the DSP literature (Fine and Stoneman, 1996; Fine and Rustomjee, 1996; Fine 2004a, 2006c, 2007b and 2010e and f; and

---

18   As an illustration, see the debate between Wade (2010 and 2011) and Lin (2010). which is remarkable for the extent of what is excluded as much as for the marginal shifts towards state developmentalism being signalled in World Bank scholarship and rhetoric, if not, it should be emphasised, policy other than in reflecting changed circumstances. See also debate between Lin and Chang (2009) and debate that accompanies Lin and Monga (2011a) in the same issue. Note just how much is excluded by Lin's various contributions, of which the developmental state is the most obvious absence. Indeed, Lin and Monga (2011a) might be thought to be not so much taking a step towards re-introducing industrial policy as attempting to constrain it with striking substantive parallels to the World Bank's (1993) *East Asian Miracle Report*. The notion touted by Lin and Monga of latent comparative advantage as the source of success is almost inevitably an ex post tautology and rationale for limiting the role of the state just as is the earlier notion of the state conforming to the market. See previous Chapter.

Ashman et al. 2010), with emphasis placed upon two different ways in explaining how successful development has been and might be achieved, this being the goal of the developmental state literature.[19]

For one, termed the economic school, the focus is on those (economic) policies, often narrowly drawn and conceived, that are necessary for an economy to achieve development. Drawing primarily on the idea that markets do not work perfectly and, correspondingly, upon (imperfect market) economics as a discipline, the state is required to accrue, for example, the economies of scale and scope, to coordinate investments within and across sectors, to harness positive and eliminate negative externalities, and so on. For the economic school, then, it is a matter of identifying the appropriate policies, with the presumption that they will be implemented by a developmental state because they need to be.

By contrast, and completely complementary, the political school with its own disciplinary origins predominantly from within political science (to some degree sociology, but certainly separate from economics), is remarkably aloof from consideration of the economy itself and the nature of the economic policies required to bring about development. Rather, the political school is concerned with the nature of the state itself and whether it has the potential in general, and the independence in particular, to adopt the necessary policies more or less irrespective of what these might be. Here, emphasis is placed upon the necessity for the developmental state to be free from capture by particular interests, and so to be able to adopt developmental policies, whatever they might be.

Taken together, the economic and political schools address what policies are to be adopted and what allows them to be adopted. Successful cases of development in practice can be interpreted through this dual prism, and such is a major methodological thrust of both schools. For each has been highly inductive in practice, examining the role of economic policy in bringing about development and the nature of the states adopting such policies. This is not to suggest, however, that the developmental state literature has been without theory or analytical content. The economic school, for example, strongly emphasises the significance of market imperfections and the role of a developmental state in addressing, if not necessarily correcting them. In highlighting the departure from neoliberalism, Amsden (1989) famously declared that it was a matter of "getting relative prices wrong", of not conforming to the

---

19   These earlier contributions offer extensive surveys of the evolving literature, with the discussion here more focused on the more recent contributions.

dictates of the market.[20] In principle, the economic school could have drawn upon orthodox economics and its deductive methods, especially in its emphasis upon market imperfections. In practice, though, as indicated, it has been drawn towards more inductive and case study methods, and it has generally been characterised as displaying a suspicion towards orthodoxy even when the latter is based on market imperfections.[21]

Similarly, the political school has tried to identify empirically what characterises the nature of the states, and the societies containing them, in which development has proven possible. Posing this in terms of the independence of the state from economic or other interests has itself presumed an analytical approach in which society is structured along the lines of the state as opposed to the market, with the addition of civil society to fill out the remaining economic, political and ideological space. In this way, not only is the (developmental) state seen as potentially independent, the term favoured is autonomous, it is also perceived to evolve interests of its own that prevail over those of the market and civil society, especially where these conflict with developmentalism. This approach of the political school is admirably captured in the notion of "Bringing the State back in" as an agent of development in its own right (Evans and Rueschemeyer, eds, 1985).[22]

Across both economic and political schools, then, there is a predilection to set up an opposition between state and market. For the economic school, the state overrules the market and so is able to improve upon it. For the political school, the state needs to stand aloof from the market, and the economic interests found within it. The result has been to downplay the role of class in the analysis (Radice, 2008). With the economic school, it does not tend to appear at all for it is simply a matter of identifying the right policies and not whether they have sufficient support to be implemented, and on whose behalf or to

---

20   In an interview, she answers in response to the question, "What made your work on industrialization and on Korea so influential?", she replies, "Showing that Korea developed by getting the prices 'wrong'", van der Hoeven (2008, p. 1093).

21   Significantly, the leading orthodox proponent of the consequences of increasing returns to scale, Paul Krugman, has advised against drawing policy conclusions from his deductive theory, even though they clearly offer a rationale for state intervention, on the grounds that policy is liable to be captured by special interests (something he, paradoxically, ignores in developing his theory of uneven development). See Fine and Milonakis (2009) and Fine (2010a) for a discussion.

22   See Stubbs (2009) for this point amongst others in a useful retrospective on the developmental state. But note that he manages to avoid discussion of class altogether, with the exception of one reference to the middle class! See also Beeson (2009) for an overview of East Asian developmental states.

whose benefit. On the other hand, matters are not so simple for the political school. It is not that class or more general economic interests are absent but it is important that the state has the capacity to neutralise if not to override them. And, of overwhelming importance if so much taken to be granted as more or less to remain unstated, there is a total pre-occupation with the nation-state and its capacity to bring about development irrespective of the impact of international or global factors.[23] This does not mean that the global is absent, only that it needs to be incorporated as a positive (availability of catch-up technology, for example) or as a negative (competition from imports), influence in the policies to be adopted or the attainment of independence in policymaking.[24]

Such are the general characteristics of the economic and political schools, but the developmental state literature has a rhythm of greater or lesser prominence and a more detailed content in conformity with more general events and intellectual trends. Early traces of the economic school are to be found in the protectionism associated with Friedrich List in the nineteenth century and, for the political school, developmentalism is associated with nation-building through industrial and military strength.[25] Latin American import substitution industrialisation from the 1930s until the 1980s is seen as successful (economic school) until radical populism placed undue burdens upon the state (political school).[26] But the developmental state comes of age with the rise of

---

23   Note that for Yazid (2007, p. 39), "the success of a developmental state requires external support from external powers". Does this apply to China?

24   See Pirie (2008), and also Radice (2008), for a strong statement of the constraints imposed on prospective developmental states by the impact of globalisation and neoliberalism, but also Khondker (2008) and Pereira (2008) for continuing possibilities in case of Singapore. See also below.

25   For the past, see Blecher (2008, p. 171) for the view that, "Bonapartism was not just a forerunner of modern authoritarianism, but also of the capitalist developmental state". And, for the present, see Lange (2009) for the potential for crises to prompt nation-building developmental states, drawing upon Botswana and Malaysia as case studies, and also Barbara (2008) for post-conflict economies as potential developmental states. See also Kim (2009) for the importance of the historical origins of contemporary developmental states, de Haan (2010) and Di John (2010) for developmental state building, and Berger and Ghosh (2010, p. 586) for the interesting proposition that the end of the Cold War has witnessed "an important shift from developmental nationalisms to cultural nationalisms", with correspondingly negative implications for developmental states as "the nation-state system itself is sliding deeper into crisis against the backdrop of the global framework of 'genuinely existing' liberal capitalism".

26   The Latin American experience raises the question of whether a developmental state can survive without being authoritarian, confronting the demands both for democracy and from an organised labour movement the more it is successful. Note, though, that for Draibe and Riesco (2007, p. 1), the Latin American developmental welfare state (LADWS) is a crucial factor for success, not a disintegrating cause derived from radical populism,

the East Asian NICs in the post-war period. The classic case study derives from Johnson (1982) from within the political school, with his emphasising the role played by the Japanese trade and industry ministry, MITI. Significantly, this study, from a former CIA analyst, was confessed to be motivated by support for the United States in its Cold War aspirations, advising that the unrealistic and abstract propositions derived from neoliberalism would not bring capitalist development, judging from the experience of Japan, and would make Soviet prescriptions more attractive; and he is particularly scathing of the propositions derived from mainstream economics (Johnson, 2006).

But, although still acknowledged as a classic contribution that stands alone in its own way in modern times in its message of the need for a powerful state agent to underpin industrialisation (and with a close account of Japan as late-comer as case study), the ensuing literature on the developmental state focused its critical attention entirely upon the target of neoliberalism in general and the Washington Consensus in particular whose own version of neoliberalism could only have been anticipated by Chalmers just a few years before. By contrast, by the mid-1980s, inspired by the developmental successes of the East Asian NICs and the unremitting hostility to state intervention being displayed by both the World Bank and the IMF, the DSP became one of the two leading strands of criticism of the conditions being attached to these organisations' offers of aid.[27] Apart from Amsden's (1989) study of South Korea's industrialisation, Wade's (1990) account of Taiwan's, offering the mantra of "Governing the Market", also rapidly became a classic.

The growing intellectual momentum of the DSP in the wake of the success of the East Asian NICs, and the incontrovertible evidence of extensive state intervention in these countries, was complemented by the growing sense of failure, indeed a crisis of legitimacy, of the Washington Consensus as the 1980s was appropriately seen as a lost decade as far as development elsewhere in the world was concerned. In the early 1990s, the Japanese funded a study to reassess the role of the state in the East Asian NICs. It had three good reasons to do so. First, the Washington Consensus denied the historical reality of its own

---

"The core argument ... is that LADWS was the original historical form that drove forward social and economic development in the particular conditions of the region during the twentieth century". See below but especially next Chapter on bringing welfare back into the DSP.

27   The other being the social costs of the policies, adjustment without a human face. For critical presentation of the Washington Consensus and its aftermath as Post-Washington Consensus, see Fine et al. (eds) (2001), Jomo and Fine (eds) (2006) and Bayliss et al. (eds) (2011).

latecomer success. Second, it was on the point of becoming the leading donor to developing countries. And, third, most important of all, its own industrial strategy, of contracting out less technology-intensive production to countries within the Asia-Pacific Rim, required for success that this be supported by appropriate local industrial policies. Japan could hardly be expected to continue to pay for policies that it knew both to be based on falsehood and to be against its own interests![28]

In the event, the World Bank's (1993) report on the East Asian NICs proved a remarkable piece of intellectual acrobatics. It did not deny that the state had intervened extensively but suggested that it had done so in a way that was market-conforming, doing what the market would have done had it been working perfectly, an unassailable but vacuous position in support of the market. It further suggested that the conditions which had allowed for this were not to be found replicated elsewhere. Essentially, the relevance of the East Asian NICs as a model or models for development were discounted except to confirm the rule of following, or conforming to, the market.[29]

Whether such a contorted logic could have prevailed for long is a moot point, especially given the shifting contradictory relationship between the scholarship, rhetoric, policy and representation of reality that emanates from the World Bank (Bayliss et al. eds, 2011). But the logic did not persist in any case but for reasons that witnessed not the triumph of the DSP but its demise from the second half of the 1990s. First and foremost, the Asian financial crises of 1997/98 cast a long shadow over the region's economic miracle, some economists even denying that it had ever occurred and arguing that it had simply reflected the heavy accumulation of resources as opposed to disproportionate increases in productivity.[30] Second, though, the second half of the 1990s also witnessed the shift in the World Bank from the Washington to the PWC, inspired and launched by Joe Stiglitz in 1997 as Chief Economist at the Bank. Underpinning this shift in paradigm from neoliberalism is the idea of market and institutional imperfections as the source of failing economic performance,

---

28   See Wade (1996).

29   For continuing but long-established recognition of a variety of models across developmental states, see Bardhan (2010). He contrasts India and China with one another and with east Asian NICs – politically, regionally, by relations between public and private sectors, sources of finance, role of conglomerates and foreign capital, and role of state officials.

30   See Young (1994 and 1995) and Krugman (1994b), although a simple visit to factories throughout the region might have offered a contrary view over the progress made in the adoption of new technologies (as opposed to simply accumulating on the basis of the old).

and for policy to be addressed at correcting these in a piecemeal fashion. In addition to a more favourable stance in principle to the state, the Bank (or its research ethos) also placed emphasis upon good governance, the elimination of corruption, empowerment, and democracy, all elements that were supposed to enable the state to act developmentally.

As a result, if in its own way, and at a microeconomic as opposed to a systemic level as far as the economics is concerned, the concerns of the developmental state had been at least partially addressed by the new Bank orthodoxy but also in a way that meant that the term never had to be used. The market versus state agenda set by the World Bank gave way to one of market plus state. Symbolically, the person who continues to be seen as a leading proponent of the developmental state, Ha-Joon Chang, both tends not to use the term himself and aligned himself with the PWC, at least to the extent of editing a volume of Stiglitz's contributions on his new paradigm (Chang, ed. 2001).[31]

For a decade or so following the Asian crisis, then, the DSP went into decline. But it is important to recognise that doubts about its continuing relevance had already been sewn amongst its own practitioners before the crisis struck, particularly as far as South Korea is concerned. The South Korean model of the developmental state eventually involved a focus on what might be termed the Giants of Asia's Next Giant, to be found within the conglomerate chaebol system. Even before the financial crisis of 1997, it was being argued that the developmental state had become a victim of its own success, possibly as a general rule. For, in South Korea for example, it had spawned the chaebol and, hence, a powerful class of capitalists who were now in a position to challenge and, ultimately, to prevail over the state.[32] In addition, the working class also becomes more numerous, organised and powerful with development (as industrialisation), together with demands for democratisation that challenges the authoritarian origins of the state's autonomy.[33]

Indeed, such insights inevitably informed the eruption of diagnoses over the causes of the crisis that emerged so rapidly despite the failure to anticipate its occurrence. In crudest form, these placed emphasis on corruption and rent-seeking at the expense of the role of the state and of coordinated

---

31   See Pirie (2009) for an exposure of the ambiguities in Chang's analytical stance.

32   But see Hundt (2009) for this in the context of a continuing if shifting developmental alliance between the state and capital in South Korea.

33   See Pereira (2008) for a clear statement of the developmental state death hypothesis but the use of Singapore as a counterexample in case the capitalist class remains relatively marginal and the working class is incorporated, thereby allowing the state to continue to be developmental.

industrial policy; more subtle was the idea of the demise of powers of the state over the chaebol as they pursued its favour through diversified profitable outlets in industry as well as property, financial and international markets; and, as already mentioned, there were those prepared to deny there had ever been a miracle, and yet others who emphasised the failure of the state to be able to hold off any longer the interventions of international capital as it sought, not without willing domestic partners, both to deregulate the state's control of finance and to open the economy's productive basis and markets to foreign multinationals.[34] In short, following the crisis, the DSP suffered for a decade or so from being outflanked by the new PWC orthodoxy at the Bank and, paradoxically, with the DSP not finding itself on the more state-friendly PWC agenda, being caught by a pincer movement between the consequences of developmental success (capitalists emerge to challenge autonomy) and apparent revisionist interpretation of failure in the wake of the Asian financial crisis.

Yet, without wishing to blame the victim, one of the unnoticed and essential features of the original DSP literature, which persisted with minor exceptions up to the new millennium (see below), is the extent to which it has been extraordinarily self-limiting, especially within the economic school. From the review given above, it is instructive to examine this in some detail. First and foremost, based on its inductive method of identifying developmental states, and explaining them in terms of the policies adopted and the capacity to adopt them, case studies within the developmental state literature have been self-selecting. Elsewhere, this has been parodied as a law of economics (Fine, 2010f), that wherever there is developmental success, the developmental state paradigm will be more or less casually applied and prosper.[35] Of course, this is a process of self-limitation in practice rather than in principle. For, from a logical point of view, failed developmental states should also fall within the paradigm as case studies, those economies that did not adopt the right policies or were unable to do so.

In the event, this latter logic has not been followed other than cursorily. Rather, the literature, has proceeded primarily, but not exclusively, by providing a cumulative basket of successful case studies, with East Asia to the fore, and

---

34   See Phelps (2008) for a discussion of the role of, and need for, the developmental state in forging developmental clusters out of multinational corporate investment. Note that this involves a state versus market approach, primarily within the economic school, in which MNCs are a proxy for the market. See also Cherry (2007) on the South Korean developmental state in light of crisis, neoliberalism and foreign direct investment.

35   For two arbitrarily and unfairly selected examples, see Kumar (2008) for India and Xia (2008) for China.

a few bright spots elsewhere such as Botswana, Mauritius, and the Republic of Ireland, Maundeni (2002) and Robinson (2009), Meisenhelder (1997), and O'Hearn (2000) and Riain (2000), respectively, for example. For the economic school, this has commendably led to the conclusion that there is not a single model for the developmental state, as they share insufficient in common across the different East Asian economies. In a sense, this is all illustrated by the thrust of Chang's (2002 and 2007) work and message: that the developmental states of the past (the developed countries of today) did experience a wide variety of conditions and causes but these all diverged from the recommendations for both economic and non-economic policies that they currently offer to the developing world (especially as regards neoliberalism and the premature burdens of democracy and modernisation). In this way, failed developmental states or, more exactly, failed development is at most implicitly explained by divergence from one or other developmental state model as opposed to close examination of such failures themselves from within the broader application of the DSP itself.

For the political school, there has been much less single-minded preoccupation with those developmental states that have succeeded, with the attempt to tease out the surrounding conditions explaining why appropriate policies could be adopted rather than being subverted by special (non-developmental) interests derived, normally, from the economy but also potentially from civil society. Recall that the rationale underlying the gathering of case studies is to identify where the state is able to act independently and/or even to have an interest of its own. Indeed, initially, the presence of a developmental state (as reflected in MITI for Japan for example) was taken as sufficient evidence of the required state autonomy. But, obviously, this does not probe very deeply into the social, political, cultural and ideological circumstances that both create such pre-conditions and allow them to prevail over other causal factors and interests. The search, again within an inductive framework, was mounted for the sources of what became known as relative and/or embedded autonomy[36] – a growing recognition for the paradigm that the state had to be both independent of, and yet, responsive to and controlling of other structures, processes and agents "in thick social relationships with various institutions of society" (Khondker, 2008, p. 36). This seems to be a matter of

---

36   Whilst the notion of relative autonomy derives from the Althusserian school (and Poulantzas) and embedded autonomy from Polanyi, their use tends to fail to acknowledge these roots and to depart from them both in substance, sophistication and tension in content and application.

bringing back in what has been left out from the state when previously bringing it back in as an autonomous agent!

Not surprisingly, the more case studies of relative, embedded autonomy were addressed, the more (refined) conditions, or their absence, were found to be of relevance. The literature has offered attention to consensus, institutions, political participation, authoritarianism, inclusion and exclusion, the international environment, bureaucratic cohesion, depoliticisation, weakness and strength, efficacy, adaptability, networks, politics in all of its forms (leadership choice, regime maintenance, and interaction between economic performance and coalition formation), and social structure comprising class, gender, ethnicity, culture and religion.[37] In this respect, at least for the political school, the paradox is that limitation to political capacity to deliver developmental policy has led to unlimited scope of case studies to incorporate both successes and failures.

The difference with the economic school, and its tendency to shy away from failure, despite a common inductive methodology, is explained by the extent to which much state failure in economic policy cannot in and of itself be readily distinguished from the instances of success from within the economic school as both breach with the dogma of relying exclusively upon the market – as it were, where does developmentalism end and rent-seeking and corruption take over? By contrast, because it does not look at the economy as such, and takes the distinction between successful developmental states and unsuccessful states as starting point, the political school can round up the evidence across as many states as it chooses, and across as many variables likewise, and seek to discover empirical regularities in the determination of success or not. In this, it has some sort of advantage over the economic school which can only, for example, insist that some degree of protection is essential for developmental success but cannot guarantee it. On the other hand, the results of the political school are far from solid and are unable to offer simple nostrums around the relationship between authoritarianism, say, and developmentalism. There are also too many variables that can be added to the unpicking of relative, embedded autonomy, and there seems no fixed interactions between them, although the results swing towards democracy against authoritarianism as we move forward in time (in line with more progressive stances along the lines that equality is good for growth, etc). But, by being more rounded than the economic school in addressing state success *and* failure, the political school becomes vulnerable to being outflanked by a literature that addresses the same issue

---

37   See especially White (1998), Chan et al. (1998) and Leftwich (2000 and 2005).

whilst totally ignoring the DSP, precisely as good governance, institutional analysis, etc, come to the fore, not least with the desire to identify and explain the African dummy for poor performance for example (Jerven, 2011).

The limitation to successful developmental states, most notably for the economic school (other than in critique of the rest as relying too heavily upon neoliberal prescriptions, something that need not arise for the political school more concerned with internal politics and external influences upon it), has inevitably involved a self-limitation with regional bias towards East Asia as the preferred area of application of the developmental state paradigm. Africa, for example, is notable for the relative absence of corresponding case studies (Mkandawire, 2001). But, surely, if interventionist policy is able to explain success in East Asian NICs by adoption of the right interventionist policies, it ought equally to be able to explain failure elsewhere by their lack of adoption or of the wrong policies. The point here, and it will recur across other issues around the self-limiting scope of the DSP, is to question to what (extent) does the approach apply, how wide is its explanation, does it explain success as well as failure and, is this a matter of self-confinement in its causal principles or analytical framework or not. For simple propositions concerning the necessity of state intervention because markets do not work perfectly seem to be extremely wide in application, more or less without limit, as opposed to being confined to developmental success alone (and within particular regions of the globe). And, by the same token, the concerns of the political school around the conditions which allow for efficacy in state intervention (whatever that might be in practice) are also not confined to accounts of developmental success in particular parts of the world for particular phases of development, especially in large-scale statistical cross-country exercises as opposed to more informal individual case studies for which choice of success over failure continues to loom large even for the political school.

Not surprisingly, given its emphasis on East Asian NICs, and the particular phase in the process of development attached to latecomer, catch-up industrialisation, the DSP has been drawn to assess industrial policy at the expense of other policy and aspects of the process of development and even of other stages of development including those of industrialisation itself other than latecomer catch-up. Most obviously absent is the role of agriculture, in and of itself, and as a crucial catalyst to industrialisation as a source of surplus for investment thereby alleviating savings constraints, labour for industrial employment, demand for domestically produced industrial goods, and measures to enhance productivity of agriculture itself. The same applies to the role of other primary products in development not least oil. As Ikpe (2011) argues in seeking to extend the DSP to Nigeria (as a failed instance):[38]

Developmental states are expected to address the noted constraints on industrialisation by:

- managing *savings constraints* by extensively taxing the agricultural sector; and manipulating foreign exchange rates with regard to agricultural exports;

- alleviating *marketed surplus constraints* by adopting policies to appropriate food from producers at low prices; obliging producers to pay for land and inputs and credit repayments in food; making widespread efforts to raise agricultural output and productivity levels through investment in infrastructure, including irrigation and provision of subsidised inputs; and protecting the domestic agricultural sector from foreign competition;

- limiting *industrial demand constraints* by ensuring the protection of the domestic industrial sector from foreign competition; and pursuing agricultural investments to enhance agricultural output and supporting pluriactivity to improve agricultural incomes; and

- mitigating *labour constraints* by locating industrial activity in rural areas to enable pluriactivity; investing in rural infrastructure and social services including education to enable rural industrial activity as well as preparing the rural workforce for industrial employment; and driving investment in land and labour saving technology to ease the outflow of labour from agriculture.

- ... and strengthening the agricultural sector by ensuring *fiscal linkages* between agriculture and mineral resources by enabling fiscal transfers to the former for rural infrastructural developments, provision of subsidised inputs and credits to producers.

It is, of course, not accidental that such considerations derive from seeking to extend and strain the DSP to incorporate the classic concerns of the old development economics. And, by the same token, whilst there are extensive literatures on both agriculture and development (not least for the successful developmental states), this does not tend to have been incorporated into the DSP itself.

This discussion offers the following lessons for LDCs insofar as they seek to become or, more exactly, aspire to learn from the experiences of erstwhile (East Asian) developmental states either from their golden periods of

---

38   See also Ikpe (2013).

industrialisation or from those foundational periods that preceded them.[39] First and foremost is the need to focus state policy on agriculture (and other primary sectors) to bring about productivity increase for which leaving the sector to the market to exploit comparative advantage and be disciplined by competitive forces is totally inadequate. Second, this must be targeted as both a goal and a means to development. Third, as already indicated to some extent, corresponding policy for agriculture will dovetail with the classically conceived challenges of development in which the state plays a significant role across expanding food and raw material supply, creating a surplus for investment, surplus labour for transfer to other sectors, and surplus product for export to earn foreign exchange, and creating both supply and demand linkages for sectors serving agriculture (fertiliser, seeds, etc) and served by it (food processing). Fourth, the range of potential policies involved are extensive and their suitability and potential highly complex and diverse, and contingent upon crop, climate, land quality and location, and potential for mix of products (by quality and for domestic or export markets), infrastructural provision (transport, irrigation, etc), potential for land reform, integration or not into global (or domestic) value chains, traditional patterns of work and consumption, and so on. In this light, as amply confirmed by the overview of Chang (2009), the task is to identify the appropriate policies for agriculture to be developmental drawing upon a wealth of historical and continuing experience rather than seeking to emulate some elusive market-led route to efficiency. Whilst Chang is mainly concerned with policy for raising agricultural productivity in light of historical and continuing experience, similar considerations apply to, and inevitably mix in with, achieving the broader developmental goals associated with industrialisation. On the basis of case studies, and broader overview, it is found that the state can play a significant role in relation to land tenure, land degradation, either over-fragmentation or over-concentration of landholdings, agricultural research, extension services, rural credit, irrigation, transport, fertilizers, seeds, price and income stabilities, trade shocks, agro-processing, marketing, electrification and education.[40] Last, then, and by no means least, and

---

39   See Ikpe (2011) for account of developmental states and agriculture (and primary production) before they were such and the lessons to be drawn, with an application to Nigeria and both rice economy and oil. Note that Lin and Monga (2011a) more or less totally ignore agriculture and, by default, the corresponding challenges for LDCs in addressing the "dynamics of industrial change" however well this may have been understood otherwise. Significantly, their contribution falls unwittingly into a weak form of contribution to the economic school of the DSP albeit without any reference to it whatsoever.

40   See also Chang (ed.) (2012) which includes case studies from Chile, Ethiopia, Ghana, India, Mexico and Vietnam.

as suggested implicitly by extension of the political school attached to the DSP, there is no avoiding the politics of agriculture and the complex of interests and public and private, national and international, institutions with which such politics is embroiled. These range from the multinational biotechnology corporations down through more or less wealthy landowners and tenants to landless, casualised wage-labourers.

Indeed, the formation, implementation and monitoring with feedback of policy must be sensitive to the structures and processes through which these interests are formed and exert influence and, equally, how they interact with the emergence and/or strengthening of new constituencies as development proceeds, or not. It is also essential to be mindful of the speed and unexpected directions that might be taken as oil-rich middle east economies (and China) buy up agricultural land in developing countries (especially in Africa) to address their own food sustainability (and, of more longstanding duration, the displacement of agricultural production for domestic production for cash crop production for western European luxury and/or all-year consumption).

Significantly, in light of these issues, it is indicative that the International Assessment of Agricultural Knowledge, Science, Technology for Development (IAASTD) recommended broad conclusions and mixed methods of analysis for dealing with the diversity and complexities of food supply.[41] And even the World Bank, which has tended to neglect agriculture except for the occasional blitzed focus from one decade to the next, finds it difficult, if not impossible, to specify one policy fits all on targets and instruments for agricultural policy even though it does have an ethos of favouring private property rights, minimal state intervention, and the promotion of multinational corporation interests as suppliers to, and customers for, agriculture.[42]

And much the same is true of closer consideration of different stages of industrial development themselves other than that of latecomer catch-up. The exception in this respect is the 'flying geese' approach. This has two aspects. On the one hand are the dynamic linkages from one sector to another with

---

41   For the seven-volume report of IAASTD, see McIntyre et al. (2009). It sat from 2004 to 2008 and incorporates the participation of over 400 authors and a wide range of national and international agencies. See also Ishii-Eiteman (2010).

42   For the analytical acrobatics involved in the World Bank's attempts to reconcile populist land reform with market promotion, see Oya (2011). Prospects for agriculture also need to take account both of the newly more prominent problems associated with climate change and environmental spoliation, as well as pre-empting the emergence of the food diseases of affluence (obesity) that are reaching epidemic proportions in developed countries for which developing countries need to be mindful through careful negotiation of the interaction between food and health policy, see Fine (1998e).

potentially increasing degree of technical sophistication and value added as we move through the flock. Here, once again, there have been limitations by taking the Washington Consensus as point of departure. For the neoliberal reliance upon getting the prices right, perceiving the state as a source of corruption and rent-seeking, and denying its capacity to pick and promote winners, induced corresponding counterclaims on these terms alone. Consequently, the result was also not only to focus upon industrial policy but also to frame it in a narrow way, straying little beyond trade policy, preferential access to finance, and coordination and promotion of investment within and across sectors. But this tends to leave a number of vital elements of industrial policy (or factors within industrial policy) out of the picture – such as skills and the labour market, the role of the financial system more generally than directed finance, and technology policy.[43] These seem more or less to have been assumed to fall into place by virtue of other policies as prime movers.

On the other hand, 'flying geese' serves to highlight the shifting international division of labour between, or across, national economies as those at lower levels of development and wages and skills take on the relocated manufacturing roles of those already upgrading or upgraded to higher stages of industrialisation. The classic case is Japan's investment strategy into the Asia-Pacific Rim in the last decades of the twentieth century although China currently presents a more complex picture as it both leads the geese of follower nations and competes with them. This and closer examination of historical experience in terms of, or increasingly at the expense of the metaphor adopted, suggests questioning whether geese fly in a two-dimensional V-shaped pattern or formation alone, and might not other birds or creatures either join the flock and even challenge hierarchy within it. Otherwise is to suggest a limited form of technological determinism that strains both the evidence and the potential for policies that breach with, or progress beyond, confinement to latecomer catch-up that preserves the existing order in the international division of labour, ones that have indeed been broken by the East Asian NICs in the past, with China possibly ready to repeat the exercise in its own fashion.[44]

Thus, certainly, labour-intensive industries in the first instance can then form the basis for a 'flying geese' pattern of upgrading into linked higher value,

---

43   For the latter, for a late exception, see Lee, K. (2009).

44   Thus, Masina (2010) deploys the common metaphor from global network approaches of Vietnam's recent successes being dependent upon its position in relation to manufacturing hubs, with corresponding constraints on moving through higher stages of industrial upgrading and on retaining independence over industrial policy given reliance on foreign direct investment and technologies.

skilled and more capital-intensive production (Shafaeddin, 2005, p. 1153; and Haque, 2007, p. 6).[45] What will mark the (success of the) earlier stages of such processes is the extent and sustainability of markets against volatility and competition. This means both a premium on export markets, and on domestic production for domestic markets deploying domestic resources. The latter can neatly dovetail with the provision of a number of basic needs. But it remains essential to acknowledge that such stylised forms of progress may not be the only ones, and must be subjected to investigation as such, even if they were the only options available, in order to identify shifting potential in light of techno-logical imperatives and domestic and global market and other economic and social conditions.

This is also, however, to raise the issue of global factors both logically and analytically. Not all can catch up otherwise there would never be leaders despite the pressures towards gaining and sustaining technological advance. Indeed, much of the DSP's latecomer catch-up perspective not only neglects earlier stages of industrialisation but also the later stage of being on, or beyond, the frontier itself (as if once at the finishing line, the story is over). That this is not so simple nor automatic is evidenced by Japan's industrial travails over the past two decades, whilst the record of the East Asian NICs more generally of getting beyond the frontier remains mixed, contingent on the nature of the technologies, consumer products and the strategies of incumbents (the origi-nal geese).[46]

And as mentioned, the closely studied impact of China is also relevant in and of itself as well as being indicative of much more widely dispersed sources of origin and sectors for application for direct foreign investment from multi-national corporations and corresponding countries of origin for such invest-ment (with such investment previously heavily dominated by the USA, with

---

45   But see Hart-Landsberg and Burkett (1988) for an early critical review of the potential of
       flying geese strategies for development.
46   See Ohno (2009) both for five stages of catching-up industrialisation, from zero to four –
       which may or may not (be designed to) have affinities with Rostovian stages – and for
       the suggestion that there is the prospect of a middle-income trap, or "invisible 'glass ceil-
       ing'", between his Stage Two ("Have supporting industries, but still under foreign guid-
       ance") and Stage Three ("Management & technology mastered, can produce high quality
       goods"), p. 28. The passage between these two stages is seen as depending upon capabil-
       ity for "technology absorption", and depending on "creativity" for the transition between
       Stage Three and the last, Stage Four (Full capability in innovation and product design as
       global leader). Various countries are distributed across these stages as are other charac-
       teristics as specified for other stages. See also Al-Jazaeri (2008 and 2013) for the problems
       of getting beyond catch up, and Karo and Kattel (2010) for the complexities of the deter-
       mination of innovation policy, practice and outcome.

the UK significant but far behind in second place). Thus, the increasing spread of sources of foreign direct investment is indicative both of enhanced opportunities (availability of, and competition between, sources) and of the erosion of potential for national developmental strategies insofar as there is dependence on global value chains/networks.

But for China itself, there are both lessons and impact to be assessed on which there are burgeoning literatures. Here, a few simple assertions are offered from this literature.[47] First, in the past, Chinese economic development has been primarily based on rapidly expanding *domestic* markets. This has been accompanied by relatively rapid growth in labour productivity, contingent upon very high levels of investment and has given rise to increasing real wages and the emergence even of shortages for skilled labour.

Second, export growth has been of increasing importance more recently, with corresponding widening of China's trade surplus, but this has been more associated with lower levels of wages, for employment in sectors attached to foreign direct investment, particularly geared towards the processing trade. Whilst this has been large enough at least to account for China's total trade surplus, its contribution to value added is no more than 5% of Chinese GDP, more or less conforming to an enclave-type economy, typically found across multinational corporation activity across the world within export-processing zones, etc. But this should not be taken as typical of, nor predominant in, the Chinese economy and its success.

Third, the dependence of China upon banks for finance for industrial investment is staggering. As Carney (2009) reveals, it is proportionately roughly four times higher than for the United States, and at least double that of most other countries. This is, however, indicative of the *limited* extent of financialisation of the Chinese economy, since finance has derived primarily from state-owned banks that have been policy driven and instructed. Of course, this does not guarantee developmental success in the absence of other conditions but these are precisely what have been present in China where, nonetheless, development is fraught by the tensions associated with sustaining international competitiveness and domestic economic and social stability.

Fourth, this is indicative of the much more extensive reliance of China upon policies that have totally broken from the Washington Consensus in general and those for transition economies in particular, where the outcomes by comparison with Eastern Europe are salient.[48] Significantly, for a short period,

---

47   What follows draws heavily on Lo and Zhang (2011) and Lo (2010).
48   As well as, for example, for Vietnam, see Masina (2010).

China did succumb in the mid-1990s to some degree to policies inspired by the Washington Consensus but, as a matter of pragmatism in wake of the crisis this induced, it immediately abandoned them for policies of Keynesian expansionism led by welfare provision, a renewal of the role of the state sector, and reversal of foreign sector liberalisation.

Fifth, in this light, it is hardly surprising that a very wide spectrum of opinion from across different positions regarding the sources of China's success and its responsibility, or not, for prompting, aggravating or ameliorating the current crisis, have some common positions on how it should proceed – by expanding domestic production to serve both higher wages and higher levels of social provision, and reducing the overall level of domestic investment as a proportion of GDP. Indeed, such postures are in line with those being adopted by China itself.[49]

Nonetheless, sixth, myths do prevail concerning China and its role in the world economy. These tend to originate from an ethos of blame either incorrectly specifying factors or their causal roles in response to problems that derive other than from China itself. These include the idea of a global savings glut, unreasonable trade surplus and competitiveness from too low an exchange rate, and China's export growth at the expense of domestic consumption. In contrast, it should be emphasised that China's success or impact in these terms, properly interpreted, can only be of considerable benefit to the world economy (as well as its own) although the incidence of such benefits are uneven and possibly negative for some. Failure to realise these benefits is no fault of China and that they do not accrue for other, unrelated reasons, of which financialisation elsewhere is clearly culpable, is no reason to displace blame onto China.

More specifically, as far as China might serve as an enabling factor in the promotion of developmental states elsewhere, its size and diversity give rise to a complex mix of complementary opportunities and sources of competition. Inevitably, these are variously spread across different countries, at different stages of development, across different sectors, technological capabilities and levels of value-added, and corresponding position within global value chains/networks (Kaplinsky, 2008, on sub-Saharan Africa for example). Across the literature more generally, the levels of uncertainty and unevenness involved is conducive to appeal to metaphor as China is variously understood as "Engine, Conduit, or Steamroller?" (Haltmaier et al. 2007), or as a perpetrator of "Flying

---

49   See, for example, Lippit et al. (2011), Zhu and Kotz (2011), Hart-Landsberg (2011) and
        Piovani and Li (2011) in special issue of *Review of Radical Political Economics*, vol 43, no 1.

Geese or Sitting Ducks" (Ahearne et al. 2006). For Haltmaier et al. (2007) in particular, China offers large, growing and varied markets (including its own growing foreign tourism), as well as competition in own domestic and third-party markets for other countries. And it is a conduit for regional manufacture and assembling of goods across internationally fragmented production processes and markets and, p. 25:

> As China has moved up the value chain in recent years, increasing its presence in electronic high-tech exports in particular, there have also been shifts in the pattern of production in the other economies in the region. For instance, Japan and Korea have further increased their presence in the medium-tech automotive industry and Singapore has developed its biomedical sector. At the same time, the Philippines has increased its revealed comparative advantage in exports of electronic high-tech products, a large proportion of which are parts and components. However, our analysis of product displacement suggests that China's increasing export share has not reduced export growth for the other countries in the high-tech industries, although it has had a negative effect in the medium-tech and low-tech industries.

Further, though, the following implications are drawn, with the first proposition no doubt being tested much earlier than could have been anticipated:[50]

> First, although China's rise as an economic powerhouse is undisputed, at this point it is unlikely that emerging Asia could weather a significant slowdown in the U.S. economy, for example, without being noticeably affected. Second, our results on displacement of exports and changes in product mix of exports suggest that for some countries the rising trade in parts and components may be an endogenous response to competition from China, as these countries try to find areas of complementarity with China rather than compete head-to-head. Third, China's impact on the economies of the region is not uniform.

---

50   See also Zebregs (2004) for a detailed discussion of the rise of intraregional trade in Asia but who is quoted by Ahearne et al. (2006, p. 15) to the effect that, "the rise in intraregional trade is largely driven by rapidly growing intra-industry trade, which is a reflection of greater vertical specialization and the dispersion of production processes across borders. This has led to a sharp rise in trade in intermediate goods ... but the EU, Japan and the United States remain the main export markets for final goods".

And they continue, "Finally it should be emphasized that the debate on these issues is still evolving (the present paper included) and is difficult to settle. Additional research is needed".

Similarly, Ahearne et al. (2006, pp. 2–3) point to the varied manners in which global production is organised, possibly allowing for complementary patterns of growth:

> As an example of how vertical integration might make export growth rates similar, take the example of a small electronic device like a DVD player. The manufacturing of some components – e.g., motherboards, memory, etc. – might be handled in one or several of the ASEAN economies or the NIESs. Those components are then exported to, say, China, where they are assembled into the DVD player. The DVD player is then shipped out to its final destination. Several economies in the region might thus provide value-added to a single device. Hence, as demand for DVD players fluctuates, one would expect export growth to be positively correlated across economies.

However, they add, p. 14:

> When one looks at the sectoral data on U.S. imports from Asia, there is no doubt that China is displacing other Asian economies across a wide spectrum of markets. Not all of this displacement is symptomatic of competition. First, a significant portion of the final assembly of Asian-made products takes place in China.

And, further complicating matters, they observe that, "to some extent the changes in trade shares reflect a longer-term trend of China moving into the product space vacated by the Asian NIEs as they move to higher value-added products", p. 14, but also quoting McKinnon and Schnabl (2006), who suggest yet another role around intra- and inter-regional assembly for which, "China is merely the face of a worldwide export surge into American consumer markets", p. 15.

Here, given the diverse and shifting roles to be played by China, it is necessary to be mindful of the most recent lessons to be drawn from the Japanese experience. Prior to the emergence of China, it was seen as driving the Asian region and, with it, the potential for developmental states to emerge (Chia, 2007, for example). Its own malaise over the past two decades, and its turn towards a new 'industrial policy' based on infrastructure and social welfare, possibly to be reinforced by the tragic consequences of the tsunami, is a telling testimony not only of the need for continuing research in and of itself but because of how rapidly circumstances can change. And, as a result, as Haltmaier et al. (2007, pp. 25–6) suggest, "In particular, acquiring a more detailed understanding of the country-specific responses to the rapid emergence of China would be a fruitful line of further inquiry".

More generally, the DSP might paint too rosy a picture of what will be attempted, and what can be achieved at the national level in light of neoliberal globalisation and the constraints that this imposes. The extent to which these constraints prevail, in or out of global crisis, is yet to be tested and depends upon how it is addressed at both global and national (and other) levels.[51] For Hayashi (2010), for example, this means that neoliberal globalisation has not undermined the potential for developmental states.[52] Indeed, far from being outdated, they are necessary in order to integrate into the world economy, rather than protect from it, p. 62:

> the developmental state is a model of state-led industrialization for developing countries, where the market mechanism is underdeveloped or the market itself does not exist. The underdevelopment (or nonexistence) of the market means that the market does not signal which industries should grow or disappear. Under the circumstances, the government should be more proactive than just leaving any economic activity to the market: the government should identify which industries should be targeted and actually promote such industries. However, the means to promote particular industries do not have to equate to trade protectionism. Southeast Asian countries have implemented state-led industrialization by utilizing MNCs, and have been successfully upgrading their economic structure through FDI. Their experience provides an important insight when considering future strategies that today's developing countries could pursue.

This stands in sharp contrast to developmental state agnostics, not least Pirie (2013), who argues that the prospects for successful industrial policy on a broad and national front are limited by virtue of first-comer advantages of competitors and the scale of domestic markets that would need to be available to be

---

51 See Gray (2008) for the suggestion for South Korea, and possibly of wider relevance, that more prominent labour movements and democratic participation can be associated with incorporation into more favourable negotiating of neoliberal globalisation.

52 See also Rock et al. (2009) for discussion of developmental state, technological change and environmental sustainability in the context of globalisation.

able to compete even if protection were a viable policy option. The alternative is offered of national promotion of social provision as some insulation from global dominance.[53] Yet, the burden of these arguments surely depends upon the nature of the sectors concerned, how they are or can be organised and integrated nationally and internationally, and how domestic and international interests are forged and realised. This suggests the need to finesse a number of (false) dualisms – reformism versus revolution; nation-state versus globalisation; state versus market; and democracy versus authoritarianism, and so on. Each of these can only fit uncomfortably within the DSP itself as traditionally posed.

Yet, over the most recent period, the DSP has experienced a limited revival, to some degree stretching beyond the limitations previously highlighted here but without regaining the prominence previously enjoyed as a leading form of critique of the Washington Consensus. But it has done so in a way that tends to depart from its original ethos of examining the systemic role of the state in bringing about development (conceived as latecomer catch-up development). Instead, scope of application has been extended by incorporating any positive role played by the state as evidence of presence of a developmental state. First, for example, especially but not exclusively through the South Korean experience, the DSP has attracted renewed attention. Reports of its death have been taken to be exaggerated as the Asian crisis and its preconditions and aftermath have neither entirely dismantled state intervention but nor has the latter been detached from the influence of the chaebol, with corresponding consequences for the nature and depth of recession and speed and extent of recovery.[54] Consequently, different but continuing state intervention of different types, in different circumstances, and under different influences, lead the DSP to be invoked once more, with emphasis upon continuing state intervention to support both industrial and financial restructuring and the relations between them. After all, both state and development are involved, and so more or less casually constructed descriptors are deployed to resurrect the developmental state. Thus, for Chu (2009), there is a "reconfigured developmental state",

---

53 See Pirie (2013) for an even more pessimistic take on the potential of the developmental state model in an era of globalisation.

54 See Lee (2008) and also Kalinowski (2008) who supports Weiss (1999) and Thurbon and Weiss (2006) against Pirie (2005, 2006 and 2008) to the effect that the developmental state has not succumbed to neoliberalism in the wake of the crisis, although it does, for him, seem to be in its last death throes! Note that Bae and Sellers (2007) find for South Korea that democratisation can strengthen the developmental state in urban policy as technocracy is married with middle class interests as opposed to individualised pursuit of profitability.

geared towards the knowledge economy, in which "Korea remains inclined towards development and does so by serving as a leader and an arbitrator of interests. In seeking to attain its development goals, the Korean state articulates visions and deploys public resources to structure the market and shape innovation", p. 291 and see also Lim (2010) and Lee, K.-S. (2009), and Lee and Kwak (2009) for a comparative account of South Korea and Japan.

Wider afield, Kuriyan and Ray (2009), in an account of ICT industries in India, perceives public-private partnerships as a form of developmental state and, in a sophisticated analysis of the Tema port in Ghana, Chalfin (2010, p. 580) concludes that, emphasis added:

> The result is a port dominated by what can be described as a *neo(-liberal)* developmental state maintaining select features of an earlier statism rooted in the expansion of bureaucratic oversight and the protection of national interests and market share, now repurposed in line with a neo-liberal agenda focused on trade facilitation, multinational corporate advantage, and financial speculation.

The counterposing of neoliberal with developmental state is striking but raises the question of just how far the two can be accommodated with one another, conceptually and in practice.

Second, as suggested, the DSP has now come to serve as a blanket term for any circumstance in which there is state involvement and some aspect of development.[55] This also allows a certain promiscuity in forging relations between the DSP and other paradigms. For Yeung (2009), the development state is situated in relation to global production networks and regional integration; Gomez (2009) incorporates firm organisation by appeal to Chandler's approach to big business; Kwon and Yi (2009) and Kwon (2009) address poverty reduction and international policy transfer, respectively; Eimer and Lütz (2010) offers a comparative study of HIV/AIDS drugs policy across India and Brazil; Aiyede (2009) questions whether federalism can overcome predatory fragmentation; and de Haan (2010) is concerned with corruption, clientelism, patronage, resource curse, and rent-seeking, p.109:[56]

---

55   Reflecting more general features of development literature in which, for example, globalisation is attached to anything that is international or social capital to anything that is in civil society, etc. See Cornwall and Eade (eds) (2010) on buzzwords and fuzzwords in development discourse, for which the developmental state (and the state more generally other than the 'fragile') is notable for its total exclusion. Promotion of concepts by the World Bank is clearly necessary to make a buzz or fuzz!

56   See below for further examples of widening scope of application of the DSP.

So neo-patrimonial states do not have to democratize, liberalize and out-law corruption before they can become developmental states. But their political-administrative elites *do* have to feel a need – because of political pressure from society – to engage in a social contract for economic growth with their population instead of just engaging in a redistribution system of state revenues based on patronage and a fat bank account abroad.

Interestingly, such a prognosis within the political school is entirely without roots within particular economic activities at whatever stage of development.

The DSP is, in principle, and to some degree then in practice, of univer-sal applicability. Further, such widening of the scope of the approach is also unsurprising as those who are newly, or continue to be, attached to it, seek to find new avenues for their research. Mok (2007), Green (2007) and Gopinathan (2007) are concerned with the developmental state and (higher) education as East Asian NICs have responded to crisis; Neo (2007) with the environment; and Fritz and Menocal (2007), Sindzingre (2007), and Randall (2007) with aid, taxation and political parties, respectively. And industrial policy also benefits from a broader perspective, as Park (2007) examines the treatment of SMEs, Lazonick (2008) is mindful of entrepreneurship, Lee and Tee (2009) take on cluster analysis for the bio-medicine sector in Singapore, and Bowen (2007) weds global production networks to aircraft manufacture in the Asia-Pacific Rim.[57]

And, third, as in the past, newly emerging developmental states provide the raw material for further contributions, not least with China's economic miracle to the fore.[58] What is more novel is the goal of identifying developmental states

---

[57]   Block (2011) even refers to the USA's "hidden developmental state" in light of its high-tech dependence on state funding to military research. See also Peres and Primi (2009, p. 15) who refer to the US government, "permitting exclusive licenses for patented innova-tions only when the innovation is to be manufactured in the United States (section 204). Selecting US firms as the beneficiaries of these exclusive licenses – an action in line with the national strategy to protect the competitiveness of the country's industry – is clearly a de facto industrial policy, even though it takes the form of intellectual property rights management".

[58]   With some emphasis on provincial or local developmental states and their relations with the centre, see Liu (2008), Thun (2006), and Ferdinand (2007) for which Russia has become a developmental state alongside, if later and less effective, than China. Note that Cao (2009) examines the role of urban property in China for the presence, or not, of a (local) developmental state. See also Blecher (2008) for the ubiquitous emphasis on contradictions between local and central states across planning and promotion of private capital. For a contrary view around the retrenchment to the centre for major investment projects, see Kun-Chin (2007). See also Bateman et al. (2011) for a Colombian local devel-opmental state!

in the making. This is true of the hopes placed for a new developmental state on more progressive governments in Latin America, Moudud and Botchway (2008) and Caldentey (2008), as well as on Africa, Matlosa (2007) and Moudud and Botchway (2007). Barbara (2008, p. 311) views post-conflict states as potentially developmental since, "The economic environments of failed states provide extreme examples of market failure". And, in a bizarre way, developmental state optimism takes extreme form after a decade or more of neoliberalism, with the self-declaration of post-apartheid South Africa as a prospective candidate, all evidence to the contrary (Fine, 2010f; and Ashman et al. 2010). This is ironic given that most developmental states were, at least initially, blissfully unaware of their status as such whilst experiencing, let alone anticipating, it! They needed western academics to tell them what they were after they had already been it.

In short, the attempt to realise the goals of the DSP can potentially make a major contribution to the progressive transformation of global capitalism and national capitalisms although it does not offer a model or collection of models from which appropriate policy can be picked from the shelf. The DSP serves at most as a stepping stone that must be surpassed both analytically and strategically. But for the moment, at least, as neoliberal scholarship, ideology and policy in practice remain severely unchallenged in the alternatives being offered in the wake of global crisis, the DSP is worthy of critical attention as opposed to deliberate and far from benign neglect and marginalisation.

3 Industrial Policy

In many respects, discussion of industrial policy, especially for economists, has suffered a similar fate as the DSP. It has gone out of fashion. And, where it has clung onto survival at the margins, it has been marked and limited by its neoliberal alter ego of leaving everything to the market, reducing its methods, substantive content and scope of application. For, the new orthodoxy (market- and institutional-imperfections approach) around industrial policy still accepts a basic division as starting point between state and market, but accepts that there is a role for each, and that they can be complementary rather than antagonistic. Thus, for Hausmann and Rodrik (2006, p. 25):

> the government is only focused on providing complementary inputs to the market. It is not an issue of state vs. market. If the government does not provide the inputs, market efficiency will be low. In this world, laissez-faire is a dead-end street. Instead, the ideal alternative is for the

government to provide all the complementary inputs to all potential [market] activities.

Significantly, though, with the pro-active state only making up for the deficiencies of the market, this is all set within an analytical framework firmly grounded upon microeconomic principles and corresponding market imperfections. The latter are general and drawn from the microeconomics that has emerged over the past two decades to greater prominence and without development initially in mind as an application. It involves universal notions of potential market failure derived from the presence of externalities, scale economies, informational problems and those of coordination (Haque, 2007, p. 3, for example). And, although occasional and even inevitable reference is made to the macro or systemic aspects involved in development and industrialisation, especially in pursuit of structural change (however understood), the thrust of the approach is to favour the market (or globalisation) other than in piecemeal and selective interventions to correct market imperfections. In this respect, the limited departure from the Washington Consensus is striking. For the latter also offers no concept of development as opposed to a putative mechanism to deliver it, reliance upon market forces. By the same token, enhancing or complementing the market by piecemeal state intervention offers little more insight into the nature of development and industrialisation.

As a result, the Washington Consensus can be seen to have had the effect of narrowing down how industrial policy has been conceived, not least if ironically in the opposition to its neglect over the past decade. This has occurred on a number of levels. One has been, as already suggested, in the extent to which industrial policy has been transformed from a mechanism for systemic industrialisation and development into an instrument for correcting market imperfections. At a second level, what counts as industrial policy has been unduly circumscribed. Whilst in principle anything falling under the rubric of market imperfections could count as a prompt to corrective industrial policy, the Washington Consensus has funnelled attention into a few, particular directions. The most obvious and prominent has been trade policy, followed closely by privatisation. This does itself reflect a more longstanding feature within the industrial policy literature of its being subject to fashions and shifting, but limited, focus on particular factors – trade policy, competition policy, promotion of SMEs, privatisation, skills, technology, and so on. Industrial policy has tended to search out and hit upon either highlighted obstacles to be remedied or removed, or magic bullets to be targeted, with specific factors and case studies being unduly generalised. In a sense the Washington Consensus is an extreme case with the market as the golden shot, and the state as the impediment.

At a third level, and by the same token, the goals of industrial policy have been unduly reduced to some sort of notion of (international) competitive success and survival as if market criteria for the firm or industry were sufficient in and of themselves. In the limit, market success has been taken as the ultimate and exclusive goal. Or such success could be understood to be an efficient and effective way to allow for other objectives to be pursued in principle without examining whether this occurs in practice (exports to earn foreign exchange are taken as sufficient in and of themselves without examining whether these earnings are retained or shifted abroad for example). And the same neglect applies to the broader, systemic goals and drawbacks of development whether it be industrialisation or environmental degradation, respectively.

Further, whilst it has now become fashionable to emphasise diversity, complexity and context in considering industrial policy, these are often endowed with a shallow content, no more than is necessary to move beyond the one model fits all point of departure, and one that tends to be removed from broader economic and social goals and the transitions associated with, and as a component part of, development and industrialisation themselves. Consequently, and in contrast, industrial policy should both elaborate broader goals than simply attaining competitive survival and incorporate or integrate them with other processes and policies. The goals and means of modernisation attached to what might be termed the Pre-Washington Consensus, as it were, need to be reinterpreted and reformed in light of historical experience and the transformations to contemporary conditions.

It would be a mistake, however, to see each individual contribution or all contributions taken collectively as simply collapsing the goals and instruments of industrial policy. Rather, it is more useful to recognise that there are tensions within the literature. As already remarked, whatever the practice, the principle underpinning much discussion of industrial policy is that it is necessary to correct market imperfections, and these are extraordinarily wide-ranging across the literature especially when case studies are gathered together. For these cover each and every aspect of industrial performance – technology, finance, markets, skills, competition, trade and so on. Further, as Haque (2007, p. 1) notes, "Contrary to a general perception – born out of the current sway of the neoliberal orthodoxy – industrial policy is alive and well". And Rodrik is cited to the effect that, "The reality is that industrial policies have run rampant during the last decades – and nowhere more so than in those economies that have steadfastly adopted the agenda of orthodox reform". A literature search on the scholarship over the past few years reveals thousands of examples of industrial policy successfully implemented, although much of this both focuses upon (new) technology and is not to be found heavily present within the mainstream economics literature.

As mentioned, this raises questions over whether the market imperfection theoretical approach to industrial policy can accommodate the evidence gained from case study material. Consider trade policy for example. The Washington Consensus offers an approach in which it is advised that levels of effective protection should be reduced in order that developing countries should be disciplined by world prices. This presumes, however, that the notion of effective protection is itself well-founded, that it can be appropriately measured, and that a policy of reducing effective protection is advantageous. As summarised in Deraniyagala and Fine (2001 and 2006) by reference to various contributions to the literature, such propositions depend upon a series of wildly unrealistic assumptions ranging over there only being two sectors in the economy, perfect competition in all markets, full employment of resources, no intra-affiliate trade, on which see Bhaduri (2005), no non-tradeables, no scale effects, even uncertainty of outcomes across sectors of different capital-intensity, and so on (including absence of smuggling and transfer-pricing!).

Similar considerations will apply to other elements of industrial policy where the incidence of market imperfections are equally legion. The issue is not so much that this renders the Washington Consensus nirvana of the free market as otiose, as it does, as how to pose alternatives across a multitude of so obviously relevant factors in influencing industrial performance. In this light, the response from the orthodoxy that still favours the market is significant. For Pack and Saggi (2006, p. 267) accept the case for industrial policy in principle if rejecting it in practice because of the complexities involved, particularly in view of globalisation (as the "dominance of international production networks"). Indeed, "Overall, there appears to be little empirical support for an activist government policy even though market failures exist that can, in principle, justify the use of industrial policy".

In practice, however, their argument in favour of this conclusion is *not* drawn from the empirical evidence but from speculative reasoning around the capabilities of government, even leaving aside "the possibilities of rent-seeking", p. 282. They suggest that the breadth and depth of knowledge necessary for a policymaker are too demanding. Indeed, "They would have to be accurately informed about an enormous range of complex questions, understand their relevance, and be able to accurately evaluate subtle differences". They go on to list what is involved as a minimum, pp. 281/2:[59]

- The firms and industries that generate knowledge spillovers.
- The firms and industries that benefit from dynamic scale economies – the precise path of such learning and the magnitude of the cost disadvantage at each stage of the learning process.
- The sectors that have a long-term comparative advantage.
- The size of scale economies of different firms and sectors, to facilitate investment coordination.
- An ability superior to that of individual firms to learn about their potential competitiveness.
- The nature and extent of capital market failures.
- The magnitude and direction of interindustry spillovers.
- The relative amount of learning by individual firms from others and from their own experience.
- The extent to which early entrants generate benefits for future entrants.
- The extent of heterogeneity of firms' learning abilities.
- Whether consumers learn the quality of a good after consuming rather than by inspecting it.
- Whether firms that are trying to reduce production costs also begin a simultaneous effort to improve their product's quality to obtain a better reputation.
- The potential effects of FDI or international trade on coordination problems, including a detailed knowledge of which of tens of thousands of intermediates are tradable.
- A forecast of which firms can create new knowledge and discover better production methods.
- The spillover effects of FDI and the likely intensity of foreign purchase of domestic intermediates.

The conclusion drawn is that no state is capable of meeting these demands and, paradoxically, doubts are cast on whether the private (consulting) sector could do it either, "Quite apart from the dangers of optimal policy being subverted by industries and firms that would benefit, the sheer knowledge and skill requirements would exceed that possessed by almost any institution, including the best consulting firms".

Through this prism, it is remarkable that any development continues to take place at all, given that the same demands will have to be met by the private

---

59   See also Pack (2011) in commenting on Lin and Monga (2011a).

sector in the absence of the state. In effect, this is simply the argument about the state being unable to create or pick winners raised to a higher and more detailed level. These and other demands upon the state in making industrial policy have to be assessed against goals, what would happen otherwise and what can be achieved rather than simply denying "that government officials might be this omniscient". What is interesting here, then, is less the dogma of relying upon the market – even on its own terms, the issues raised do not lead to this conclusion – as the acknowledgement of the complexity and diversity of considerations to be broached by the state. Strikingly, the laissez-faire argument has shifted from one of the free market being a simplistic choice against the alternative of state, to one of being the only satisfactory way to deal with the complexity of market and other choices.

Yet, those more favourable to state intervention to promote industry do not depart substantially from a similar conclusion. For Hausmann and Rodrik (2006, p. 25), as noted above, the ideal is for the state to intervene perfectly to complement the market. It cannot do so for two reasons. First is because "it is unaffordable. The government cannot address all potential infrastructure needs or fix all the standards and rules affecting all existing and potential economic activities. It would overwhelm its financial, managerial and political resources". Second, "the list of interventions is unknowable ex ante. Institutions and markets co-evolve and this implies that transaction costs and problems will be revealed as new transactions appear and new markets develop. Solutions have to fit the specifics of the context. This may be the reason why there is such an enormous variability of institutional arrangements across industrial countries". As a result, Hausmann and Rodrik recommend that the state limit itself to providing the framework within which the private sector can best seek out the way forward, a process of enhancing what they term "self-discovery" in another paper (Hausmann and Rodrik, 2003). Analytically, then, there is very little to distinguish Hausmann and Rodrik from Pack and Saggi. One is just a little more state-friendly than the other in supporting the private sector, and arbitrarily so in denying a more extensive intervention because it cannot be perfect. Indeed, emphasis on correcting static market imperfections has given way to a parallel universe in which a neo-Austrian commitment to the free market as a recipe for innovation is complemented by some degree of state support to facilitate that innovation or path of discovery.[60]

---

60   See also Lin and Monga (2011a) with the added false nostrum that failed industrialisation in the past must be due to failed industrial policy (as opposed to failed market forces which have not been, for them, adequately corrected).

Interestingly, part of the argument of Hausmann and Rodrik is that, empirically, there is no consistent relation between comparative advantage based on factor endowments and patterns of production and trade. This is because they see comparative advantage as evolving over time in a path-dependent way, using the analogy of a monkey jumping from tree to tree in a dense forest, with the result that outcomes depend upon differing co-evolving institutional arrangements. But this all points to a much deeper conclusion to the effect that either comparative advantage is a tautology (you are competitive in what you are competitive) or it has no analytical purchase (there are no underlying and fixed determinants of industrial performance such as factor endowments). As Hausmann and Rodrik rightly argue, this renders industrial development to be context specific. But their understanding of context, as well as path dependence, is relatively limited depending upon a monkey-swinging in-the-forest analogy at one extreme and co-evolving institutions and markets at the other. Whilst this marks a welcome and explicit shift away from the one model fits all associated with the earlier Washington Consensus, with emphasis instead placed upon piecemeal correction of institutional and market imperfections, this shift is itself both piecemeal and insufficient in remaining heavily marked both by its origins within mainstream economics and by taking the Washington Consensus as critical point of departure. In a sense, the new approach, which claims both universal applicability and wide consent, might be dubbed a "one model of one model does not fill all". Significantly, as already observed, Rodrik's own recent collection of essays is entitled, *One Economics, Many Recipes*, and Hausmann and Rodrik (2006) see "Industrial Policy as Predicament".

Corresponding limitations in approach can be seen from a different perspective, and from what is in general a different literature, one more concerned with understanding and reflecting upon industrial policy in practice through case study rather than speculative reasoning. This immediately confronts the problem of providing a definition of industrial policy. As Välilä (2008, p. 101) puts it:

> It is difficult to define industrial policy unambiguously ... Against this background, it is hardly surprising that the quest for a common definition of industrial policy is often abandoned in favour of a looser delineation of the concept or even in favour of outright agnosticism ... 'Industrial policy' is the label that has come to be used to describe a wide-ranging, ill-assorted collection of micro-based supply-side initiatives which are designed to improve market performance in a variety of occasionally mutually inconsistent ways. Even in the absence of a universally agreed definition, industrial policy has nevertheless been recognised as a distinct

area of economic policy in its own right, so there has to be a way to characterise it, if not define it.

At one extreme, as already suggested, there have been fashions in which particular policies have come in and out of favour as definitions of industrial policy. This suggests that a more comprehensive definition would gather these together as a composite set of policies that might be used to promote industry.[61]

The result is to move close to, but not as far as the opposite extreme to single policies, in which industrial policy is perceived to be synonymous with any policy that affects the performance of industry. As Lin and Monga (2011b, p. 304) put it:

> It is useful to start by stressing that every country in the world, intentionally or not, pursues industrial policy ... This is surprising only if one forgets that industrial policy broadly refers to *any* government decision, regulation or law that encourages ongoing activity or investment in a particular industry.

In general, this is seen to be too far-ranging as almost all policies will have some effect on some industries. Consequently, Pelkmans (2006, p. 47) structures "policies (somehow) affecting industry" into two broad categories – those "NOT for industry" and those that are. The latter is itself then subdivided into what are still not designated as industrial policy (regional planning and price control, for example) and those that are included in a "(Wide concept of) industrial policy", comprising three categories – framework aspects, and horizontal and sectoral/specific industrial policy (see below). Otherwise, there are intermediate definitions, as is the one favoured by Memiş and Montes (2008, p. 45) in following Chang (1993), "It is useful here to summarize the key points of this paper. Industrial policy is the application of selective government interventions to favour certain sectors so that their expansion benefits the productivity of the economy as a whole".

Not surprisingly, the conundrum surrounding what is industrial policy is complemented by similar doubts about how. For Välilä (2008, p. 101):

---

61   For some discussion of these conundrums, see Peres and Primi (2009, p. 13) who observe, "The literature defines industrial policy in different ways, emphasizing various aspects of State intervention in support of industrialization". Note they also distinguish between macro and micro interventions although it can be argued these distinctions are questionable given how vertical and horizontal factors straddle macro/micro.

There is in general no public agency devoted to industrial policy, nor is there a legal framework for industrial policy. Second, and again in contrast with most other areas of economic policy, industrial policy does not have a well-identified and universally recognised set of goals to achieve. Industrial policy has goals, such as innovation support or protection of sectors in decline, but those goals change over time and from country to country. And finally, industrial policy does not possess a clearly identifiable tool kit of policy instruments that would be devoted exclusively to achieving the goals of industrial policy.

In similar vein, Bianchi and Labory (2006, p. 23–4) conclude that, "Our definition of industrial development policies implies a new view of the debate: what is relevant is not whether selective or functional policies are useful but what is the appropriate mix of measures to determine industrial development. Industrial development policies are programmes or strategies consisting of a variety of measures (both rules and capabilities), the mix of which is specific to a country's conditions and historical experience". Thus, "the 'new' industrial policies consist of large sets of measures that aim at providing the appropriate framework for industrial development to take place, via both the creation of firms and sectors (creation of comparative advantages) and the structural change of existing firms (structural change)". And, in relating competition to industrial policy, Lorentzen and Møllgaard (2006, p. 130) conclude that, whilst "competition policy is rule-bound ... By contrast, industrial policy can afford to be much more eclectic: what works, works ... Hence there is no one-size-fits-all".

Across such literature, industrial policies tend to be divided into three categories: the horizontal which, in principle, could influence each industry, as in trade, competition or innovation policy; the vertical that is targeted to particular sectors; and the structural that are designed to promote a compositional shift in economic activity, either in downsizing or expanding particular sectors (although this might be thought to be part of, or to straddle, the other two categories), see Välilä (2008, p. 103) for example. Especially for the first of these, there is a very large number of factors involved in terms of the determinants of industrial performance even in the narrow sense of competitive success. And each of these factors commands a rich and contested literature over the role of trade, competition, and innovation as well as finance, sources of investment, skills, labour markets, regulation, privatisation, and so on. By the same token, the intersection of these factors within particular sectors is bound to be different from one sector to another and from one country to another for the same sector (and across global value chains and networks).

This diversity is itself complemented by two further complicating factors, both of which have already been raised. On the one hand, possibly reflecting the amorphous nature of industrial policy, it tends to be subject to a mix of policy-making institutions, more or less dedicated to the purpose. These range over competition boards, regulatory authorities, sectoral associations, quite apart from the various government departments and ministries. There are inevitably problems of insufficient powers to make policy as well as of coordination of powers where they do exist in policymaking. The corresponding potential for lack of instruments, goals and institutions in the making of industrial policy leads Välilä (2008) somewhat precipitously to presume that it is, or even should be, narrowed down in scope. In a perverse way, this point, concerning both the scope of industrial policy and its interaction if not inclusion with other forms of policy and policymaking, is revealed by the way in which international trade disputes (as one element of industrial policy) have spilled over into issues around unfair competition through discriminatory pricing, competition policy, subsidies to training and research and development, and so on. As it were, anything that the state does that might improve industrial performance is open to be deemed to be unfair in a trade dispute.

On the other hand, particularly in the context of industrialisation and development, the goals of industrial policy need to be expanded to incorporate much more than competitive success (as well as questioning what success means), with achievement to be assessed in terms not only of growth, productivity increase, trade balance but also of employment generated, wages and conditions in general and across different socio-economic strata, skills engendered, linkages to other sectors, and so on.

On this last point, Mackintosh et al. (2007) confirm that the blinkered analysis of industrial policy derived from the one market model fits all has closed down the breadth of considered policy space. In addition, though, this has precluded consideration of the relationship between social sectors and industrial policy. More specifically, for Paci and Schweitzer (2006, p. 301), "The health sector is made up of a significant number of inter-connected industries that produce health services and manufactured goods, including pharmaceuticals and medical equipment". They identify three clusters of industries: healthcare providers, financiers and manufacturers. This leads to the conclusion that, "Policy towards health could be reconsidered, in order to take account of this broad concept of the health industry, as a system of intertwined actors and thus also industrial policy, can be implemented in this field", p. 302. It inevitably follows that there are synergies between health and industrial policy, and the same would apply to other elements of economic and social provision, including basic needs such as housing and education, as these too incorporate and/or are attached to industrial sectors.

This all leads here to a different and novel approach to the definition of industrial policy, one that does not seek a more or less arbitrary general definition of narrower or wider scope that can be applied in specific instances. Instead, first, it allows for case study and policy analysis itself to identify the key areas for intervention although, as will be seen, this does not imply neglect of the various factors that inform policymaking and industrial performance. In other words, context and specificity is understood in a different way, to be empirically induced rather than imposed by choice of model and corresponding configuration of given factors. Perhaps, although it can also be misleading, the most appropriate analogy is with the idea of national culture for which general models are neither appropriate for the diversity within and between countries although general considerations can be identified. Similarly, industrial policy will have its own culture or cultures, deeply rooted in the economic and social history and the continuing structures, relations, agencies and practices within the economy and, for which, the approach associated with national systems of innovation offers some insight. This is because of its emphasis on empirically grounded attention to evolution, institutions, networks and so on.

Second, emphasis is placed upon how the state and market are integrally related, especially in the context of development, and that one is not necessarily or simply at the expense, or even the complement, of the other. As a result, it is a matter of exploring the *underlying* factors that allow for synergy between state and market and how to mobilise these for development. This is recognised in the older development economics where industrialisation is not simply seen as structural change in the sense of changing composition of output but as part and parcel of a wider process of transition involving class relations, urbanisation, agricultural transition, and so on, as indicated by the admittedly heavily disputed notion of modernisation.

Third, traditional measures and achievement of industrial success are important (competitiveness and productivity increase, etc) but they have to be set against wider goals related to economic and social development. These wider goals are what constitutes horizontal or strategic factors that are both the conditions and consequences, and hence the instruments and targets, of industrialisation. Not only employment generation, but what kind of employment in terms of wages and conditions as well as the creation of, and transformation in, labour markets form one such horizontal factor.

Fourth, industrial policy does need to be targeted to specific sectors and the location of such sectors within the economy in terms of its inputs and outputs and impact upon economic performance narrowly conceived (most narrowly in input-output terms but more broadly in terms of the agents, structures and processes involved in provision). Such a vertical approach, however, needs to be complemented by a horizontal approach, incorporating the strategic requirements and contributions attached to industrial performance. These range over finance for investment, technology, skills, environment, markets, infrastructure, employment intensity and creation, balance of payments impact, poverty alleviation, and so on. Conversely, such horizontal factors need to be addressed as part and parcel of industrial policy – how the financial system functions, how technology and skills are to be generated and retained, gender, regional, environmental and other balances, and so on.

Fifth, the heady and diverse mixes of horizontal and vertical factors within and between economies, with correspondingly different priorities and content in policies, is the reason why 'industrial policy' as such needs to be context specific. But there is equally the danger of overlooking the macro or systemic functioning within which industrial policy and transformation is occurring. So, it is also important to take a view on the structure and dynamic of the economy and society within and through which policy is being directed in order to gauge both potential feasibility and impact.

Sixth, readily overlooked and treated as secondary, is organising the systematic collection of adequate data for the policy process. Without such data, it is neither possible to formulate policy adequately nor to monitor its effects. Further, government departments must have the skills and motivation to carry out the necessary policy work. And there must be the determination to overcome, or incorporate, underlying economic and political interests in formulating, implementing and monitoring (and providing feedback to) policy. These aspects must be carried forward together with, for example, data collection responding to the impact analysis of policy work, and policy responding to and informing monitored outcomes.

Last, and as a special instance of much that has gone before, the most recent financial turbulence on a global scale has revealed the extent to which the increasing financialisation over the past thirty years is now proving extraordinarily dysfunctional for economic performance in general and for industrial policy in particular. The impact of financial crises on industrial performance can be devastating, both more or less directly in collapsing market demand and finance for investment, and indirectly through the resources and capabilities that are gathered to shore up the financial sector itself at the expense of other activities and provision. In this light, careful attention needs to be paid to how industrial (and other policy) can be insulated from, rather than subordinated to, finance with testing issues to be addressed in terms of the internal workings of the domestic financial system and its integration into global finance.

This bears further consideration, not least because the dysfunction attached to financial crisis ought necessarily to raise the issue of the extent to which this is normal in some sense as opposed to exceptional for being particularly acute. The central concern must be to what extent has the rise of finance met the aims of economic and social development, not only in providing financial services (and profits) but also in generating finance for industry and for government expenditure more generally. And, in the realms of both policy and resource allocation, there are questions concerning whether the vested interests and (free market) ideology of finance has prevailed at the expense of other interests and stances, not least given the extent to which finance has currently shown itself to be excessively dependent upon the state to save both itself and the wider economy from collapse.

In this respect, the experience of China offers a salutary lesson in terms of the extent to which finance has, to a large degree, remained under central control. In making the contrast between China and elsewhere, Lo (2007, p. 207) suggests, "There is thus an intrinsic contradiction with financialization: the speculative pursuits of profitability tend to crowd out productive activities, therefore resulting in systemic demand deficiency and undermining the sources of profitability". More generally, as argued in detail by Jomo (2008), the financialisation associated with neoliberalism has failed to deliver on any of its putative benefits for the functioning of individual economies and for the global economy as a whole. Moreover, remedial measures need to be extensive at national and international levels. In this respect, the relatively recent, but now largely set aside, distinction between bank-based and market-based financial systems needs to be revived as well as refined and developed now that the previously triumphant market-based approach has been thoroughly discredited. It is a matter of placing finance at the service of industrial policy and investment, and of developmental goals more generally, and the same applies to macroeconomic policy (for which it is significant how huge sums of government funding can be found to support the financial system during a crisis whilst these were denied for health, education and welfare during more prosperous circumstances). Significant is the extent to which the East Asian NICs subordinated both finance and macro-policy to developmental goals rather than vice-versa. In addition, the deregulation of the financial system has both raised volatility and removed the mechanisms for handling it, other than through extremely costly holdings of foreign reserves (quite apart from capital flight both legal and illegal) (Rodrik, 2006; and Ndikumana and Boyce, 2008).

Of course, finance, and corresponding financial systems across varieties of markets and functions, each of which will have its own country-specifics as well as integration with international and state finance, is just one of a number of horizontal or strategic factors that will need to be addressed in and of itself and in its particular incidence upon industrial policy in its vertical or sectoral aspects. The issues involved are very different in case of direct foreign investment of a multinational corporation as opposed to small-scale enterprises serving localised markets. And the same applies to the difference in the role of finance in case of primary commodity exports (themselves to be differentiated from agriculture through to precious metals) as opposed to clothing, say, or casualised and informal sectors.

For industrial policy, required across each of these horizontal factors is to break not only with the mantra of the Washington Consensus but also with the limited departure from the laissez-faire approach that has already been delineated. This entails an analytical departure from the market/institutional imperfection framework and a more extensive empirically grounded input from historical experience as begins to be provided by the developmental state approach. In case of direct foreign investment, for example, it can offer varieties of benefits from increased exports through to technological upgrading. But this is far from the inevitable consequence of adopting policies in pursuit of a spurious business-friendly environment or competing in sweet-heart deals for investment by affiliates (Memiş and Montes, 2008, p. 3). Rather, the accrual of benefits from direct foreign investment have to be anticipated in advance, not only in principle, but also through negotiation and by putting in place the mechanisms and policies by which there is technological and other spill-over.

In this context, technology itself needs to be unpicked with a considerable degree of sophistication that goes far beyond either the pursuit or sustaining of "self-discovery" or the more general orthodoxy that perceives technological progress as a shift in a production function whether through expenditure for that purpose (R&D) or through some induced but undervalued externality such as spill-over or learning-by-doing. In the latter respect, the literature taken as a whole has recognised the complexity of what is involved, with the potential for learning not only by doing but also by exporting, importing, adopting, adapting, licensing and so on. This only begins to draw out the complexities of both the nature of technology and the causes and consequences of the ways in which it evolves. There are differences across sectors as well as in the demands between catching up in technology and moving beyond what is always itself an evolving technological frontier, and how each of these aspects fits differentially and over time into the chains of activities that comprise industrial linkages and interactions, see previous discussion of flying geese, etc.

The role of the state sector is also imperative. It is, after all, a large consumer itself and can use its purchasing power as a lever for other policies. It plays a major role in the provision of economic and social infrastructures,

themselves a part of, or heavily linked to, industry. The marked shift away from
the dogma of privatisation is, in terms of perceiving the state as supporting the
private sector to deliver and responsible for improving conditions of competition and regulation, sorely inadequate as the backdrop and basis for industrial policy. Taken together, there is no guarantee that what is generally the
limited scope of interventions that can be made by trade, competition and
regulation authorities is sufficient to generate sufficient levels of investment,
appropriate technologies, skills and welfare of the workforce, and so on. The
issue is, however, not simply to counterpose state versus private enterprise –
the commanding heights versus the free market or somewhere in between –
but to formulate strategic and sectoral goals and examine how they might best
be achieved, in which the incidence of form of ownership is just one part. In
this respect, it may be necessary to reform the institutions for making industrial policy so that the allocation and coordination of responsibilities across
government departments is rationalised and coherent. Specific sectors may
require their own authorities rather than relying upon the government departments set up for general purposes, to bring together and integrate the various
elements involved such as training, technology, investment levels, pricing, and
so on (Fine, 1998d for a telling example drawn from South African steel whose
prognoses have been borne out).

And, apart from being a consumer, the state is a filter and funnel for many
other policy goals that should be accommodated by industrial policy, whether
as intermediate targets (such as export earnings), meeting basic needs, reducing poverty and inequality, etc. Some form of social cost-benefit needs to be
made to inform policymaking, but there is no reason to presume that the
weights given to objectives should remain constant over time or across different horizontal or vertical issues (as a big push might be made for skills or health
from time to time). Nor is it the case that the enhancement of employment
and working conditions must be at the expense of other goals otherwise, of
course, the more developed countries would have even worse such conditions
than the developing! As found in Sri Lanka, for example, the consequences
of labour repression, in pursuit of wage reduction and undermining of trade
unions, can be counterproductive by precluding the potential for orderly collective bargaining and prompting economic and social disruption in its place.
As Teitelbaum (2007, p. 830) puts it:

> Beginning in the late 1970s, the Sri Lankan government adopted a labour-
> repressive export-oriented strategy of development ... repression of pri-
> vate sector unions during this period destroyed the legitimacy of tradi-
> tional left unions and the structure of institutionalised bargaining that

was in place prior to Sri Lanka's authoritarian period. This erosion of the system of institutionalised bargaining eventually led workers to shift their support to more radical, 'new left' unions and culminated in a wave of extreme and violent forms of protest that chased away much needed foreign direct investment. The chaotic consequences of the labour repression suggest two primary conclusions: (a) that prior democratic mobilisation may make labour repression untenable over the long term; and (b) that repression may backfire, creating bursts of highly visible and destabilising protest that undermine the developmental objectives of neoliberal reforms.

Similar, if far from identical, considerations apply to the role played by the use of migrant labour to undermine secure pay and conditions, whether this leads to xenophobic protests and/or low-wage, low-cost, low productivity employment as opposed to upgrading and improved working conditions (Selwyn, 2007 for grape production in Brazil; and Champlin and Hake, 2006 for a fascinating study of meatpacking within the most developed country).

For reasons that should be apparent, there has been an inclination in discussing industrial policy to jump between a number of models, whether corresponding or not to different ideal types of developing countries at different stages of development and/or with particular characteristics such as composition of outputs, balance of exports, etc. One set of models is pitched at the macro-level although it comes in a number of forms. It may be driven by Kaldorian notions of demand-led productivity increase, motivated by the salience of (dynamic) economies of scale and scope, or by import-substituting or export-oriented industrialisation. It may draw upon the notion of linkages from consumer to capital goods, from low-skill, low-technology, low value-added production to its high counterparts. And it may focus upon enhancing one or more indispensable factor in the processes involved, generically organised under notions of productive capabilities. Further, models of (industrial) development are increasingly recognising the skewed but shifting impact of global factors, around the patterns of access to trade, finance and (international) investment as well as insertion into global value chains and networks.

The point is less to accept or reject these models as such rather than to acknowledge that each offers some insight if take in conjunction with other relevant factors (or those judiciously chosen from other models). This is just to reiterate the previously argued proposition that industrial policy should be inductively derived from which the broad models around stages, processes and targets and instruments of policy, associated with the corresponding literature, can offer rich lessons, if not, to emphasise once more, models and

blueprints to be emulated. To some extent, such uncertainties and complexities have been implicitly acknowledged but in two ways that are constructive
in the form taken.

One of these is to be associated with Dani Rodrik and his collaborators, see
above. In a sense, this offers an unwitting and diluted form of the DSP (which
it otherwise ignores). It is vehemently opposed to the Washington Consensus,
viewing state intervention as imperative to successful industrialisation. And,
equally, it accepts that the contextual specificity of discovering, exploiting and
developing comparative advantage is complex, diverse and difficult to model
and capture. Accordingly, the conclusion drawn is that the state's (industrial
policy) interventions should be limited to those that facilitate "self-discovery"
on the part of entrepreneurs through publicly provided support to infrastructure, training, skills, etc.

Crucially, this conclusion of light intervention does not follow from the correct premise of the diversity, complexity and contextual content of industrial
policy. The agency of the state may well perform better in self-discovery quite
apart from consideration of broader goals of development itself, of incorporating interests and participation of interests other than entrepreneurs, and of
developing institutional capacities of the state to promote self-discovery (or
more) where or whether this is, indeed, the appropriate focus for industrial
policy in particular circumstances. In short, the support self-discovery model
of industrial policy is this and no more; one model amongst many, of limited
applicability on its own in the absence of, and integration with, other models
and aspects of development. It also avoids, rather than addresses, the what,
where and how of industrial policy as far as the extent of state intervention is
concerned. There is also a notable absence of account of interests and determinants other than those conjured up out of state-entrepreneur relations
engaged in an exercise of self-discovery. This is at the expense of the other
constituencies (such as labour, and corresponding meeting of basic needs) and
other processes at both macro- and micro-levels, particularly as entrepreneurs
may be induced to discover the short-term rewards of capital flight, financial
speculation, and credit-induced consumption at the expense of productive
investment.[62]

Essentially, the Rodrik school eschews more extensive interventionism
because of (recognition of) complexities, etc. At the other extreme, especially
in the context of LDCs being heavily dependent upon a few agricultural or

---

62   For a debate on these issues in the context of South Africa, see Fine (2009b and c) and
      Hausmann and Andrews (2009).

primary products and with the most limited presence even in elementary manufacture, there is an understandable inclination to locate such economies and industrial policy as belonging at a particular, early stage of development. Consequently, industrial policy can be perceived relatively simply in abstract terms as involving the shift to the next stage of industrialisation.

This, however, begs a number of questions concerning the nature and dynamic within and across stages of (industrial) development. How do we know what is the current and next stage and how do we achieve it? As evidenced by the BRICS, and especially China, such economies simultaneously span and encompass all of these stages of development on both domestic and global scales. Of course, most LDCs are considerably smaller than the BRICS, and market size and scale of domestic resources are germane considerations (although, for example, shift to global networks in agriculture to serve affluent markets in the north both leapfrogs stages of development to some degree and offers local opportunities for industrialisation depending on how such production is served in its manufactured inputs whether at set-up or in passing on capacity and capability as part of conditions attached to foreign investment and participation). In any case the inductive approach to industrial policy is not primarily motivated, nor exhausted, by the presence of a more or less simple industrial structure. Rather, the complexity and diversity of industrial policy, and the need for an inductive if theoretically informed approach, derives from contextual specificity not from complexity of industrial structure or composition of output as such (although these are of considerable importance in an inductive approach itself in terms of integration of policy needs and performance within and across sectors). Once again, the specification of LDCs at an early stage of (pre-)industrialisation is a model (with variable and contested content) with corresponding strengths and weaknesses for policy-making, although equally offering rich lessons from comparative and historical experience.

Such considerations are brought to the fore in locating industrial policy in a wider developmental context, specifically in targeting both the meeting of basic needs and economic and social transformation. For, many of the activities associated with early stages of industrial development and meeting basic needs are labour-intensive and are open to domestic production. This is especially so for (the inputs into) social and economic infrastructure. The same applies to clothing and food processing. It is essential that these are seen as part and parcel of industrial policy, with corresponding attention to the inductively incorporated horizontal and vertical factors previously delineated. And models and blueprints, or categories of LDCs at different stages of development, of general applicability can at most serve as a guide for more contextually-sensitive analysis.

4   South-South Cooperation by Way of Conclusion

From our previous accounts, it is apparent that each of developmental state and industrial policy serves as an umbrella term. They do so for a complex, diverse, shifting and selective amalgams of factors with equally varied incidence across historically, socially, institutionally and country specific causes and outcomes. Necessary to take into account, there are different *stages* and *aspects* of development for putative developmental states to negotiate. These range far beyond latecomer catch-up industrialisation to earlier and later stages of development. For this, corresponding technological and production paradigms are potentially more varied and more liable to be misled than led by notions of flying geese (and other metaphors). Industrial policy needs to be derived inductively through case-by-case study from refined consideration of a multitude of horizontal and vertical factors specific to sectors and countries. Horizontal factors are generic across the economy as whole such as levels of employment and skills. Vertical factors relate to the chain of activity specific to the industrial sector itself. It is necessary to reject the notion that one or more models can suffice to fit all circumstances, even if selected from a portfolio for application. This is also so of inappropriately relying upon mantras, or dogmas, concerning privatisation, trade liberalisation or not, and so on. Developmental states also need to address other aspects of development such as the role of agriculture, welfare, the shifting nature and incidence (and corresponding constraints and opportunities offered by) global factors, and relations beyond those between state and industry (to incorporate the role of labour and democratisation and institutions beyond those that facilitate industrial policy directly).

Similarly, in and of itself and as a key element for developmental states and development itself, it is necessary that social policy is neither specified merely as a safety net nor as poverty relief alone. Indeed, these should be rejected even as defining the core of social policy although they do represent important functions and goals. Rather social policy should be understood as comprising a mix of sectors of the economy, differentiated by sector and context and appropriately understood as such. Health, education, and economic and social infrastructure more generally are very different from one another and are even appropriately understood as forms of industry in their own right with characteristics of their own along their chains of provision. In short, they are health and education systems, etc. As such, this equally defies off-the shelf models as a guide to understanding and policymaking, whether these be attached or not to state provision, targeting, user-charging, privatisation, public-private part-nerships, privatisation and so on.[63]

Further, in a globalised and increasingly globalised world, the latter itself needs to be unpicked as it is subject to multiplicities of contents, meanings and understandings, each of which is subject to differing incidences, ranging over trade, finance and investment through aid and IFI policy to the ideologies of neoliberalism and its various opponents and their policy proposals. This means it is more and not less imperative that national policymaking should be systemic and holistic, not piecemeal and blinkered. It is necessary not to set aside the inevitable and unavoidable elephant in the room of globalisation that constrains national policymaking. But nor is it necessary to defer either to globalisation's putative beneficial effects as would be claimed by neoliberals or to its rigidly determining influence as some of its opponents would have it. Rather, it is neither helpful nor accurate to view the role of the state as either more or less salient in the contemporary world. In its nature and forms, and in the underlying economic, political and ideological interests through which its actions are determined, it remains complex, shifting and contradictory as it always has been.

It is important, however, to acknowledge that the current financial crisis has substantially increased both the role of the state and its prominence in economic affairs. This has, however, tended to be confined to be driven by, and on behalf of, finance. This is doubly unfortunate. On the one hand, it seems to seek to restore the status quo ex ante which, despite favourable circum-stances for more favourable outcomes, has been associated with relatively low and uneven rates of growth globally, especially across the poorer developing countries, with lost decades as a result. On the other hand, three decades of neoliberalism and its close associate, financialisation, have been responsible for squeezing out the potential for formulating and implementing alternative policies. A thorough and wide-ranging rethink of the role of the state is essen-tial that breaks with the experiences and ideologies of the past but which, nonetheless, remains sensitive to the lessons that can be drawn from the expe-riences of successful, and failed, developmental policy and the role the state has played within it.

---

63   Although mainly drawing upon the (deleted) section on social policy, this paragraph has been retained for substance and continuity of flow of text.

These observations point to outcomes at opposite extremes. One is of pessimism for, on the one hand, the complexities and diversities involved in policy-making would appear to defy the possibility of ever making any (well-founded) policy at all. On the other hand, as adopted here, a realistic as opposed to an optimistic stance is one which recognises that there has been a vast flow of policy with mixed content and outcome on which to draw. Indeed, not making policy is not an option as this is itself a policy and one which has rarely prevailed in the pure form demanded by neoliberal postures. Extensive intervention has predominated in practice and that this is so, of course, is true not only in national arenas but also in international collaborations, South-South or otherwise. The result has been a proliferation of deals, with Baldwin (2008) for example viewing "Factory Asia" as suffering a "Noodle Bowl" syndrome as far as its tangle of bilateral trade deals alone are concerned (quite apart from the conflicts of interests that arise from those who feed directly or indirectly, or even accidentally, from the bowl). Further, Baldwin poses questions such as "who should take the lead?" and "what should be the long-run goals?" as far as cooperation is concerned and, unsurprisingly, concludes that these have no easy answer and so have been left unanswered. He also asserts that the time for an East Asian vision is gone with a greater need now for East Asian *management*, not *vision*.[64] And for Chia (2007), South-South cooperation across the dimensions of regionalism, bilateralism and multilateralism is captured through the metaphor of a "spaghetti bowl".[65] As will be seen below, this raises what should be the unavoidable issues of management and vision for whom and by whom, with answers not necessarily being reduced to constituent countries and the international cooperative organisations on which they rely or form.

Similar considerations apply to the spaghetti and noodle bowls of other regions, most notably Africa and Latin America. For these as well, if possibly less so, the mere presence of China looms large. As already discussed, its impact is equally mixed, complex and diverse, defying simple nostrums even if attracting a proliferation of metaphors – as developmental engine, conduit, lead or lagging flying goose, exploiter of sitting ducks, steamroller, piggy for piggy-back, and so on. This appeal to metaphor is itself indicative of the difficulties of formulating appropriate general theory or analysis, as is equally reflected by the mix of the metaphors themselves. In a sense, so large and diverse and rapidly if unevenly developing itself is China that as far as South-South cooperation is concerned, it offers the full range of conundrums

---

64   With wishful thinking he sees the answer as being provided elsewhere other than within
      Asia itself by the EU and WTO leading and managing on its behalf!
65   See also commentaries on her contribution in the same issue.

across the spectrum – as source of demand in global networks, as source of demand to growing middle-class consumerism and working class basic goods, as competitor in cheap assembly, as leader or intermediate producer in higher value products, as foreign direct investor within and across public and private sectors, as competitor for inward foreign direct investment, as conduit and competitor for export markets in developed countries as well as import competitor with domestic production for domestic demand, and as a major source of global demand for primary products with corresponding strategic political imperatives for this and other reasons.

This suggests a different metaphor of its own for understanding how to approach South-South cooperation from an analytical perspective, with the literature understandably having suffered from an inadequacy of tools and principles necessary to address the complexity and diversity of the issues involved. This is to view (South-South) cooperation through the prism of aid or, more fully, aid and development. The reasons for doing so are that, even if roughly, South-South or other cooperation can be viewed as if it were aid across its various dimensions. Of course, such cooperation is generally free of the hierarchy associated with the donor-recipient syndrome, including the presence of international organisations and NGOs, etc. These have a mixed record as far as serving as facilitators, drivers, or impediments, for development. However, whilst the donor-recipient relationship characteristic of aid and development is absent in the context of (South-South) cooperation, this does not mean that there is an equal absence of unequal relations between the countries involved and that all can participate on an equal basis (as indicated by the China syndrome). Indeed, if without the donor-recipient relationship as such, it is apparent just how much the issues associated with (South-South) cooperation match those associated with aid and development across the causes and outcomes involved and the means that might be used to achieve them.

The (South-South) cooperation literature, from an initial grounding in the trade creation versus trade diversion approach derived from customs union theory, has evolved to fill the spaghetti/noodle bowl. Unsurprisingly, the literature on aid has suffered a similar fate. To parody, the mainstream literature divides into two extremes, with agnostics situated somewhere between the two (Tarp, 2006 for an overview from these perspectives).[66] Aid is good and promotes development or aid is bad, has little or no effect and can even be counterproductive in reinforcing the obstacles to development that seem to

---

66   See also Arndt et al. (2010) for a more recent review, and re-estimation, of the aid-growth nexus, coming out in favour of a positive relationship.

make it necessary in the first place. It is, of course, no accident that these positions tend, respectively, if imperfectly to reflect positions on the state versus market dichotomy (with more leftwing adherents collectively if inconsistently caught between demanding more aid and also seeing it as an instrument of control if not exploitation). Time and space do not offer the opportunity to review this literature in depth, and so yet a further metaphor might, necessarily clumsily and inexactly, do the work. Consider advertising not least in light of the dictum of Lord Lever, historically leading entrepreneur in the provision of household goods to the British Empire and beyond, that, "I *know* that 50% of *my advertising works*, but I just don't *know* which 50%". Of course, this is not the 50–50 of tossing a coin but a recognition that the processes of how advertising works, or not, remains complex and possibly mysterious.

Much the same 50–50 syndrome would appear to apply to (South-South) cooperation although the exact probabilities and distribution of costs and benefits are not necessarily so even. As with aid, it is important to recognise why this is so in order not to throw out the baby with the bathwater on the grounds that neither cooperation nor aid is worth the toss (although advertising, like these, tends to grow from strength to strength other than in times of stress when, of course, protectionism and more become more prominent in consideration as potential policy levers). Significantly, in reviewing Asian aid other than for Japan, Kondoh et al. (2010) observe of its "Emerging Donors" that, p. 1:

> The aid patterns employed by the emerging donors are divergent. Chinese aid has shifted from the overtly political and ideological to the commercialist; thus, current Chinese aid is closely tied to Chinese state-owned enterprises (SOEs). Korean aid has consistently been commercialist, but recently it has incorporated universal and humanitarian considerations. Thailand has maintained a keen interest in aid as a stabiliser of its neighbouring countries. The Indian aid program was initially formed during the Cold War consonant with the ideology of the Non-Aligned Movement, but from the 1990s economic considerations became more important. Indian aid is influenced also by regional strategies, namely the stabilisation of neighbouring countries.

This demonstrates the continuing lack of an aid model (or the only model is that there is no model) so diverse across time and place, motive and outcome, etc, are the determinants and consequences of aid. Once again, in light of the analogy between aid and cooperation, this suggests how inappropriate it is to seek to construct general models for either.

And for Japan itself, the most significant development over the past few decades has been the sharp decline in the volume of aid, reversing the trend that saw it become the world's largest donor in the 1990s (Palanovics, 2006 for an account).[67] However, the less Japan spends on aid the more it seems to become pre-occupied with interrogating its goals, administration and impact, as reflected in the ODA (2007) Manifesto. This incorporates more general trends in official thinking (i.e. those of the IFIs), such as promoting private sector participation (Task 9 and Proposals 23–26) and rewarding model countries (Task 10, Proposal 29). It is, however, far from clear how a holistic vision and strategy (Task 1) can be targeted when it can range over so much complexity of both development itself and the diverse contexts with which it is associated.

Thus, to reiterate, if South-South cooperation is, as it were, mutual aid by other means, exactly the same applies to its shifting origins, levels, motives, forms and outcomes. But this is tied into a closely-related but separate issue from which considerable insight, possibly lessons, can be learned from the aid syndrome. This is to interrogate the capacity to deliver cooperation and what are the determinants of its content and outcomes in principle and practice. For, on occasion, the criteria for managing and assessing aid are constructed through grand theme or nostrum concerning development – as in modernisation and neoliberalism for example, although each of these is comprised of varieties of scholarship, ideology and policy in practice when examined in detail. But in principle and in accelerating practice over at least the last two decades, aid has itself been situated across a multiplicity of elements around development. These ought to be familiar enough to those in the aid business if exercising some degree of circumspection but is strikingly illustrated by the collection edited by Cornwall and Eade (2010), entitled *Deconstructing Development Discourse: Buzzwords and Fuzzwords*. The latter B and F words include entries on poverty reduction, social protection, globalisation, participation, citizenship, empowerment, social capital, gender, sustainability, rights, NGOs, social movements, country ownership, transparency, accountability, corruption, governance, fragile states, and knowledge.

This proliferating lexicon of developmental considerations is matched by an equally alarming volatility in the nature and incidence of aid itself across types, volume, goals, outcomes and impact. In case of Africa, for example, which receives more aid absolutely and in per capita terms than elsewhere, it is not simply a matter of destabilising fluctuations in the volume of aid, but

---

67   But note that as a percentage of GDP, Japanese aid then peaked at only 0.35, ranking it near the bottom of leading donors Arase (2005, p. 4). A figure of net spending of 0.27% is also given, p. 6.

the emergence and exponential growth of an "aid complex" (Oya and Pons-Vignon, 2010, p. 180, drawing on Riddell, 2007):

> Each individual recipient country deals with an average of 26 different official donors ... over 35,000 separate official aid transactions were reported in 2004 ... individual African ministries are overloaded by aid proliferation. For example, Tanzania had over 2000 donor projects ongoing in the early 1990s, while the Ministry of Health in Mozambique alone managed over 400 projects recently.

It is as if aid has become the surrogate goal, so that managing aid for development becomes a substitute for development itself. For, as Oya and Pons-Vignon conclude, the capacity of the state is itself concentrated on relating to donors and managing aid as well as being undermined by the antipathy to the state under the Washington Consensus. Indeed, p. 176:

> The burden of aid management, coordination and execution, as well as the biases introduced in public administration through technical assistance and conditionality-led loss of policy space, have contributed to the formation of states (a) that now seem unable to deal with long-term strategic issues; (b) are ill-suited to creative and innovative policy thinking; (c) are far too constrained by the fragmentation and ideological biases of the aid complex; and (d) remain more preoccupied with managing and maximizing aid than with long-term development goals.

Further, p. 186, in citing Chang (2006), the range over which the aid complex needs to be managed is limitless, for "these days, there is virtually no area on which the Bank and the Fund do not have (often very strong) influence – democracy, judicial reform, corporate governance, health, education, and what not".

The consequences of such spread are various and go beyond, or different from, what might be termed mission creep, or even gallop, under which aid is attached to a proliferating portfolio of conditionalities and criteria of assessment. There is simply created huge scope for discretion. Aid can, for example, be considered successful because it has achieved one or more, if not many, of any number of goals (however accurately and honestly assessed). By the same token, aid can be deemed unsuccessful for failure on one or more, of any number, of goals across the buzz and fuzz. And, equally, the goal of development itself can either fade into the background as some specific target serves as proxy for it (poverty reduction for example) or development is foregrounded but by reducing it to one or other target (growth per capita) as a magic bullet for achieving development.

Once again, considerable insight into cooperation can be extrapolated from piggy-backing on aid and the aid literature. This is so around issues of proliferation of goals, agencies, and the criteria and standards of assessment of performance (allowing for self-selecting reviews of success or failure). And, possibly most important, there is a need for close consideration of the institutional and political capacity to deliver across these factors, taking account of delivery by whom and for whom given the different constituencies that drive outcomes within, between and across nations (in a world of globalisation).

As yet, if only because of being a newer or lesser mature kid on the block than aid (South-South) cooperation, is less promiscuous (if far from monogamous) in terms of the factors by which it is determined and assessed. But, as indicated by the noodle/spaghetti bowl syndrome, it clearly does already range over the broadest terms from forging political alliances across nations to promoting more narrowly defined economic progress within and across them. And, here, the evidence from the capacity to deliver appropriate national policies does not offer comfort for those wishing to extend these policies and policy making to South-South cooperation. This is often admirably driven by a wish to complement, or even to displace, the dominance of North-South economic ties and policy influence that is taken to be responsible for lack of development in the South. But, even to the extent that national policy making can be prised away from North-South ties and influences (which can themselves benefit from, and even be strengthened by, South-South cooperation), such prospects should not be viewed through rose-coloured spectacles, dreaming that such cooperation will kick-start a reverse process of enhancing national policy by virtue of knock-on or demonstration effects or be driven through the necessity of feedback effects on national policy derived from South-South cooperation. A significant problem within the South, as well as between South and North, is the uneven levels of development, capacities, and powers, as evidenced by the rise of China for example. These cannot be brushed aside any more than the unavoidable presence of the North as South-South cooperation is engaged. South-South cooperation is no panacea and nor can it be presumed that there is solidarity or unity of purpose within and across the South by virtue of the shared incidence of being relatively poor or, for the privileged minority, of being amongst the poor.

In short, capacity to engage in South-South dialogue and cooperation is not simply some technical issue of merely negotiating for mutual gain in the absence of Northern interests and influence (as for the economic school's approach to the developmental state, see above, shifted from the national to the international level). Nor is it simply a matter of the creating of the appropriate institutions, with sufficient autonomy over nations, capable of promoting positive sum outcomes for its constituents (as for the political school's approach to the developmental state, see above, shifted from the national to the international level). Rather, South-South cooperation will need to derive from a dialogue across political and economic factors that both reflect, but also cut across, participating nations. In a nutshell, in case of finance, for example, this is both national and international and so will not fit neatly with national interests which will, in any case, be contested. The same applies both to trade and production insofar as these are attached, as they are to a significant extent, to global networks and value chains, with corresponding configurations of conflicts of interest within the South as well as between it and the North.

In short, the noodle/spaghetti bowl syndrome is a reflection both of these fragmented and conflicting interests across a multitude of diverse factors and an indication that South-South cooperation requires capacity that goes beyond simply negotiating between one nation and another for mutual gain. For, such gains, if realised, divide within and across nations and are not simply national as such. Further, there are serious questions over the levels and sources of such capacity to negotiate. For, as Mkandawire (2010) observes following Evans (2004), all policy capacity let alone action, following decades of neoliberalism, has been subject to "institutional mono-tasking" favourable to the promotion of private capital, what Mkandawire (2009) himself refers to as "institutional mono-tasking". Nor is it surprising that the IFIs should back-pedal on (South-South) cooperation given that their priority has been to get national policy in order with a content that will, in any case, tend to exhibit antipathy to state intervention at national let alone higher levels of governance.

Mkandawire (2010, p. 51) also points to the extent to which aid, and corresponding policy perspectives, have shifted 'empowerment' to the micro level and complemented this by disempowerment at the macro level (or possibly, more accurately, re-assigned power by shifting it within and away from national sources to national and international elites, and especially if by no means exclusively to those attached to finance). This corresponds in the world of scholarship to the shift in understanding of development (policy) from the systemic (old development economics and its focus on macro/structural change) to piecemeal considerations (the new development economics and its focus on the micro and piecemeal change). Indeed, if in the context of social policy and poverty alleviation in his discussion but of much wider relevance for other areas of policy, this reconfiguration of (dis)empowerment from macro to micro is associated with corresponding shift in power across various constituencies, p. 44:

New social policy and poverty agendas are driven by NGOs, international organisations, and national elites with very different agendas than the progressive movements that inspired the formation of welfare states in the past.

And, by the same token, both institutional capacity and willingness to deliver, and driven by whom and in whose benefit, are liable to be telling determinants of the creation and outcomes of (South-South) cooperation. This is necessarily so given the multiplicity of forms and content that these can and will adopt across countries at different and diverse stages of development and with different and diverse capacity for, and drivers of, policymaking in national let alone international arenas.

In short, on past experience, there is surely little doubt that South-South cooperation will proliferate, albeit in the 'polluted' environment and impure forms associated not only with mixed motives and mixed participation and influence from outside the South but also on the basis of equally uneven and diverse capacities and motives from within economies within and across the South itself.[68] This suggests that South-South cooperation is best addressed through what might be termed a highest common factor rather than lowest common multiplier approach. In other words, this is not to facilitate, support and proliferate agreements as they arise but to advise a softly-softly stance in pursuit of secure benefits, promoted by and accruing to targeted and deserving constituencies, subjecting such agreements and policies for cooperation to a circular process of policy formulation, implementation and monitoring of outcomes that feed once more into policy formulation (and corresponding institutional capacity building within and across participants for the processes). On this basis, much more secure foundations will evolve for national and cooperative policymaking in equitable and developmental terms, offering a bit more and a bit more variety of protein in the noodle/spaghetti bowls on offer.

More specifically, what are the lessons that we might learn for South-South cooperation from the experience of China (and earlier developmental states) and from the experiences of the impacts of China (and ditto)? First is that, for the prospects and goals of South-South cooperation, such cooperation tends to be a consequence not a cause of development. In other words, national policy making must be on a sound footing as a precondition for sound cooperation.

---

68   See Sally and Sen (2005) for the numbers and varieties of trade agreements arising out of diversity of national policies.

Second, in this respect, the origins (and proliferation) of cooperation in trade agreements (and, to a much lesser extent, monetary unions) can be the source of possibly counter-intuitive and misleading indicators as far as approaches to (South-South) cooperation are concerned. For, whilst trade may be the leading and most prominent form taken by South-South economic relations, there is no reason to presume that it is of prime or sole importance in national policy making nor that such issues in cooperation across nations can be handled independently of other policy issues within them.

Third, then, what are the issues of significance for national policy making which must be addressed as a precondition for success in South-South cooperation. Broadly, and overgeneralising, it is not simply national policymaking that still remains crucial but that, in contemporary conditions, especially in the wake of the current crisis, developmentalism and a corresponding positive role for the state depend upon: insulating the mobilisation and allocation of finance from financialisation in all of its forms; the promotion of secure domestic provision of goods for domestic consumption especially as far as the meeting of basic needs and poverty alleviation are concerned; and a strong commitment to state provision of social and economic infrastructure attached to a developmental welfare state, and targeted industrial (and other) strategies designed to expand employment and productivity in line with corresponding increases in wages.

Finally, and with a flourish, if such policies could be put in place within countries of the South, considerable strides could be made in harnessing them to the positive benefits of (South-South) cooperation. But, by the same token, far from South-South cooperation being appropriately served and underpinned by national policymaking, it is also national policymaking that should be served and not constrained by such cooperation. If we have one lesson to learn from the lost decades, it is that North-South cooperation, formal or informal, market or otherwise, is not the model to be emulated within the South, even if it could be.

This last reservation, for example, is germane in relation both to South-South and, slightly or considerably different, regional cooperation. For both, levels and types of development of participating economies are liable to be mixed and uneven. For regional development in particular, the sorts of "spaghetti" to be found in the bowl of cooperation (and, possibly, integration but not, for example, for sub-Saharan Africa with South Africa as pole, strongly oriented towards the North, and similarly for middle-east oil-rich economies), are liable to be those inspired on a case-by-case basis in light of costs of transport and communication. For the latter, of course, finance has increasingly come to the fore with new developments increasingly attached to North-South with at most regional and subordinate hubs, not least as financial systems have been liberalised. In consideration of transport costs, though, in contrast, regional integration and cooperation (other than for primary products destined for use in the North for manufacturing or consumption) trade agreements are liable to be promoted.

These may serve the developmental goals of participating economies. But, as with all trade policy, these will serve, represent and promote some constituencies at the expense of others as well as commanding and building institutional capacities within and between states. That trade is easiest to identify, and possibly to negotiate, does not necessarily mean that it is most important and beneficial. What has been observed more in the breach of both South-South and regional cooperation (and international integration more generally) is the issue of migration. Here, an appropriate starting point in part by way of explanation for this exception, is the political sensitivity and corresponding conflict around representation of interests involved which tend to defy national let alone international resolution.

There are the interests of the migrants themselves in terms of wages and conditions and security of livelihoods. Also involved are employers looking for wider sources of recruitment, possibly at exploitative wages and conditions, possibly with skilled labour at the expense of the economy of origin, although equally a source of remittances and potential return of skills and experience. And there are also the interests of native workers who can consider their jobs, wages and conditions and bargaining power as undermined by competition from migrant workers, or even that the latter gratifyingly undertake paid employment for undesirable jobs on terms that would be unacceptable to others. Further, like migration itself, such interests and how they are represented, with what outcomes, are fluid not least in the wake of the global crisis. At least, no one doubts just how important are migrant workers to the economies of LDCs in terms of both employment and remittances as international financial flows.

In addition, each of these issues is irreducibly attached to social policy, broadly conceived, as migrant workers, at least in principle, are dependent upon conditions governing provision of, and access to, basic needs, with the attendant risk of denial of their rights, alongside inferior wages and conditions, and even dangers of attacks upon them contingent upon levels of public provision and conditions of access to them. This suggests that a key issue both for South-South and regional cooperation is the formulation of policy in relation to migration that goes beyond legal rights, border controls and access to one another's labour markets as such. Indeed, migration might be considered to be the most tangled and unrecognised of the pastas (or is it the sauce) in the spaghetti bowl, both most deserving of attention and most likely to reap 'highest common factor' rewards of consolidating and building mutual capacity for South-South cooperation and integration in relation to (1) enhancing North-South relations; (2) building capacity for further cooperation and beneficial integration; (3) incorporating social into industrial policy; (4) sharing policy perspectives, lessons and experiences across industrial, social and labour policy.

These insights are illustrated by the experience of the Southern African Development Community (SADC), which first signed a trade protocol in 1996, following the demise of apartheid.[69] As SARDN (2011a, p. 1) puts it, "progress in the region to reap the benefits purported to accompany regional economic integration appears limited". Levels of trade within the region remain low, and in expanding outside the region with limited diversification into new products. There is an acknowledged need for greater coordination across targeted infrastructure and an acknowledged "lack of political will among SADC member states towards practically unlocking the benefits that accompany regional economic integration", p. 2. Significantly, in meeting poverty alleviation let alone broader developmental goals, attention is placed on the impact of volatile and peaking fuel and food prices, and the interaction between them, as subsidised bio-fuel "threatens poor households' food supplies" (SARDN, 2011b, p. 1), a problem that needs to be addressed through the Southern African Customs Union, SACU.[70] Indeed, it is suggested that (SARDN, 2011c, p. 2):

> Food security is at the core of the poverty problems and hence gains from regional economic integration, specifically from gains from trade, can improve food security through increased agricultural and agro-industry cross-border investment.

---

69   What follows draws upon the work of the SARDN, only founded in 2007, itself indicative of the decimation of independent capacity in research following the assault on African higher education under the Washington Consensus, with economics hit particularly hard as far as alternatives are concerned. This is acknowledged by SARDN (2011d) itself insofar as the leading economic power in the region, South Africa, also dominates university education across the continent (reportedly responsible for the top ten universities apart from the American University in Cairo). Elsewhere, it is suggested that, "In the longer term, Botswana can serve as an alternative to South African institutions, as was the case with Zimbabwe before the political challenges" (SARDN, 2011e, p. 2). For a proposal for more independence, capacity and own ethos in African research, see Mamdani (2011).

70   SACU and SADC have considerable overlap but are distinct, indicative of the spaghetti bowl!

Significantly, attention is also paid to issues of migration and more general policy harmonisation and how to reconcile national with regional interests (and to handle the attraction of seeking more readily achieved short-term gains through non-regional integration). The point is less that these issues can be settled once and for all but that they should be acknowledged and addressed on a systematic and pragmatic basis.

The Continuing Enigmas of Social Policy

Postscript as Personal Preamble

In the previous Chapter, a wide take on developmental state and industrial policy, the opportunity was briefly taken to set the personal and contemporary scene. The current Chapter, addressing social policy, was drafted only a few years later (Fine, 2011a and 2014, respectively). Unsurprisingly, its context is marked by considerable continuities and commonalities. Equally unsurprisingly, there are some changes. I still seemed to be extremely energetic but with social capital and economics imperialism occupying much less of my time than previously, possibly a reflection of the "watershed" subsequently identified as characterising the decline in prominence of economics imperialism (Fine 2024a–c), quite apart from the World Bank's abandonment of social capital as much as a decade earlier (even if having propelled it with sufficient momentum to keep it going without its own continuing participation).[1]

Most significant in keeping me occupied was the rise of 'financialisation', by then already in its adolescence as opposed to its earlier infancy with increasing presence within each social science and across all of them (with the bizarre but telling exception of mainstream economics).[2] But, for me, 'finn' had a further major aspect over and above specifying it both theoretically and empirically. It allowed me to specify neoliberalism as a stage of capitalism with finn as its central distinguishing feature, with neoliberalism evolving through three different phases although the third had yet to be identified in this Chapter even if no longer prospective – in retrospect, I see it as preceding the Global Financial Crisis (GFC) of 2007/8. Such is the lag between contemporary developments and scholarship. Significantly, neoliberalism itself had been subject to scholarly specification for at least two decades in ways with which I had never been satisfied (as generally reflecting criteria and features present across capitalism in general or at least for periods other than the neoliberal). That

---

1   The World Bank's abandoning of the social capital juggernaut left it heavily listing on the efforts of Robert Putnam, whom I dubbed the Ronald McDonald of the social sciences. See Fine (2010b, but also 2002b).

2   See Fine (2013–14) for an early overview, and Fine (2022a) for the latest of a long line of contributions, plus Mader et al. (eds) (2020) for extensive coverage.

neoliberalism is distinguished by finn but not reducible to it served as a Eureka moment for me.

This is because of the engagement at all levels with the relationship between finn and not only neoliberalism as such but also all aspects of globalisation, economic and social reproduction, everyday life, material culture and, ultimately, bringing all of these together, in focusing upon the evolving nature and incidence of social policy. My interest in, and contributions to, the study of social policy was far from new. In an indirect way, it had begun with what some might think of as esoteric debates over the nature of productive and unproductive labour, but even these intersected with concerns around the nature of 'domestic' labour and the distinctiveness, in economic and social reproduction, of state expenditure and the role of the sectors it supported, if not commanded, such as health, education and 'welfare'.[3] Part of capitalism, undoubtedly, but part of capital or not considerably more challenging not so much in terms of yes or no but how and how evolving.

Social policy had also been of significant interest in the early 1990s in my contributing chapters on health, education, electrification and housing to the MERG Report (1993), commissioned by Nelson Mandela in 1992 but ditched in 1993 as it was about to be published, a stunning indication of the direction that post-apartheid policy was about to embrace both rapidly and extensively.[4] At the time, I wrote a more general take on social policy to serve as an umbrella introduction to the sector-specific chapters but it was not included in the published volume (Fine, 1996). In retrospect, it contained two vital ingredients that by chance in origins but by choice in going forward, have continued to inform my study of social policy. On the one hand, 'apartheid' served as too dull an analytical instrument or descriptor to deal with what were entirely different levels and forms of provision across different sectors even though these were characterised by the most severe and overt forms of racial inequality and oppression. On the other hand, my approach to social policy arose out of extending longstanding work on (commodified, private) consumption through the system of provision approach, to public sector systems of provision – bearing in mind that scholarship on consumption, especially in the wake of postmodernism, tended to confine itself to private, individualised consumption without a thought for public or collective consumption, nor for the consumption derived from public services and the welfare state. These two

---

3 Corresponding debates reflected deeper differences across Marxist political economy, especially with neo-Ricardianism/Sraffianism.

4 For my own, retrospective, account of the MERG process and its significance, see Fine (2022b). Otherwise, see Padayachee and Niekerk (2019).

insights – that social policy under apartheid is differentiated by sector as well as by race, and that (public sector) systems of provision are distinct from one another – have remained mutually reinforcing, leading to an abiding insistence on what I am keen to pinpoint as variegation in social policy across time, place, sector and forms of, and access to, delivery.

Despite these early forays into social policy, I only dealt with the topic intensively and extensively through invitations to do so by UNRISD and for a conference in India in which I suspect I was matched to an uncovered topic, not by expertise.[5] By the end of the noughties, I began to draft what has become this Chapter, commissioned to provide a theoretical framing for approaching social policy across the developing world. Finn and SoPs were in the air, but I also engaged in an extremely intensive and extensive review of the welfare state and social policy literature. Here, I found an unresolved tension between homogenising grand theory or framing, and its lack of sensitivity to the empirical evidence of variegation. In particular, I took a strong dislike, contempt even, for the Welfare Regimes Approach, WRA, which uncomfortably or, more exactly, unsuccessfully sought to fit social policy into a small number of specific regimes.[6] I was also concerned over the absence of finn from the discussion of social policy, in part because it was a new kid on the block and yet to be incorporated and in part because the neoliberalisation of social policy was complacently perceived as being well- and long-understood in terms of macro austerity and commercialisation/privatisation (reduce the state and rely upon the market, as long in the tooth as Mrs Thatcher).

Most important, though, at a personal level, was that this Chapter was drafted around the time of applying for and initiating the FESSUD research project (fessud.org). It is covered in great detail in Volume 4 of this series (Fine et al. 2024), with comparative case studies across water and housing in particular but also broaching pensions, health and well-being. This Chapter is also notable for a review of Conditional Cash Transfers (on the rise at the time, now well-established) and for lining up in favour of a developmental welfare state despite the harsh account I have given of the developmental state paradigm (as in the previous Chapter). One reason for this was to support UNRISD initiatives (Kwon, ed. 2005, for example), another was to see welfare provision

---

5 See Fine (2005b, 2009d and e, and 2014).
6 Also important, like many other grand approaches put forward in the decades around the turn of the millennium, the post-war boom and understanding of its conditions formed the template for understanding neoliberalism as a deviant from the Keynesian period rather than neoliberalism being seen as a stage of capitalism in its own right (and longer lasting than its predecessor).

as developmental as opposed to safety netting, and a third was to prise understanding of welfare provision away from something necessarily separate and distinct from industry. From a system of provision approach, the principles under which social policy and industrial policy are to be understood should be the same.[7]

Finally, most so far has been focused on the personal context in shifting from UNCTAD (previous chapter) to UNRISD (this one). As far as contemporary social policy is concerned, as comprehensively and brilliantly covered by the work of Isabel Ortiz and Matthew Cummins (look on web), an initial if uneven response to the GFC was to expand some compensating social support. But it was soon to give way to austerity or business as usual. Much the same, if more so, has happened in response to the pandemic, to which I would add that the removal of extraordinary measures in its wake offered the opportunity both to cut back more and provide differently in conformity to neoliberal imperatives.[8]

1   **Introduction and Overview**

The purpose of this Chapter is to provide a way of framing both the understanding of social policy and how to approach the making of social policy itself.[9] In doing so, it faces a number of difficulties. First and foremost, social policy is extremely diverse across different countries, different programmes and over time and circumstance. At the very least, any framing of social policy will need to be able to allow for such diversity. What sort of country, at what sort of stage and with what sort of dynamic of development; what welfare service, such as health or education, or income transfer such as pensions or social security; and who is served, the old or the young, male or female, etc.

Second, this diversity does not mean that social policy is free of common influences or determinants, and these should be identified. Leading candidates for such factors, particularly in the contemporary world, include the role

---

7   For the South Korean DWS, and its integration with industrial policy, see Barbosa (2024). Similar considerations apply to other more or less arbitrary distinctions between sectors, Cramer et al. (2022) on agriculture as industry, for example, and there are also the interpretative and empirical problems posed by the subcontracting by industry of its 'services' inputs, in light of deindustrialisation and shifting compositional shares of GDP.

8   For the extensive continuing work on social policy and beyond, arising out of the Fessud project, see Fine et al. (2024 Chapter 1, Appendix 3, and Appendix 2 for Fessud work itself).

9   This paper draws heavily from other papers of mine, occasionally verbatim for a paragraph or more.

of globalisation and neoliberalism and, most recently, the response to severe crisis. There is also the role played by ideational factors such as the presence and strength of goals and ethos of meeting human rights, basic needs, alleviating poverty, and so on. This creates a dual task of both specifying what these controversial common determinants are or mean, for they are themselves contested in how they are understood, and whether they are positive or not for welfare policy and more generally, how they allow for what are unavoidably heterogeneous outcomes.

Third, unsurprisingly, there is a huge literature on social policy ranging from grand comparative posturing at a general level to close and detailed studies of particular programmes in particular countries at particular times, and with impact upon particular sections of the population – by age, gender, location, or socioeconomic status. This wealth of literature and experience is both helpful in providing the raw materials for framing an approach, but daunting in its own volume and diversity.

Fourth, disappointingly if unsurprisingly, the vast bulk of the social policy literature, especially that concerned with framing the understanding and making of policy, derives from developed countries and Europe in particular, with both the United States and Japan, not prominent as examples for understanding social policy. Indeed, there has been a degree of conceptual imperialism as far as social policy is concerned, with the analysis and policies for developing countries following the putative lead of development, whether it be in erstwhile goals of modernisation or the more recent turn to market mechanisms. This raises the issue of how to learn from the literature without becoming its slave, and whether initiatives such as the Millennium Development Goals (MDGs) and poverty alleviation offer a way of escaping unduly pre-determined ways of thinking.[10]

Fifth, yet again unsurprisingly, the literature is well-established and runs along a number of well-oiled grooves. Social policy and the welfare state have been around for long enough for us to be able to debate, if not explain, whatever is happening or might happen. We have, after all, seen it all before, whether it be fast or painfully slow convergence to modern forms of welfare provision; the response to or setbacks due to crises; the impacts of neoliberalism and globalisation; the emergence or strengthening of new concerns such as gender; or the path dependence built into institutional and policy inertia

---

10   The MDG programme and similar are not covered in this paper. See Lancet Commission (2010).

(see Section 3). Surely, we already have more than enough toolkits for assessing and proposing social policy?

This Chapter suggests otherwise on the basis of two wide-ranging, if necessarily selective, reviews of the literature. One was prepared shortly after the current crisis broke and the other over the last year by way of an updating and stock-taking of responses to the enduring global crisis.[11] Of necessity, such reviews were guided by four key threads to assess the literature critically and, where appropriate, be challenged by it.

The first thread, and unusual for framing social policy, other than in the latest neoliberal fad of treating citizens as consumers, is to relate social policy to long-standing work on consumption (Fine, 2013d for a retrospective account). This offered two insights. One was to see private, commercial consumption in terms of commodity specific chains of provision, or systems of provision as they have been termed (SOPs), significantly distinct from one another as with food, fashion, energy, housing systems, etc. (Fine and Leopold, 1993). The other was to recognise how the huge expansion in the study of consumption across the social sciences in the decades of postmodernism had studiously neglected *public* consumption. In a sense, it has been as if social policy simply does not exist when it comes to the study of consumption. As I have argued, there are good and understandable reasons for this. As soon as consumption becomes recognisably public, it tends to be redefined as something else, most notably as the welfare state or social policy. This places it outside the realm of consumption studies as such, once again with the reservation of what has been termed, under neoliberalism, the recommodification of social policy so that the latter does to some degree become more market-like, and the citizen deemed to be and made more putatively consumer-like.[12]

While social policy does depart from market forms of consumption to a greater or lesser degree, this is no reason for abandoning how studying consumption sheds light on public provision. Without in any way reducing social provision to private consumption, this leads me to argue that social policy can be addressed in terms of what has been dubbed *public sector* systems of

---

11   Early in 2009, I presented upon request a paper on neoliberalism and social policy (Fine, 2009e) to a conference in Mumbai. This was subsequently submitted for consideration for an UNRISD Conference on social policy later in the year, and delivered revised and under the title "Financialisation and Social Policy", before ultimately appearing, to some degree shortened, revised again and partially updated, in the edited volume from the conference (Fine, 2012d).

12   For a discussion of the literature on the citizen made (financial) consumer especially in the context of housing, and ideology of owner occupation, see Robertson (2014b).

provision (PSSoPs) (Fine, 2002d; Bayliss and Fine, eds, 2008; and Bayliss et al. 2013).This is taken up in Section 6 where the PSSoP approach can be seen to have a number of advantages, especially in light of the difficulties previously raised. For it does emphasise the diversity of social policy by time, place, programme and context; it does take an integral or holistic view of such policy rather than focusing on a particular aspect such as public or private provision, mode of financing, presence or not of user charges; it does locate social policy in its wider context such as neoliberalism and globalisation as well as country-specific factors; and the PSSoP approach allows the critical incorporation and assessment of the existing literature by relating whatever it contributes to the functioning of the PSSoPs under consideration.

The second thread in my take on social policy was to emphasise the role of financialisation with its significance projected to new heights by the form and depth of the global crisis. However financialisation is understood – and it is a new concept deriving predominantly from diverse heterodox traditions with equally diverse theoretical underpinnings, meanings and foci – no one can doubt that the direct and indirect impact of financial imperatives on social policy has been nothing short of decisive over the intervening years. Yet, as far as the social policy literature is concerned, financialisation might just as well not exist. The reason for this in part is that the role of financial imperatives in the (re)making of social policy have long been studied in the light of previous crises. This is especially true in the wake of the end of the post-war boom and the subsequent stagflation, and the ethos of assaults on state expenditure associated with neoliberalism. But do such longstanding analyses fully capture the extent to which finance has itself influenced, if not captured, the making of social policy at a systemic level as well as at the level of detail? In Section 5, an account is given of financialisation which relates it not only to neoliberalism and globalisation but also to the underlying factors that give rise to diverse effects in the making of social policy. As a result, while there are a number of models and typologies of different types of capitalism, seeking to distinguish from the social democratic Scandinavian at one extreme to the neoliberal United States at the other, neither these in themselves, nor their implications for social policy, have satisfactorily addressed the issue of financialisation and how it influences and constrains policy making.

This is closely linked to the third thread, especially also derivative from the first, which is an antipathy to the welfare regimes approach (WRA) to social policy. As shown in Section 2, it cannot be overemphasised how this has dominated the social policy literature over the last two decades. It has sorted welfare provision into a number of models or ideal types. Initially, this started with three models based on developed countries. The WRA has subsequently expanded the number of models in order to include more countries, more of the advanced countries, as well as East Asian and Latin American regimes, thereby addressing empirical anomalies or outliers as far as fit with the initial models is concerned.

While the WRA has allowed an enormous amount of informative empirical work to be undertaken, it has led to increasingly serious deficiencies. It has been denuded of any explanatory or theoretical content. It is incapable of explaining change – if a regime is classified as a model of one sort, how does it become another? WRA fails to explain why different social policies should have the characteristics of different regimes within the same country, not least because it necessarily imposes undue homogeneity across, from my perspective, diverse PSSoPs whether by sector (for example, housing is different from education, meaning that different principles will apply to outcomes even if underpinned by common determinants however identified) or by country. It is incapable of offering significant policy advice for change since policy is caught within its specified regime.

In short, welfare regimes have become a buzzword and fuzzword in the social policy literature, not least with proliferating regimes as ideal types.[13] With one major exception, it is almost impossible to discuss social policy without reference to the WRA. Yet, as argued here, it is time to abandon this approach despite or even because of what it has offered. Indeed, it might be argued that the more we have learned about regimes, the more we have found them to be deficient. Thus, the WRA has shown itself to be well beyond its use-by-date not least in the sense that if we undertake the hypothetical exercise of suspending history and put the WRA forward anew now, it would almost certainly be of limited appeal contingent upon what fills the vacuum created by its absence. But what the approach has demonstrated, to some extent by neglect and omissions as well as by what it has positively shown, is that theories of social policy must accommodate a variety of structural determinants, how they interact across agencies, processes, relations and institutions to give rise to a diversity of shifting outcomes (as opposed to mixes of ideal types) within and across countries and sectors. With this emphasis on diversity as opposed to ideal types as a starting point, there is the potential for more and deeper consideration of theoretical issues and their historically specific and

---

13   For buzzwords and fuzzwords in development – those that have been used so universally and casually that they border on the meaningless and ideological – see Cornwall and Eade (eds) (2010). Surely the welfare regimes have become buzz and fuzz when, for example, reference can be made to "Mao's socialist welfare regime" (Ngok, 2013, p. 107).

comparative location, for which the theme of financialisation and the framing by the PSSoP approach offers an alternative for the contemporary world.

The one area where the WRA has been less successful in making its presence felt, although lost ground is being made up, is in the context of development. This is a welcome reflection of the distance between social policy, and the prospects for it, in developing countries and those of the developed world. In this respect, the WRA might be dubbed a failed buzzword for, in the context of development, buzzwords are often created by being adopted by the World Bank.[14] Significantly, a search on the World Bank website does not reveal a single reference to "welfare regimes".[15] It is not unusual for the putative Knowledge Bank to overlook the literature it does not like, and the WRA does model itself on the ethos of Scandinavian interventionism. But this is peculiar where the neglected approach has such a strong presence in the mainstream literature, albeit generally orthogonal to development. The WRA has to some degree compromised with newly emerging (World Bank) mainstream approaches to social policy. This is based on the idea that social policy needs to respond to market imperfections, both in terms of the market inevitably generating the need for social support (broadly conceived), and because of potential exploitation of such support by individuals not in need, or other inefficiencies due to lack of markets. This has the effect, thereby, of narrowing down both the analytical content of how social policy is conceived (towards emphasis on a narrow understanding based on those individuals at social risk for reasons that remain primarily unexplored other than as due to market and/or institutional imperfections) and the ambition of policies themselves (towards residual relief as opposed to economic and social transformation).

A fourth thread, then, is to have acknowledged the overwhelming influence of new mainstream orthodoxies on the understanding of social policy, with an increasing role for the World Bank in the context of development. The previous couple of decades have not only witnessed the demise of the political economy of welfare approaches (and its substitution by an evolving WRA) but also an increasing erosion of the welfare state as such as the gold standards and goals for social policy itself. Symbolically, the UNRISD programme on social policy, with its frame of developmental welfare state (DWS) stands out

---

14 For this in the case of the developmental state, see Fine (2013a), as opposed to the temporarily World Bank promoted social capital (Fine, 2010b and c, and 2011b).

15 Interestingly, though, the same is true of the Marmot Report on the social determinants of health which similarly does not find it necessary to mention welfare regimes nor Esping-Andersen, although it does mention tax, trade, intellectual property rights and even dairy regimes (CSDH, 2008)!

as exceptional in all respects in this regard, although I should add that, in my own work, the notion of developmental state as such is far from unproblematic (most recently, Fine, 2013a). However, in Section 6, the deficiencies of the new orthodoxy are revealed through the prism of the alternative offered by seeking to marry the DWS and PSSoP approaches, with such a union having the added advantage of remedying some of the deficiencies of the developmental state paradigm (DSP), not least its undue reduction to industrial policy, and of industrial policy itself to an economic and political relationship between state and business.

In preparing this Chapter, then, I decided to revisit the social policy literature in light of these threads to see how it had evolved, or not, over the intervening period since my earlier review. I did so by inspecting articles that had been published over the past six years in select leading journals, reviewing hundreds of contributions and paying them anything from casual disregard to close reading, depending upon the interest generated by their titles, abstracts and/or substantive content. I am happy to report that the DWS and PSSoP approaches are together fit for purpose as is illustrated in the penultimate section by critical review of the literature on conditional cash transfers (CCTs), the new kid on the block as far as social policy in developing countries is concerned. The concluding remarks summarise what can be learned for framing social policies.

2   From Welfare Regimenting ...

The most striking aspect of the recent social policy literature is the continuing presence, dominance even, of the WRA. In their "audit" of welfare modelling, Powell and Barrientos (2011, p. 69) find that "the 'welfare modelling business' ... initially a one person firm (Esping-Andersen, 1990) has become in recent years a multinational corporation".[16] Given this, it is unsurprising that there are considerable attractions – even merits – within the WRA. It does seek to identify, and possibly as a first step, begin to explain, diversity across different national systems of welfare provision. It does so by looking at templates for the specification of provision, the different welfare regimes themselves (see

---

16   As Scruggs and Allan (2006, p.69) put it earlier, "It is hard to overstate the significance of the impact of *The Three Worlds of Welfare Capitalism* on comparative studies of the welfare state". See also Kam (2012, p.108), "Since Esping-Andersen presented the three worlds of welfare typology thesis, the study of the classification of welfare regimes has been dominated by his work and the debates surrounding it".

below). It allows for intra- and inter-country empirical analysis of provision – what are the differences by one or more elements of provision between countries, and what are the differences within countries across different elements of provision in case the regimes within a country differ according to what is provided. The WRA also readily accommodates a variety of theories, causal variables and methodologies although these are often middle-range, casual or not closely specified. Consequently, we have gained much from the WRA, which has been bountiful in organising our understanding and knowledge of welfare provision. And, by the same token, it has underpinned colossal programmes of research and publications over the past two decades and more.

However, despite its many positive features, there is a huge tension across the contributions collectively as well as from particular contributions that take the WRA as critical point of departure without breaking with it. The need to break with the WRA is the conclusion drawn here. To put it polemically, whatever purposes the WRA has served in the past, it has long since passed its use by date. Or, in understanding the continuing evolution of welfare provision, it is only with a huge sense of relief that we should unburden ourselves by discarding the baggage of tyranny that goes with the WRA. I am not the first to be drawn to this drastic solution (Bambra, 2005, pp. 53–54).[17]

> Five substantive critiques of this [WRA] typology have emerged: the range of countries and number of regime types; the methodology used; the usefulness of the regime concept; the analytical dominance of income maintenance schemes over welfare services; and the omission of gender in the analysis ... Some assert that a distinctive fourth type of welfare state regime is emerging in the countries of the Latin rim of the European Union (Spain, Portugal, Greece and to a lesser extent Italy) and [some] argue that the UK, Australia and New Zealand constitute another 'radical' fourth type of welfare state regime. ... Esping-Andersen's methodology has been widely critiqued ... and the use of cluster analysis has also suggested that there could be four or five 'worlds of welfare' ... questioned [has been] the validity of the regimes concept itself, asserting that instead of internal policy homogeneity or cohesion, welfare states and welfare regimes exhibit significant variation across different areas of provision. Esping-Andersen's decision to organise the principle of classification around the study of cash benefit programs, ignoring the fact

---

17   Devastating general criticisms if in the context of her own study of infant mortality rates as outcomes rather than as policies or processes.

that welfare states are also about the actual delivery of services, has also been a source of contention. ... Feminist commentators ... have offered the most extensive critique, arguing that Esping-Andersen's 'three worlds of welfare' typology is deeply flawed because it marginalises women.

Letting go, however, is not a purely negative exercise. Its critical rejection allows for the constituent parts and ethos of alternatives to be identified. I deal with a number of such issues in turn.

First, it is apparent that the more the WRA is applied, the more it is found to be inadequate. But corresponding criticism has not led in practice to the rejection of the WRA, but to its extension. This, in part explains its increasingly heavy and continuing presence as it absorbs criticism. Thus, the most favoured sort of contribution to the literature is through empirical case study, ranging across regimes as a whole for more or fewer countries to focusing upon particular programmes within particular countries. As is well-known, Esping-Andersen initially proposed three ideal types of welfare regimes – the Scandinavian social democratic, the Bismarckian corporatist-statist, and the Anglo-Saxon liberal. These, though, have long been supplemented by a proliferating set of extras to accommodate empirical diversity. There has been the Southern European or Mediterranean welfare model,[18] with emphasis on familial provision, to which there has been added a Middle Eastern regime (or even five of them, as in Jawad and Yakut-Cakar, 2010) as well as Latin American and East Asian ideal types. Varieties of cluster analyses give rise to varieties of outcomes, with five regimes for Bambra (2007) (looking at defamilisation), five also for Kuitto (2011) investigating varieties of cash transfers, four ways of supporting the working-aged for Pfeifer (2012) across fourteen European countries.[19] Equally, it is now acknowledged that there is not a one-to-one

---

18   See Gal (2010, p. 283) who extends this regime to cover Cyprus, Greece, Israel, Italy, Malta, Portugal, Spain and Turkey but sees these as underpinned by "religion, family and the role of clientelist-particularist relations in the structuring and functioning of welfare state institutions". For what follows, see also MacGregor (2013) for Antipodean, East Asian, Mediterranean and transition regimes; Mayes and Mustaffa (2013) for diversity of regimes across an enlarged EU; and for Choi (2013), the apt observation that the Republic of Korea and Taiwan Province of China are entirely different developmental states, so they give rise to very different welfare systems, let alone conform to a putative east Asian regime, itself rejected for Japan by Kasza (2006). Should there be a BRICS welfare regime (Midgley and Piachaud, eds, 2013)? On east Asian welfare provision more generally, see Ku and Finer (2007).

19   Delineated as "an *extensive safety nets type* operating well with functioning labour markets; a *liberal protection type* dealing with low levels of unemployment; a *targeted*

relationship between countries and regimes, with an attempted resolution through appeal to hybrids. Thus, for Aybars and Tsarouhas (2010, p. 761), "The picture painted above is mixed and points to the 'hybrid' character of the Turkish welfare regime, illustrating important features of both the Middle Eastern and Southern European welfare models, but remaining an outlier to both in certain respects".[20] And, as Mätzke and Ostner (2010, p. 390) observe, "'hybridization' increases once family policies are studied comparatively ... and even more so when change is taken into account – rendering comparisons across Esping-Andersen's 'worlds' problematic".[21]

Much the same applies to the transition economies of Eastern Europe, whose existence, of course, post-dates the welfare regime approach (Greve, 2009, p. 103):[22]

> the welfare states in Eastern Europe moving very much towards a more liberalistic approach, but at the same time maintaining in principle a universal approach in relation to health care. The mix between public and private is perhaps thus not dependent on the welfare state type or society we are looking at, but instead more dependent on the welfare sector we look into.

Similar conclusions arise for country- and/or sector-specific regime studies with ideal types proving elusive, as with Willemse and de Beer (2012, p. 105), for whom, across nineteen developed Western countries:

> by applying the central concepts of welfare state analysis of decommodification and stratification, as proposed by Esping-Andersen, to the field of higher education ... We conclude that including higher education in comparative welfare states analysis might result in a less clear-cut

---

protection type combined with an insider-outsider divide on the labour market; and lastly, a *patchy safety nets type* facing high unemployment levels" (Pfeifer, 2012 p. 13).

20   See also Gal and Greve (2010, p. 657), and van Hooren and Becker (2012) for hybrid varieties for child, as opposed to elderly, care in Netherlands.

21   As an alternative fix to hybrids (if retaining proliferation of regimes), Hudson and Kühner (2012) add an East Asian productive regime but limit their ambitions to 'fuzzy' fits, or fuzzy set ideal type analysis (FSITA)!

22   To some degree, this reflects the extent to which financialisation has been at the heart of social policy restructuring in Eastern Europe, and promoted by international organisations, in the absence of previously existing internal financial interests as such, but with correspondingly contested and diverse outcomes.

categorization of welfare regimes than when the analysis is restricted to social protection and labour market policies.

For Berggren et al. (2010, p. 409–410), in the context of care management in a study of provision for the elderly and psychiatric disabled in Sweden, a "move from 'ideal types construction' to 'real types descriptions' in positioning and understanding welfare state differences and similarities would be fruitful".[23] This study allows for variation within national provision according to how it is decentralised to the local, as is confirmed by Künzel (2012) who has this to say about minimum income policies across France and Germany, p. 4:

> At the local level, however, we have discovered very different outcomes of active inclusion reforms, ranging from market-oriented, integrated and participatory variants of active inclusion to the persistence of standardized benefits.

More broadly, Wendt (2009) finds that there is no reason for health regimes to match with welfare regimes, especially as more countries are taken into account as well as in addressing the specificities of health itself.[24] In short (Powell and Barrientos, 2011, p. 75):[25]

> Regimes are broader than individual programmes such as pensions, and broader than the welfare state ... A number of authors have attempted to apply Esping-Andersen's typology to specific programmes, or groups of programmes ... Their findings are mixed. Some find the welfare regime typology works, while others find it does not ... Britain – supposedly the

---

23   Albeit from a perspective of suggesting "This shift implies a move from ideology/structure and policy to values/administration and outcome" (Berggren et al. 2010, p. 410), something which is unlikely to offer much beyond a particular empirical focus and narrative.

24   Although, Kam (2012, p. 108) looking at health through the prism of decommodification, finds, "the existence of significant differences in the welfare systems between the East Asian countries and the 18 OECD countries studied by Esping-Andersen (1990) and the existence of significant similarities in the welfare systems between East Asian countries".

25   See also Kasza (2006, p. 153), "Regime analysis fails as a way to categorize welfare systems according to their programmatic differences because the welfare policies of each country have different histories, discrete sets of policy actors participate in various fields of welfare policy making, variations in the policy-making process affect policy substance, and borrowing from foreign models introduces inconsistencies into each country's welfare package. Each of these factors dilutes the relationship between the class politics of a country's ruling party in a given period and its welfare programs, stripping welfare systems of the consistency required by a regime typology".

residualist welfare state – had the largest social rented sector; French economic policy was the most orthodoxly neo-liberal; and corporatist Germany had gone furthest in privatizing social housing ... focus on 'social assistance regimes' or 'poverty regimes' ... find only a limited relationship to wider welfare regimes ... welfare regimes tend to be based on transfers rather than services, but the relationship between them is far from clear. Moreover, there are important differences between the patterns of health and social care ... welfare states are composed of different approaches to different social risk, and the approach to each social risk is often 'hybrid'.

Proliferating hybrids of proliferating regimes increasingly suggests a chaotic classificatory scheme.

Even those contributions that remain (unquestioningly) faithful to the welfare regime approach find it necessary to qualify or supplement it.[26] Kuitto (2011, p. 348) finds five clusters across 28 European countries, with welfare states differing primarily "along their emphasis either on cash transfers for the elderly or on social services and cash transfers for the working-age population".[27] Franzoni and Voorend (2009 and 2011) whether looking at the distributional impact of welfare regimes or the potential for CCTs "to become stepping stones to universal social policy" (Franzoni and Voorend, 2009, p. 279), in Chile, Costa Rica and El Salvador, find it necessary to look at the role of societal coalitions. Gough and Sharkh (2011) draw on five 'I's as the determinants of social

---

26   For a spirited defence of the WRA, in part upon the grounds that ideal types have been displaced by typologies in the passage from Esping-Andersen's original formulation, see van Kersbergen (2013). However, while one is never supposed to be realised purely in practice, and the other is through classification, neither suffices to deal with the issues raised here of the diversity of regimes, and their determinants, across and within countries. See also Ferragina and Seeleib-Kaiser (2011, p. 597) for whom, emphasis added, "Our literature review confirms the existence of three worlds of welfare capitalism in the light of ideal types. We propose a classification of rich democracies on a *continuum* from the most purely social-democratic (Sweden) to the most liberal country (the United States)". And see Kammer et al. (2012) for support for the WRA by examining redistribution at the household level, albeit with Belgium and Netherlands as hybrids across social democratic and conservative models.

27   While "European welfare states cluster along these two spending dimensions in a way that to a great extent coincides with the well-known delineation of welfare regimes based on institutional characteristics", yet "the results attest to the emergence of a variety of welfare arrangements in the post-communist region ... with a general orientation toward a Bismarckian or conservative model". Furthermore, "The results of this analysis demonstrate that disaggregated welfare expenditure measures retain considerable importance in elucidating the realities of contemporary welfare policy" (Kuitto, 2011, p. 348).

policy: industrialisation, interests, institutions, ideas and international influences, and use cluster analysis to identify welfare regimes lettered A through
H, with only partial association with meeting welfare/security needs. In a
separate paper, Sharkh and Gough (2010, p. 28) suggest the "regime approach
remains a fruitful paradigm for thinking about social policy across the developing as well as the developed world". For this, they give three justifications:

> First, it situates modern 'welfare states' within a wider *welfare mix*: gov-
> ernments interact with markets and families to produce and distribute
> welfare. Second, it pays attention to welfare *outcomes*, the final impact
> on human security, need satisfaction and wellbeing. Third, it is a *political
> economy* approach that embeds welfare institutions in the 'deep struc-
> tures' of social reproduction: it forces researchers to analyze social policy
> not merely in technical but in power terms.

But, as argued, the increasing diversity across welfare states and mixes tends
to undermine the approach. In the extreme and in practice, not least in their
own contribution and that of others, the political economy or other theoretical
approaches, let alone genuine reference to deep structures and power, tend
to be overlooked in deference to the use of statistical methods in identifying
regimes. Accordingly, despite their welcome departure from a "one-size-fits-
all" approach to social policy across the global South, this is not remedied by
a many-size-fits-all replacement in which, "there is greater scope for policy
learning within regime clusters".

   Far from justifying the extension of the WRA to developing countries, Sharkh
and Gough (2010) explicitly open up the potential for critical commentary on
three further aspects: its scope of application, its theory and its policy implications. Initially, especially in light of its subsequent coverage, the scope of application of the WRA was both ambitious (categorising different welfare states
as a whole) and, paradoxically, relatively limited in two significant aspects.
On the one hand, it was confined to a sample of developed countries. On the
other hand, although a product of the neoliberal era by timing (early 1990s),
its origins are heavily marked by the lingering influences of the conditions of
the post-war boom and its association with Keynesian welfarism, however
this might be interpreted. As a result, there is at least an implicit presumption
that the welfare states or regimes concerned are at a mature stage, rather than
being in the process of being established, and in the context of advanced capitalist economies in which Keynesianism still appears to be a viable intellectual
and policy option. Inevitably, this places considerable logical and historical
limitations on the scope of applicability of the WRA, irrespective of its merits,

for understanding the conditions that have spawned it and which have long been in the process of being dissolved. The WRA is confined, initially, to those advanced societies that have benefitted from the post-war boom even if subsequently, they were deep in the period of neoliberalism.[28] Scholarly ethos at the time when the WRA emerges focuses in the main on explaining relatively minor differences in performance across otherwise similarly (potentially) expanding economies – especially for growth, with Germany and Japan, for example, at the fore, and welfare provision, where Scandinavia takes the lead.

Most obviously, this means societies in which average incomes are high, formal employment and working conditions are normal, and unemployment is variable but contained. There will be a modern industrial sector, possibly in relative decline by weight of economic activity, and long-established and well-functioning (government) bureaucracies and institutions. The family of welfare regimes in such narrowly delimited circumstances will only show minor differences compared to regimes spread wider over both historical (long before and longer after the post-war boom) and logical (different stages of development) canvases.

In addition, the WRA was primarily focused upon income transfers as opposed to welfare services, something equally more prominent in the sorts of societies under consideration at a particular stage in their development. Now, with the hindsight of a further two decades of neoliberalism and the extensive application of the WRA to a range of other societies, it is scarcely surprising that it should not be able to stand on the relatively slender foundations on which it was constructed. Why should the specific approach to select welfare states around the period of the post-war boom be of general applicability to other times, places and programmes?

Indeed, the expansive scope of the WRA is indicative of a narrow Eurocentric conceptual imperialism,[29] in which other countries are illegitimately seen

---

28 Interestingly, much the same can be said of the varieties of capitalism (VoC) approach, emerging at the same time, indeed the last possible moment for it to do so, with the prospective projection forward of the favoured Keynesian interventionist model that had already been rendered redundant by neoliberalism (Ashman and Fine, 2013). For an attempt to marry WRA and VoC, see Lehndorff (2012).

29 See Izuhara (2013) for this in the context of East Asia, with China especially challenging to the WRA as new kid on the block with particularly rapid shifts in policy and provision. See also Walker and Wong (2013). Such conceptual imperialism can also be unwitting, as with the productivist and developmental interpretations of East Asian welfare provision corresponding to longstanding Western productivist and ends-oriented approaches, respectively (Wong, 2013). Interestingly, it is also the case that welfare policy is often seen in terms of the path dependency derived from colonial heritage but this cannot be taken

through its prism with modification to suit where the fit is poor, blurred or even more or less non-existent. And the ultimate option remains to add another ideal type. This is indicative of the poverty of theory attached to the WRA which should, at least in principle, delimit its historical and logical scope of application, rather than bordering on the universal in its substance. Is the theory suitable for other societies than those that gave it birth and for welfare programmes at other points in world history and national stages of development?

Such considerations are a reflection of a deeper theoretical malaise across the welfare regime approach. As put by Arts and Gelissen (2002, p. 155) more than a decade ago, "A better formulation of the theory on which it is based deserves priority". This is amply confirmed by the more recent review of Powell and Barrientos (2011, p. 81):[30]

> The main conclusion of the article is that the 'welfare modelling business' requires investment in its more neglected elements. There has been a great deal of attention on the empirical validity of Esping-Andersen's *Three Worlds*. However, apart from the feminist critique and de-familization, the conceptual and theoretical aspects which the typology was expected to facilitate remain under-developed. It is a little ironic that a work aiming to lay bare the 'theoretical substance of welfare states' (Esping-Andersen, 1990, p. 19) has led to a largely atheoretical debate.

To some extent, this theoretical deficiency is a reflection of the neglect of Esping-Andersen's original intentions concerning theoretical scrutiny of the role of resources and power as the structural underpinnings for factors such as decommodification and stratification, and how these give rise to complex outcomes across ideal types of welfare regimes. These reflect the previously delineated intellectual origins of the WRA in the conditions of the post-war boom, and the potentially progressive roles played by an industrial working class and its organisations, politics and ethos. Subsequently, specifying a proliferation of regime types has taken precedence over explaining and understanding their nature, with casual appeal to a range of other considerations and categorisations such as hybrids, gender, decommodification and defamilisation.

---

for granted, and what does or does not get passed on needs to be explained (Chang and Ku, 2013).

30   This is not, though, to accept that the theoretical way forward is that, "more attention must be directed at the how issues of social rights, stratification, the welfare mix and social risks – the key analytical elements of Esping-Andersen (1990, 1999) – combine in welfare states" (Powell and Barrientos, 2011, p. 81).

There are a number of issues involved here. The first is whether whatever theory is present is appropriate to its object of study, specifying and understanding the provision of welfare presumably across some form of geographically, historically and logically delimited application associated with capitalist development. There will be a need to finesse the general (capitalism), the historical (over what period and how characterised), and the specific (provision of what, to whom, through what mechanisms). The initial power-resources hypothesis deployed by Esping-Andersen is arguably inadequate for purpose along a number of dimensions, not least because it is universal in method (all societies deploy power and resources), fails to address explicitly the nature and period of capitalism under consideration (although, as already argued, it is itself very much a product of the Keynesian period, or just beyond into its decline),[31] and equally fails to have the potential to fill the gap between the more abstract theoretical considerations and the chain of causation linking these to outcomes (see the third point below).

Second is that the theory underpinning the WRA has not remained static. Indeed, as observed, it has stagnated or even decayed in deference to, or even because of, the strain imposed by empirical case studies involving regime classification and extension. Reference to power and resources as explanatory factors are increasingly, even absolutely, notable for their absence. This decline might reflect an unconscious response to the rise of neoliberalism and a corresponding shift in balance, composition, and organisation of forces across and within capital and labour. Thus, the theory underpinning the WRA may well be a victim of its own limitations, the weight of empirical studies in its image, and the demise of the Keynesian period that inspired it.

With this decline and shift in WRA theory, it would, of course, be unduly harsh to blame such developments in the literature in this regard on Esping-Andersen himself. He can hardly be held responsible for his followers. But nor would blaming him be entirely a case of blaming the innocent victim. As argued as early as Fine (2002d), Esping-Andersen himself seems to have abandoned the power-resources theory for flirtation with, if not embrace of, mainstream concepts such as collective risk management and market failures.

---

31   And, of course, there are also historically delimited elements within the conceptual apparatus employed by Esping-Andersen and his followers, such as decommodification, which presume, however explicitly, a particular stage of capitalism. Note though, in passing, that the use of the term decommodification is casual, merely representing some strengthening of labour's position in its social and economic reproduction. It does not signify the abolition of labour power as a commodity, in the same way as for decommodified goods and services. See Saritas (2016).

Esping-Andersen (1999, p. 36) heads a section, "The Foundations of Welfare Regimes: Risk Management", with opening sentence, "social policy means public management of social risks". Compare this with his classic text Esping-Andersen (1990, p. 11) for which "the central question, not only for Marxism but for the entire contemporary debate on the welfare state, is whether, and under what conditions, the class divisions and social inequalities produced under capitalism can be undone by parliamentary democracy".

In his subsequent work, *The Incomplete Revolution*, Esping Andersen (2009, p. XVIII) informs us that, "Some years ago I solemnly promised to myself that I would from then on dedicate my research and writing to anything but the welfare state". Here, as previously, he has commendably taken the criticism of neglect of gender considerations to heart, redefining welfare provision in terms of household life chances from cradle to grave, especially emphasising early years of life and, "to conclude that if the welfare state can help accelerate the revolution of women's roles, we will probably also harvest major equality and efficiency gains across the board" (Esping-Andersen, 2009, p. 174). Otherwise the volume is marked by: (i) continuing identification of ideal types (associated with gender roles and their broader economic and social situation and life chances), not least through a traditional male breadwinner model set against defamilialisation and masculinisation of women as they engage in work; (ii) ironically in light of ideal types, attention to the proliferation and diversity of living arrangements and familial choices; and (iii) the taking of Gary Becker and Talcott Parsons as points of departure and yet incorporation of casual reference to multiple equilibria, Pareto efficiency, the knowledge economy, inequality and homogamy, human capital, social investment, information failure, and the troika of family, market and government. This might be thought not so much to be completing an intellectual revolution as consolidating a counterrevolution.[32]

But, third, what then of the policy implications of the WRA that are, for example, claimed in principle by Sharkh and Gough (2010), not least for developing countries? Across the literature, there is primarily a stunning, if

---

32   As Powell and Barrientos (2011, p. 74) suggest, "The new emphasis on social risk effectively replaces the political-economy, power resources, approach to building welfare regimes in the three worlds, with a more functional response to perceived threats to welfare". They also observe, p. 70, "It has been criticised for being too centred on Scandinavian debates; ignoring the development of feminism as one of the most important and creative forces in social sciences over the past two decades; not being well-adapted to encompass the postmodern development of industrial society; being ill-adapted to understand the differences between welfare states in the politics of retrenchment; and not paying sufficient attention to the political differences between consensus and majoritarian regimes".

unobserved, silence. This is for good reason, despite what I suspect is an inclination to favour expanded welfare provision through the state and the erstwhile, golden-age standards, and evolving developments, of Scandinavian levels and forms of provision. The problem is that the WRA almost inevitably offers little by way of policy advice for two compelling and complementary reasons. One reason is that, in welfare as in many other things, we all want to be Scandinavian. But either the WRA offers no advice on how to transition from one regime to another in view of lack of theory, or, what theory there is, such as appeal to power and resources, suggests that transitions are pre-empted by underlying determinants such as history, the organisation and balance of class or other forces and their corresponding politics and ethos. So, "become like Sweden", is either unhelpful or infeasible. The second reason is, with welfare regimes as ideal types, whether grounded in underlying power and resources or not, there is little scope for the intermediate relations, processes, structures, agencies and ideational factors that influence, if not determine, policy in detail to be incorporated into the analysis. The WRA essentially precludes policy considerations at the levels of both grand regime determination and passage to policy and outcomes in detail.

These observations are borne out to a large degree by Jensen (2011a) who highlights the extent to which the WRA has been based upon income transfers as opposed to welfare services, and how much more challenging it is to broaden the approach from concentration on pensions and social security. What work there is on welfare services tends to fall into three categories: (i) programme-specific drawing on health care, childcare or education, for example; (ii) typologies to assess whether services fall into welfare regimes in cross-country comparisons; and (iii) attempts to gauge whether there are close relations or not between the sorts of income transfers that occur and the provision of welfare services. While those under (i) tend to overlook broader influences and implications, those under (ii) and (iii) beg the question of why should the same ideal types prevail, or be determined by the same factors, for income transfers as for welfare services.

Jensen supports this conclusion by drawing upon the idea that a broader set of constituencies, rather than a stereotyped strengthening of labour movements and left-wing governments, are now involved in making welfare policy. Moreover, there are not just different interests but these interests are differently and more narrowly focused. Indeed, p. 409:

> Two points should be noted here. First, the policy development of individual welfare programmes is difficult to understand by relying on macro-level factors, such as the power of the left. Much more important is the

strength of sector-level interest groups. Second, the strength of these sector-level interest groups may vary considerably from one sector to the next ... this entails that it becomes difficult to talk of *the* welfare state in a country because the policy dynamic is likely to be very different in different welfare programmes. The within-country variation is, in other words, likely to be as great as, or greater than, the between-country variation.

More specifically, Jensen argues welfare services are distinct from income transfers because they involve provision, "the production mode", that "entails a transformation of the input (money) into an output (the actual in-kind service)". As a result, vested interests are created in the process of provision itself and, in addition, this tends to induce both the participation of the state and more complex conflicts over the levels and forms of provision. Indeed, the "effect of these different production modes is quite dramatic", p. 410, with reference made to vested, possibly conservative, interests of those attached to the processes of provision as opposed to macro-goals and ideational factors around equality, p. 411:

> The welfare service component is tricky to analyse compared with the transfer component, not least because the individual services constituting this component are of such varied quality. Healthcare, education and social care are hugely different fields characterised by very different policy dynamics.

As will be argued, there is much to commend in Jensen's conclusion, but it suffers from being derived from distinction between welfare as income transfers and as services. This is not simply because there are comparable difficulties for the WRA for both but also because the fact that one is produced and other is not, in some sense, is insufficient in explaining why welfare provision as a whole is differentiated. State involvement, vested sectoral interests and processes of provision are equally applicable to income transfers. This is, especially and increasingly obvious in case of pensions and where public provision might involve private agencies (subcontracting the assessment for disability, housing or other benefits for example).[33] Income transfers as much as welfare

---

33   In a separate contribution on welfare service provision, Jensen (2011b) offers eight factors as determinants: left-party strength; vested interests; capacity of left-wing parties better able to deliver austerity; technical complexity; veto points; deindustrialisation increasing childcare; globalisation; and women's social demands. But these, and other factors, also apply to a greater or lesser extent to income transfers.

services equally "are hugely different fields characterised by very different policy dynamics", p. 411. This has been particularly highlighted by the most recent events around the crisis even if it does not originate with them, as will be seen from the next section but one.

3   ... to Convergence through Path Dependence to Crisis

It is useful to acknowledge that not all welfare analysis is confined to the WRA, although its presence is heavy even upon those who depart from it. There have been other takes on the nature and evolution of welfare, especially within if not originating from the rise of neoliberalism and reinforced by its current global crisis. Particularly prominent across the more recent literature have been two considerations, neatly summarised as whether and how social policy has exhibited convergence (because of neoliberalism and globalisation) and whether and how it has been subject to path dependence (which has meant in social policy terms, resistance or obstacles to changes in response to neoliberalism, globalisation *and* crisis).[34] As with the welfare regime approach, the literature has become heavily empirically driven, with more or less casual reliance upon conceptual points of reference for the criteria, let alone the processes of whether or not there is convergence, with the same applying, rather than questioning, what were the criteria of difference in the past.[35] Not surprisingly in view of earlier discussions, there is a mix of contributions and conclusions across countries and programmes.

Thus, for example, Guo and Gilbert (2007) investigate continuity and change across welfare regimes and family policy, focusing on the role of defamilisation and decommodification. They find that the two are mutually supportive but in an unstable relationship with one another. For Southern European welfare states, Greve (2008a, p. 105) finds that:

---

34   Note that much of the literature overlooks how social policy has to change in light of secular trends in household composition, feminisation of the workforce and an ageing society (Grimshaw and Rubery, 2012; and Rubery, 2011). The nature of labour markets has also changed, as emphasised by Heintz and Lund (2012), with multinational corporations heavily involved in flexible subcontracting to which social policy does, or does not have to, respond.

35   Schmitt and Starke (2011, p. 131), for example, conclude for OECD welfare states that, once correcting for conditioning factors, "the speed of welfare state convergence is influenced by the degree of globalization, EU membership and welfare regime type".

certain distinct characteristics still prevail in the Southern European welfare states, while ... movement towards the rest of Europe is also taking place. A more active welfare state with universalism at least in the area of health care, although with space for a private sector as well, might gradually move the welfare state away from its more classical highly familialistic framework.

Chung and Thewissen (2011, p. 16) suggest, framing around welfare regimes, that responses to unemployment in Germany, Sweden and the United Kingdom are strongly path-dependent in the short run according to "different dynamics than the more structural long-term policy developments". And Lewis et al. (2008, p. 21) conclude that, "There is very little evidence of convergence towards a dual, full-time worker model family outside the Nordic countries, although the balance between the hours which men and women spend in paid work is becoming less unequal".

There is, then, some evidence of erosion of difference with core distinctions remaining, especially at the two extremes of the United States and Scandinavia. For the former, Alber (2010, p. 108) is concerned to highlight, "*three aspects of Americanization in Europe and two aspects of Europeanization in the US*" having observed that, p. 114:[36]

in many respects the American welfare state is different and complex rather than incomplete, because it uses a host of different instruments, including not only social insurance, but also minimum wage legislation and tax credits for the working poor, as well as some other measures ... such as loan guarantees and other subsidies in housing, the regulation of employment conditions, and tort law ... within the realm of social security the American welfare state is more similar to European welfare states than the term 'residual welfare state' suggests, because it is also dominated by *public* provisions for welfare, among which social insurance programmes, particularly Social Security and Medicare, predominate; because its public pension scheme is more universal, redistributive, and generous than the German pension insurance system, because social programmes have also been growing over time in recent decades; and because it is moving closer to Europe with respect to extended public health care schemes ... [But] noteworthy differences to Europe remain, most notably a stronger reliance on private schemes in pensions and

---

36   See also Greve (2008b).

health, a stronger emphasis on work-conditioned benefits, and a greater importance of selective or targeted schemes, which represent about one third of the total social spending in the American welfare state if Medicaid is included.

This leads him to reject the idea of the United States as a residual welfare state for concealing both the nature and the peculiarities of provision.[37] But the centre of gravity of the convergence literature is oriented around what is happening to the Scandinavian model. For Greve (2011, p. 113), "profound changes have taken place and the Nordic model is no longer so distinct and special as it has been in a historical perspective", although this is seen to be consistent with continuing, possibly widening, differentiation across countries. For Jørgensen and Schulze (2011), there has been the erosion of the Danish corporatist model, especially with regard to the strength and presence of trade unions, and Jochem (2011) sees this as important across the Nordic countries in responding to unemployment, especially with the decline of centralised national bargaining, although active support to access to labour markets remains through education for lifelong skills. More generally, for Kvist and Greve (2010, p. 146), using the Danish example:[38]

> The Nordic welfare model is undergoing a fundamental transformation ... Although Denmark still offers universal coverage in core welfare state areas, the increased use of occupational and fiscal welfare as well as changes in public schemes has gradually transformed the nation into a multi-tiered welfare state that is more dualistic and individualistic, with participation in the labour market becoming still more important for entitlement to benefits. These profound changes have taken place in such a way that although core characteristics are still in place, new structures and understandings of the welfare state are also developing. Thus classical typologies need revision, so that they include more focus on this combination of universality and institutional attachment to the labour market. Moreover, measures of what welfare comprises should include not only public but also private elements.

---

37   But see Adésínà (2009) for the idea, that for developing countries, the Washington Consensus marks the transition from transformative to residual social policy.

38   Although, for family policy, as already covered, Tunberger and Sigle-Rushton (2011) observe more continuity than change.

The reference, almost in passing, to the private sector is crucial not least in the context of neoliberalism. For social policy is not a sealed unit within the state, or between it and its citizens, but also interacts with the private sector in complex and shifting ways at both macro and micro levels, both in conditioning what is to be addressed by social policy and how it is addressed.

Such is brought out by Haynes' (2011, p. 130) study of income support for older people in countries of the OECD and the potential gender impact of movement toward (private) occupational pension schemes. For:

> In Scandinavia, the move towards occupational welfare and pensions seems less likely to disadvantage women because of their high participation in the labour market. In countries where women are encouraged and incentivized to take traditional caring roles over and above employment and where participation in the labour market is low, occupational welfare systems may pauperize women.

Significantly, then, the introduction of the private sector can displace both public service provision and familial dependence, as argued by Pavolini and Ranci (2008, p. 257–258) in their study of long-term care (LTC) across Western European countries:

> the reforms introduced in the six countries considered converge on a 'mixed' model of intervention with a growing intermediate level of public coverage of LTC needs, while the organization of care systems endeavours in various ways to combine the service-led model with an informal care-led model. This convergence is the paradoxical result of two opposing trends: while the countries traditionally closer to a service-led model have shifted to new forms of intervention based on greater flexibility (supposedly best guaranteed by the introduction of market mechanisms) and more attention to the family care giving capacity; the countries historically based on an informal care-led model have extended the public coverage of dependency needs and have progressively shifted to more organized forms of intervention where families are supported in their care giving through the introduction of market mechanisms and new measures aimed at helping the caring families.

Similar restructuring, and tensions, across forms and levels of provision are highlighted by Mendes' (2009) study of Australian (neoliberal) welfare state reform with workfare measures, and corresponding cuts to wages and welfare, complemented by continuing family payments systems as a way of addressing poverty. This should not blind us, though, to the possibilities that qualitative and quantitative welfare retrenchment can proceed together, mutually reinforcing one another, as argued by Jutila (2011) for Finland over the past twenty years.

And, at least until the dust settles, comfortable notions of convergence, and path dependence[39] appear somewhat bizarre in the context of the global crisis, especially to the citizens of Greece for example, with the double whammy of explosion of need and implosion of provision.[40] Nonetheless, crises are seen as opportunities (Ramesh, 2009), and as Prasad and Gerecke (2010, p. 236) argue:[41]

---

39   See Isuani (2010) for path dependence and resistance to change in the Argentine welfare system but Hertel-Fernandez (2009) for a critique of path dependence on the grounds that institutions can be turned to entirely different purposes once circumstances change, using the example of Chile.

40   See Arcanjo (2012, p.16) for varieties of unemployment reform across France, Germany, Portugal and Spain with diversity of outcomes despite reform towards "weaker social rights and stronger obligations". See also Yerkes and van der Veen (2011, p. 430) for the suggestion that, "the current economic crisis, in combination with previous reforms and changing social risks, creates the potential for an even greater transformation of social rights". Further, Vis et al. (2011, p. 338) point to the added complexities across the mix of welfare regimes, path dependence, convergence or not, and the phasing of responses to the crisis, "If ever there was momentum to roll back the welfare state, it is the (aftermath) of the financial crisis of 2008–09. All theoretical perspectives within comparative welfare state research predict radical reform in this circumstance, but does it also happen? Our data indicate that – at least so far – it does not. Focusing on a selection of advanced welfare states (the UK, the USA, Germany, the Netherlands, Denmark and Sweden), we find that these countries face similar problems and that their initial response to these problems is also similar. The latter is surprising because, theoretically, we would expect varying responses across welfare state regime types. Rather than retrenchment, we observe a first phase of emergency capital injections in the banking sector and a second of Keynesian demand management and labour market protection, including the (temporary) expansion of social programmes. Continuing public support for the welfare state was a main precondition for this lack of immediate radical retrenchment. However, the contours of a third phase have become apparent now that budgetary constraints are forcing political actors to make tough choices and introduce austerity policies. As a result, the question of who pays what, when, and how will likely give rise to increasingly sharp distributional conflicts".

41   See also Taylor-Gooby (2012) on whether it is cuts or restructuring in the United Kingdom, and Doetter and Götze (2011, p. 488) for its health system for which, "while acute economic crises create windows of opportunity for change, it is the interaction of system-specific deficits and the role of ideas and political factors that largely condition the content and timing of reforms". As, Dukelow (2011, p. 408) puts it for Ireland, "if Ireland continues on the path it has instigated, the liberal disposition of the Irish welfare state will intensify". See also Sacchi et al. (2011, p. 484) on short-time working across Austria, Germany and Italy, concluding that, "programme level convergence gives way to rather

social security regimes have often been born out of crisis. In addition, on average, social security spending increases over the course of a crisis; however, there is wide regional variation, with advanced countries exhibiting the most countercyclical spending ... crises can be used as an occasion to improve and strengthen social security; in doing so, countries not only mitigate the worst effects of the crisis, but also create better social policy and improve long-term crisis preparedness ... the countries that have avoided fiscal discipline during past crises have typically been more successful.[42]

Nonetheless, whether crises prompt enhanced or reduced social policy, it is once more imperative to finesse this by context, ranging from migration to child labour. Deacon (2011, p. 147) points to "the unwillingness of national social policies to meet the social protection needs of an increasingly mobile global population, which will increase with the global climate change crisis inducing environmental migration". On a more optimistic, if unrealistic, note, why is a crisis necessary for this? Patel (2009, p. S51) suggests:

> As long as governments and international organizations keep their eye on the ball and maintain a focus on free and compulsory primary education; immunization; micronutrient supplementation (iodized salt, vitamin A, and zinc for children and iron folate for pregnant and lactating women); behavioral change programs such as sex education; the importance of breast feeding; oral rehydration during episodes of diarrhea; and, sleeping under mosquito nets in malarial areas, children in East Asia will continue to thrive – and to guarantee the future dynamism of the region.

Easier said than done. Kane (2009) points to the lack of any simple causal relationship between poverty and the incidence of child labour, with the corresponding prospect of crisis-induced increases in some places and greater protection in others.[43]

---

differentiated trajectories of development which tend to reinforce existing divergences between Germany and Austria, on the one hand, and Italy on the other".

42   See also Pavolini and Ranci (2008) for crises as a stimulus for progressive reform and Riesco (2009b) for the consequences for (privatised) pensions in Latin America.

43   And for Mahon (2010, p. 172), "Although the Organisation for Economic Co-operation and Development (OECD) and the World Bank are often (rightly) associated with the diffusion of ideas and practices underpinning neoliberal globalization, a closer examination of their policy discourses over the last decade suggests that they have clearly gone beyond the brute neoliberal prescription of welfare cuts and structural adjustment. This shift is particularly evident in their advocacy of public investment in childcare/child

On a wider canvas, there is a remarkable resonance between the longer-established globalisation and crisis literatures in terms of impact upon social policy in view of their common either/or outlook, each deriving this from the ambiguous responses to similarly perceived stimuli of external pressures. Thus, for Koster (2008, p. 291), there are a number of arguments about the effects of globalisation, such as:[44]

> the welfare state cannot be sustained as globalisation increases for the reason that, due to mobility of capital, countries will no longer be able to maintain the high taxes that are required to fund the welfare state ... Others argue that there is a positive relationship between globalisation and welfare spending because financially open countries require substantial welfare state investment to shield citizens from external shocks caused by fluctuations on international markets.

Kim and Zurlo (2009, p. 131), drawing on Blackmon (2006), are even more explicit in addressing how globalisation affects welfare states as mediated by the ubiquitous welfare regimes in their account:

> The *efficiency hypothesis* ... argues that globalisation is the cause of welfare state decline. On the other hand, a positive perspective, called the *compensation hypothesis* ... claims that the emerging internationalisation of economies is related to a high demand for social security, which in turn facilitates an upward shift of taxation and social spending levels.

In this way, together with other refinements, we can always chart, even explain, what happens as a combination of efficiency and compensation.

---

development programs, as 'investing in children' has come to be seen as a critical component of the paradigm. Different versions of this discourse, however, reflect a greater or lesser break from neoliberal canons". Further, Mahon (2009) suggests the OECD can play a softer line in reconciling family and work lives, as it does not have to put (aid) money where its mouth is.

44   He adds that the impact of globalisation should be acknowledged in its political and social as well as its economic dimensions. See also Koster (2009).

4 This Time (Social Policy) Is (and Was) Different(iated)[45]

At the time of writing (February 2014), no one can doubt that the nature and impact of the current crisis is both deep and yet uneven from and within one country to another. Youth unemployment, for example, is soaring towards 60 per cent in Greece and Spain, relative to levels of less than half this for their populations as a whole. Reduce this by a further four-fifths for Germany. Across the European Union (EU), similar sharp contrasts are to be found for wage levels, with falls in real terms over the course of the crisis in Greece of the order of 22 per cent, of over 10 per cent in Hungary, Lithuania and Romania, of moderate declines (less than 10 per cent) in many countries, and even moderate increases in Belgium, Bulgaria, Croatia, the Czech Republic, Finland, France, Germany and Sweden .

Inevitably, the impact of the crisis is in some, if not major, part, a consequence of the policies adopted in response to it. Initially, there was some fiscal stimulus, although this rapidly morphed, especially in the United Kingdom and the United States, into quantitative easing followed by deflationary measures from 2010. In this light, it is worth quoting at length from Ortiz and Cummins (2013a, p. 1) who have reviewed spending projections and prospects for between 170 to 180 countries drawing upon IMF studies.[46] For them:

> In a first phase of the global economic crisis (2008–09), most governments introduced fiscal stimulus programs and ramped up public spending, as the world was able to coordinate policies. However, premature expenditure contraction became widespread in 2010, which marked the beginning of the second phase of the crisis, despite vulnerable populations' urgent and significant need of public assistance. In 2013, the scope of public expenditure consolidation is expected to intensify significantly, impacting 119 countries in terms of GDP, and then steadily increase to reach 132 countries in 2015. The latest IMF projections suggest that this trend will continue at least through 2016.
>
> One of the key findings of this analysis is that fiscal contraction is most severe in the developing world. Overall, 68 developing countries are projected to cut public spending by 3.7% of GDP, on average, in the third phase

---

45 See Reinhart and Rogoff (2010) with title "This Time is Different: Eight Centuries of Financial Folly".

46 See also Ortiz and Cummins (2013b) where impacts of austerity on women are addressed although, significantly and understandably, by reference to knock-on effects of policies given limited attention to gendered requirements of social policy!

of the crisis (2013–15) compared to 26 high-income countries, which are expected to contract by 2.2% of GDP, on average. Moreover, comparing the 2013–15 and 2005–07 periods suggest that a quarter of countries are undergoing excessive contraction, defined as cutting expenditures below pre-crisis levels. In terms of population, austerity will be affecting 5.8 billion people or 80% of the global population in 2013; this is expected to increase to 6.3 billion or 90% of persons worldwide by 2015.

Regarding austerity measures, a desk review of IMF country reports published since 2010 indicates that governments are weighing various adjustment strategies. These include: (i) elimination or reduction of subsidies, including on fuel, agriculture and food products (in 100 countries); (ii) wage bill cuts/caps, including the salaries of education, health and other public sector workers (in 98 countries); (iii) rationalizing and further targeting of safety nets (in 80 countries); (iv) pension reform (in 86 countries); (v) healthcare reform (in 37 countries); and (vi) labor flexibilization (in 32 countries). Many governments are also considering revenue-side measures that can adversely impact vulnerable populations, mainly through introducing or broadening consumption taxes, such as value added taxes (VATs), on basic products that are disproportionately consumed by poor households (in 94 countries).

A different take on such impacts of the crisis is offered by van Dijk (2013) who studies the experience of financial crises over the period 1970–2009, during which all but two of the 126 countries covered suffered at least one banking crisis, and 1.5 on average. Of course, not all crises are the same, and the current episode is notable for bucking the outcome of an average inflation of prices of 30 per cent over six years, although the current stands out for far exceeding GDP declines and unemployment increases of 2 per cent.[47] But, in addition, "A wider-angle lens exposes broad-ranging implications for society. For example, in the six years following a crisis, average life expectancy declines by nine

---

47   See also Ball et al. (2013, p. 1), "Using episodes of fiscal consolidation for a sample of 17 OECD countries over the period 1978–2009, we find that fiscal consolidation has typically had significant distributional effects by raising inequality, decreasing wage income shares and increasing long-term unemployment. The evidence also suggests that spending-based adjustments have had, on average, larger distributional effects than tax-based adjustments. That such postures should be emanating from the IMF is striking but should also be viewed with some suspicion insofar as it has primarily played a legitimising role as translation into policy response is negligible in terms of the strong dissonance between such scholarship and policy practice".

months, primary school enrolment drops by 3.5%, and fertility falls by 5.5% (but adolescent fertility rises by 4.5%)" (van Dijk, 2013, p. 1).[48]

These narratives can hardly come as a surprise and, especially in light of pre-occupation in the current crisis with financial developments as precursor if not cause, have given rise to the invention of an ideal-type of household of the following sort (heavily driven by stereotyped US experience). In short, households have been subject to: a pincer movement of neoliberalism and rampaging finance in which real wages have been held down; provision through social expenditures has been privatised, reduced or even withdrawn; credit has necessarily been used to sustain norms of consumption across commodities and, recently and increasingly, commodified forms of social provision; and capital gains from housing bubbles have underwritten expansion of credit-fuelled consumption. Also the coincidental rise of both neoliberalism and finance has exacerbated income inequality, fuelling speculative investment by the wealthier.[49] As Crouch (2011, p. 114) puts it:

> Two very different forces came together to rescue the neoliberal model from the instability that would otherwise have been its fate: the growth of credit markets for poor and middle-income people, and the emergence of derivatives and futures markets among the very wealthy. This combination produced a model of 'privatized Keynesianism' that occurred initially by chance, but which gradually became a crucial matter for public policy. Instead of governments taking on debt to stimulate the economy, individuals and families did so, including some rather poor ones.

Consequently, the current crisis is seen as both reflecting these developments of the past and intensifying the problems of the present and into the future. There are questions over this account for a number of reasons. First is to doubt whether the weight of 'financialisation' of households, let alone its dynamic, is primarily marked and driven by those on low incomes, deprived of social services, realising expenditure on the basis of evaporating capital gains in housing and unduly dependent on indebtedness through sustaining consumption by credit. This is an empirical question where averages may conceal more than

---

48   See also Stuckler and Basu (2013) for a striking account of the impact of austerity and austerity policies on health in general and various mortality rates in particular.

49   Such developments have been understood within a Marxist perspective in terms of financial exploitation of workers, for which see Lapavitsas (2009 and 2013) for an account and Fine (2010d and 2014) for an alternative and critique. For similar postures from a post-Keynesian perspective, see Fadda and Tridico (2013).

they reveal, not least as the household pressures experienced in the crisis are not necessarily representative of what has gone before. And even across the separate elements of the stereotypical household, there are liable to be different impacts from one household to another rather than all coming together for all in a bundle (Zakrevskaya and Mastracci, 2013).

Second, not only are households differentiated by how they are affected by the crisis, and the conditions that preceded it, so are the extent and forms of financial developments across different countries and sectors of the economy. While, especially for households, mortgage and pension finance may have been at the fore, these have neither been uniformly nor evenly attached to a homogeneous forward march of financial markets.[50]

Third, both more generally than for mortgages and pensions alone, how finance has interacted with the separate areas of provision, quite apart from old age and for housing, has differed. This is so by sector and by country and by interaction with social policy more generally. Each area of provision will have its own specific dynamics and traditions that will not been homogenised by its interaction with, what is in any case, the uneven incidence and forms of financial development.

Fourth, it must also be recognised that both finance and neoliberalism are not homogenising forces of introducing the market. Even in some sort of pure form, they leave, for example, a residue of those for whom the market is dysfunctional even if that is seen as a personal responsibility. This gives rise to the hard to house, the hard to provide for in old age, the hard to raise out of poverty, and the hard to educate, provide for health, etc. In short, even the hardest neoliberals are liable to be faced with a Polanyian double (or multidimensional) movement albeit arguably of their own making (if also subject to conflict and pressure) and on a greater or smaller residual of the population as opposed to social policy of universal scope (Rubery, 2011, p. 658):

> First, European social models are being asked to extend social support to meet new needs associated with the ageing society, changes in citizens' aspirations and behaviour and the reduced reliability of support from employers and the family. How nations respond to these new needs varies according to current gaps in provision and to political will, but most states up to the crisis were expanding their range of social interventions, sometimes leading to hybridization of their traditional social models.

---

50   See the Fessud research papers, Bayliss et al. (2013), Karacimen (2014), Saritas (2014), Churchill (2014), Fine (2013b) and Robertson (2014a and b).

Second, deconstruction of social models to implement neoliberalism and reconstruction to meet new needs are often two sides of the same process.

Precisely because such dysfunctions in provision for the hard to serve are multi-dimensional and uneven in their incidence, individual anomalies are liable to be created across them either in the form of either what are perceived to be undue benefits (to be cut) or undue harshness (to be alleviated). Not surprisingly, in context of crisis and recession, there are pressures both to reduce individual and overall benefits and to protect the most vulnerable, even if it tends to be an uneven contest between the two. Nonetheless, this creates a different sort of double or multi-dimensional movement of policy in squeezing and simplifying what has evolved in the past, thereby providing fertile ground for piecemeal amendments to protect the most vulnerable as its consequence, reinforcing the heterogeneity associated with neoliberalism. This even leads some to the point of the denial of neoliberalism on the basis of this diversity and faint resonances of welfarism (see below).

By virtue of the response to the crisis over the past few years, as indicated by Ortiz and Cummins (2013a), social policy in the aggregate can go in different directions, not least in response to greater need and vulnerability as opposed to the presumed predilection for austerity imperatives especially associated with neoliberalism, just as the Keynesian post-war boom or periods of growth might be associated with a remorseless expansion of welfarism. Not surprisingly, at lower levels of disaggregation to individual policies, the incidence of differentiated responses is liable to be even more variegated, not least given the specific nature of provision and mixed configuration of determinants over and above macro-determinants. The purpose of the rest of this section, through selective illustration, is to highlight just how multi-dimensional the determinants of policy are, irrespective of the more immediate considerations that have arisen in the wake of the current crisis.

For example, in terms of outcomes for minimum income (MI) support across the EU, Figari et al. (2013, p. 12) suggest:[51]

---

[51]   Thus, "our results seem to confirm that we are still some way from either institutional conformity ... or convergence of social protection in the EU" (Figari et al. 2013, p. 13). Matos (2013, p. 882) says, of transition economies, "there was no clear shift from social to individual insurance and no move from universal to means-tested benefits. Indeed, Hungarian and Latvian welfare reforms recombined these systems. The national arrangements were dissimilar and different benefits involved a specific *bricolage* of social protection systems. In general, family provisions and pensions were the most resilient, whereas

If coverage and adequacy are accepted as key dimensions of antipoverty effectiveness, then variation in effectiveness seems to be as significant *within* welfare regimes and/or social assistance types as it is *between* them ... Moreover, the apparently reasonable notion that coverage and adequacy must be strongly and positively correlated with each other (as countries move along a continuum from rudimentary to comprehensive social safety nets) is actually not borne out here. We have found that the correlation between our two dimensions of effectiveness is weak and negative (and very far from being statistically significant). Hence, while some countries offer better coverage and more adequate MI benefits than others, elsewhere in the EU, an implicit trade-off seems to be present: While some countries have opted for narrowly targeted but relatively generous MI support, others have chosen the exact opposite.

More generally, it might be concluded that the proposition of multiple determinants and diversity of outcome is pushing against an open door as far as the literature is concerned. In a Background Paper, framing "New Social Policy for the 21st Century", UNRISD (2014) offers five separate lists of factors, 26 elements in turn, ranging from aging to the environment.[52]

Otherwise, and foremost in assessing the complexity and diversity of social policy is the central role played by labour markets, in respect of both diversity of determinants and the interaction across them and corresponding policies. This is especially highlighted in the context of developing countries. Labour markets are both to be served, and compensated for, by social policy.[53] In this respect, the notion of decommodification derived from the WRA is unfit for purpose, failing to get to grips with the working poor (Iwata, 2013) – for example, the formal/informal divide in work and, whether contributions from, and benefits to, the formal sectors are extended to the informal for social security

---

unemployment benefits were more easily curtailed. These benefits have distinct beneficiaries and various levels of popularity".

52 See also Greve (ed.) (2013) for diversity of considerations in welfare provision; and Devereux et al. (2013) for multiplicity of factors in evaluating policy. Other factors promoting diversity include the ideational and institutional as in Buxton (2013) for social policy in Venezuela, and health provision in Thailand as in Yivayanond and Hanvoravongchai (2013), and Brazil, d'Ávila Viana and da Silva (2013).

53 Buendia and Palazuelos (2014) view the welfare/growth nexus in terms of four pillars: the first concerns the labour market with four elements – labour market policies, job creation by the public sector, industrial relations, and degree of solidarity around wage policy; the second is social security; the third is welfare provision; and the fourth is broader fiscal stance.

as in Indonesia (Suryahadi et al. 2014), and for health in Russia (Cook, 2013). There are issues relating to national and international migration, for social policy for China (Wong, 2013), together with urban/rural divides for social protection in India (most notably Mehrotra et al. 2013). Overlaying all of these, and many other issues, are gender inequalities, especially around paid and unpaid work and corresponding design and implementation of social policy which may reflect, consolidate or even temper structured discrimination without addressing underlying determinants of disadvantage in economic and social reproduction. Thus, for Cook and Razavi (2012, p. 3):

> three key points emerge from a gendered analysis of markets: first, women and men do not come to the market with the same resources (whether material or social); hence, women often cannot take advantage of new economic opportunities because they lack assets, resources (including time) and social contacts. Second, women and men have very different roles and relationships to the unpaid economy or the reproductive sector, which impinge on their links to the market. And third, following from the first two factors, gender inequalities in the market cannot be explained away in terms of choices made by individual women and men regarding the use of their time or the ignorance and prejudice of employers; rather, gender inequalities are structured into the way markets operate by discriminatory practices inherited from the past as well as by the differential exercise of power by different market actors.

For our purposes, two crucial points follow from this. First, the position of social policy is situated within, and interacts with, broader element of economic and social reproduction. Second, while focused upon gender, especially in light of this broader analytical sweep, similar if far from identical considerations apply to inequalities across other social groups whether by race, age or otherwise. As concluded by Kennett et al. (2013, p. 261), pointing to the diversity of social policy across other factors such as role of institutions and level of government intervention:[54]

> Constellations of social protection are translated within specific national and local contexts and are mediated by institutional structures, norms and practices, as well as power relations between and within states, and between men and women. Dimensions of gender, status (place, and

---

54   See Ronald (2013) for similar conclusion for East Asia in the context of housing policy.

length of residence, political elites and local cadres), class and ethnicity, as well as type of employer, are dynamics which mediate and shape access to social protection.

5   Social Policy – It's Financialisation, Stupid[55]

There are, then, a number of well-established toolkits for understanding social policy. It might possibly be best viewed as having been underpinned by intellectual plumbing rather than architecture, given the paucity of theory as opposed to framed empirical and statistical analysis around broadly defined explanatory factors such as globalisation, and structurally determined outcomes especially by reference to welfare regimes, or to convergence and path dependence. These perspectives are often difficult to operationalise empirically, given the availability of data and potential multiplicity of criteria and methods by which they are measured and investigated. As already emphasised, the results display extreme heterogeneity of outcome and change across and within programmes and countries. This is even more apparent once attention is directed at more detailed accounts, or those including other factors, such as comparative work organisation (Daly and Szebeheley, 2012) or long-term residential care for the aged in Sweden and Canada; bureaucracy on health (Greer, 2010); cultures and values on religion (Jo, 2011); on universalism versus selectivism (Kuivalainen and Niemelä, 2010); on values and attitudes (Muuri, 2009; and van Oorschot and Meuleman, 2012); and on the displacement of social spending by social investment (Jenson, 2010).[56]

As a result of these perspectives, social policy literature might best be seen as having worked but subject to springing leaks. Pursuing this metaphor further, it might be added that the leaks have, in the wake of the global crisis if not before, burst and transformed into a scarcely acknowledged flood. And, in moving from metaphor to parody, the social policy literature has been subject to an unduly complacent convergence around the welfare regimes approach with a corresponding deadweight of path dependence. For, to a large degree, social policy literature has been a victim of its early and longstanding success in deploying the leading concepts drawn from the social sciences. It knows how to deal with globalisation and neoliberalism. Crises such as the present one have often been experienced and responded to in the field of welfare and

---

55   See Fine (2012c) for the relationship between neoliberalism and financialisation.
56   For my own take on the material culture of social policy, see Fine (2013d).

social policy. It seems to be a matter of more of the same possibly with the added wrinkle of addressing the 'new kids on the block', CCTs and China. The result has been that the current global crisis has been treated as social policy business as usual, other than the addition of more empirical evidence, without reflecting seriously on how the present crisis might warrant a reconsideration of analytical frameworks to understand the past, present and future.

Such harsh criticism is justified if we consider what is not present within the literature. The most striking absence is 'financialisation'. Across the hundreds of articles reviewed, it appears just four times,[57] and only in passing: in Akan (2011, p. 372) where, for a Turkish Islamic sect, with "real production-centred economic investment and the elimination of the overfinancialisation of the aggregate economic activity, there would not be unemployment but full employment"; in the "Digest" for *Global Social Policy* (2010), which "reminds us of the role of the International Finance Corporation section of the [World] Bank in encouraging the financialisation of pensions and health care in developing countries"; as the financialisation of households in the short-lived New Labour Child Trust Fund in the United Kingdom (Prabhakar, 2013); and, almost certainly in the Jung and Walker (2009, p. 434) study of the Republic of Korea in which "the neoliberals, whose position is strengthening constantly, have demanded the financialisation of the NPF [National Pension Fund]".

This absence of financialisation is a devastating weakness both in terms of how it underpins other absences and in how it constrains understanding of what I have taken to be the key conundrum in addressing social policy: the diversity of outcomes across countries and sectors despite common underlying determinants of which, of course, financialisation is but one.[58] Further, the absence of financialisation from the social policy literature is indicative of weakness in understanding the relationship between it and globalisation. For,

---

57   Not surprisingly, financialisation is a more prominent term in the pensions literature. See Dixon and Sorsa (2009) for example which, unsurprisingly, finds variegated presence of finance and pension provision across Europe, (see below).

58   For a striking illustration of this point, see de Haan (2013, p.15) who correctly identifies the complexity, diversity and contextual nature of social policy across a number of dimensions, "Central to the argument in this article is that social policy is not merely about the redistribution of income or wealth generated by economic growth. Instead, social policy is integral to the way economic processes are structured, a role that changes but obtains heightened significance as economies open up. Like economic governance institutions, these social policies show a great deal of path dependence and are closely intertwined with national histories, ideologies and models of citizenship and inclusion. While globalisation plays a critical role in setting the parameters of social policies, history and path dependence continue to shape characteristic features of social policy". Yet no mention of financialisation.

while the *'Global Social Policy* school' has appropriately questioned the methodological nationalism of much social policy analysis, it is far from clear that it has done so with sufficient depth and breadth. Deacon (2011, p. 147) questions the UNRISD approach to poverty alleviation for ignoring the following terms:[59]

> (1) the continuing global contestation between agencies for the right to shape national social policy and for the content of that policy, which has come to a head in the context of the global economic crisis; (2) the unwillingness of national social policies to meet the social protection needs of an increasingly mobile global population, which will increase with the global climate change crisis inducing environmental migration; and (3) the consequential need to go beyond aid dependency not in the direction of reverting to only national funding but onwards in the direction of global public good funding.

At most, this only implicitly and indirectly addresses, for example, the role of financialisation (and its interactions with international and national agencies and the levels and forms taken by aid and global public funding), not least in generating instability in labour, energy and food markets, so significant for social policy. Indeed, it might be argued that treating the global in this way is worse than subordinating it to national considerations. Of course, globalisation is not to be reduced or confined to finance, and *Global Social Policy* commendably offers, for example, a contribution on the global strategies of the tobacco industry (Holden and Lee, 2009). But, for considerations of health, we also need to take account of the diseases of affluence of which smoking is but one globally profitable part, not least with the rise of philanthro-capitalism, with the Gates Foundation to the fore, and the location of national and international agencies within a world of financialisation.[60]

But what exactly is financialisation and why is it so important? Across a new but rapidly expanding – predominantly heterodox and diverse – literature, it has pointed to a number of different features of contemporary capitalism, mainly drawing upon the United Kingdom and the United States as its leading

---

59   The second of these has already been cited above.
60   See Stuckler et al. (2011) and, with the "global fight against obesity" hailed as a "mega-investment theme", Bank of America Merrill Lynch has targeted the obesity epidemic as it will "present opportunities for those selling pills, weight-loss programmes or health foods to governments" or, as it headlines, "Ride the obesity wave and supersize your returns", suggesting, possibly in parody, the prospect of futures markets for slimming products, *Your Money*, 12 July 2012, http://www.pressdisplay.com/pressdisplay/viewer.aspx.

sites, but with varying depth and breadth of incidence and impact across the globe, especially in the wake of the global crisis. In brief, financialisation has involved the phenomenal expansion of financial assets relative to real activity (by three times over the last 30 years); the proliferation of types of assets, from derivatives through to futures markets with a corresponding explosion of acronyms; the absolute and relative expansion of speculative as opposed to or at the expense of real investment; a shift in the balance of productive to financial imperatives within the private sector, whether financial or not; increasing inequality in income arising out of weight of financial rewards; consumer-led booms based on credit; the penetration of finance into ever more areas of economic and social life such as pensions, education, health, and provision of economic and social infrastructure; and the emergence of a neoliberal culture of reliance upon markets and private capital and corresponding anti-statism, despite the extent to which the rewards to private finance have in part derived from state finance itself. Financialisation is also associated with the continued role of the US dollar as world money despite, at least in the current crisis, its deficits in trade, capital account, the fiscus, and consumer spending, and minimal rates of interest.[61]

However financialisation is characterised, its consequences have been reductions in overall levels and efficacy of real investment as financial instruments and activities expand at its expense even if excessive investment does take place in particular sectors at particular times (as with the dotcom bubble of a decade ago); prioritising shareholder value, or financial worth, over other economic and social values; the pushing of policies towards conservatism and commercialisation in all respects; extending influence of finance more broadly, both directly and indirectly, over economic *and* social policy; placing more aspects of economic and social life at the risk of volatility from financial instability; and, conversely, placing the economy and social life at risk of crisis from triggers within particular markets as with the food and energy crises that preceded the financial crisis. While financialisation is a single word, it is attached to a wide variety of different forms and effects of finance with the United Kingdom and the United States at the fore. And, even if exposed in acute form by the crisis, its expansion over the last few decades has been at

---

61   I observe in passing that the policies adopted by the United States and some other developed countries have been exactly the opposite of those advised, or that have been imposed, on developing countries experiencing similar crises in the past. Ha-Joon Chang can be interpreted as being at the forefront of arguing in the context of historical paths to development, that those that have traversed it insist, "Do not do as we *did*, do as we say" to which should be added the nostrum, "Do not do as we *do*, do as we say".

the expense of the real economy, despite otherwise extraordinarily favourable 'fundamentals' for capitalist economies in terms of availabilities of new technologies, expansion in supplies of labour, weakening of labour and progressive movements more generally, slow increases in economic and social wages under the influence of neoliberal policy, and the end of the Cold War.

Against these perspectives, the significance of financialisation is twofold. One is in influencing the conditions of economic and social reproduction of which social policy is both a part and to which it is perceived to respond. Thus, the overall performance of economies, and the levels and composition of (un)employment, wages, working conditions and the inequalities of income[62] and access to consumption that they generate, have been profoundly underpinned by financialisation. By the same token, as remarked, financialisation has exerted a profound influence on social policy itself given its strong associations with globalisation and neoliberalism and their imperatives.[63]

Such postures are, though, extremely blunt in dealing with the diversities of social policy. For them to become more refined, it is germane to pinpoint the relationship between financialisation and neoliberalism, especially as the latter is often ill-defined and liberally – and inconsistently – used as a pejorative explanation of negative outcomes in contemporary conditions across huge diversity with corresponding inconsistencies and ambiguities, as the same policies and arguments are often associated with neoliberals and their opponents. Leading progressive scholars such as Castree (2006) and Ferguson (2007) have even doubted whether neoliberalism is a legitimate category of analysis.[64] And it is significant, especially in the academic world, that there are very few who label themselves as neoliberals as opposed to much more liberal application of the moniker to others. It is, however, no accident that financialisation and neoliberalism should coincide with one another over the period of the last thirty years. This is certainly true at the ideological level as the imperative of freeing markets has been applied first and foremost to those

---

62   See especially Palma (2009) who shows, especially in Latin America (and southern Africa) how the neoliberal art of democracy has been for those in the top decile of income to be able to gain at the expense of those at the bottom and even to squeeze the middle. See also Lloyd-Sherlock (2009, p. 359) who "demonstrates how high levels of social spending in Latin America contribute to social inequalities, rather than reducing them".

63   In scatter diagrams, Tridico (2012) finds correlations between financialisation and both inequality and labour market flexibility. By the same token, the example of China demonstrates potential for economic performance and reform of social policy in the absence of financialisation.

64   For an excellent finessing of the diversities and contextual substance of neoliberalism, see, for example, Hart (2002 and 2008).

supposedly pure markets associated with finance. But finance has also been associated with the emergence, strengthening and influence of financial elites at both national and international levels.[65]

As a result, I do not see financialisation as a simple associate of neoliberalism but as its defining or underlying aspect, with a reach that goes far beyond financial markets themselves. This is not to reduce neoliberalism to financialisation but to see the latter as its central aspect, and from which other aspects derive. This is so in two senses. On the one hand, financialisation has prospered on what are taken to be more general developments and policies associated with neoliberalism: freeing markets, making labour flexible and reducing wages and working conditions, privatisation, and so on, as with Washington Consensus conditionalities. On the other hand, financialisation has more generally underpinned the pursuit of such processes and policies and, thereby, sustained their mutual presence and interaction over an extended period. This is in contrast, for example, to the preceding Keynesian/welfarist period.

To make sense of and even to defend these postures, two further points need to be made. The first is to highlight significant connections but also inconsistencies across the ideologies, the scholarship and policies in practice of neoliberalism. These have a shifting relationship to one another across time, place and topic. I have argued this at great length elsewhere, particularly in the context of development (Fine, 2001 and 2010b; Fine et al. eds, 2001; and Bayliss et al. eds, 2011). It is crucial that, despite its scholarship and rhetoric, neoliberalism has always been heavily associated with state intervention.[66] As Amable (2011, p. 4) cleverly puts it, "In its popular representation, neoliberalism is reduced to a fight against 'state interventionism' and any public intervention in the economy is consequently held to be a victory by its most naïve opponents, even when this intervention actually follows the neoliberal precepts". Similarly (Hartman, 2005, p. 70):

> Critics of neoliberalism point to the widening economic disparities it has produced on a global scale and many take the localized discourses of welfare dependency at face value, appearing to believe that eventually all forms of state assistance will be rescinded. This article has attempted to show that though neoliberalism may exacerbate inequality on a massive

---

65   This raises issues of the role of the 'middle classes' in welfare provision (Deacon and Cohen, 2011). Does the strengthening of financial elites make them more or less important and how and in what ways (in terms of levels and forms of provision)? See also Haarstad (2011).

66   See, for example, Konings (2009).

scale, welfare provision in wealthy countries is integral to its continued success. At first glance they may seem antagonistic, but if this analysis is correct, neoliberal and welfare rationalities are bedfellows nonetheless.

In the specific context of Swedish pensions,[67] Belfrage and Ryner (2009, p. 258) observe that:[68]

> neoliberal*ism* in pure form is difficult to implement due to 'rigidities and dynamics of structure.' But this does not preclude that a broad strategy of neoliberal*ization* has had profound effects. These effects manifest themselves in composite and often contradictory outcomes of renegotiated settlements, whose character and iterative direction are predominantly shaped by neoliberal norms. This is at least what our study suggests.

A similar conclusion follows from Block's (2003, p. 8) discussion of Polanyi, "he argues that market liberals wanted to embed society in the autonomous economy but their project *could not* succeed. ... Even in market societies, ways have to be found to embed labor, land and money in social relations".

And, of course, this is true of all commodities, not just a troika of Polanyian 'fictitious' commodities of land, money and labour, but neoliberalism is not just caught in a Polanyian trap, it positively embraces it on an extensive scale. This has primarily been intervention to promote private capital in general and finance in particular, not to compensate for their consequences by virtue of a counter-movement. The response to the current crisis is no exception, and extraordinarily revealing, in which the crisis within – and not of – neoliberalism has been associated with extraordinary measures of support to finance both in levels of finance and even in nationalisation of failing financial institutions. Indeed, so powerful has been finance's influence over policy in the wake of the crisis that it has jokingly been described as "socialism for the bankers" and not as a case of government treasuries nationalising the banks but of the banks nationalising the treasuries.

---

67   For similar tensions across neoliberal approaches to health and welfare of single women parents and getting them back to work, see Cook (2012).

68   It is, then, a moot point, though, whether neoliberalism can exist, and so whether it should be defined, in pure form as it is necessarily mixed in substance. As is concluded, hybrids are the name of the game, "It remains to be seen if this hybridic construct is sturdy enough to withstand the economic and legitimatisation challenges that events such as the contagion effects of the U.S. subprime crisis (which are unfolding at the time of writing) are likely to pose" (Belfrage and Ryner, 2009, p. 279). But such hybrids in pension provision are commonplace (Saritas, 2014; and Churchill, 2014).

This is all indicative of a further feature of the relationship between financialisation and neoliberalism, which is that, very roughly, the latter falls into two phases divided by the early 1990s. The first phase is aptly characterised as shock therapy in which, most strikingly, first in Latin America and, subsequently, in the former Soviet bloc, the promotion of private capital proceeded without regard to the consequences. The second phase has been, if only in part, a reaction to the consequences of the first phase in terms of the dysfunctions created, not least in social welfare provision. It is also more marked by explicit intervention by the state to sustain the processes of and underpinning financialisation, as is again starkly demonstrated by responses to the crisis in terms of support to banks as the top priority over everything else. On the other hand, this second phase is equally illustrated by initiatives such as the social investment paradigm, active labour market policy and so on, in which (however much described as otherwise) more progressive interventions and intentions are part and parcel of neoliberalism as opposed to a break or compromise with it,[69] not least as the direct and indirect thrusts of financialisation remain unchallenged.

For this and other reasons detailed above, the extent and forms taken by financialisation, and the policy responses to it in general, are crucial in setting the conditions to which social policy responds. But, as already indicated, financialisation is closely associated with the formulation and implementation of social policy more directly. This is most obvious in terms of the pursuit

---

69   For these self-confessed ambiguities, tensions and limited purchase in practice, see Morel
      at al. (2012) and Gilbert and Besharov (2011), and Jenson (2009) for social investment as
      a compromise between the welfare state and neoliberalism. Note, for Triantafillou (2011,
      p. 577), the OECD has problematised structural unemployments since the mid-1970s,
      "Demand management and other ways of tackling unemployment were dismissed in
      favour of interventions seeking to stimulate the self-governing capacities of the unem-
      ployed, entrepreneurs, students and others. While this emphasis on the self-governing
      capacities of citizens may be characterised very broadly as a supply-side strategy, it has
      really nothing to do with a laissez-faire approach that assumes the existence of perfect,
      self-governing markets". Further, in what might almost be a manifesto for neoliberal
      unemployment policy in practice, p. 578, "the new structural problematisation of unem-
      ployment has come with a set of governing mechanisms that are at once more *indirect*
      in that they target institutions believed to be conducive to the boosting of employment
      and much more *comprehensive* in that they target not only the aggregate economy and
      the unemployed, but also a wide range of institutions and citizens deemed of importance
      to the competitiveness of society. This is not only about the disciplining of the workforce
      through diverse technologies of power. Today, it is difficult to see which institutions or
      which citizens could convincingly be claimed not to be of relevance to national compet-
      itiveness and thereby escape the gaze and potential interventions informed by this new
      problematisation of unemployment".

of privatisation in general and of pensions in particular,[70] as well as in the broader ways in which finance has inserted itself into public forms of economic and social provision. As highlighted by the collection edited by Savage and Williams (2008), the role of elites in general and of those attached to finance has been sorely neglected by social science even as they have emerged in new forms and strengthened over the period of neoliberalism at national and international levels. But, to coin a phrase, the state cannot simply act as an instrument to manage the affairs of the financial bourgeoisie although it might, however successfully, be thought to have done so more extensively and overtly in the wake of the global financial crisis. And, over the period of neoliberalism as a whole, there has been a shift in the balance of forces operating on the formation of social policy, not only in cuts to projected levels of expenditure and in moves towards more commercialised forms of provision, but also together with a neoliberal hollowing out of the policy-making process itself as governance is subject, for example, to new forms of public sector management and to token and transformed forms of decentralisation and participation.[71]

What the social policy literature reveals then, unsurprisingly, is the multiplicity of factors that go into the making of policy itself with diversity across and within countries and programmes. This has already been repeated often enough, but a further point is how to understand the nature and determinants of that diversity, probing deeper than the proximate determinants of, and forms taken by, policy. For the literature tends to view it in terms of location between extremes, dualisms even, with more or less neoliberalism, globalisation, stratification, residualism, selectivity, universalism, commercialisation, decommodification, path dependence or radical restructuring, and so on. This approach is, however, questionable as these factors should be seen more as contradictory, or subject to conflicting tendencies, rather than as linear oppositions.

Consider privatisation, for example. As is well-known, this takes a multiplicity of forms from deregulation through subcontracting, user-fees and public-private partnerships to denationalisation.[72] But a neoliberal push towards

---

70 For this in the context of the shifting relationship between scholarship, ideology and policy in practice in the shift from Washington to Post-Washington Consensus, see Bayliss and Fine (eds) (2008), not least as privatisation has given way to public-private partnerships.

71 Almost unimaginably revealed by the formation of unelected and/or powerless governments in the EU!

72 See, for example, Khoon (2011, pp. 145–146) on health care in Malaysia, "Less apparent in the calls to privatize healthcare for the middle classes in Malaysia [to allow more funds for the poor] is the fact that Malaysian government agencies, at both federal and state levels, are heavily invested in the commercial healthcare sector. In effect, they now own

private provision can create countervailing pressures for intervention by the state, to subsidise those, for example, who are too poor to pay by whatever criteria. Similarly, in case of social security, as with contributory schemes for unemployment, health or private pensions, such quasi-commercialisation inevitably creates a residue that is not covered and which becomes the responsibility of the neoliberal state irrespective of the level at which it provides. In this light, quite apart from their own complexities, residualism, selectivity and so on, are not simply neoliberal policy choices, but the consequence of the complexities of neoliberal policymaking, especially in the second phase of neoliberalism in which the dysfunctions and inequities of the first phase have come to the fore to a greater or lesser extent as problems to be addressed.

Further, for concepts such as (de- or re-)commodification, this is also not a matter of more or less, whether for labour market participation or for economic and social provision more generally (access to health, education, housing, etc.). Rather, for example, as with the Scandinavian model, generous provision of childcare allows for dual parent labour market participation. Indeed, it is not so much that decommodification and re-commodification are at the expense of one another but that there is a tension between them in which both can expand together. This is something which, of course, tends to be concealed by posing them in terms of shares which necessarily are at one another's expense.[73] So the issue is not so much whether we have more or less (de- or re-)commodification but how the tensions between them are resolved, the crucial point being that contemporary capitalism does so on the basis of an era of neoliberalism underpinned by financialisation as opposed to the Keynesian/modernisation/welfarism era of the post-war boom.

Care must also be taken, when acknowledging the diversities and specificities of social policy, not to isolate individual elements of welfare provision

---

or operate three parallel systems of healthcare providers: The regular Health Ministry facilities (as well as the health facilities of the Ministry of Defence); Corporatized, publicly owned hospitals (National Heart Institute, university teaching hospitals); The Pantai chain of hospitals (the second largest in the country), operating as commercial hospitals with Khazanah (the Malaysian sovereign wealth fund) as a controlling shareholder, similarly with the KPJ chain of hospitals (the largest), controlled by the Johor state government through its corporate arm, the Johor Corporation".

73 This point has been emphasised in my much earlier work on female labour market participation (Fine, 1992), in considering the balance between commodity and non-commodity consumption (Fine, 2002d), and in interpreting the world economy in terms of underconsumption (Fine, 2012a), which is erroneous not only for viewing capitalism as incapable of generating sufficient consumption and, hence, reliant on non-capitalist markets, but as failing to recognise that capitalism also expands the realm of such markets (as well as non-market provision) while also absorbing them.

from one another and from broader functioning, not least labour markets and gender relations for example. One way to do so is to locate welfare in relation to economic *and* social reproduction. Consider pensions:[74] on the face of it, pensions are a simple thing – the provision of income upon retirement and/ or in old age. But, as will be apparent in what follows, pension systems are extremely complex for a number of reasons. First, there are different types of pension systems in terms of levels of benefits and contributions, who pays, over what period, the retirement age itself, and so on, and this is what is usually interpreted as representing different pension systems and proposals to move between them – too narrow a conceptualisation from my perspective. Second, there is a corresponding mix across public and private systems. Third, pensions are part and parcel of broader systems of economic and social provision, interacting with health and housing provision, for example, as well as with policies for poverty alleviation. Equally, pension provision can be integral to the functioning of both labour and financial markets. Fourth, there are both shorter- and longer-term influences on pension systems ranging over shifting dependency ratios (the contributing relative to the benefitting), the global crisis, and the policies, practices and influences of neoliberalism. Fifth, there are ideational factors attached to pension provision ranging from welfarism to individualism (state, collective or personal responsibilities). Sixth, cutting across some of the earlier points, pension systems are perceived to be embedded within national contexts most notably, for example, by reference to welfare regimes, varieties of capitalism, or according to the depth and longevity of financial markets. All of this raises the issue of what we mean by a pension system, prior to seeking to distinguish between them.

Indeed, in light of this mix of factors, it is hardly surprising that any survey of pensions systems in practice reveals them to be extremely complex and diverse, and that the perceived imperative of classifying them through appeal to a number of ideal types is at best only liable to be successful in a rough and ready fashion, and possibly remain stable only over a short period. By virtue of a pension as a source of income, it necessarily conforms to specification of who pays and who receives, and how much in return for what. And, to the extent, that the latter at least nominally involves the individual, the pension system can be interpreted as a special sort of financial asset in which saving

---

74   Similar considerations apply most clearly in case of health, for example, as has been well-illustrated in the debate over universal health care, the forms it should take (private, if possibly state-funded insurance versus free public provision as extremes), the role of international agencies, etc. See Sengupta (2013), Oxfam (2013), Álvarez and Acharya (2012) and Anon (2012).

(contributions) gives rise to benefits (returns). Of course, from this perspective, pensions can be treated like other assets subject to more or less favourable treatment by the state in terms of tax advantages and/or subsidies. Such treatments by the state can themselves be the basis for distinguishing pension systems.

Such a view is at least complicit with the idea of pensions as part and parcel of more or less imperfectly working financial markets with a lean towards privatising pensions to the extent that financial markets and the citizen/consumers who participate in them are deemed to be able/to be made to work perfectly. But there is an alternative and, in many respects, more traditional view that pensions have little to do with financial markets and are simply part and parcel of social policy and the welfare state or, in grander abstract terms, they are attached to social reproduction, if of those in retirement/old age, as opposed to those to some degree in education, ill-health or need of some other sort of state-supported need. The rich have always accrued assets that may or may not be deployed to provide for their old age with or without various forms of tax advantages. But this is not necessarily a reason for perceiving pension provision in this way, although it is understandable that a shift in perception would accompany pension privatisation and more individualistic and less collective forms of provision.

The alternative view, departing from the previous of pensions as a subsidised or market-imperfection-correcting asset, locates it less in terms of uncertain individual saving/investment decisions over time and more as influence, conflicts even, over levels of collective provision both across levels of contributions and benefits and the forms by which these are determined. Accordingly, different pension systems for the first view are nothing of the sort from the second perspective. Instead, they merely reflect different arrangements for providing income in retirement/old age as part of, and in interaction with, other aspects of (non-market) provision that otherwise would appear to have nothing to do with pensions as such; from personal wealth to poverty, housing, and so on.

Such is the position adopted here, but it has methodological implications. It involves rejecting the idea that pension systems, as a mix of ideal types or not, are *determined* by their context for an understanding of pension systems as being *defined* by their contexts. In other words, pension systems are to be understood as contingent upon the economic and social system within which they are embedded and not simply to be a product of that embedding.[75]

---

75   For a similar inductive approach to industrial policy, see Fine (2011a), and for social policy, Fine (2012d).

Consequently, it is hardly surprising that we should find that pension systems display commonalities, as would housing, clothing or most systems of
provisioning by virtue of what they provide, and yet display considerable differentiation within and across countries and over time. This remains the case
despite the common pressures that have been experienced by, or imposed
upon, pension systems. Thus, the rhythm of pension privatisation associated
with financialisation, the neoliberalisation of social policy, and the fiscal and
other knock-on effects of the crisis are not homogeneous in themselves nor in
their interaction with pension and social provision, quite apart from the different character of national economies within which pension policy is made,
if not free of global influences. In other words, as with many other aspects
of financialisation and neoliberalism, the implications of financialisation for
pension provision is necessarily variegated as opposed to mixed ideal-typical.
In short, a pension system as such cannot be properly understood or explained,
independently of its own context, although it remains possible to distinguish
between them through different arrangements of common elements around
benefits, contributions, age of retirement, etc. It should be added that how
pensions are gendered is of crucial importance with an unavoidable reference to economic and social reproduction as a whole, given different degrees
of attachment to, and rewards within, labour markets. This is in part because
of inequitable positions within social reproduction outside of labour markets,
and how this and labour market participation are supported, or not, by social
policy (Marin and Zólyomi, eds, 2010). Such issues are more extreme for developing countries contingent on what forms participation in labour markets
takes, with corresponding benefits, and so on, quite apart from factors such as
education, health and housing. As Arza (2012, p. 26–27) concludes in a Latin
American context:

> Virtually all elements of social protection can have an impact on gender
> equality. In pension policy, gender inequalities result from the combi-
> nation and interaction of labour market and demographic factors, gen-
> der roles, and pension design features. Women have lower participation
> rates and more career breaks over their working lives than men. Under
> contributory pension systems, this reduces their chances to qualify for a
> pension of their own. In most Latin American countries, women are also
> more likely to be unemployed, work in the informal sector, and receive
> lower average earnings than men. Different pension designs process
> these labour market features in different ways. Systems that require a
> long period of contributions to obtain benefits tend to penalize women
> for their shorter and often interrupted participation in the labour market.

Benefit formulas also matter. Purely earnings-related systems tend to reproduce earnings inequalities in retirement. Defined-contribution systems which calculate benefits from individual savings and life expectancies strengthen the link between labour market and demographic factors, on the one hand, and pension benefits, on the other. When gender-specific mortality tables are used, as in Latin American private systems, further differentiation between men and women is introduced. Other features such as flat-rate or minimum benefits can favour women. Indexation is also important. If pensions are not properly adjusted to reflect rises in prices and earnings the living standards of women can be especially affected because women live longer in retirement. Other design features, such as retirement ages and mechanisms to compensate for time spent in caring and household work, are also relevant for gender equality.

Three grand conclusions can be drawn for social policy: the first is to emphasise the diversity of social policy both within and between different programmes; the second is that this is fundamentally characteristic and not a denial of neo-liberalism, as financialised and commercialised forms of provision are not only diverse themselves but also induce equally diverse responses; and the third conclusion is that this is only imperfectly captured by a sort of uneven Polanyian double, more appropriately multi-dimensional and contradictory, movement across and within different elements of social policy.[76]

6   Towards Alternatives

How, then, to frame social policy in light of general determinants, broader context of global crisis and the diversity of outcomes? To some extent, an answer can be found by drawing the contrast with what has been termed the developmental state paradigm (DSP), and its situating of industrial policy. Significantly, at least until recently, one of the major limitations of the DSP has been its neglect of social policy.[77] The position adopted here is very different

---

76   For Grimshaw and Rubery (2012, p. 122), "There is also the longer term, Polanyian argument that neoliberalism needs social and public expenditure, both to make up for gaps in welfare that its product market and labour market policies produce and to maintain demand in the private sector in a context of strong public–private linkages". For them, New Labour offers neoliberal residualism with some stronger floors.

77   As well as the role of labour movements, see Chang (2013) for an exception. For a critical account of the DSP for this and more generally, see Fine et al. (eds) (2013).

in drawing upon and departing from the DSP. Significantly, this neglect, as Mkandawire (2010) observes, is complemented by the presumption that developmental states no longer offer the potential on which to construct social policy, let alone to include it as part of the developmental state. "One quite remarkable feature of the new social policy focused on MDGs or PRSPs is that the status and the requisite capacity of the state differ radically from the historical 'success stories'. Thus far, these policies are tethered to the demise of the 'developmental state', both as a reality and as an aspiration". (Mkandawire, 2010, p. 50).

First, there is no need to treat social policy as different from industrial policy as outlined previously, recognising that social policy does itself offer general, horizontal or social provision beyond its immediately acknowledged goals.[78] The education, housing and health systems are imperative for industrial performance, and industrial policy neglects them at its peril. Second, by the same token, even if often primarily within the public sector, social is akin to industrial policy because it is sectoral, using inputs through a chain of provision to provide outputs even if these might be designated as public goods, welfare services or whatever, with income transfers an obvious exception (see below).

In the past, the developmental state has been to industrial policy as the welfare state is to social policy, each setting a broader transformational frame of reference and ethos, respectively, and with the two parallel to one another. To a large extent, reflecting its own path dependence, the social policy literature continues to hold to this vision, with the Scandinavian model and some form of social compacting and neocorporatism[79] as the gold standard to be emulated and against which to assess shortfalls of achievement. Increasingly, though, both aspirations and framing have been eroded, marginalising the attachment of social policy to the transformational goals associated with the welfare state as a key element in development/modernisation.[80] To some degree, this is the responsibility of the evolving presence and predominance of the WRA. But at least as important has been the increasing appropriation of social policy by orthodox (development) economics, especially in the form of the new welfare economics which has taken neoliberal antipathy to welfare (and its own commitment to privatisation and user charges) as the point of departure, to see

---

78   On industrial policy from the perspective offered here, see Fine (2011a).

79   See Mkandawire (2012) and Fine (2012b).

80   To some degree, Standing's (2011) notion of the precariat and the policy and strategy of basic income is acknowledgement, however justified and explicit, of limited aspirations for welfare provision and the forces and organisations to achieve it. For a critique of Standing, see Breman (2013).

welfare provision as a game in which the state and individual citizen strategise in relation to one another on the basis of different information and objectives (meeting minimum standards of living at minimum cost for the state, for example, but maximising income for minimum work by the individual).[81] Currently, the World Bank and IMF are pushing this new welfare economics, as it allows the different elements of welfare provision to be arbitrarily attached to one another (as with conditional cash transfers) and to build upon, and appear to be departing from, the previous policies of user charges and privatisation by promoting state support for private participation in welfare and economic and social infrastructure provision (on all of this, see below).

This new approach is, unsurprisingly, seriously deficient in at least two major respects. First, in specifying social policy as a response to individual risk and vulnerability, it overlooks the systemic nature of economic and social reproduction, treating social policy as if it were the response to short-term shocks as opposed to a component part of development itself. Second, like the WRA, even if based on universal deductive principles (merit goods, optimisation, market imperfections, etc.) as opposed to ideal types, the new welfare economics is insensitive to the contextual differences that mark both countries and policies in terms of individual aspects of welfare provision. Child education means different things in different places at different levels of development, and the way it is provided and the challenges it poses differ by context.

The issue, then, is how to deal with the specificity of particular elements of social policy, in terms of their diversity of causes, content and consequences, without losing grip of the bigger picture. For the latter, pioneered by UNRISD, emphasis has been on locating welfare provision within the framework of the DWS.[82] This has the advantage of foregrounding systemic change in both targeting development, welfare and the role of the state. The approach also remains sufficiently open to be able to accommodate different aspects and trajectories to development and welfare provision.

---

81   See Fine (2002d, Chapter 10) for a critique not least in the context of the WRA which, in Esping-Andersen's hands, has been influenced by corresponding issues of risk management and asymmetric information. For a recent example of the genre, examining whether high will support low waged for collective social policy in context of wage bargaining in presence of adverse selection, see Castaneda and Marton (2013).

82   See Mkandawire (ed.) (2005) and subsequent volumes in the series. Not surprisingly, hopes are placed on Latin America (Riesco, 2009a, p. S22), "an unambiguous shift in direction has been taking place in Latin America since the 1997 economic crisis ... a new developmental welfare state model is in the making. How will it evolve over the wider space of an increasingly integrated Latin America?". See also Draibe and Riesco (2009).

Where does this leave the promotion of social policy and alternative forms of public sector provision in the future? We can draw two general lessons. First, there is a need to insulate public provision from financialisation, the direct or indirect effects of turning provision into a financial asset however near or distant. Privatisation does incorporate finance directly with provision potentially becoming subject to the vagaries of stakeholder value on the stock market and other forms of speculative finance;[83] subcontracting does it indirectly as the firms involved require their own financial imperatives to be observed. Finance must be placed in a subordinate not dominant position. This is easier said than done not least because, prior to the crisis, this was said to be true of the role played by the financial system in terms of its efficient mobilisation and allocation of funds for investment and its trading in risk. But financialisation continues to impinge upon public provision in multifarious ways that can only be guarded against as opposed to being absolutely eliminated, at least for the foreseeable future.

Second, the vulnerability of public sector provision to erosion and distortion is a consequence of the absence of broader supportive institutions and policies in the wake of three decades of neoliberalism. Alternative public sector provision and new, broader policy capacities, and corresponding means and sources of finance must be built in tandem.

Beyond these two generalities, I would emphasise the need to address the specificity of particular types and circumstances of public sector provision in terms of the diversity of causes, content and consequences to which they are subject, but without losing grip of the bigger picture. In particular, my own approach has been to posit the notion of PSSoP. Specificity is incorporated by understanding each element of public provision as attached to an integral and distinctive system – the health system, the education system and so on. Each PSSoP itself should be addressed by reference to the structures, agencies, relations, processes, power and conflicts that are exercised in material provision itself, taking full account of the whole chain of activity bringing together production, distribution, access and use, and the conditions under which these occur.

There is extremely strong support from an unexpected source for the PSSoP approach, in the context of the environmental impact of water, energy and other systems, to be found in OECD (2002, p. 8):

---

83   For a striking illustration of which, see Bayliss (2014) on UK water provision for which
      ownership and deployment of secure revenues are incorporated into byzantine corporate
      pyramids ending in the Cayman Islands!

To analyse the key forces shaping consumption patterns, the report use *the system of provision framework*. The systems of provision approach analyses consumption as an active process, with actors seeking certain lifestyles, and constructing their identity by selective consumption and practices. The "systems of provision" is defined as the chain that unites particular systems of production with particular systems of consumption, focusing on the dynamics of the different actors (producers, distributors, retailers as well as consumers). In this light, it becomes clear that by the way governments design and transform energy, water and waste systems can either enable or obstruct household behaviour towards sustainable consumption.

The *systems of provision* framework for understanding consumption patterns stresses the importance of exploring the mechanisms that shape everyday practices related to commodities and services and the extent to which they can be seen to support or impede sustainable consumption behaviour. In this light, household consumption is not the sum of individual behavioural patterns, each consciously motivated and evaluated by the actor. Instead, household consumption is a whole set of behavioural practices that are common to other households ... They are social practices carried out by applying sets of rules and shared norms. They are also connected to production and distribution systems (technological and infrastructure network) that enable certain lifestyles that connect consumers to one another.

Thus, the PSSoP approach has the advantage of potentially incorporating each and every relevant element in the process of provision, investigating how they interact with one another, as well as situating them in relation to more general systemic functioning. This allows for an appropriate mix of the general and the specific and, policy-wise and strategically, signals where provision is obstructed, and why and how it might be remedied. This is in contrast to unduly focused approaches, those that emphasise mode of finance alone for example, as has frequently been the case for housing both before and after its current crisis. This is opposed to emphasis on who is building what, how and for whom, with what means of access. At the opposite extreme are unduly universal approaches such as those that appeal to market and/or institutional imperfections, and which accordingly fail to recognise that water provision is very different from housing provision in and of itself as well as in different contexts.[84]

The PSSoP approach has been addressed in Fine (2002d, 2005b, 2009d and e, 2011a and 2012d) for the welfare state and social policy, and in Bayliss and Fine (eds) (2008) for electricity and water.[85] I do not aim to develop, let alone impose, the PSSoP approach more fully for it is essential to see it as an approach that needs to be contextually driven rather than as a source of the ideal types or universal theory that characterises, and even mars, much of the current literature (with ideas such as leaving things to the market, or correcting market and institutional imperfections to fit into and enhance a welfare regime). I aim rather to argue for the need for something akin to the PSSoP approach, irrespective of the methods and theories with which it is deployed. These will, no doubt, continue to be controversial, alongside the nature, depth and breadth of economic and social transformation essential for any significant change in provision to be secure.

Further, though, this does allow for the results of existing studies to be incorporated into the PSSoP approach to the extent that they do identify, however partially, the factors involved in provision and how they interact with one another. Of course, in practice, sectorally grounded approaches by electricity, health and water appear to be adopted as if by second nature. But this has not necessarily been true of how they are analytically broached, where sectoral and contextual sensitivity often gives way to universal prescription driven by the neoliberal or anti-neoliberal fashion of the moment, whether privatisation, user charges, public-private partnerships or renewal of state provision, control or ownership. At the very least, the PSSoP approach offers a framework within which to address policy needs in light of identifiable provisional deficiencies, broadly interpreted, as opposed to general models and blunt recipes drawing

---

84   See Blank (2000, p. C47–C48), for example, critically cited in Bayliss and Fine (2008, p. 238), for whom public or private provision of services is a matter of gauging: "The degree of concern with agency problems and the degree of belief in government's ability to be wisely paternalistic. The degree of concern over the difficulty in collecting and disseminating information on quality of services. The extent that equity and universalism is emphasised. The level of trust in the public sector".

85   More recently, the approach has, in particular, been pursued for water and housing in a comparative study, mainly based upon (but not confined to) the EU, bringing out general and country and sector specific considerations. See Bayliss et al. (2013) and other relevant FESSUD Working Papers. The approach has also been used for the major UK iBuild and INDEMAND research programmes, see https://research.ncl.ac.uk/ibuild/ and http://www .ukindemand.ac.uk/, respectively.

to the fullest extent upon the 'market' (private capital and finance) in practice, even when recognising its deficiencies in principle.

In addition, as highlighted in earlier accounts of the approach, not only is each PSSoP uniquely and integrally organised in provision, by country and sector, but each will also be attached to its own meaning and significance for those engaged with or excluded by it. For example, whether public provision is seen as household risk management against vulnerability or collective provision towards developmental goals is both cause and consequence of material provision itself and, equally, subject to debate – or rather not subject to it not insofar as different approaches exist in parallel with one another according to context. As also argued in the approach, the cultural system, in the widest sense, attached to each PSSoP is also integral with material provision and is generated along and around that provision itself. The culture and meaning of public provision, thereby, becomes subject to what has been termed the 10Cs. The material culture of provision is: Constructed, Construed, Commodified, Conforming, Contextual, Contradictory, Closed, Contested, Collective, and Chaotic (on which see Fine, 2013d, for example). This is important for developing and understanding the meanings attached to public or social provision, not least in prising them away from the negative stance attached to the neoliberal ideology of flawed public provision.

Understanding the meaning of provision is also crucial for finessing the tricky terrain of the role of ideational factors in both provision and policy. This is well-illustrated by the discourses surrounding, for example, universal health care. In the case of the United States, for example, it is fairly clear that pushing through the idea of universal provision is less important than defeating the alliance of forces that oppose it (or seek to swing it to their advantage in form and content), including the private insurance industry (Fine, 2011b). Otherwise, appeals to human rights, basic needs, poverty alleviation and equity all have variable and contested meanings, and chances of being adopted and exerting an influence. The PSSoP approach has been extended, through the 10Cs, see above, to address how ideational and material factors mutually influence one another.[86]

One apparent weakness of the PSSoP approach[87] – a consequence of its strength of examining provision comprehensively within sectors – is its

---

[86]   For example, with applications separate from provisioning such as financing and the ethics of economics, see Fine (2013c).

[87]   Another weakness is its focus on welfare service delivery as opposed to income transfers (note, the mirror image of the WRA!). But for an extension of the PSSoP approach to pensions, see Saritas (2014) and Churchill (2014).

distance, at least initially, from the synergies and interactions across sectors, as with the role of 'horizontal' factors (as opposed to the 'vertical') such as equity, labour conditions, and macroeconomic impacts. Arguably, however, these need to be addressed in their own right *and* in the context of particular sectors within which they are rooted. Indeed, the dialogue between generic and sectoral issues is vital in designing, understanding, promoting and defending public sector alternatives.

By way of illustration, reference can be made to the first application of the PSSoP approach, if not explicitly in terminology,[88] as part of a policy programme for the economic and social infrastructure for post-apartheid South Africa covering, in particular, health, schooling, housing and electrification (MERG, 1993). As universally recognised, there can be little doubt about the contextual specificity, and deep-rooted nature of the inherited provision in South Africa, with numbers of elements in common across the separate sectors of provision, or PSSoPs, in light of the particular forms taken by apartheid. Nonetheless, it was and remains crucial to acknowledge the inherited differences in existing manner, levels and incidence of provision as well as the sectorally specific challenges involved within the wider context of the continuing dynamic (and transformation) of the South African economy and society more generally (Fine, 2007b). Significantly, in adopting what are generally acknowledged to have been neoliberal policies at macro- and, to some degree and as a consequence, micro-levels, it is only now that this is being seen as a serious case of mismanagement as far as public sector service delivery, not least as a developmental state is now being touted as an alternative approach.

But the virtues of the PSSoP approach can also be acknowledged through the wider evidence on service delivery across the developing world, with wide disparities in success and failure with limited correlation with per capita income (and corresponding implications for such correlations with the Human Development Index/ HDI). Thus, levels of literacy and health provision in Kerala and Cuba are exemplary and offer lessons in a comparative exercise for how corresponding PSSoPs might be addressed in other countries by contextually informed emulation. As Katz (2004, p. 763) puts it in critical response to the Sachs Report (Commission on Macroeconomics and Health, 2001), "Primary health care is, of course, one of the public services required to provide the conditions for good population health". Yet, "We have 100 years of solid public health experience demonstrating that access to decent food, clean water, adequate sanitation, and shelter are the major determinants of health"

---

88   See Fine (1996 but also 2007b, Appendix 2).

(Katz, 2004, p. 756). And much the same, if also different by context and meaning, could be said of education, nutrition, housing, water, and so on.

The PSSoP approach is in marked contrast to that taken by the World Bank whose current stance on social policy incorporates five fundamental characteristics (Fine, 2012d). The first is the continuing influence of its roots within the rhetoric, scholarship and policy perspectives of the Washington Consensus. There is a corresponding lingering presumption of social protection as the response to random shocks that induce individual or household vulnerability that requires at most temporary relief in deference to market solutions. Second, though, is the flexibility and discretion that is exercised in putative departure from the Washington Consensus.[89] Anything can be incorporated on a piecemeal or umbrella basis. This is precisely where the World Bank falls short despite the two other features: departing from the Washington Consensus and incorporating anything as social policy.

For, as a third aspect of the Bank's new social policy, it becomes developmental without any notion of development, able to include anything that is associated with development: good or bad, to be promoted or alleviated, and, inevitably, technicist for the purposes of economic and social engineering. Putting aside the scope of what is included and the marginally more favourable stance towards the state as against the market, this marks a major continuity with the Washington Consensus, for each shares in common a *method* to get development without a specification of what it is. For the Washington Consensus, it is reliance upon market forces, whereas its successor depends upon correcting market and institutional imperfections as well as their accompaniments of poverty, bad governance, inequality and so on to include anything else for legitimacy or discretion in policy. What is particularly disturbing here is the way in which the World Bank as "Knowledge Bank" has evolved in such a way that all economic and social development and policy has come under its compass, since all factors and outcomes are mutually conditioning; that the social is increasingly reduced to market imperfection economics; and market imperfection economics in principle, and even more so in practice, is wedded to a tempered neoliberalism across scholarship, rhetoric and policy in practice (Bayliss et al. eds, 2011; and Fine, et al. 2024).

---

89   But see Van Waeyenberge (2009) for the extent to which traditional Washington Consensus assessments for aid have hardened in the era of its Post-Washington Consensus successor. Note also in the current crisis how the IMF can play the role of good cop, especially in the troika governing EU conditionalities through which its own formal requirement to be politically neutral can also be neutered and complement by its partners. See Grahl and Teague (2013).

Fourth, despite the increased attention to social dimensions of development, the World Bank has adopted a fragmented approach. Moser (2008, p. 47) complains:

> The World Bank does not have a specifically defined social policy as such. Within the institution, three predominant social policy 'domains' can be identified: social sectors, social protection, and social development. The fact that each has a distinct location within the organization has served to create artificial conceptual and operational barriers to a holistic social policy.

Of these domains, social development is seen as the least developed. While Moser's jointly edited volume (Moser and Dani, eds, 2008) showcases the role of 'assets' as a means of pursuing social policy, her own take on its *absence* from the Bank might better be seen as *being* the social policy itself to which piecemeal and fragmented correctives are now being appended.[90] The review of Holzmann et al. (2009, p. 1) of World Bank policy over the course of the first decade or so of the new millennium reports that,[91] "the first social

---

[90] Of course, most people's most important 'asset' is the ability to work, which sits uneasily in World Bank discourses concerning social policy, given high levels of unemployment, and low pay and working conditions as a result of market forces. The discursive consequences, in the case of youth unemployment, are brought out by Fergusson and Yeates (2013, p. 68) around four neoliberal themes, "The first theme we identified by means of critical discourse analysis concerns the (mis)match between young people's skills and the perceived skills needs of specific labour markets. The second focuses on the dynamics of labour supply and demand in relation to young people as they are realised through labour costs and wage levels, particularly concerning minimum wages and social protection. The third theme concerns the WB's interpretation of the coincidence of the crisis with the so-called 'Youth Bulge' in some countries. The final theme takes the form of the new WB interest in the relationship between (un)employment and social cohesion, which includes a focus on criminality and civil unrest and disorder". In short, youth unemployment is the result of wrong sorts of skills, too high wages and social protection, demographic factors and, yet, the need to focus on potential for consequential rebellion!

[91] As the *Global Social Policy Digest* (2010, p. 421–2), reports, "Critics of the part played by Robert Holzmann in privatising pensions and advocating a risk management approach to social protection when he was head of the Social Protection section of the World Bank will be pleased to learn of his retirement and his replacement by Arup Banerji, who is striking a different note with regard to both pensions and social protection. In a presentation delivered at a conference preparing for the second European Report on Development, Banerji outlined initial thinking towards a review of the Bank's Social Protection Strategy to take place in late 2011. He argued social protection should consist of protection (cash transfers, etc ...), prevention (social security and other insurances), and promotion (employment strategy). A recent bank paper endorses universal social pensions in Latin

funds were prepared in the late 1980s to help communities cope with short-term adverse impacts of structural reforms. These funds expanded rapidly to become a central part of the Bank's poverty reduction efforts in low income countries". Following on from the pensions and financial crises of the 1990s, ad hoc arrangements eventually gave way to a new framework integrating social protection and labour, "based on the conviction that risk and access to risk management instruments matter for development" (Holzmann et al. 2009).

Fifth, the Bank's own figures, though, tell a different story in terms of the levels of support given to social policy. Over the eight years from 2000, total expenditure on "Social Protection and Labor Lending" amounted to a little less than a mere $10 billion.[92] However in relation to the dollar a day poverty count, this is in the region of a dollar per year for the world's poor. Much more significant is the number of country Risk and Vulnerability Assessments for which funds will have been used in financing consultants, with a total of 127 such assessments over the period. At about $10 million offered per country per assessment per year, the Bank might be thought to have purchased any corresponding influence over policy at an extremely low price.

This is brought out very clearly in the contributions of Holzmann and Kozel (2007a and b) with social policy perceived as social risk management (SRM), with little regard to endemic and systemic poverty, which is hardly a risk to be managed. Poverty and social policy/protection cannot legitimately be treated as if attached to income and 'shocks' alone. As Guenther et al. (2007, p. 17) put it, "In policy terms, SRM leads to interventions that focus on transitory income shocks rather than on structural determinants of poverty". Indeed, the presence of the analytical and policy tensions involved in all of this is confirmed by Ravallion's suggested response to the financial crisis in "Bailing out the World's Poorest". Is poverty short-term or long-term; do we target temporary or permanent measures? For Ravallion (2008, p. 21):

> Even a highly successful effort to protect the living standards of the world's poorest from the global crisis will leave a reality in which poor people face multiple risks on a daily basis, well after the crisis. If the crisis does create the opportunity for building an effective safety net then it

---

America. However as always the Bank presents different faces to different audiences and its different sections pursue different agendas". And so, as already cited, the Digest (2010, p. 422) "reminds us of the role of the International Finance Corporation section of the Bank in encouraging the financialisation of pensions and health care in developing countries".

92   See pp. 6–9 for more details by different programmes and regions.

should become permanent, dealing simultaneously with crises and the more routine problems of transient poverty in normal years. It will be an integral part of the country's poverty-reduction strategy, recognizing that the impact of a shock is intimately connected to deeper problems of underdevelopment: credit and insurance market failures, underinvestment in local public goods, and weak institutions. The synergies between safety net interventions and longer-term poverty reduction can be reinforced by explicit de[s]ign [sic] features, such as incentives to encourage the children of poor families to stay in school or emphasis on building assets of value to poor communities.

So, everything is connected to everything else in both analytical and policy terms, and Ravallion (2008, p. 21) can close:

There will no doubt be relatively low frequency events, such as the current global financial crisis, for which extra external aid will be needed, and certainly justified on moral grounds when it was the rich countries of the world that were largely responsible for the crisis. However, the domestic resources should be sufficient to cover a normal sequence of shocks as well as modest demand in normal years. The budgetary cost of such a permanent safety net need not be very high and it could well bring longer-term efficiency gains to the economy. The budgetary outlay could well be highly variable over time in risk-prone settings, entailing some fiscal stress.

But if developing countries can and should take responsibility for themselves except when subject to financial crises other than of their own making, how does this relate to a more systemic role not only in "promoting longer-term recovery" – the term deployed in Ravallion's abstract for his working paper, and begging the question of recovery to what – but also in bringing about economic and social transformation? This, implicitly at most, raises the issue of how to locate social policy in the broader contexts of systemic analysis and development as transformation but, unsurprisingly, offers no answers.

There are, then, considerable and shifting tensions in the World Bank's positions on social policy across ideology, scholarship and policy. These can be highlighted by addressing the one major innovation that has marked policy over the recent past and continues to sustain considerable momentum, conditional cash transfers.[93] CCTs have rapidly shot to prominence over

---

93   With corresponding parallel prominence in the recent literature, alongside welfare regimes and convergence for developed countries.

the past decade, particularly in Latin America but also elsewhere, including Bangladesh, Cambodia, Kenya and Pakistan. According to the World Bank (2009a, p. 32–33):[94]

> Paralleling the rise in the number of countries (now 29) with programs has been an increase in the size of some programs. Mexico's program started with about 300,000 beneficiary households in 1997, but now covers 5 million households. Today, the federal Bolsa Família program [in Brazil] serves 11 million families or 46 million people. In other countries, the increase in size has been less explosive, but still notable.

There are, however, wide variations in both absolute and relative coverage of such programmes by country, in their substantive content as well as their cost as a percentage of GDP, and the generosity of benefits as a percentage of mean household consumption. Thus, as Ramesh (2009, p. 96) reports:

> According to ILO's projections for a sample of 12 low-income countries in Africa and Asia, governments can establish social protection programs offering universal basic old age and disability benefits at the cost of between 0.6 and 1.5% of annual GDP (ILO Social Security Department, 2008). For perspective, note that the fuel subsidy in Indonesia at its height cost the government nearly 4% of GDP. In comparison, the Bolsa Familia program in Brazil reached 11 million households and cost the government only 0.5% of GDP in 2006. Core elements of all social protection systems should include free and compulsory primary education, access to secondary education that is affordable to all, and free or low-cost access to basic health services.

It is a moot point whether this indicates the limited resources that underpin social policy in general, and CCTs in particular, or what can be achieved with such limited resources.[95]

---

94   For overview of Latin America in particular, see Bastagli (2009).
95   It is hardly rocket science, even as Caminad et al. (2012, p. 123) report, using multiple regressions, "our results suggest that public income transfers indeed seem to be an effective policy instrument in alleviating poverty". And for Kangas (2010, p. S57), "Generally speaking, for the life expectancy of a population to improve, it is better to have broader coverage or universal access to care than to have more generous benefits that are channelled to a limited circle of citizens. The very same story is told by pensions: it is better to give an adequate amount to all than to give lavishly to too few".

For the World Bank, CCTs serve in some respects as an ideal instrument in response to the second phase of neoliberalism in crisis.[96] Yet, as then Chief Economist, Justin Lin, puts it (World Bank, 2009a, p. XI–XIII):[97]

> Even the best-designed CCT program cannot meet all the needs of a social protection system. It is, after all, only one branch of a larger tree that includes workfare, employment, and social pension programs ... As the world navigates a period of deepening crisis, it has become vital to design and implement social protection systems that help vulnerable households weather shocks, while maximizing the efforts of developing countries to invest in children. CCTs are not the only programs appropriate for this purpose, but as the report argues, they surely can be a compelling part of the solution.

Accordingly, the level and design of the programmes in practice are discretionary; the boxes of addressing the poor, children, and health and education are ticked; there is potential for institutional and other externalities into broader social provision; ambition in potential is matched by modesty of aspiration; and, analytically, there is scope for spillovers, and general equilibrium effects, empirical investigation of short-run as opposed to long-run impact, and for theory drawing upon market and institutional imperfections to be corrected on a piecemeal basis.[98]

Most telling, though, is the detachment of CCTs from broader economic and social provision other than as the context in which they may or may not succeed. As Ballard (2013) suggests, CCTs involve the detachment of the treatment of poverty from its causes. Further, in closing, p. 817:

---

96   See Azevedo and Robles (2013) for whom, as World Bank employees, multi-dimensional targeting of CCTs is more effective in meeting goals of, for example, poverty alleviation and education of children. Addressing the causes of deficiencies in the first place, let alone policies to eliminate them, does not get onto the agenda. CCTs as social policy are reduced to more or less effective targeting models.

97   Subsequently, Lin (2012a) has put forward a proposal for a new structural development economics which, remarkably, does not mention social policy. See Fine and Van Waeyenberge (2013a and b) for a critique.

98   Almost laughably, reasons for CCTs include "imperfect information, myopia, and incomplete altruism", that "governments typically do not behave like textbook benevolent Dictators", and "levels of human capital investment by the poor ... might not be *socially* optimal because of the presence of market failures, particularly, externalities" (World Bank, 2009a, p. 50).

> Cash transfers have been championed by a social justice lobby which rec-
> ognizes that the poor do not bear complete responsibility for their poverty
> and that universal, non-conditional and increasingly generous distribu-
> tional systems are required to achieve social justice and human rights ...
> Cash transfers have also been enfolded within mainstream development
> approaches which locate responsibility for transcending poverty ... upon
> the poor themselves and use grants to alter the behaviour of the poor ...
> The role of cash transfers within broader structures of social reproduc-
> tion has emerged as a fundamental development problem.

In any case, conditioning income support on accessing health and/or education is contingent upon these being available. As noted by the World Bank
(2009a, p. 202), "Clearly, a supply of health and education services of adequate
quality must be developed ... Cash transfers may be the right policy instrument to alleviate poverty in the short run, but their contribution to longer-
term poverty reduction also will depend on what happens on the supply side".
And as Soares (2009, p. 1) concludes:[99] "CCTs are not panaceas to strengthen
the (emergency) resilience of families and states. But they have features that
can be used to lessen the impact of a crisis as long as they are integrated in a
broader social protection strategy whose goal is not solely to work as a minimal
and temporary safety net".

Such integration cannot, of course, be guaranteed. Mattei and Sánchez-
Ancochea (2010), for example, find that while the Brazilian Bolsa Familia has
offered some poverty relief, it has done very little for longer-term educational
and health outcomes, with conditionalities either merely being met in a token
fashion or given levels of provision being redistributed across the poor. A per-
sistent and welcome theme across the literature is for CCTs to be integrated
contextually into a broader range of developmental goals (St. Clair, 2009) and
to serve as a stepping stone from residualism to universalism, developmentalism, a welfare state, not least through broader political participation rather
than on the basis of individualised recipients (Franzoni and Voorend, 2011;
Haarstad and St Clair, 2011; and Sering, 2009). If to belabour the points, for
Sánchez-Ancochea and Mattei (2011, p. 313):[100]

---

99   Whether such problems render unconditional transfers more palatable, as would be
     argued by proponents of a Basic Income Grant, remains an open question (see the issue
     of *Basic Income Studies*, "Should Feminists Endorse Basic Income?", available at http:
     //www.bepress.com/bis/announce/20090128/).

100 But, in contrast, for the most upbeat of attachments to CCTs, see various contributions
     from the UNDP's IPC-IG, especially one-pagers where breadth and depth of impact is

Most of the evidence points out to Bolsa Família's positive contribution to the reduction of poverty and inequality in the short run ... Bolsa Família cannot, however, deliver a sustained improvement in health and education outcomes and a reduction of poverty and inequality in the long run. These goals will only be met through an expansion in health and education services and, especially, an improvement in their quality – together, of course, with the transformation of the economic system ... however, deeper reforms that reduce inequalities in provision between regions and classes are increasingly important.

Future research and debate thus needs to move beyond debates on the short-term effects of Bolsa Família – and most other CCT programmes for that matter – and consider the way they overlap with the rest of the social policy regime. We must explore the extent to which the programmes are consolidating residual social systems in some instances while contributing to the expansion of universal services in others. The ultimate impact of CCTs will not only depend on their specific design but, more significantly, on the way they influence the political behaviour of the poor and the opportunities for broader and more encompassing social coalitions.

On the other hand, Freeland (2007, p. 75) dismisses CCTs as "Superfluous, Pernicious, Atrocious and Abominable". Drawing upon Samson (2006) and a South African case study, he finds, "it is typically the poorest and most vulnerable who will find it most costly to comply with any conditionalities, and are therefore the most likely to be deprived of benefits if they fail to do so" (Freeland, 2007, p. 77). Conditioning transfers on meeting criteria of children's health and education falters on lack of facilities to deliver and/or access these, and weak capacity to deliver conditioned transfers. There are also issues of whether CCTs reinforce or break with traditional gender roles and stereotyping (Quijano, 2009).

Further, even programmes that meet certain criteria of success may prove unsustainable administratively or politically. Despite various achievements, the Nicaraguan CCT programme, attached to child education and health, was discontinued. According to Moore (2009) this was due to a lack of understanding

---

assessed with references to supporting papers, http://www.ipc-undp.org/PubSearc hResultType.do?language=1&idtype=2&online=1 Typically, for Rasella and Paes-Sousa (2013), drawing on Rasella et al. (2013), "Our study provides evidence that a multisectoral approach, comprising a conditional cash transfer programme acting on the social determinants of health, with a primary health care programme responding to basic health demands of the population, can substantially reduce childhood morbidity and mortality from poverty-related diseases in low- or middle-income countries".

and misrepresentation of its achievements upon transfer of responsibility from one ministry to another. She closes with the observation that, "Although RPS [Red De Protección Social] had a disappointing conclusion, all is not lost". For, "in its own uniquely complex environment [we] can remind policymakers to be aware of the balance they must keep in performing well for international stakeholders while securing domestic acceptance of their own programmes", p. 36. But how to guard against the transfer from one ministry to another, the shifting interests of external (and domestic) agencies and so on? As Barrientos (2013, p. 12) puts it:

> The main argument, grounded on the evolution of Bolsa Família, was that this required managing two key progressions and satisfying one condition. The two progressions relate to the need for growing institutionalisation of human development income transfer programmes, on the one hand, and to an associated development of the conceptual framework underpinning them. The presence of positive policy-to-politics feedback effects capable of sustaining political support for social assistance provides a fold for these two progressions.

But it is a moot point whether such progressions and conditions are best delivered through CCTs, not least given that they have been situated in a neoliberal context in which individualisation and commodification are the order of the day in the absence of a pre-existing welfare state providing corresponding services. As Lavinas (2013, p. 40) puts it:

> The social protection paradigm that emerged at the end of the 19th century and developed, in parallel with the workers' movements, during the 20th, aimed to protect and equalize access and opportunities, irrespective of income level and social status. By contrast, the hegemonic paradigm of the 21st century holds that market mechanisms are the key to improving general welfare; cash transfers and expanded household debt, the latter underwritten by the former, are the key elements in this framework, in which decommodified provision is to be pared to the barest bones.

Indeed, it would appear precisely because CCTs have proven themselves to be potentially consistent with, rather than antagonistic to, private, possibly state-supported, forms of provision of social and economic infrastructure, that the World Bank's initial scepticism is now one of relatively warm embrace as it involves itself in the goal of using the state to support the private sector in such provision where privatisation has proven impossible or unsuccessful (Fine and Hall, 2012).

In this respect, like all social policy, outcomes necessarily both reflect *and* contest entrenched structures, relations, processes, powers and agencies.[101] At a specific level, let alone more generally, the idea that there will be universal solutions on how to balance (or more exactly transform and promote, respectively) one outcome against the other borders on the ridiculous in both analytical and strategic terms.[102] Also, something that is possibly overlooked, is the political content of CCTs as both a site of conflict and means to temper it and gain electoral support relatively cheaply in terms of cost and extent of reform. In short, while there are those that express support for CCTs as a major success with continuing potential, albeit subject to careful, contextual implementation (Fajth and Vinay, 2010), the more sceptical perceive CCTs as welcome, simply for providing momentum towards universalism in social policy. "Its ultimate success depends on a simultaneous expansion and improvement of universal services in health and education" (Mattei and Sánchez-Ancochea, 2010, p. 2). Universalism is set against the conditional, targeted ethos of CCTs, and viewed as more effective and secure in practical and political terms.[103]

Here, there is a stunning silence across the World Bank literature, and much more besides. It is as if the *welfare state* as the embodiment of universalism and public provision does not and has never existed.[104] And, of course, much the same is true of the absence of the (radical) political economy of welfare literature that approached the status of orthodoxy a generation or so ago,

---

101 For critical approaches to CCTs on these terms, see both Lavinas (2013) and Saad-Filho (2015) for Brazil, with the latter's abstract claiming, "The Brazilian *Programa Bolsa Família* (PBF) is the most successful conditional cash transfer programme in the developing world. Examination of the conceptual foundations of PBF, its historical roots, key features, impact and limitations shows that it belongs within a strictly neoliberal framework. PBF distributes conditional and very small tax-funded alms to the 'deserving destitute', as part of a strategy of management of poverty and inequality. In doing this, PBF also subsidises low wages and helps to perpetuate the conditions which it purports to address. While PBF can improve the conditions of the very poor at the margin, it is, by design, insufficient to block the reproduction of poverty and inequality".

102 See special issue on CCTs, *Global Social Forum*, vol 9, no 2, 2009.

103 See Chiwele (2010) for a useful discussion of the costs of implementing CCTs, the need for institutional capacity to deliver, and the prospects for corruption – all of which might best be addressed across a broader range of policies and provision.

104 Note that a search on the World Bank website for "welfare state" reveals just one hit, for lawyers in the Netherlands claiming legal aid as part of the welfare state! There are 22, 897 for "welfare", 69, 265 for "state", and 8517 for both to be found separately in document texts. Note there are 2,038 hits for CCT* and 5,656 for "conditional cash transfer*", 24 February 2014, where the * allows search on extended terms, eg CCTs.

focusing on the design and function of welfare for advanced capitalism.[105] These absences are hardly surprising for the Washington Consensus, not least with its neoliberal and Americanised inspirations, but why should it be so for the Post-Washington Consensus with the rediscovery of its own version of Keynesianism, market imperfections, public and merit goods, and so on? By contrast, the modernisation aspirations of what might be termed the Pre-Washington Consensus were heavily influenced by the notion of emulating the welfare states of western Europe. For this, in contemporary developing country circumstances, we need a marriage of the PSSoP approach with that of the DWS. Again, in acknowledgement of the political school of the DSP, such an approach is liable both to promote the interests of, and strengthen the presence of, those who have most to gain by its developmental content as opposed to consolidating neoliberal forms of governance that have so signally failed for LDCs over the past decades.

7   Conclusions as Starting Points

The global crisis, together with an international climate that is at least nominally committed to human rights, basic needs, poverty alleviation, improvements in human development indices and well-being, etc., has put the issue of social policy on the agenda as never before, not only in the differentiated and differentially impacted developed world but also across the equally diverse developing economies. In this light, how are social policies to be understood, explained and made? A number of lessons can be drawn from the extensive literature survey undertaken, leading to conclusions that might be thought as nothing more than a new common sense. Nonetheless, deeply embedded conventional wisdom remains entrenched despite its relatively recent vintage in the historical sweep of welfare provision, and the salient lessons that might have been drawn from the crisis that such conventional wisdom had deemed preventable. Such postures derive primarily from the imperatives and experience of neoliberalism just as their Keynesian/modernisation/welfarist predecessor exercises at most a lingering, nostalgic nudge to those who seek alternatives.

---

105   Note that Ravallion's (2008) own contribution only references at most a few pieces from outside the immediate orbit of the World Bank, an endemic feature of its research as commented upon by the Deaton Report (Deaton et al. 2006) on which see Bayliss et al. (eds) (2011) for a critical appreciation.

First, then, is to acknowledge the diversity of social policies across time, place, context, programme, causes, content and meaning, and influence of conditioning factors and variables. The idea that, for example, the South African health system can be understood in the same frame as the UK water system is simply nonsensical even allowing for variations in typologies, models or whatever.

Second, this implies, on a more begrudgingly positive note, that grand, inflexible approaches to the understanding of social policy are neither doomed to failure nor without insight. They achieve whatever they do, though, only on the basis of more or less useful, and casual, empirical specifications of social policies and the determinants and outcomes associated with them. This is especially true of the welfare regimes approach that dominates the literature but equally of other typologies and schemes for assessing the nature and dynamics of social policies such as whether there is convergence, divergence and/or path dependence in their evolution.

Third, this is not to throw up one's hands in horror, eschew general theory and historical narrative, specify the nature of contemporary conditions, and conclude that everything is so complicated and contextually determined that we can only expect to realise heterogeneous case studies across countries and policies. On the contrary, it is essential both to address the nature and significance of underlying and general influences. These include the nature and influence of neoliberalism and globalisation and, as emphasised here and in departure as yet from the existing literature, the role of financialisation in determining social policies both directly and indirectly. Further, as demonstrated, these grand variables are not at all forces for homogenising social policies but are fundamental in bringing about their heterogeneity.

Fourth, insofar as there have been shifts in social policy thinking over the neoliberal period, it has been towards reducing how it is understood and what it constitutes. Drawing upon mainstream economics and notions of the state as simply a mediator in the market and institutional imperfections faced by individuals, and especially in the hands of the World (Knowledge) Bank – whose scope of policy making increasingly accepts no bounds, except in conception – social policy has been understood as temporary, residual relief. What is notable in such an approach, apart from its predilection for the market forms of provision and its potential for discretionary intervention, is the absence of an explanation for the need for social policy in the first place, other than to alleviate the results of 'shocks', dependence upon universal principles that are not attuned to country- and policy-specific contexts, and the absence of the role that social policies play in the processes of development.

Fifth, then, and more constructively, a particular approach to framing social policy has been put forward that, at least in principle, addresses these identified deficiencies. This is to treat each social policy as an integral system in its own right, tracing provision from beginning to end as in a health system, education system, housing system, pension system and so on. This has been dubbed the public sector system of provision (PSSoP) approach. Further, while the initial focus is upon the functioning of such systems in providing core outcomes, it is equally recognised that they are embedded in a broader economic and social dynamic that also needs to be specified, with implications, as for all policies and for which the comparison with industrial policy, for example, is salient, for employment, gender relations, equity, etc.

Last, as already indicated, it is inappropriate to locate the progressive making of social policy purely in terms of residual, safety net or whatever as opposed to its reflection of, and contribution to, economic and social change, or development. For this reason, it is proposed that the PSSoP approach be integrated with the notion of a developmental welfare state. While the DWS, like social policies themselves, is liable to be heterogeneous in its presence, content and meaning, by incorporating it into policy making there is some guarantee that broader issues will be forced into consideration in terms of both causal factors and targeted outcomes, just as the welfare state served as analytical and policy template in the Keynesian era.

References

Acemoglu, D., S. Johnson and J. Robinson (2001) "The Colonial Origins of Comparative Development: an Empirical Investigation", *American Economic Review*, vol 91, no 5, pp. 1369–1401.

Acharya A., S. Vellakkal, F. Taylor, E. Masset, A. Satija, M. Burke and S. Ebrahim (2012) *Impact of National Health Insurance for the Poor and the Informal Sector in Low and Middle-Income Countries: a Systematic Review*, London: EPPI-Centre, Social Science Research Unit, Institute of Education, University of London.

Adam, C., W. Cavendish, S. Percy and J. Mistry (1992) *Adjusting Privatisation: Case Studies for Developing Countries*, London: James Currey Ltd.

Adésínà, J. (2009) "Social Policy in Sub-Saharan Africa: a Glance in the Rear-View Mirror", *International Journal of Social Welfare*, vol 18, no S1, pp. S37–S51.

Aghion, P. and S. Durlauf (eds) (2006) *Handbook of Economic Growth*, Amsterdam: North Holland.

Ahearne, A., J. Fernald, P. Loungani and J. Schindler (2006) "Flying Geese or Sitting Ducks: China's Impact on the Trading Fortunes of Other Asian Economies", Board of Governors of the Federal Reserve System, International Finance Discussion Papers, no 887.

Aiyede, E. (2009) "The Political Economy of Fiscal Federalism and the Dilemma of Constructing a Developmental State in Nigeria", *International Political Science Review*, vol 30, no 3, pp. 249–69.

Akan, T. (2011) "Responsible Pragmatism in Turkish Social Policy Making in the Face of Islamic Egalitarianism and Neoliberal Austerity", *International Journal of Social Welfare*, vol 20, no 4, pp. 367–80.

Akerlof, G. (1984) *An Economic Theorist's Book of Tales*, Cambridge: Cambridge University Press.

Akyüz, Y. (2011) "Capital Flows to Developing Countries in Historical Perspective: Will the Current Boom End with a Bust", South Centre, Research Paper, no 37, http://www.southcentre.org/index.php?option=com_content&view=article&id=1529%3Acapital-flows-to-developing-countries-in-a-historical-perspective-will-the-current-boom-end-with-a-bust&catid=142%3Aglobal-financial-and-economic-crisis&Itemid=67&lang=en.

Alber, J. (2010) "What the European and American Welfare States Have in Common and Where They Differ: Facts and Fiction in Comparisons of the European Social Model and the United States", *Journal of European Social Policy*, vol 20, no 2, pp. 102–25.

Al-Jazaeri, H. (2008) "Interrogating Technical Change through the History of Economic Thought in the Context of Latecomers' Industrial Development: the Case of the

South Korean Microelectronics, Auto and Steel Industries", University of London, unpublished Phd Thesis.

Al-Jazaeri, H. (2013) "Always the Latecomer, Never the Leader: the South Korean Microelectronics Industry beyond Catch-up?", in Fine et al. (eds) (2013), pp. 110–145.

Álvarez, M. and A. Acharya (2012) *Aid Effectiveness in the Health Sector*, Working Paper no 2012/69, ReCom, United Nations University and UNU-WIDER.

Amable, B. (2011) "Morals and Politics in the Ideology of Neo-Liberalism", *Socio-Economic Review*, vol 9, no 1, pp. 3–30.

Amsden, A. (1989) *Asia's Next Giant: South Korea and Late Industrialization*, New York: Oxford University Press.

Anon (2012) "The World Bank's Infrastructural Turn: Implications for Global Health", mimeo.

Arase, D. (2005) "Introduction", in Arase (ed.) (2005), pp. 1–20.

Arase, D. (ed.) (2005) *Japan's Foreign Aid: Old Continuities and New Directions*, London: Routledge.

Arcand, J.-L., E. Berkes and U. Panizza (2012) "Too Much Finance", IMF Working Paper, no wp/12/161, http://www.imf.org/external/pubs/ft/wp/2012/wp12161.pdf.

Arcanjo, M. (2012) "Unemployment Insurance Reform – 1991–2006: a New Balance between Rights and Obligations in France, Germany, Portugal and Spain", *Social Policy and Administration*, vol 46, no 1, pp. 1–20.

Arndt, C., S. Jones and F. Tarp (2010) "Aid, Growth, and Development: Have We Come Full Circle?", *Journal of Globalization and Development*, vol 1, no 2, Article 5, http://www.bepress.com/jgd/vol1/iss2/art5.

Arnold, B. and F. Kay (1995) "Social Capital, Violations of Trust and the Vulnerability of Isolates: the Social Organization of Law Practice and Professional Self-Regulation", *International Journal of the Sociology of Law*, vol 23, no 4, pp. 321–46.

Arrow, K. (2000) "Increasing Returns: Histographic Issues and Path Dependence", *European Journal of History of Economic Thought*, vol 7, no 2, pp. 171–80.

Arts, W. and J. Gelissen (2002) "Three Worlds of Welfare Capitalism or More? A State-of-the-Art Report", *Journal of European Social Policy*, vol 12, no 2, pp. 137–58.

Arza, C. (2012) "Pension Reforms and Gender Equality in Latin America", UNRISD Research Paper, no 2012–2, March, Geneva.

Ashman, S. and B. Fine (2013) "Neo-Liberalism, Varieties of Capitalism, and the Shifting Contours of South Africa's Financial System" *Transformation*, no 81/82, pp. 145–78.

Ashman, S., B. Fine and S. Newman (2010) "The Developmental State and Post-Liberation South Africa", in Misra-Dexter and February (eds) (2010), pp. 23–45.

Aybars, A. and D. Tsarouhas (2010) "Straddling Two Continents: Social Policy and Welfare Politics in Turkey", *Social Policy and Administration*, vol 44, no 6, pp. 746–63.

Azevedo, V. and M. Robles (2013) "Multidimensional Targeting: Identifying Beneficiaries of Conditional Cash Transfer Programs", *Social Indicators Research*, vol 112, no 2, pp. 447–475.

Bae, Y. and J. Sellers (2007) "Globalization, the Developmental State and the Politics of Urban Growth in Korea: a Multilevel Analysis", *International Journal of Urban and Regional Research*, vol 31, no 3, pp. 543–60.

Baer, W. (1996) "Changing Paradigms – Changing Interpretations of the Public Sector in Latin American Economies", *Public Choice*, vol 88, no 3/4, pp. 365–79.

Baldwin, R. (2008) "Managing the Noodle Bowl: the Fragility of East Asian Regionalism", *Singapore Economic Review*, vol 53, no 3, pp. 449–78.

Ball, L., D. Furceri, D. Leigh and P. Lounganil (2013) "The Distributional Effects of Fiscal Consolidation", IMF Working Paper, no WP/13/151, Research Department, June, http://www.imf.org/external/pubs/ft/wp/2013/wp13151.pdf.

Ballard, R. (2013) "Geographies of Development II: Cash Transfers and the Reinvention of Development for the Poor", *Progress in Human Geography*, vol 37, no 6, pp. 811–21.

Bambra, C. (2005) "Health Status and the Worlds of Welfare", *Social Policy and Society*, vol 5, no 1, pp. 53–62.

Bambra, C. (2007) "Defamilisation and Welfare State Regimes: a Cluster Analysis", *International Journal of Social Welfare*, vol 16, no 4, pp. 326–38.

Banerjee, A. and E. Duflo (2011) *Poor Economics: Barefoot Hedge-Fund Managers, DIY Doctors and the Surprising Truth about Life on Less Than $1 a Day*, London: Penguin Books.

Barbara, J. (2008) "Rethinking Neo-Liberal State Building: Building Post-Conflict Development States", *Development in Practice*, vol 18, no 3, pp. 307–18.

Barbosa, P. (2024) "The Developmental Welfare State in South Korea under Globalization", *Brazilian Journal of Political Economy*, vol 44, no 1, pp. 145–67.

Bardhan, P. (2010) "The Paradigm of Capitalism under a Developmental State: Does It Fit China and India?", *Singapore Economic Review*, vol 55, no 2, pp. 243–251.

Barnes, T. (2001) "Retheorizing Economic Geography: From the Quantitative to the 'Cultural Turn'", *Annals of the Association of American Geographers*, vol 91, no 3, pp. 546–65.

Baron, J. and M. Hannan (1994) "The Impact of Economics on Contemporary Sociology", *Journal of Economic Literature*, vol XXXII, no 3, pp. 1111–46, reproduced in Swedberg (ed.) (1996), pp. 530–66.

Barrientos, A. (2013) "Human Development Income Transfers in the Longer Term", International Policy Centre for Inclusive Growth, UNDP, Working Paper, no 116.

Barrientos, A. and M. Niño-Zarazúa (2010) "Effects of Non-Contributory Social Transfers in Developing Countries: a Compendium", Geneva: ILO.

Bastagli, F. (2009) "From Social Safety Net to Social Policy? The Role of Conditional Cash Transfers in Welfare State Development in Latin America", International Policy Centre for Inclusive Growth, Working Paper, no 60, December.

Bateman, M., J. Ortiz and K. MacLean (2011) "A Post-Washington Consensus Approach to Local Economic Development in Latin America? An Example from Medellín, Colombia", ODI Background Note, April, https://papers.ssrn.com/sol3/papers.cfm?abstract_id=2385197.

Bayliss, K. (2014) "The Financialisation of Water in England and Wales", FESSUD Working Paper Series, no 52, https://fessud.org/wp-content/uploads/2015/03/Case-study-the-financialisation-of-Water-in-England-and-Wales-Bayliss-working-paper-REVISED_annexes-working-paper-52.pdf.

Bayliss, K. and B. Fine (1998) "Beyond *Bureaucrats in Business*: a Critical Review of the World Bank Approach to Privatization and Public Sector Reform", *Journal of International Development*, vol 10, no 4, pp. 841–55. See Chapter 2.

Bayliss, K. and B. Fine (2008) "Conclusion and Alternatives", Bayliss and Fine (eds) (2008), pp. 235–48.

Bayliss, K. and B. Fine (eds) (2008) *Privatization and Alternative Public Sector Reform in Sub-Saharan Africa: Delivering on Electricity and Water*, Basingstoke: Palgrave MacMillan.

Bayliss, K. and B. Fine (2020) "Financialisation and the Future for SOEs", in Bernier et al. (eds) (2020), pp. 354–71.

Bayliss, K. and B. Fine (2021a) *A Guide to the Systems of Provision Approach: Who Gets What, How and Why*, Basingstoke: Palgrave.

Bayliss, K. and B. Fine (2021b) "Food, Diet and the Pandemic", *Theory and Struggle*, vol 122, no 1, pp. 46–57.

Bayliss, K. and B. Fine (2022) "From Addressing to Redressing Consumption: How the System of Provision Approach Helps", *Consumption and Society*, vol 1, no 1, pp. 197–206.

Bayliss, K. and B. Fine (2024) "Locating the World Bank: the Unmaking and Remaking of Development Economics in Its Shifting Vision", in Schmidtke and Vetterlein (eds) (2024), pp. 38–50.

Bayliss, K., B. Fine and M. Robertson (2013) "From Financialisation to Consumption: the Systems of Provision Approach Applied to Housing and Water", FESSUD Working Paper Series, no 02, https://fessud.org/wp-content/uploads/2013/04/FESSUD-Working-Paper-021.pdf.

Bayliss, K., B. Fine and M. Robertson (2018) "The Systems of Provision Approach to Understanding Consumption", in Kravets et al. (eds) (2018), pp. 27–42.

Bayliss, K., B. Fine and M. Robertson (eds) (2018) *Material Cultures of Financialisation*, London: Routledge, reproduced from special issue of *New Political Economy*, 2017, vol 22, no 4.

Bayliss, K., B. Fine, M. Robertson and A. Saad-Filho (2024) "Reports of My Death Are Greatly Exaggerated: the Persistence of Neoliberalism in Britain", *European Journal of Social Theory*, vol 27, no 4, pp. 540–60.

Bayliss, K., B. Fine and E. Van Waeyenberge (eds) (2011) *The Political Economy of Development: the World Bank, Neo-Liberalism and Development Research*, London: Pluto Press.

Bazbauers, A. and N. Madkour (2024) "Gender and the Multilateral Development Banks: From WID to GAD to Retroliberal WID", *Progress in Development Studies*, vol 24, no 2, pp. 165–84.

Bazerman, M. and D. Malhotra (2012) "Economics Wins, Psychology Loses, and Society Pays", in De Cremer et al. (eds) (2012), pp. 263–80.

Beall, J. (1997) "Social Capital in Waste – a Solid Investment", *Journal of International Development*, vol 9, no 7, pp. 951–61.

Bebbington, A. (2004) "Social Capital and Development Studies 1: Critique, Debate, Progress?", *Progress in Development Studies*, vol 4, no 4, pp. 343–49.

Bebbington, A. and K. Foo (2024) "Social Capital and Development", in Dauncey et al. (eds) (2024), pp. 186–90.

Bebbington, S., M. Woolcock, S. Guggenheim and E. Olson (2004) "Grounding Discourse in Practice: Exploring Social Capital Debates at the World Bank", *Journal of Development Studies*, vol 40, no 5, pp. 33–64.

Bebbington, A., M. Woolcock, S. Guggenheim and E. Olson (eds) (2006) *The Search for Empowerment: Social Capital as Idea and Practice at the World Bank*, Bloomfield: Kumarian Press.

Becker, G. (1996) *Accounting for Tastes*, Cambridge: Harvard University Press.

Bédécarrats, F., I. Guérin and F. Roubaud (eds) (2020) *Randomized Control Trials in the Field of Development, a Critical Perspective*, Oxford: Oxford University Press.

Beeson, M. (2009) "Developmental States in East Asia: a Comparison of the Japanese and Chinese Experiences", *Asian Perspective*, vol 33, no 2, pp. 5–39.

Belfrage, C. and M. Ryner (2009) "Renegotiating the Swedish Social Democratic Settlement: From Pension Fund Socialism to Neoliberalization", *Politics and Society*, vol 37, no 2, pp. 257–88.

Benjamin, B. (2007) *Invested Interests: Capital Culture and the World Bank*, Minneapolis, MN: University of Minnesota.

Berg, N. and G. Gigerenzer (2010) "As-If Behavioral Economics: Neoclassical Economics in Disguise?", *History of Economic Ideas*, vol 18, no 1, pp. 133–66.

Berger, M. and D. Ghosh (2010) "Geopolitics and the Cold War Developmental State in Asia: from the Culture of National Development to the Development of National Culture in Independent India", *Geopolitics*, vol 15, no 3, pp. 586–605.

Berggren, U., S. Blomberg and J. Petersson (2010) "Traits of a Representative Welfare State: the Swedish Example", *International Journal of Social Welfare*, vol 19, no 4, pp. 402–411.

Bernier, L., M. Florio and P. Bance (eds) (2020) *Handbook on State-Owned Enterprises*, London: Routledge.

Bhaduri, A. (2005) "Macroeconomic Policies for Higher Employment in the Era of Globalization", Employment Strategy Papers, Employment Analysis Unit, Employment Strategy Department, ILO, http://www.ilo.org/public/english/employment/strat/download/esp2005-11.pdf.

Bhargava, V. (2024) "Reflections on World Bank Engagement on Governance and Anticorruption: Insider and Outsider Perspectives", in Schmidtke and Vetterlein (eds) (2024), pp. 357–69.

Bianchi, P. and S. Labory (2006) "From 'Old' Industrial Policy to 'New' Industrial Development Policies", in Bianchi and Labory (eds) (2006), pp. 3–27.

Bianchi, P. and S. Labory (eds) (2006) *International Handbook on Industrial Policy*, Cheltenham: Edward Elgar.

Bianchi, S. and J. Robinson (1997) "What Did You Do Today? Children's Use of Time, Family Composition, and the Acquisition of Social Capital", *Journal of Marriage and the Family*, vol 59, no 2, pp. 332–44.

Björkman-Nyqvist, M., L. Corno, D. de Walque and J. Svensson (2013) "Evaluating the Impact of Short Term Financial Incentives on HIV and STI Incidence among Youth in Lesotho: a Randomised Trial", *Sexually Transmitted Infections*, vol 89, Supplement 1, https://sti.bmj.com/content/sextrans/89/Suppl_1/A325.1.full.pdf.

Blackmon, P. (2006) "The State: Back in the Center of the Globalisation Debate", *International Studies Review*, vol 8, no 1, pp. 116–19.

Blanchard, O. (2008) "The State of Macro", NBER Working Paper, no 14259, http://www.nber.org/papers/w14259.pdf, published as Blanchard (2009).

Blanchard, O. (2009) "The State of Macro", *Annual Review of Economics*, vol 1, pp. 209–28.

Blanchard, O., G. Dell'Ariccia, and P. Mauro (2010) "Rethinking Macroeconomic Policy", IMF Staff Position Note, 12th February, SPN/10/03, http://www.imf.org/external/pubs/ft/spn/2010/spn1003.pdf.

Blank, R. (2000) "When Can Policy Makers Rely on Private Markets? The Effective Provision of Social Services", *Economic Journal*, vol 110, no 462, pp. C34–C49.

Blecher, M. (2008) "Into Space: the Local Developmental State, Capitalist Transition and the Political Economy of Urban Planning in Xinji", *City*, vol 12, no 2, pp. 171–182.

Block, F. (2003) "Karl Polanyi and the Writing of *The Great Transformation*", *Theory and Society*, vol 32, no 3, pp. 275–306.

Block, F. (2011) "Pulling away the Curtain: the US Government's Role in Technology Development", http://triplecrisis.com.

Bowen, J. (2007) "Global Production Networks, the Developmental State and the Articulation of Asia Pacific Economies in the Commercial Aircraft Industry", *Asia Pacific Viewpoint*, vol 48, no 3, pp. 312–29.

Breman, J. (2013) "A Bogus Concept", *New Left Review*, no 84, Nov/Dec, pp. 130–38.

Broad, R. (2006) "Research, Knowledge and the Art of 'Paradigm Maintenance': the World Bank's Development Economics Vice-Presidency (DEC)", *Review of International Political Economy*, vol 13, no 3, pp. 387–419.

Bronk, R. (2010) "Models and Metaphors", in Skidelsky and Wigström (eds) (2010), pp. 101–109.

Brown, L. and D. Ashman (1996) "Participation, Social Capital, and Intersectoral Problem Solving: African and Asian Cases", *World Development*, vol 24, no 9, pp. 1467–80.

Bryceson, K., K. Gough, J. Rigg and J. Agergaard (2009) "Critical Commentary. The World Development Report 2009", *Urban Studies*, vol 46, no 4, pp. 72–38.

Buckley, R. (2009) "Commentary: Discontent with the World Bank's Excursion into Economic Geography: Lions and Butterflies Once More?", *Environment and Planning A*, vol 41, no 12, pp. 2806–15.

Buendía, L. and E. Palazuelos (2014) "Economic Growth and Welfare State: a Case Study of Sweden", *Cambridge Journal of Economics*, vol 38, no 4, pp. 761–77.

Burt, R. (1992) *Structural Holes*, Cambridge: Harvard University Press.

Burt, R. (1997) "A Note on Social Capital and Network Content", *Social Networks*, vol 19, no 4, pp. 355–74.

Busumtwi-Sam, J. (1996) "Models of Economic Development in Africa: Lessons from the Experiences of Ghana, 1975–95", *Journal of Commonwealth and Comparative Politics*, vol 34, no 3, pp. 174–98.

Buxton, J. (2013) "Social Policy in Venezuela: Bucking Neo-Liberalism or Unsustainable Clientelism", Towards Universal Social Security in Emerging Economies: Process, Institutions and Actors, UNRISD Background Paper.

Calabrese, L., R. Jenkins and L. Lombardozzi (2024) "The Belt and Road Initiative and Dynamics of Structural Transformation", *European Journal of Development Research*, vol 36, no 3, pp. 515–47.

Caldentey, E. (2008) "The Concept and Evolution of the Developmental State", *International Journal of Political Economy*, vol 37, no 3, pp. 27–53.

Camerer, C. (2003) *Behavioral Game Theory: Experiments in Strategic Interaction*, Princeton, NJ: Princeton University Press.

Camerer, C. and E. Fehr (2004) "Measuring Social Norms and Preferences Using Experimental Games: a Guide for Social Scientists", in Henrich et al. (eds) (2004). pp. 55–95.

Camerer, C. and G. Loewenstein (2004) "Behavioral Economics: Past, Present, Future", in Camerer et al. (eds) (2004), pp. 3–51.

Camerer, C., G. Loewenstein, and M. Rabin (eds) (2004) *Advances in Behavioral Economics*, Princeton, NJ, and Oxford: Princeton University Press.

Caminad, K., K. Goudswaard and F. Koster (2012) "Social Income Transfers and Poverty: a Cross-Country Analysis for OECD Countries", *International Journal of Social Welfare*, vol 21, no 2, pp. 115–26.

Cao, J. (2009) "Developmental State, Property-Led Growth and Property Investment Risks in China", *Journal of Property Investment and Finance*, vol 27, no 2, pp. 162–79.

Carney, R. (2009) "Chinese Capitalism in the OECD Mirror", *New Political Economy*, vol 14, no 1, pp. 71–99.

Carrier, J. and D. Miller (eds) (1998) *Virtualism: the New Political Economy*, London: Berg.

Case, A. and A. Deaton (2020) *Deaths of Despair and the Future of Capitalism*, Princeton: Princeton University Press.

Castaneda, M. and J. Marton (2013) "Employer-Provided Health Insurance and the Adverse Selection Problem", *Public Finance Review*, vol 41, no 1, pp. 3–36.

Castree, N. (2006) "Commentary", *Environment and Planning A*, vol 38, no 1, pp. 1–6.

Cecchetti, S. and E. Kharroubi (2012) "Reassessing the Impact of Finance on Growth", paper to the Reserve Bank of India's Second International Research Conference in Mumbai, India, February, http://sirc.rbi.org.in/downloads/4Cecchetti.pdf.

Cesaratto, S. (2009) "Endogenous Growth Theory Twenty Years on: a Critical Assessment", Department of Economics, University of Siena, Working Paper, no 559, http://repec.deps.unisi.it/quaderni/559.pdf.

Chalfin, B. (2010) "Recasting Maritime Governance in Ghana: the Neo-Developmental State and the Port of Tema", *Journal of Modern African Studies*, vol 48, no 4, pp. 573–98.

Champlin, D. and E. Hake (2006) "Immigration as Industrial Strategy in American Meatpacking", *Review of Political Economy*, vol 18, no 1, pp. 49–69.

Chan, S., C. Clark and D. Lam (1998) "Looking beyond the Developmental State", in Chan et al. (eds) (1998), pp. 1–8.

Chan, S., C. Clark and D. Lam (eds) (1998) *Beyond the Developmental State: East Asia's Political Economies Reconsidered*, London: MacMillan.

Chang, D.-O. (2013) "Fetishised State and Reified Labour: the Developmental State Theory of Labour", in Fine et al. (eds) (2013), pp. 85–109.

Chang, H.-J. (1993) *The Political Economy of Industrial Policy,* London: Macmillan.

Chang, H.-J. (2002) *Kicking away the Ladder: Policies and Institutions for Development in Historical Perspective*, London: Anthem Press.

Chang, H.-J. (2006) "Policy Space in Historical Perspective – with Special Reference to Trade and Industrial Policies", *Economic and Political Weekly*, vol XLI, no 7, February 18–24, pp. 627–33.

Chang, H.-J. (2007) *Bad Samaritans: Rich Nations, Poor Policies, and the Threat to the Developing World*, London: Random House.

Chang, H.-J. (2009) "Rethinking Public Policy in Agriculture: Lessons from History, Distant and Recent", *Journal of Peasant Studies*, vol 36, no 3, pp. 477–515.

Chang, H.-J. (ed.) (2001) *Joseph Stiglitz and the World Bank: the Rebel Within*, London: Anthem Press.

Chang, H.-J. (ed.) (2003) *Rethinking Development Economics*, London: Anthem Press.

Chang, H.-J. (ed.) (2012) *Public Policy in Agriculture in Historical Perspective*, Rome: FAO.

Chang, H.-J. and A. Singh (1993) "Public Enterprises in Developing Countries and Economic Efficiency: a Critical Examination of Analytical, Empirical and Policy Issues", *UNCTAD Review*, no 4, Geneva.

Chang, H.-J. and A. Singh (1997) "Can Large Firms Be Run Efficiently without Being Bureaucratic?", *Journal of International Development*, vol 9, no 6, pp. 865–75.

Chang, K.-S., B. Fine and L. Weiss (eds) (2012) *Developmental Politics in Transition: the Neoliberal Era and Beyond*, Basingstoke: Palgrave MacMillan.

Chang, Y. and Y. Ku (2013) "Social Policy and Its Implications to Structural Shifts: a Comparison between Taiwan and Korea in the Colonial Era", in Izuhara (ed.) (2013), pp. 65–85.

Cherry, J. (2007) *Foreign Direct Investment in Post-Crisis Korea: European Investors and "Mismatched Globalization"*, London: Routledge.

Chia, S. (2007) "Whither East Asian Regionalism? An ASEAN Perspective", *Asian Economic Papers*, vol 6, no 3, pp. 1–36.

Chiwele, D. (2010) "Assessing Administrative Capacity and Costs of Cash Transfer Schemes in Zambia: Implications for Rollout", International Policy Centre for Inclusive Growth, Country Study, no 20, February, http://www.ipc-undp.org/pub/IPCCountryStudy20.pdf.

Choi, Y. (2013) "Developmentalism and Productivism in East Asian Welfare Regimes", in Izuhara (ed.) (2013), pp. 207–25.

Chu, Y. (2009) "Eclipse or Reconfigured? South Korea's Developmental State and Challenges of the Global Knowledge Economy", *Economy and Society*, vol 38, no 2, pp. 278–303.

Chung, H. and S. Thewissen (2011) "Falling Back on Old Habits? A Comparison of the Social and Unemployment Crisis Reactive Policy Strategies in Germany, the UK and Sweden", *Social Policy and Administration*, vol 45, no 4, pp. 354–70.

Churchill, J. (2014) "Towards a Framework for Understanding the Recent Evolution of Pension Systems in the European Union", FESSUD Working Paper, no 12, https://fessud.org/wp-content/uploads/2013/04/Towards-a-framework-for-understanding-the-recent-evolution-of-pension-systems-in-the-European-Union-FESSUD-working-paper-12.pdf.

Clark, D. (ed.) (2006) *The Elgar Companion to Development Studies*, Cheltenham: Edward Elgar.

Clegg, L. (2024) "Housing and the World Bank: Mortgaging Development", in Schmidtke and Vetterlein (eds) (2024), pp. 320–30.

Clemens, M., C. Montenegro and L. Pritchett (2008) "The Place Premium: Wage Differences for Identical Workers across the US Border", World Bank Policy Research Working Paper, no 4671, Background Paper to the 2009 World Development Report, available at http://siteresources.worldbank.org/INTWDR2009/Resources/4231 006-1204741572978/Clemens-Montenegro-Pritchett.pdf.

Coleman, J. (1987) "Norms as Social Capital", in Radnitzky and Bernholz (eds) (1987), pp. 133–55.

Coleman, J. (1988) "Social Capital in the Creation of Human Capital", *American Journal of Sociology*, vol 94, Supplement, S95–S120, reproduced in Swedberg (ed.) (1996), pp. 319–44.

Coleman, J. (1990) *Foundations of Social Theory*, Cambridge: Harvard University Press.

Commission on Macroeconomics and Health (2001) *Macroeconomics and Health: Investing in Health for Economic Development*, Report of the Commission on Macroeconomics and Health, chaired by Jeffrey D. Sachs, http://whqlibdoc.who.int /publications/2001/924154550x.pdf.

Cook, K. (2012) "Neoliberalism, Welfare Policy and Health: a Qualitative Meta-Synthesis of Single Parents' Experience of the Transition from Welfare to Work", *Health*, vol 16, no 5, pp. 507–30.

Cook, L. (2013) "Constraints on Universal Health Care in the Russian Federation: Inequality, Informality, and the Failures of Medical Health Insurance Reforms", Towards Universal Social Security in Emerging Economies: Process, Institutions and Actors, unrisd Background Paper.

Cook, P. (1997) "Privatization, Public Enterprise Reform and the World Bank: Has 'Bureaucrats in Business' Got It Right?", *Journal of International Development* vol 9, no 6, pp. 887–897.

Cook, P. and C. Kirkpatrick (eds) (1988) *Privatisation in Less Developed Countries*, Brighton: Wheatsheaf.

Cook, P. and C. Kirkpatrick (eds) (1995) *Privatisation Policy and Performance: International Perspectives*, New York: Prentice Hall.

Cook, S. and S. Razavi (2012) "Work and Welfare: Revisiting the Linkages from a Gender Perspective", UNRISD Research Paper, no 2012–7.

Corbridge, S. (2007) "The (Im)possibility of Development Studies", *Economy and Society*, vol 36, no 2, pp. 179–211.

Cornwall, A. and D. Eade (eds) (2010) *Deconstructing Development Discourse: Buzzwords and Fuzzwords*, Oxfam and Rugby: Practical Action Publishing.

Cramer, C., J. Di John and J. Sender (2022) "Classification and Roundabout Production in High-Value Agriculture: a Fresh Approach to Industrialization", *Development and Change*, vol 53, no 3, pp. 495–524.

Crouch, C. (2011) *The Strange Non-Death of Neo-Liberalism*, Cambridge: Polity Press.

CSDH (2008) *Closing the Gap in a Generation: Health Equity through Action on the Social Determinants of Health*, Final Report of the Commission on Social Determinants of Health, Geneva: World Health Organization, https://www.who.int/publications/i/item/WHO-IER-CSDH-08.1.

d'Ávila Viana, A. and H. da Silva (2013) "Universalization in Brazilian Health Policy: the Impact of the SUS on Political, Economic and Social Institutions", Towards Universal Social Security in Emerging Economies: Process, Institutions and Actors, UNRISD Background Paper.

Daly T. and M. Szebehely (2012) "Unheard Voices, Unmapped Terrain: Care Work in Long-Term Residential Care for Older People in Canada and Sweden", *International Journal of Social Welfare*, vol 21, no 2, pp. 139–48.

Damodaran, S., S. Gupta, S. Mitra and D. Sinha (eds) (2023) *Development, Transformations and the Human Condition: Volume in Honour of Professor Jayati Ghosh*, New Delhi: Routledge, forthcoming.

Dauncey, E., V. Desai and R. Potter (eds) (2024) *The Companion to Development Studies*, London: Routledge.

Davis, J. (2008) "The Turn in Recent Economics and Return of Orthodoxy", *Cambridge Journal of Economics*, vol 32, no 3, pp. 349–66.

Davis, J. (2013) "Economics Imperialism under the Impact of Psychology: the Case of Behavioral Development Economics", Department of Economics Working Paper, no 13–01, Milwaukee, WI: Marquette University.

De Cremer, D., M. Zeelenberg and J. Murnighan (eds) *Social Psychology and Economics*, Mahwah, NJ: LEA.

de Haan, A. (2013) "The Social Policies of Emerging Economies: Growth and Welfare in China and India", Working Paper, no 110, June, International Policy Centre for Inclusive Growth, UNDP.

de Haan, L. (2010) "Perspectives on African Studies and Development in Sub-Saharan Africa", *Africa Spectrum*, vol 45, no 1, pp. 95–116.

de Walque, D., W. Dow, C. Medlin and R. Nathan (2012a) "Stimulating Demand for AIDS Prevention: Lessons from the RESPECT Trail", NBER Working Paper, no 17865. Cambridge, MA: National Bureau of Economic Research.

de Walque, D., W. Dow, R. Nathan and R. Abdul (2012b) "Incentivising Safe Sex: a Randomised Trial of Conditional Cash Transfers for HIV and Sexually Transmitted Infection Prevention in Rural Tanzania", *BMJ Open*, vol 2, no 1, e000747.

Deacon, B. (2011) "The Global Politics of Poverty Alleviation in the Context of Multiple Crises", *Global Social Policy*, vol 11, no 2/3, pp. 146–49.

Deacon, B. and S. Cohen (2011) "From the Global Politics of Poverty Alleviation to the Global Politics of Social Solidarity", *Global Social Policy*, vol 11, no 2/3, 233–49.

Deaton (2009a) "Instruments of Development: Randomization in the Tropics, and the Search for the Elusive Keys to Economic Development", the Keynes Lecture, British Academy, October 9th, 2008, available at https://www.nber.org/papers/w14690.

Deaton, A. (2009b) "The World Development Report at Thirty: a Birthday Tribute or a Funeral Elegy", in Yusuf (2009), pp. 105–14.

Deaton, A. (2010a) "Instruments, Randomization, and Learning about Development", *Journal of Economic Literature*, vol 48, no 2, pp. 424–55.

Deaton, A. (2010b) "Understanding the Mechanisms of Economic Development", *Journal of Economic Perspectives*, vol 24, no 3, pp. 3–16.

Deaton, A. (2020) "Introduction: Randomization in the Tropics Revisited, a Theme and Eleven Variations", in Bédécarrats et al. (eds) (2020), pp. 29–46.

Deaton, A., A. Banerjee, N. Lustig and K. Rogoff with E. Hsu (2006) "An Evaluation of World Bank Research, 1998–2005", http://siteresources.worldbank.org/DEC/Resour ces/84797-1109362238001/726454-1164121166494/RESEARCH-EVALUATION-2006 -Main-Report.pdf.

Deaton, A. and N. Cartwright (2018) "Understanding and Misunderstanding Randomized Controlled Trials", *Social Science and Medicine*, vol 210, pp. 2–21.

Deaton, A. and J. Muellbauer (1980) *Economics and Consumer Behavior*, Cambridge: Cambridge University Press.

Demir, F. (2009) "Financial Liberalization, Private Investment and Portfolio Choice: Financialization of Real Sectors in Emerging Markets", *Journal of Development Economics*, vol 88, no 2, pp. 314–24.

Deraniyagala, S. and B. Fine (2001) "New Trade Theory Versus Old Trade Policy: a Continuing Enigma", *Cambridge Journal of Economics*, vol 25, no 6, pp. 809–25.

Deraniyagala, S. and B. Fine (2006) "Kicking Away the Logic: Free Trade is neither the Question nor the Answer for Development", in Jomo and Fine (eds) (2006), pp. 46–67.

Devarajan, S., W. Easterly, H. Fofack, D. Go, A. Izquierdo, C. Petersen, L. Pizzati, C. Scott, and L. Serven (2002) "A Macroeconomic Framework for Poverty Reduction Strategy Papers", available in one form at http://www.csae.ox.ac.uk/conferences/2002-UPaGi SSA/papers/Devarajan-csae2002.pdf.

Devereux, S., K. Roelen, C. Béné, D. Chopra, J. Leavy and J. McGregor (2013) "Evaluating outside the Box: an Alternative Framework for Analysing Social Protection Programmes", Centre for Social Protection, CSP Working Paper, no 010, Institute of Development Studies.

Dezalay, Y. and B. Garth (1997) "Law, Lawyers and Social Capital: 'Rule of Law' versus Relational Capitalism", *Social and Legal Studies*, vol 6, no 1, pp. 109–41.

Di John, J. (2010) "The Concept, Causes and Consequences of Failed States: a Critical Review of the Literature and Agenda for Research with Specific Reference to Sub-Saharan Africa", *European Journal of Development Research*, vol 22, no 1, pp. 10–30.

Dixit, A. and J. Stiglitz (1977) "Monopolistic Competition and Optimum Product Diversity", *American Economic Review*, vol 63, no 2, pp. 297–308.

Dixon, A. and V.-P. Sorsa (2009) "Institutional Change and the Financialisation of Pensions in Europe", *Competition and Change*, vol 13, no 4, pp. 347–67.

Doetter, L. and R. Götze (2011) "Health Care Policy for Better or for Worse? Examining NHS Reforms During Times of Economic Crisis versus Relative Stability", *Social Policy and Administration*, vol 45, no 4, pp. 488–505.

Dolan, P., M. Hallsworth, D. Halpern, D. King and I. Vlaev (2010) "Mindspace: Influencing Behaviour through Public Policy", London: Cabinet Office and the Institute for Government.

dos Santos, P. (2011) "A Policy Wrapped in 'Analysis'– the World Bank's Case for Foreign Banks", in Bayliss et al. (eds) (2011), pp. 18–214.

Draibe, S. and M. Riesco (2007) "Introduction", in Riesco (ed.) (2007), pp. 1–17.

Draibe, S. and M. Riesco (2007) "Latin America: a New Developmental Welfare State Model in the Making?", in Riesco (ed.) (2007), pp. 21–113.

Draibe, S. and M. Riesco (2009) "Social Policy and Development in Latin America: the Long View", *Social Policy and Administration*, vol 43, no 4, pp. 328–46.

Dukelow, F. (2011) "Comparing Irish Policy Responses in the 1970s and 1980s with the Present", *Social Policy and Administration*, vol 45, no 4, pp. 408–29.

Durlauf, S., P. Johnson and J. Temple (2004) "Growth Econometrics", Working Paper, no 61, October, Vassar College, Department of Economics, available at https://www.researchgate.net/publication/23698255_Growth_Econometrics, reproduced in Aghion and Durlauf (eds) (2006), pp. pp. 555–677.

Edigheji, O. (ed.) (2010) *Constructing a Democratic Developmental State in South Africa: Potentials and Challenges*, Cape Town: Human Sciences Research Council Press.

Eimer, T. and S. Lütz (2010) "Developmental States, Civil Society, and Public Health: Patent Regulation for HIV/AIDS Pharmaceuticals in India and Brazil", *Regulation & Governance*, vol 4, no 2, pp. 135–53.

Eitinger, L. and R. Wade (2024) "US 'Hegemony' in the World Bank", in Schmidtke and Vetterlein (eds) (2024), pp. 118–28.

Elmslie, B. (2010) "One Small Step for Man: Paul Krugman, the 2008 Nobel Laureate in Economics", *Review of Political Economy*, vol 22, no 1, pp. 1–17.

Esping-Andersen, G. (1990) *The Three Worlds of Welfare Capitalism*, Princeton: Princeton University Press.

Esping-Andersen, G. (1999) *Social Foundations of Postindustrial Economies*, Oxford: Oxford University Press.

Esping-Andersen, G. (2009) *The Incomplete Revolution*, Oxford: Polity Press.

Evans, P. (1996a) "Introduction: Development Strategies across the Public-Private Divide", *World Development*, vol 24, no 6, pp. 1033–37.

Evans, P. (1996b) "Government Action, Social Capital and Development Reviewing the Evidence on Synergy", *World Development*, vol 24, no 6, pp. 1119–32.

Evans, P. (2004) "Development as Institutional Change: the Pitfalls of Monocropping and Potentials of Deliberation", *Studies in Comparative International Development*, vol 38, no 4, pp. 30–52.

Evans, P. and D. Rueschemeyer (eds) (1985) *Bringing the State back in*, Cambridge: Cambridge University Press.

Fadda, S. and P. Tridico (ed.) (2013) *Financial Crisis, Labour Markets and Institutions*, London: Routledge.

Fadda, S. and P. Tridico (2013) "Introduction", in Fadda and Tridico (ed.) (2013), pp. 1–16.

Fajth, G. and C. Vinay (2010) "Conditional Cash Transfers: a Global Perspective", MDG Insights, http://mdgpolicynet.undg.org/ext/MDG_Insight/MDG_Insights_Feb_2010 .pdf.

Fasenfest, D. (ed.) (2022) *Marx Matters*, Leiden: Brill.

Fedderke, J., R. de Kadt and J. Luiz (1998) "Growth and Social Capital: a Critical Reflection", mimeo, published in *Theory and Society*, vol 28, no 5, 1999, pp. 709–45.

Fellmeth, A. (1996) "Social Capital in the United States and Taiwan: Trust or Rule of Law?", *Development Policy Review*, vol 14, no 2, pp. 151–72.

Ferdinand, P. (2007) "Russia and China: Converging Responses to Globalization", *International Affairs*, vol 83, no 4, pp. 655–80.

Ferguson, J. (2007) "Formalities of Poverty: Thinking about Social Assistance in Neoliberal South Africa", *African Studies Review*, vol 50, no 2, pp. 71–86.

Fergusson, R. and N. Yeates (2013) "Business as Usual: the Policy Priorities of the World Bank's Discourses on Youth Unemployment, and the Global Financial Crisis", *Journal of International and Comparative Social Policy*, vol 29, no 1, pp. 64–78.

Ferragina, E. and M. Seeleib-Kaiser (2011) "Welfare Regime Debate: Past, Present, Futures?", *Policy and Politics*, vol 39, no 4, pp. 583–611.

Figari, F., M. Matsaganis and H. Sutherland (2013) "Are European Social Safety Nets Tight Enough? Coverage and Adequacy of Minimum Income Schemes in 14 EU Countries", *International Journal of Social Welfare*, vol 22, no 1, pp. 3–14.

Fine, B. (1982) *Theories of the Capitalist Economy*, London: Edward Arnold.

Fine, B. (1990a) *The Coal Question: Political Economy and Industrial Change from the Nineteenth Century to the Present Day*, London: Routledge.

Fine, B. (1990b) "Scaling the Commanding Heights of Public Sector Economics", *Cambridge Journal of Economics*, vol 14, no 2, pp. 127–42.

Fine, B. (1992) *Women's Work and the Capitalist Family*, London: Routledge, reproduced as Routledge Revival, 2011.

Fine, B. (1995) "From Political Economy to Consumption", in Miller (ed.) (1995), pp. 127–63.

Fine, B. (1996) "Some Perspectives on the Provision of Social and Economic Infrastructure", Prepared for, but not presented at, Workshop for South African Policy Makers, June, 1996, https://eprints.soas.ac.uk/32961/1/MERGINTR.docx.

Fine, B. (1997a) "Industrial Policy and South Africa: a Strategic View", NIEP Occasional Paper Series, no 5, Johannesburg: National Institute for Economic Policy.

Fine, B. (1997b) "The New Revolution in Economics", *Capital and Class*, no 61, Spring, pp. 143–48.

Fine, B. (1997c) "Privatisation and the Restructuring of State Assets in South Africa: a Strategic View", NIEP Occasional Paper Series, no 7, Johannesburg: National Institute for Economic Policy.

Fine, B. (1997d) "Playing the Consumption Game", *Consumption, Markets, Culture*, vol 14 1, no 1, pp. 7–29.

Fine, B. (1998a) *Labour Market Theory: a Constructive Reassessment*. London: Routledge.

Fine, B. (1998b) "From Bourdieu to Becker: Barbarism Confronts the Social Sciences", mimeo, but see Fine (2024a, Chapter 5).

Fine, B. (1998c) "The Triumph of Economics: Or 'Rationality' Can Be Dangerous to Your Reasoning", in Carrier and Miller (eds), pp. 49–73.

Fine, B. (1998d) "Vertical Relations in the South African Steel Industry", NIEP Occasional Paper Series, no 13, Johannesburg: National Institute for Economic Policy, originally a report for NUMSA Investment Company, December, 1997.

Fine, B. (1998e) *The Political Economy of Diet, Health and Food Policy*, London: Routledge.

Fine, B. (1999a) "The Developmental State Is Dead – Long Live Social Capital?", *Development and Change*, vol 30, no 1, pp. 1–19, reproduced with afterword, in Moore (ed.) (2007), pp. 121–44. See Chapter 3.

Fine, B. (1999b) "A Question of Economics. Is It Colonising the Social Sciences?", *Economy and Society*, vol 28, no 3, pp. 403–25.

Fine, B. (2000) "Endogenous Growth Theory: a Critical Assessment", *Cambridge Journal of Economics*, vol 24, no 2, pp. 245–65.

Fine, B. (2001) *Social Capital versus Social Theory: Political Economy and Social Science at the Turn of the Millennium*, London: Routledge.

Fine, B. (2002a) "Economics Imperialism and the New Development Economics as Kuhnian Paradigm Shift", *World Development*, vol 30, no 12, pp. 2057–70.

Fine, B. (2002b) "They F**k You up Those Social Capitalists", *Antipode*, vol 34, no 4, pp. 796–99.

Fine, B. (2002c) "The World Bank's Speculation on Social Capital: Bursting the Bubble", in Pincus and Winters (eds) (2002), pp. 203–21.

Fine, B. (2002d) *The World of Consumption: the Material and Cultural Revisited*, London: Routledge.

Fine, B. (2003a) "New Growth Theory", in Chang (ed.) (2003), pp. 201–17.

Fine, B. (2003b) "Social Capital: the World Bank's Fungible Friend", *Journal of Agrarian Change*, vol 3, no 4, pp. 586–603.

Fine, B. (2004a) "Beyond the Developmental State: towards a Political Economy of Development", in Hirakawa et al. (eds) (2004), (in Japanese), pp. 2–43, with English version in Lapavitsas and Noguchi (eds) (2005), pp. 17–33.

Fine, B. (2004b) "Social Capital for Africa?", *Transformation*, no 53, pp. 29–52.

Fine, B. (2004c) "Contesting Social Capital: a Response to Elke Zuern", *Transformation*, no 55, pp. 113–15.

Fine, B. (2005a) "If Social Capital Is the Answer, We Have the Wrong Question", in Runnymede Trust (2005), pp. 75–81.

Fine, B. (2005b) "Social Policy and Development: Social Capital as Point of Departure", in Mkandawire (ed.) (2005), pp. 80–96.

Fine, B. (2006a) "Financial Programming and the IMF", in Jomo and Fine (eds) (2006), pp. 87–100.

Fine, B. (2006b) "New Growth Theory: More Problem than Solution", in Jomo and Fine (eds) (2006), pp. 68–86.

Fine, B. (2006c) "The Developmental State and the Political Economy of Development", in Jomo and Fine (eds) (2006), pp. 101–22.

Fine, B. (2006d) "Social Capital", in Clark (ed.) (2006), pp. 559–63.

Fine, B. (2007a) "Eleven Hypotheses on the Conceptual History of Social Capital: a Response to James Farr", *Political Theory*, vol 35, no 1, pp. 47–53.

Fine, B. (2007b) "State, Development and Inequality: the Curious Incidence of the Developmental State in the Night-Time", paper presented to Sanpad Conference, Durban, June 26–30, https://eprints.soas.ac.uk/5611/1/sanpad.pdf.

Fine, B. (2007c) "The Historical Logic of Economics Imperialism and Meeting the Challenges of Contemporary Orthodoxy: or Twelve Hypotheses on Economics, and What Is to Be Done", paper presented at EAEPE Conference, 1–3 November 2007, Porto, Portugal, available at http://eprints.soas.ac.uk/5620.

Fine, B. (2008) "Social Capital in Wonderland: the World Bank behind the Looking Glass", *Progress in Development Studies*, vol 8 no 3, pp. 261–69.

Fine, B. (2009a) "Development as Zombieconomics in the Age of Neo-Liberalism", *Third World Quarterly*, vol 30, no 5, pp. 885–904.

Fine, B. (2009b) "Submission to the COSATU Panel of Economists on 'The Final Recommendations of the International Panel on Growth (The Harvard Panel)'", *Transformation, no 69, pp. 5–30.

Fine, B. (2009c) "A Rejoinder to 'A Response to Fine's "Harvard Group Shores up Shoddy Governance"'", *Transformation, no 69, pp. 66–79.

Fine, B. (2009d) "Financialisation and Social Policy", Prepared for Conference on "Social and Political Dimensions of the Global Crisis: Implications for Developing

Countries", 12–13 November 2009, UNRISD, Geneva, https://eprints.soas.ac.uk/7984, shortened and revised as Fine (2012d).

Fine, B. (2009e) "Social Policy and the Crisis of Neo-Liberalism", prepared for Conference on "The Crisis of Neo-Liberalism in India: Challenges and Alternatives", Tata Institute of Social Sciences (TISS) Mumbai and International Development Economics Associates (IDEAS), 13–15 March, http://www.networkideas.org/ideas act/jan09/PDF/Fine.pdf.

Fine, B. (2009f) "Political Economy for the Rainbow Nation: Dividing the Spectrum?", prepared for 'Making Sense of Borders: Identity, Citizenship and Power in South Africa', South African Sociological Association, Annual Conference, June/July, Johannesburg, available at http://eprints.soas.ac.uk/7972/.

Fine, B. (2010a) "Flattening Economic Geography: Locating the World Development Report for 2009", *Journal of Economic Analysis*, vol 1, no 1, pp. 15–33. See Chapter 4.

Fine, B. (2010b) *Theories of Social Capital: Researchers Behaving Badly*, London: Pluto Press.

Fine, B. (2010c) "Social Capital", in Cornwall and Eade (eds) (2010), pp. 123–34, reproduced from *Development in Practice*, vol 17, no 4/5, 2007, pp. 566–74.

Fine, B. (2010d) "Locating Financialisation", *Historical Materialism*, vol 18, no 2, pp. 97–116.

Fine, B. (2010e) "The Developmental State?", in Maharaj et al. (eds) (2010), pp. 101–124.

Fine, B. (2010f) "Can South Africa Be a Developmental State?", in Edigheji (ed.) (2010), pp. 169–82.

Fine, B. (2010g) "From the Political Economy of Development to Development Economics: Implications for Africa?", in Padayachee (ed.) (2010), pp. 60–82.

Fine, B. (2011a) "Locating the Developmental State and Industrial and Social Policy after the Crisis", UNCTAD, *The Least Developed Countries Report 2011: the Potential Role of South-South Cooperation for Inclusive and Sustainable Development*, Background Paper, no 3, http://www.unctad.org/Sections/ldc_dir/docs/ldcr2011_Fine_en.pdf See Chapter 7.

Fine, B. (2011b) "Social Capital and Health", in Bayliss et al. (eds) (2011), pp. 99–127.

Fine, B. (2011c) "Prospecting for Political Economy", *International Journal of Management Concepts and Philosophy*, vol 5, no 3, pp. 204–17.

Fine, B. (2012a) "Revisiting Rosa Luxemburg's Political Economy", *Critique*, vol 40, no 3, pp. 423–30.

Fine, B. (2012b) "Across Developmental State and Social Compacting: the Peculiar Case of South Africa", mimeo prepared for SANPAD, available as Fine (2016).

Fine, B. (2012c) "Neo-Liberalism in Retrospect? – It's Financialisation, Stupid", in Chang et al. (eds) (2012), pp. 51–69.

Fine, B. (2012d) "Financialisation and Social Policy", in Utting et al. (eds) (2012), pp. 103–22.

Fine, B. (2012e) "Towards a History of Development Economics", unpublished draft for APORDE volume, but see Fine (2025a, Chapter 1).

Fine, B. (2013a) "Beyond the Developmental State: an Introduction", in Fine et al. (eds) (2013), pp. 1–32.

Fine, B. (2013b) "Towards a Material Culture of Financialisation", FESSUD Working Paper Series, no 15, https://fessud.org/wp-content/uploads/2013/04/Towards-a-Material-Culture-of-Financialisation-FESSUD-Working-Paper-15.pdf, published as revised in *New Political Economy*, vol 22, no 4, pp. 371–82, reproduced in Bayliss et al. (eds) (2018), pp. 17–28.

Fine, B. (2013c) "Economics: Unfit for Purpose", *Review of Social Economy*, vol LXXI, no 3, pp. 373–89, with longer revised version as "Economics – Unfit for Purpose: the Director's Cut", SOAS Department of Economics Working Paper Series, No. 176.

Fine, B. (2013d) "Consumption Matters", *Ephemera*, vol 13, no 2, pp. 217–48, https://ephemerajournal.org/contribution/consumption-matters.

Fine, B. (2013–14) "Financialisation from a Marxist Perspective", *International Journal of Political Economy*, vol 42, no 4, pp. 47–66.

Fine, B. (2014) "The Continuing Enigmas of Social Policy", prepared for the UNRISD project on Towards Universal Social Security in Emerging Economies, UNRISD Working Paper, no 2014–10, June, http://www.unrisd.org/80256B3C005BCCF9/%28httpAuxPages%29/30B153EE73F52ABFC1257D0200420A61/$file/Fine.pdf, shortened and revised in Ye (ed.) (2017), pp. 29–60. See Chapter 8.

Fine, B. (2016) "Across Developmental State and Social Compacting: the Peculiar Case of South Africa", ISER Working Paper no. 2016/1, Grahamstown: Institute of Social and Economic Research, Rhodes University. https://eprints.soas.ac.uk/34148/1/iserwp.pdf.

Fine, B. (2022a) "From Marxist Political Economy to Financialisation or Is It the Other Way about?", in Fasenfest (ed.) (2022), pp. 43–66.

Fine, B. (2022b) "The Enigma of the Post-Apartheid Economic Transition: Insights from the Fate of MERG and a Personal Journey", mimeo available from author.

Fine, B. (2023) "Social Capital: the Indian Connection", in Damodaran et al. (eds) (2023), forthcoming.

Fine, B. (2024a) *Economics Imperialism and Interdisciplinarity: before the Watershed; Critical Reconstructions of Political Economy*, volume 1, Leiden: Brill, and Chicago: Haymarket.

Fine, B. (2024b) *Economics Imperialism and Interdisciplinarity: the Watershed and After; Critical Reconstructions of Political Economy*, volume 2, Leiden: Brill, and Chicago: Haymarket.

Fine, B. (2024c) *Cliometrics as Economics Imperialism: across the Watershed; Critical Reconstructions of Political Economy*, volume 3, Leiden: Brill, and Chicago: Haymarket.

Fine, B. (2025a) *In and against Development: from New to Newest Development Economics; Critical Reconstructions of Political Economy*, volume 5, Leiden: Brill, and Chicago: Haymarket.

Fine, B. (2025b) "The Vagaries and Volatilities of Mainstream Development Economics: a Personal Account", in Meramveliotakis and Manioudis (eds) (2025), pp. 13–28.

Fine, B. (2025c) *In and against Development: from New to Newest Development Economics: Critical Reconstructions of Political Economy*, Volume 5, Leiden: Brill.

Fine, B., K. Bayliss, M. Robertson and A. Saad-Filho (2024) *The Financialisation of Social Reproduction in the Age of Neoliberalism: from Theory to Case Studies; Critical Reconstructions of Political Economy*, volume 4, Leiden: Brill, and Chicago: Haymarket.

Fine, B. and O. Dimakou (2016) *Macroeconomics: a Critical Companion*, London: Pluto.

Fine, B. and D. Hailu (2003) "Convergence and Consensus: the Political Economy of Stabilisation, Poverty and Growth", in volume in honour of K. Borotov and O. Türel, in Turkish and, for English version, SOAS CDPR Discussion Paper, no 2202, https://eprints.soas.ac.uk/7355/1/DiscussionPaper2202.pdf.

Fine, B. and D. Hall (2010) "Contesting Neoliberalism: Public Sector Alternatives for Service Delivery", Preliminary Draft Paper for Ninth Milan European Economy Workshop, An Agenda for the New Public Enterprise: Ownership and Governance for the General Interest, University of Milan, Department of Economics, Business and Statistics, 10–11 June, revised as Fine and Hall (2012).

Fine, B. and D. Hall (2012) "Terrains of Neoliberalism: Constraints and Opportunities for Alternative Models of Service Delivery", in McDonald and Ruiters (eds) (2012), pp. 45–70, revised from Fine and Hall (2010).

Fine, B. and L. Harris (1985) *The Peculiarities of the British Economy*, London: Wishart.

Fine, B., D. Johnston, A. Santos and E. Van Waeyenberge (2016b) "Nudging or Fudging: the World Development Report 2015", *Development and Change*, vol 47, no 4, pp. 640–63. See Chapter 5.

Fine, B., C. Lapavitsas and J. Pincus (eds) (2001) *Development Policy in the Twenty-First Century: beyond the Post-Washington Consensus*, London: Routledge.

Fine, B. and E. Leopold (1993) *The World of Consumption*, London: Routledge.

Fine, B. and D. Milonakis (2003) "From Principle of Pricing to Pricing of Principle: Rationality and Irrationality in the Economic History of Douglass North", *Comparative Studies in Society and History*, vol 45, no 3, pp. 120–44.

Fine, B. and D. Milonakis (2009) *From Economics Imperialism to Freakonomics: the Shifting Boundaries Between Economics and Other Social Sciences*, London: Routledge.

Fine, B. and D. Milonakis (2011) "'Useless but True': Economic Crisis and the Peculiarities of Economic Science", The Isaac and Tamara Deutscher Memorial Prize Lecture, *Historical Materialism*, vol 19, no 2, pp. 3–31.

Fine, B. and J. Ortiz (2016) "Social Capital: From the Gringo's Tale to the Colombian Reality", SOAS Department of Economics Working Paper Series, no 195.

Fine, B. and Z. Rustomjee (1996) *South Africa's Political Economy: From Minerals-Energy Complex to Industrialisation*, Johannesburg: Wits University Press.

Fine, B., A. Saad-Filho, K. Bayliss and M. Robertson (2016a) "Thirteen Things You Need to Know about Neoliberalism", FESSUD, Working Paper Series, no 155, https://fessud.org/wp-content/uploads/2015/03/13-Things-you-need-to-know-about-Neoliberalism-working-paper155.pdf.

Fine, B., J. Saraswati and D. Tavasci (eds) (2013) *Beyond the Developmental State: Industrial Policy into the 21st Century*, London: Pluto.

Fine, B. and C. Stoneman (1996) "Introduction: State and Development", *Journal of Southern African Studies*, vol 22, no 1, pp. 5–26.

Fine, B. and E. Van Waeyenberge (2013a) "A Paradigm Shift that Never Will Be? Justin Lin's New Structural Economics", SOAS Department of Economics, Working Paper Series, no 179. See Chapter 6.

Fine, B. and E. Van Waeyenberge (2013b) "A Paradigm Shift that Never Was: Justin Lin's New Structural Economics", *Competition and Change*, vol 17, no 4, pp. 355–71.

Foch, A. (2013) "The Reasons for World Bank Support of Infrastructure Privatization in Sub-Saharan Africa: a Critical Overview", *International Journal of Transport Economics*, vol 40, no 3, pp. 349–79.

Fontaine, J.-M. and V. Geronimi (1995) "Private Investment and Privatisation in sub-Saharan Africa", in Cook and Kirkpatrick (eds) (1995), pp. 139–61.

Fox, J. (1997) "The World Bank and Social Capital: Contesting the Concept in Practice", *Journal of International Development*, vol 9, no 7, pp. 963–71.

Fox, J. (2024) "Contested Terrain: World Bank Projects and Participatory Development", in Schmidtke and Vetterlein (eds) (2024), pp. 130–42.

Frank, R. (2007) *The Economic Naturalist: Why Economics Explains Almost Everything*, London: Virgin Books.

Franzoni, J. and K. Voorend (2009) "The Role of Distributional Coalitions in Welfare Regimes: Chile, Costa Rica and El Salvador", *Social Policy and Administration*, vol 43, no 4, pp. 364–81.

Franzoni, J. and K. Voorend (2011) "Actors and Ideas behind CCTs in Chile, Costa Rica and El Salvador", *Global Social Policy*, vol 11, no 2/3, pp. 279–98.

Freeland, N. (2007) "Superfluous, Pernicious, Atrocious and Abominable? The Case Against Conditional Cash Transfers", *IDS Bulletin*, vol 38, no 3, pp. 75–78.

Fridell, G. (2011) "Joseph Stiglitz: the Citizen-Bureaucrat and the Limits of Legitimate Dissent", *New Political Science*, vol 33, no 2, pp. 169–88.

Friedmann, J. (1966) *Regional Development Policy: a Case Study of Venezuela*, Cambridge, MIT Press.

Fritz, V. and A. Menocal (2007) "Developmental States in the New Millennium: Concepts and Challenges for a New Aid Agenda" *Development Policy Review*, vol 25, no 5, pp. 531–552.

Fujita, M. and P. Krugman (2004) "The New Economic Geography: Past, Present and the Future", *Regional Science*, vol 83, no 1, pp. 139–64.

Fukuyama, F. (1995) "Social Capital and the Global Economy", *Foreign Affairs*, vol 74, no 5, pp. 89–103.

Fukuyama, F. (1996) *Trust: the Social Virtues and the Creation of Prosperity*. London: Penguin.

Furstenberg, F. and M. Hughes (1995) "Social Capital and Successful Development among at-Risk Youth", *Journal of Marriage and the Family*, vol 57, no 3, pp. 580–92.

Gal, J. (2010) "Is There an Extended Family of Mediterranean Welfare States?", *Journal of European Social Policy*, vol 20, no 4, pp. 283–300.

Gal, J. and B. Greve (2010) "Editorial Introduction", *Social Policy and Administration*, vol 44, no 6, pp. 655–57.

Galal, A., L. Jones, P. Tandon and I. Vogelsang (1992) *Welfare Consequences of Selling Public Enterprises: Case Studies from Chile, Malaysia, Mexico, and the UK*, Washington: World Bank.

Gasbarri, L. (2024) "The World Bank and Legal Studies", in Schmidtke and Vetterlein (eds) (2024), pp. 62–72.

Gerschenkron, A. (1962) *Economic Backwardness in Historical Perspective*, Cambridge: Harvard University Press.

Ghosh, J. (2012) "UNCTAD is Astute and Progressive: So Why Don't Developed Countries Like It?", https://www.networkideas.org/news/may2012/pdf/UNCTAD.pdf.

Gilbert, C., A. Powell and D. Vines (1999) "Positioning the World Bank", *Economic Journal*, vol 109, no 459, pp. 598–633.

Gilbert, N. and D. Besharov (2011) "Welfare States amid Economic Turmoil: Adjusting Work-Oriented Policy", *Policy and Politics,* vol 39, no 3, pp. 295–308.

Global Social Policy Digest (2010) Volume 10, Number 3, www.icsw.org/doc/2010-GlobalSocialPolicyDigest_10-3.docx.

Gomez, E. (2009) "The Rise and Fall of Capital: Corporate Malaysia in Historical Perspective", *Journal of Contemporary Asia*, vol 39, no 3, pp. 345–81.

Goodwin, T. (2012) "Why We Should Reject 'Nudge'", *Politics*, vol 32, no 2, pp. 85–92.

Gopinathan, S. (2007) "Globalisation, the Singapore Developmental State and Education Policy: a Thesis Revisited", *Globalisation, Societies and Education*, vol 5, no 1, pp. 53–70.

Gough, I. and M. Sharkh (2011) "Financing Welfare Regimes: Mapping Heterogeneous Revenue Structures", *International Journal of Social Welfare*, vol 20, no 3, pp. 280–91.

Grahl, J. and P. Teague (2013) "Reconstructing the Eurozone: the Role of EU Social Policy", *Cambridge Journal of Economics*, vol 37, no 3, pp. 677–92.

Granovetter, M. (1985) "Economic Action and Social Structure: the Problem of Embeddedness", *American Journal of Sociology*, vol 91, no 3, pp. 481–510, reproduced in Swedberg (ed.) (1996), pp. 239–68.

Granovetter, M. (1992) "Economic Institutions as Social Constructions: a Framework for Analysis", *Acta Sociologica*, vol 35, no 1, pp. 3–11, reproduced in Swedberg (ed.) (1996), pp. 269–77.

Gray, K. (2008) "The Global Uprising of Labour? The Korean Labour Movement and Neoliberal Social Corporatism", *Globalizations*, vol 5, no 3, pp. 483–99.

Green, A. (2007) "Globalisation and the Changing Nature of the State in East Asia", *Globalisation, Societies and Education*, vol 5, no 1, pp. 23–38.

Greer, S. (2010) "Editorial Introduction: Health Departments in Health Policy", *Social Policy and Administration*, vol 44, no 2, pp. 113–19.

Greve, B. (2008a) "Editorial Introduction: New Times and Continuity", *Social Policy and Administration*, vol 42, no 2, pp. 103–105.

Greve, B. (2008b) "Editorial Introduction: Change in Social Policy in Northern America", *Social Policy and Administration*, vol 42, no 4, pp. 319–22.

Greve, B. (2009) "Editorial Introduction", *Social Policy and Administration*, vol 43, no 2, pp. 101–104.

Greve, B. (2011) "Editorial Introduction: the Nordic Welfare States – Revisited", *Social Policy and Administration*, vol 45, no 2, pp. 111–13.

Greve, B. (ed.) (2013) *The Routledge Handbook of the Welfare State*, London: Routledge.

Grimshaw, D. and J. Rubery (2012) "The End of the UK's Liberal Collectivist Social Model? The Implications of the Coalition Government's Policy during the Austerity Crisis", *Cambridge Journal of Economics*, vol 36, no 1, pp. 105–26.

Grosh, B. and R. Mukandala (1994) "Tying It All Together: What Do We Know?", in Grosh and Mukandala (eds) (1994), pp. 245–252.

Grosh, B. and R. Mukandala (eds) (1994) *State-Owned Enterprises in Africa*, Boulder: Lynne Rienner.

Grüne-Yanoff, T. (2012) "Old Wine in New Casks: Libertarian Paternalism Still Violates Liberal Principles", *Social Choice and Welfare*, vol 38, no 4, pp. 635–45.

Guenther, B., K. Huda and Ian Macauslan (2007) "Broadening Social Risk Management: Risks, Rights and the Chronic Poor", *IDS Bulletin*, vol 38, no 3, pp. 17–19.

Guggenheim, S. (2024) "The Origins of Community-Driven Development: Indonesia and the Kecamatan Development Program", in Schmidtke and Vetterlein (eds) (2024), pp. 332–43.

Guo, J. and N. Gilbert (2007) "Welfare State Regimes and Family Policy: a Longitudinal Analysis", *International Journal of Social Welfare*, vol 16, no 4, pp. 307–13.

Gyohten, T. (1997) "Japan and the World Bank", in Kapur et al. (eds) (1997a), pp. 275–316.

Haarstad, H. (2011) "Latin American Middle Classes and Political Mobilization for Universal Welfare", *Global Social Policy*, vol 11, no 3, pp. 229–32.

Haarstad, H. and A. St Clair (2011) "Social Policy and Global Poverty: beyond the Residual Paradigm?", *Global Social Policy*, vol 11, no 2/3, pp. 214–19.

Henrich, J., R. Boyd, S. Bowles, C. Camerer, E. Fehr and H. Gintis (eds) (2004) *Foundations of Human Sociality: Economic Experiments and Ethnographic Evidence from Fifteen Small-Scale Societies*, Oxford: Oxford University Press.

Hertel-Fernandez, A. (2009) "Retrenchment Reconsidered: Continuity and Change in the Post-authoritarian Institutions of Chilean Social Policy", *Social Policy and Administration*, vol 43, no 4, pp. 382–96.

Hildyard, N. (1998) *The World Bank and the State: a Recipe for Change?*, London: Bretton Woods Project.

Hildyard, N. (2012) "More than Bricks and Mortar. Infrastructure as an Asset Class: Financing Development or Developing Finance? A Critical Look at Private Equity Infrastructure Funds", The Corner House, http://www.thecornerhouse.org.uk/resource/more-bricks-and-mortar.

Hinrich, K. (1995) "The Impact of German Health Insurance Reforms on Redistribution and the Culture of Solidarity", *Journal of Health Politics, Policy and Law*, vol 20, no 3, pp. 653–87.

Hirakawa, H., M. Noguchi and M. Sano (eds) (2004) *Beyond Market-Driven Development: a New Stream of Political Economy of Development*, Tokyo: Nihon Hyoron Sha, in Japanese.

Hitchcock, R. (2024) "The World Bank and Anthropology: Conflict and Cooperation", in Schmidtke and Vetterlein (eds) (2024), pp. 51–61.

Hodgson, G. (2008) "Prospects for Economic Sociology", *Philosophy of the Social Sciences*, vol 38, no 1, pp. 133–49.

Hoff, K., A. Braverman and J. Stiglitz (eds) (1993) *The Economics of Rural Organisation: Theory, Practice, and Policy*. New York: Oxford University Press.

Holden, C. and K. Lee (2009) "Corporate Power and Social Policy: the Political Economy of the Transnational Tobacco Companies", *Global Social Policy*, vol 9, no 3, pp 328–54.

Holzmann, R. (ed.) (2009) *Social Protection and Labor at the World Bank, 2000–2008*, Washington: World Bank.

Holzmann, R. and V. Kozel (2007a) "The Role of Social Risk Management in Development: a World Bank View", *IDS Bulletin*, vol 38, no 3, pp. 8–13.

Holzmann, R. and V. Kozel (2007b) "The Role of Social Risk Management in Development: a World Bank View – Reply to Comments", *IDS Bulletin*, vol 38, no 3, pp. 20–22.

Holzmann, R., S. Sipos and the Social Protection Team (2009) "Social Protection and Labor at the World Bank: an Overview", in Holzmann (ed.) (2009), pp. 1–10.

Hudson, J. and S. Kühner (2012) "Analyzing the Productive and Protective Dimensions of Welfare: Looking Beyond the OECD", *Social Policy and Administration*, vol 46, no 1, pp. 35–60.

Hundt, D. (2009) *Korea's Developmental Alliance: State, Capital and the Politics of Rapid Development*, London: Routledge.

Huque, A. and H. Zafarullah (eds) (2005) *International Development Governance*, London: Routledge.

Hyden, G. (1997) "Civil Society, Social Capital, and Development: Dissection of a Complex Discourse", *Studies in Comparative International Development*, vol 32, no 1, pp. 3–30.

IFC (2009) "The Business of Health in Africa", https://documents1.worldbank.org/cura ted/en/878891468002994639/pdf/441430WP0ENGLI1an10110200801PUBLIC1.pdf.

Ikpe, E. (2011) *Agriculture, the Means to an Industrialisation End: Lessons from the Developmental State Paradigm with Reference to Nigeria*, Phd thesis, University of London, in preparation.

Ikpe, E. (2013) "Lessons for Nigeria from Developmental States: the Role of Agriculture in Structural Transformation", in Fine et al. (eds) (2013), pp. 187–215.

Ishii-Eiteman, M. (2010) "Food Sovereignty and the International Assessment of Agricultural Knowledge, Science and Technology for Development", *Journal of Peasant Studies*, vol 36, no 3, pp. 663–706.

Islam, N. (2003) "What Have We Learnt from the Convergence Debate?", *Journal of Economic Surveys*, vol 17, no 3, pp. 309–61.

Isuani, E. (2010) "The Argentine Welfare State: Enduring and Resisting Change", *International Journal of Social Welfare*, vol 19, no 1, pp. 104–14.

Iwata, M. (2013) "Poverty, the Working Poor and Social Policy in East Asia: Exploring the Second Safety New Proposal in Japan", in Izuhara (ed.) (2013), pp. 434–51.

Izuhara, M. (2013) "Introduction", in Izuhara (ed.) (2013), pp. 1–12.

Izuhara, M. (ed.) (2013) *Handbook on East Asian Social Policy*, Cheltenham: Edward Elgar.

Jalilian, H. and J. Weiss (1997) "Bureaucrats, Business and Economic Growth", *Journal of International Development*, vol 9, no 6, pp 877–85.

Jawad, R. and B. Yakut-Cakar (2010) "Religion and Social Policy in the Middle East: the (Re)Constitution of an Old-New Partnership", *Social Policy and Administration*, vol 44, no 6, pp. 658–72.

Jensen, C. (2011a) "The Forgotten Half: Analysing the Politics of Welfare Services", *International Journal of Social Welfare*, vol 20, no 4, pp. 404–12.

Jensen, C. (2011b) "Determinants of Welfare Service Provision after the Golden Age", *International Journal of Social Welfare*, vol 20, no 2, pp. 125–34.

Jenson, J. (2009) "Lost in Translation: the Social Investment Perspective and Gender Equality", *Social Politics*, vol 16, no 4, pp. 446–83.

Jenson, J. (2010) "Diffusing Ideas for after Neoliberalism: the Social Investment Perspective in Europe and Latin America", *Global Social Policy*, vol 10, no 1, pp. 59–84.

Jerven, M. (2011) "The Quest for the African Dummy: Explaining African Post-Colonial Economic Performance Revisited", *Journal of International Development*, vol 23, no 2, pp. 288–307.

Jo, N. (2011) "Between the Cultural Foundations of Welfare and Welfare Attitudes: the Possibility of an in-between Level Conception of Culture for the Cultural Analysis of Welfare", *Journal of European Social Policy*, vol 21, no 1, pp. 5–19.

Jochem, S. (2011) "Nordic Employment Policies – Change and Continuity before and during the Financial Crisis", *Social Policy and Administration*, vol 45, no 2, pp. 131–45.

Johnson, C. (1982) *MITI and the Japanese Miracle*, Stanford: Stanford University Press.

Johnson, C. (2006) "Chalmers Johnson on Our Military Empire", Tomdispatch Interview, posted March 21, 2006, 07:29, http://tomdispatch.com/post/70243/tomdispatch _interview_chalmers_johnson_on_our_military_empire.

Johnston, D. (2015) "Paying the Price of HIV in Africa: Cash Transfers and the De-Politicisation of HIV Risk", *Review of African Political Economy*, vol 42, no 145, pp. 394–413.

Jomo, K. (2008) "Obstacles to Implementing Lessons from the 1997–1998 East Asian Crises", DESA Working Paper No. 66ST/ESA/2008/DWP/66, Department of Economic and Social Affairs, United Nations.

Jomo, K. and B. Fine (eds) (2006) *The New Development Economics: after the Washington Consensus*, Delhi: Tulika, and London: Zed Press.

Jørgensen, H. and M. Schulze (2011) "Leaving the Nordic Path? The Changing Role of Danish Trade Unions in the Welfare Reform Process", *Social Policy and Administration*, vol 45, no 2, pp. 206–19.

Juhász, R., N. Lane and D. Rodrik (2023) "The New Economics of Industrial Policy", NBER Working Paper Series, no 31538, http://www.nber.org/papers/w31538.

Jung, C. and A. Walker (2009) "The Impact of Neo-liberalism on South Korea's Public Pension: a Political Economy of Pension Reform", *Social Policy and Administration*, vol 43, no 5, pp. 425–44.

Jutila, M. (2011) "Narrowing of Public Responsibility in Finland, 1990–2010", *Social Policy and Administration*, vol 45, no 2, pp. 194–205.

Kahneman, D. (2003) "Maps of Bounded Rationality: Psychology for Behavioural Economics", *American Economic Review*, vol 93, no 5, pp. 1449–75.

Kahneman, D. and A. Tversky (1979) "Prospect Theory: an Analysis of Decision under Risk", *Econometrica*, vol 47, no 2, pp. 263–91.

Kalinowski, T. (2008) "Korea's Recovery since the 1997/98 Financial Crisis: the Last Stage of the Developmental State", *New Political Economy*, vol 13, no 4, pp. 447–62.

Kam, Y. (2012) "The Contributions of the Health Decommodification Typologies to the Study of the East Asian Welfare", *Social Policy and Administration*, vol 46, no 1, pp. 108–28.

Kammer, A., J. Niehues and A. Peichl (2012) "Welfare Regimes and Welfare State Outcomes in Europe", *Journal of European Social Policy*, vol 22, no 5, pp. 455–71.

Kane, J. (2009) "What the Economic Crisis Means for Child Labour", *Global Social Policy*, vol 9 (Supplement), pp 175–96.

Kangas, O. (2010) "One Hundred Years of Money, Welfare and Death: Mortality, Economic Growth and the Development of the Welfare State in 17 OECD Countries", *International Journal of Social Welfare*, vol 19 (Supplement), pp. S42–S59.

Kaplinsky, R. (2008) "What Does the Rise of China Do for Industrialisation in Sub-Saharan Africa?", *Review of African Political Economy*, vol 35, no 115, pp. 7–22.

Kapur, D., J. Lewis and R. Webb (eds) (1997a) *The World Bank: Its First Half Century. Volume 1: History*, Washington, DC: Brookings Institution Press.

Kapur, D., J. Lewis, and R. Webb (eds) (1997b) *The World Bank: Its First Half Century, Volume II: Perspectives*, Washington: Brookings.

Karacimen, E. (2014) "Dynamics behind the Rise in Household Debt in Advanced Capitalist Countries: an Overview", FESSUD Working Paper Series, no 9, https://fessud.org/wp-content/uploads/2013/04/Dynamics-behind-the-Rise-in-Household-Debt-FESSUD-Working-Paper-09-1.pdf.

Karo, E. and R. Kattel (2010) "Coordination of Innovation Policies in the Catching-up Context: a Historical Perspective on Estonia and Brazil", *International Journal of Technological Learning, Innovation and Development*, vol 3, no 4, pp. 293–329.

Kasza, G. (2006) *One World of Welfare: Japan in Comparative Perspective*, Ithaca: Cornell University Press.

Katz, A. (2004) "The Sachs Report: *Investing in Health for Economic Development* – or Increasing the Size of the Crumbs from the Rich Man's Table?, Part I", *International Journal of Health Services*, vol 34, no 4, pp. 751–73.

Kennett, P., K. Chan, and L. Ngan (2013) "Social Protection, Governance and the Dynamics of Inclusion and Exclusion in East Asia", in Izuhara (ed.) (2013), pp. 245–65.

Kenny, C. and D. Williams (2001) "What Do We Know About Economic Growth? Or Why Don't We Know Very Much?", *World Development*, vol 29, no 1, pp. 1–22.

Khondker, H. (2008) "Globalization and State Autonomy in Singapore", *Asian Journal of Social Science*, vol 36, no 1, pp. 35–56.

Khoon, C. (2011) "Aspects of Healthcare Policy in Malaysia: Universalism, Targeting, and Privatization", *Global Social Policy*, vol 11, no 2/3, 143–46.

Kim, T. and K. Zurlo (2009) "How Does Economic Globalisation Affect the Welfare State? Focusing on the Mediating Effect of Welfare Regimes", *International Journal of Social Welfare*, vol 18, no 2, pp. 130–41.

Kim, W. (2009) "Rethinking Colonialism and the Origins of the Developmental State in East Asia", *Journal of Contemporary Asia*, vol 39, no 3, pp. 382–99.

Knack, S. and P. Keefer (1997) "Does Social Capital Have an Economic Payoff? A Cross-Country Investigation", *Quarterly Journal of Economics*, vol 62, no 4, pp. 1251–88.

Kohler, H.-P. and R. Thornton (2012) "Conditional Cash Transfers and HIV/AIDS Prevention: Unconditionally Promising?", *World Bank Economic Review*, vol 26, no 2, pp. 165–90.

Kolankiewicz, G. (1996) "Social Capital and Social Change", *British Journal of Sociology*, vol 47, no 3, pp. 427–41.

Kondoh, H., T. Kobayashi, H. Shiga and J. Sato (2010) "Diversity and Transformation of Aid Patterns in Asia's 'Emerging Donors'", JICA Research Institute, October, Working Paper, no 21.

Konings, M. (2009) "Rethinking Neoliberalism and the Subprime Crisis: beyond the Re-regulation Agenda", *Competition and Change*, vol 13, no 2, pp. 108–27.

Konrad, K. (1995) "Social Security and Strategic Inter-Vivos Transfers of Social Capital", *Journal of Population Economics*, vol 8, no 3, pp. 315–26.

Koster F. (2008) "The Effects of Social and Political Openness on the Welfare State in 18 OECD Countries", *International Journal of Social Welfare*, vol 17, no 4, pp. 291–300.

Koster F. (2009) "The Welfare State and Globalisation: down and out or Too Tough to Die?", *International Journal of Social Welfare*, vol 18, no 2, pp. 153–62.

Kramarz, T. and A. Wilkinson (2024) "Environmental Partnerships in the World Bank", in Schmidtke and Vetterlein (eds) (2024), pp. 191–203.

Kravets, O., P. Maclaran, S. Miles and A. Venkatesh (eds) (2018) *The SAGE Handbook of Consumer Culture*, London: Sage.

Krueger, A. (1986) "Aid in the Development Process", *World Bank Research Observer*, vol 1, no 1, pp. 57–78.

Krugman, P. (1978) "The Theory of Interstellar Trade", mimeo, http://www.prince ton.edu/~pkrugman/interstellar.pdf.

Krugman, P. (1994a) "The Fall and Rise of Development Economics", available at http://web.mit.edu/krugman/www/dishpan.html.

Krugman, P. (1994b) "The Myth of Asia's Miracle", *Foreign Affairs*, vol 73, no 6, pp. 62–78.

Ku, Y. and C. Finer (2007) "Developments in East Asian Welfare Studies", *Social Policy and Administration*, vol 41, no 2, pp. 115–31.

Kuitto, K. (2011) "More than Just Money: Patterns of Disaggregated Welfare Expenditure in the Enlarged Europe", *Journal of European Social Policy*, vol 21, no 4, pp. 348–64.

Kuivalainen, S. and M. Niemelä (2010) "From Universalism to Selectivism: the Ideational Turn of the Anti-Poverty Policies in Finland", *Journal of European Social Policy*, vol 20, no 3, pp. 263–76.

Kukreja, V. and M. Singh (eds) (2008) *Democracy, Development and Discontent in South Asia*, New Delhi: Sage Publications.

Kumar, N. (2008) "India: a Failed Democratic Developmental State?", in Kukreja and Singh (eds) (2008), pp. 148–170.

Kumssa, A. (1996) "The Political Economy of Privatization in Sub-Saharan Africa", *International Review of Administrative Sciences*, vol 62, no 1, pp. 75–87.

Kun-Chin, L. (2007) "With Strings Attached? Improving the Administration of Central State Financed Investment Projects in the PRC", *Asian Journal of Political Science*, vol 15, no 3, pp. 319–43.

Künzel, S. (2012) "The Local Dimension of Active Inclusion Policy", *Journal of European Social Policy*, vol 22, no 1, pp. 3–16.

Kuriyan, R. and I. Ray (2009) "Outsourcing the State? Public–Private Partnerships and Information Technologies in India", *World Development*, vol 37, no 10, pp. 1663–73.

Kvist, J. and B. Greve (2010) "Has the Nordic Welfare Model Been Transformed?" *Social Policy and Administration*, vol 45, no 2, pp. 146–60.

Kwakkenbos, J. (2012) "Private Profit for Public Good? Can Investing in Private Companies Deliver for the Poor", Eurodad, http://eurodad.org/wp-content/uplo ads/2012/05/Private-Profit-for-Public-Good.pdf.

Kwon, H. (ed.) (2005) *Transforming the Developmental Welfare State in East Asia*, Houndmills: Palgrave.

Kwon, H.-J. (2009) "Policy Learning and Transfer: the Experience of the Developmental State in East Asia", *Policy & Politics*, vol 37, no 3, pp. 409–21.

Kwon, H.-J. and I. Yi (2009) "Economic Development and Poverty Reduction in Korea: Governing Multifunctional Institutions", *Development and Change*, vol 40, no 4, pp. 769–92.

Lall, S. (2004) "Reinventing Industrial Strategy: the Role of Government Policy in Building Industrial Competitiveness", UNCTAD, G–24 Discussion Paper, no 28.

Lancet Commission (2010) "The Millennium Development Goals: a Cross-Sectoral Analysis and Principles for Goal Setting after 2015", The Lancet and London International Development Centre Commission, September 13, 2010, https://rese archers.cdu.edu.au/en/publications/the-millennium-development-goals-a-cross -sectoral-analysis-and-pr#:~:text=The%20Millennium%20Development%20Go als%3A%20a%20cross-sectoral%20analysis%20and,international%20deve lopment%20centre%20commission.%20Lancet%2C%20376%20%289 745%29%2C%20991-1023.

Lange, M. (2009) "Developmental Crises: a Comparative-Historical Analysis of State-Building in Colonial Botswana and Malaysia", *Commonwealth and Comparative Politics*, vol 47, no 1, pp. 1–27.

Lapavitsas, C. (2009) "Financialised Capitalism: Crisis and Financial Expropriation". *Historical Materialism*, vol 17, no 2, pp. 114–48.

Lapavitsas, C. (2013) *Profiting Without Producing: How Finance Exploits Us All*, London: Verso.

Lapavitsas, C. and M. Noguchi (eds) (2005) *Beyond Market–Driven Development: Drawing on the Experience of Asia and Latin America*, London: Routledge.

Lavinas, L. (2013) "21st Century Welfare", *New Left Review*, no 84, pp. 5–40.

Lazonick, W. (2008) "Entrepreneurial Ventures and the Developmental State: Lessons from Advanced Economies", UNU-WIDER Discussion Paper, no 2008/1.

Lee, F. (2012) "Heterodox Economics and its Critics", *Review of Political Economy*, vol 24, no 2, pp. 337–51.

Lee, K. (2009) "How Can Korea Be a Role Model for Catch-up Development?", UNU-WIDER, Research Paper, no 2009/34.

Lee, K.-S. (2009) "A Final Flowering of the Developmental State: the IT Policy Experiment of the Korean Information Infrastructure, 1995–2005", *Government Information Quarterly*, vol 26, no 4, pp. 567–76.

Lee, S. (2008) "The Politics of Chaebol Reform in Korea: Social Cleavage and New Financial Rules", *Journal of Contemporary Asia*, vol 38, no 3, pp. 439–52.

Lee, Y. and S. Kwak (2009) "Neo-liberal Korea and Still Developmentalist Japan: Myth or Reality?", *Global Economic Review*, vol 38, no 3, pp. 277–95.

Lee, Y. and Y. Tee (2009) "Reprising the Role of the Developmental State in Cluster Development: the Biomedical Industry in Singapore", *Singapore Journal of Tropical Geography*, vol 30, no 1, pp. 86–97.

Leftwich, A. (2000) *States of Development: On the Primacy of Politics in Development*, Cambridge: Polity Press.

Leftwich, A. (2005) "Changing Configurations of the Developmental State", in Huque and Zafarullah (eds) (2005), pp. 51–74.

Lehndorff, S. (2012) "Introduction – the Triumph of Failed Ideas", in Lehndorff (ed.) (2012), pp. 1–20.

Lehndorff, S. (ed.) (2012) *A Triumph of Failed Ideas: European Models of Capitalism in Crisis*, Brussels: ETUI.

Leiterlitz, R. and C. Weaver (2005) "'Our Poverty is a World Full of Dreams': Reforming the World Bank", *Global Governance*, vol 11, no 3, pp. 369–88.

Levitt, S. and J. Dubner (2005) *Freakonomics: a Rogue Economist Explores the Hidden Side of Everything*, New York: Harper Collins.

Lewis, J., M. Campbell and C. Huerta (2008) "Patterns of Paid and Unpaid Work in Western Europe: Gender, Commodification, Preferences and the Implications for Policy", *Journal of European Social Policy*, vol 18, no 1, pp. 21–37.

Lim, H. (2010) "The Transformation of the Developmental State and Economic Reform in Korea", *Journal of Contemporary Asia*, vol 40, no 2, pp. 188–210.

Lin, J. (2003) "Development Strategy, Viability and Economic Convergence", *Economic Development and Cultural Change*, vol 53, no 2, pp. 277–308.

Lin, J. (2009) *Economic Development and Transition: Thought, Strategy, and Viability*, New York: Cambridge University Press.

Lin, J. (2010) "Six Steps for Strategic Government Intervention", *Global Policy*, vol 1, no. 3, pp. 330–331.

Lin, J. (2012a) *New Structural Economics: a Framework for Rethinking Development and Policy*, Washington: World Bank, http://siteresources.worldbank.org/DEC/Resour ces/84797-1104785060319/598886-1104951889260/NSE-Book.pdf.

Lin, J. (2012b) *Benti and Changwu: Dialogues on Methodology in Economics*, Beijing: Peking University Press, Kindle Edition.

Lin, J. and H.-J. Chang (2009) "Should Industrial Policy in Developing Countries Conform to Comparative Advantage or Defy It? A Debate between Justin Lin and Ha-Joon Chang", *Development Policy Review*, vol 27, no 5, pp. 483–502.

Lin, J. and C. Monga (2011a) "Growth Identification and Facilitation: the Role of the State in the Dynamics of Structural Change", *Development Policy Review*, vol 29, no 3, pp. 264–90.

Lin, J. and C. Monga (2011b) "Rejoinder", *Development Policy Review*, vol 29, no 3, pp. 304–10.

Lin, J. and D. Rosenblatt (2012) "Shifting Patterns of Economic Growth and Rethinking Development", World Bank, Policy Research Working Paper, no 6040.

Lin, J., X. Sun, and Y. Jiang (2009) "Toward a Theory of Optimal Financial Structure", World Bank, Policy Research Working Paper, no 5038.

Lippit, V., R. Baiman, D. Kotz, M. Larudee, M. Li, V. Lippit and S. Osterreich (2011) "Introduction: China's Rise in the Global Economy", *Review of Radical Political Economics*, vol 43, no 1, pp. 5–8.

Liu, L. (2008) "Local Government and Big Business in the People's Republic of China – Case Study Evidence from Shandong Province", *Asia Pacific Business Review*, vol 14, no 4, pp. 473–89.

Lloyd-Sherlock, P. (2009) "Social Policy and Inequality in Latin America: a Review of Recent Trends", *Social Policy and Administration*, vol 43, no 4, pp. 347–63.

Lo, D. (2007) "China's Quest for Alternative to Neo-Liberalism: Market Reform, Economic Growth, and Labor", *Kyoto Economic Review*, vol 76, no 2, pp. 193–210.

Lo, D. (2010) "China and World Development beyond the Crisis", Department of Economics, SOAS, Working Paper, no 167, https://econpapers.repec.org/paper /soawpaper/167.htm.

Lo, D. and Y. Zhang (2011) "Making Sense of China's Economic Transformation", *Review of Radical Political Economics*, vol 43, no 1, pp. 33–55.

Lohman, L. and S. Sexton (2010) "Carbon Markets: the Policy Reality", *Global Social Policy*, vol 10, no 1, pp. 9–12.

Lorentzen, J. and P. Møllgaard (2006) "Competition Policy and Innovation", in Bianchi and Labory (eds) (2006), pp. 115–33.

Lucas, R. (1987) *Models of Business Cycles*, Oxford: Blackwell.

MacGregor, S. (2013) "Welfare: Theoretical and Analytical Paradigms", Towards Universal Social Security in Emerging Economies: Process, Institutions and Actors, UNRISD Background Paper.

Mackintosh, M., J. Chataway and M. Wuyts (2007) "Promoting Innovation, Productivity and Industrial Growth and Reducing Poverty: Bridging the Gap: Introduction to the Special Issue", *European Journal of Development Research*, vol 19, no 1, pp. 1–12.

MacMillan, R. (1995) "Changes in the Structure of Life Courses and the Decline of Social Capital in Canadian Society: a Time Series Analysis of Property Crime Rates", *Canadian Journal of Sociology*, vol 20, no 1, pp. 51–79.

Mader, P., D. Mertens and N. van der Zwan (eds) (2020) *The Routledge International Handbook of Financialization*, Abingdon: Routledge.

Maharaj, B., A. Desai and P. Bond (eds) (2010) *Zuma's Own Goal: Losing South Africa's 'War on Poverty'*, Trenton, NJ: Africa World Press, Inc.

Mahon, R. (2009) "The OECD's Discourse on the Reconciliation of Work and Family Life", *Global Social Policy*, vol 9, no 2, pp. 183–204.

Mahon, R. (2010) "After Neo-Liberalism? The OECD, the World Bank and the Child", *Global Social Policy*, vol 10, no 2, pp. 172–92.

Mäki, U. (2009) "Economics Imperialism: Concepts and Constraints", *Philosophy of the Social Sciences*, vol 39, no 3, pp. 351–80.

Mamdani, M. (2011) "The Importance of Research in a University", Makerere Institute of Social Research 2011–04–21, Issue 526, http://pambazuka.org/en/category/featu res/72782.

Marin, B. and E. Zólyomi (eds) (2010) *Women's Work and Pensions: What Is Good, What Is Best?*, Farnham: Ashgate.

Maringanti, A., E. Sheppard and J. Zhang (2009) "Where Is the Geography? The World Bank's WDR 2009", *Economic and Political Weekly*, vol 44, no 29, pp. 45–51.

Martin, R. (1999) "The New 'Geographical Turn' in Economics: Some Critical Reflections", *Cambridge Journal of Economics*, vol 23, no 1, pp. 65–91.

Masina, P. (2010) "Vietnam between Developmental State and Neoliberalism: the Case of the Industrial Sector", C.Met Working Paper, no 7, Centro Interuniversitario di Economia Applicata alle Politiche per l'Industria lo Sviluppa Locale e l'Internation-alizzazione, published in Chang et al. (eds) (2012), pp. 188–210.

Matlosa, K. (2007) "The State, Democracy, and Development in Southern Africa", *World Futures: the Journal of General Evolution*, vol 63, no 5–6, pp. 443–463.

Matos, C. (2013) "The Shifting Welfare State in Hungary and Latvia", *American Journal of Economics and Sociology*, vol 72, no 4, pp. 851–91.

Mattei, L. and D. Sánchez-Ancochea (2010) "Bolsa Familia, Poverty and Inequality: towards the End of Universalism in Latin America?", mimeo, appearing in *Social Policy*, vol 11, no 2–3, 2011, pp. 299–318.

Mätzke, M. and I. Ostner (2010) "Introduction: Change and Continuity in Recent Family Policies", *Journal of European Social Policy*, vol 20, no 5, pp. 387–98.

Maundeni, Z. (2002) "State Culture and Development in Botswana and Zimbabwe", *Journal of Modern African Studies*, vol 40, no 1, pp. 105–32.

Mayer, T. (2008) "Market Potential and Development", Background Paper to the 2009 World Development Report, available at http://siteresources.worldbank.org/INT WDR2009/Resources/4231006-1204741572978/Mayer.pdf.

Mayes, D. and A. Michalski (eds) (2013) *The Changing Welfare State In Europe: the Implications for Democracy*, Cheltenham: Edward Elgar.

Mayes, D. and Z. Mustaffa (2013) "Social Models in the Enlarged European Model", in Mayes and Michalski (eds) (2013), pp. 168–89.

McArthur, J. and J. Sachs (2001) "Institutions and Geography: Comment on Acemoglu, Johnson and Robinson 2000", *NBER Working Paper, no W8114*, February.

McDonald, D. and G. Ruiters (eds) (2012) *Alternatives to Privatization: Exploring Non-Commercial Service Delivery Options in the Global South*, London: Routledge, and Cape Town: HSRC Press, http://www.hsrcpress.ac.za/product.php?productid= 2287&freedownload=1.

McIntyre, B., H. Herren, J. Wakhungu and R. Watson (eds) (2009) *Agriculture at a Crossroads: Report of the International Assessment of Agricultural Knowledge, Science, and Technology*, 7 Volumes: Synthesis Report; Global Summary for Decision Makers; Volume I: Central and West Asia and North Africa; Volume II: East and South Asia and the Pacific; Volume III: Latin America and the Caribbean; Volume IV: North America and Europe; and Volume V: Sub-Saharan Africa, Washington: Island Press.

McKinnon, R. and G. Schnabl (2006) "China's Exchange Rate and International Adjustment in Wages, Prices and Interest Rates: Japan Déjà Vu?", *CESifo Economic Studies*, vol 52, no 2, pp. 276–303.

McNeill, D. (2024) "Ethics and Human Rights in the World Bank", in Schmidtke and Vetterlein (eds) (2024), pp. 297–307.

Medlin, C. and D. de Walque (2008) "Potential Applications of Conditional Cash Transfers for the Prevention of Sexually Transmitted Infections and HIV in Sub-Saharan Africa", World Bank Policy Research Working Paper, no 4673, Washington, DC: World Bank Human Development and Public Services Team.

Mehrotra, S., N. Kumra and A. Gandhi (2013) "The Fragmented Social Protection System in India: Five Key Rights but Two Missing", Towards Universal Social Security in Emerging Economies: Process, Institutions and Actors, UNRISD Background Paper.

Meisenhelder, T. (1997) "The Developmental State in Mauritius", *Journal of Modern African Studies*, vol 35, no 2, pp. 279–97.

Memiş, E. and M. Montes (2008) "Who's Afraid of Industrial Policy?", Discussion Paper, Asia Pacific Trade and Investment Initiative, UNDP Regional Centre in Colombo.

Menashy, F. and R. Read (2016) "Knowledge Banking in Global Education Policy: a Bibliometric Analysis of World Bank Publications on Public-Private Partnerships", *Education Policy Analysis Archives*, vol 24, no 95, pp. 1–28.

Mendes P. (2009) "Retrenching or Renovating the Australian Welfare State: the Paradox of the Howard Government's Neo-Liberalism", *International Journal of Social Welfare*, vol 18, no 1, pp. 102–110.

Meramveliotakis, G. and M. Manioudis (eds) (2025) *Sustainable Economic Development Perspectives from Political Economy and Economics Pluralism*, London: Routledge.

MERG (1993) *Making Democracy Work: a Framework for Macroeconomic Policy in South Africa*, Cape Town: CDS.

Meyerson, E. (1994) "Human Capital, Social Capital and Compensation: the Relative Contribution of Social Contacts to Managers' Incomes", *Acta Sociologica*, vol 37, no 4, pp. 383–99.

Midgley, J. and D. Piachaud (eds) (2013) *Social Protection, Economic Growth And Social Change: Goals, Issues and Trajectories in China, India, Brazil and South Africa*, Cheltenham: Edward Elgar.

Miller, D. (ed.) (1995) *Acknowledging Consumption*, London: Routledge.

Milonakis, D. and B. Fine (2007) "Douglass North's Remaking of Economic History: a Critical Appraisal", *Review of Radical Political Economics*, vol 39, no 1, pp. 27–57.

Milonakis, D. and B. Fine (2009) *From Political Economy to Economics: Method, the Social and the Historical in the Evolution of Economic Theory*, London: Routledge.

Mirowski, P. (2007) "The Mirage of An Economics of Knowledge", available at https://economix.fr/uploads/source/doc/workshops/2007_history_economics/Mirowski.pdf.

Misra-Dexter, N. and J. February (eds) (2010) *Testing Democracy: Which Way Is South Africa Going?*, Institute for a Democratic South Africa, Cape Town: ABC Press.

Mkandawire, T. (2001) "Thinking About the Developmental States in Africa", *Cambridge Journal of Economics*, vol 25, no 3, pp. 289–313.

Mkandawire, T. (2009) *Institutional Monocroping and Monotasking in Africa*, Geneva: UNRISD.

Mkandawire, T. (2010) "How the New Poverty Agenda Neglected Social and Employment Policies in Africa", *Journal of Human Development and Capabilities*, vol 11, no 1, pp. 37–55.

Mkandawire, T. (2012) "Building the African State in the Age of Globalisation: the Role of Social Compacts and Lessons for South Africa", Mapungubwe Institute for Strategic Reflection, Inaugural Annual Lecture, MISTRA, https://mistra.org.za/mistra-media/building-the-african-state-in-the-age-of-globalisation-the-role-of-social-compacts-and-lessons-for-south-africa/.

Mkandawire, T. (ed.) (2005) *Social Policy in a Development Context*, UNRISD, Basingstoke: Palgrave MacMillan.

Mok, K. (2007) "Globalisation, New Education Governance and State Capacity in East Asia", *Globalisation, Societies and Education*, vol 5, no 1, pp. 1–21.

Moore, C. (2009) "Nicaragua's Red de Protección Social: an Exemplary but Short-Lived Conditional Cash Transfer Programme", International Policy Centre for Inclusive Growth, UNDP Country Study number 1, http://www.ipc-undp.org/pub/IPCCou ntryStudy17.pdf.

Moore, D. (ed.) (2007) *The World Bank: Development, Poverty, Hegemony*, Scotsville: University of KwaZulu-Natal Press.

Morel, N., B. Palier and J. Palme (eds) (2012) *Towards a Social Investment Welfare State? Ideas, Policies and Challenges*, Bristol: The Policy Press.

Moser, C. (2008) "Assets and Livelihoods: a Framework for Asset-Based Social Policy", in Moser and Dani (eds) (2008), pp. 43–84.

Moser, C. and A. Dani (eds) (2008) *Assets, Livelihoods, and Social Policy*, Washington: World Bank.

Mosley, P., T. Subasat and J. Weeks (1995) "Assessing 'Adjustment in Africa'", *World Development*, vol 23, no 9, pp. 1459–73.

Moudud, J. and K. Botchway (2007) "Challenging the Orthodoxy: African Development in the Age of Openness", *African and Asian Studies*, vol 6, no 4, pp. 457–93.

Moudud, J. and K. Botchway (2008) "The Search for a New Developmental State", *International Journal of Political Economy*, vol 37, no 3, pp. 5–26.

Muuri, A. (2009) "The Impact of the Use of the Social Welfare Services or Social Security Benefits on Attitudes to Social Welfare Policies", *International Journal of Social Welfare*, vol 19, no 2, pp. 182–93.

Narayan, D. and L. Pritchett (1996) "Cents and Sociability: Household Income and Social Capital in Rural Tanzania", Environment Department and Policy Research Department, Washington DC: World Bank, https://papers.ssrn.com/sol3/pap ers.cfm?abstract_id=604937.

Ndikumana, L. and J. Boyce (2008) "New Estimates of Capital Flight from Sub-Saharan African Countries: Linkages with External Borrowing and Policy Options", PERI Working Paper, no 166, University of Amherst.

Nellis, J. (2021) "Whatever Happened to Privatization? The World Bank and Divestiture: 1980–2020", CGD Working Paper, no 592, Washington, DC, Center for Global Development, https://www.cgdev.org/publication/whatever-happened-pri-vatization-world-bank-and-divestiture-1980-2020.

Neo, H. (2007) "Challenging the Developmental State: Nature Conservation in Singapore", *Asia Pacific Viewpoint*, vol 48, no 2, pp. 186–99.

Ngok, K. (2013) "Shaping Social Policy in the Reform Era in China", in Izuhara (ed.) (2013), pp. 105–26.

Nichols, T. (1996) "Russian Democracy and Social Capital", *Social Science Information*, vol 35, no 4, pp. 629–42.

North, D. (1963) "Quantitative Research in American Economic History", *American Economic Review*, vol 53, no. 1, pp. 128–30.

O'Hearn, D. (2000) "Globalization, 'New Tigers', and the End of the Developmental State? The Case of the Celtic Tiger", *Politics and Society*, vol 28, no 1, pp. 67–92.

O'Laughlin, B. (2013) "Land, Labour and the Production of Affliction in Rural Southern Africa", *Journal of Agrarian Change*, vol 13, no 1, pp. 175–96.

ODA (2007) "ODA Manifesto by the Group for Renovating Japanese ODA – 30 Proposals for Enhanced international Cooperation", https://gdforum.sakura.ne.jp/en/pdf_e08/manifesto(Eng).pdf.

OECD (2002) "Household Energy and Water Consumption and Waste Generation: Trends, Environmental Impacts and Policy Responses", Working Party on National Environmental Policy, ENV/EPOC/WPNEP(2001)15/FINAL.

Ohno, K. (2009) "Avoiding the Middle-Income Trap: Renovating Industrial Policy Formulation in Vietnam", *ASEAN Economic Bulletin*, vol 26, no 1, pp. 25–43.

Ohno, K. and I. Ohno (eds) (1998) *Japanese Views on Economic Development: Diverse Paths to the Market*, London: Routledge.

Oliver, A. (2013) *Behavioural Public Policy*, Cambridge: Cambridge University Press.

Ortiz, I. and M. Cummins (2013a) "The Age of Austerity: a Review of Public Expenditures and Adjustment Measures in 181 Countries", Initiative for Policy Dialogue and the South Centre, Working Paper, March, http://policydialogue.org/files/publications/Age_of_Austerity_Ortiz_and_Cummins.pdf.

Ortiz, I. and M. Cummins (2013b) "Austerity Measures in Developing Countries: Public Expenditure Trends and the Risks to Children and Women", *Feminist Economics*, vol 19, no 3, pp. 55–81.

Ostrom, E. (1994) "Constituting Social Capital and Collective Action", *Journal of Theoretical Politics*, vol 6, no 4, pp. 527–62.

Oxfam (2013) "Universal Health Coverage: Why Health Insurance Schemes Are Leaving the Poor Behind", C. Averill with A. Marriott, https://oxfamilibrary.openrepository.com/handle/10546/302973.

Oya, C. (2011) "Agriculture in the World Bank: a Blighted Harvest", in Bayliss et al. (eds) (2011), pp. 146–87.

Oya, C. and N. Pons-Vignon (2010) "Aid, Development and the State in Africa", in Padayachee (ed.) (2010), pp. 172–98.

Paci, D. and O. Schweitzer (2006) "Technology Policy and Social Policy: How Industrial Policy Applies to Health", in Bianchi and Labory (eds) (2006), pp. 298–320.

Pack, H. (2011) "DPR Debate: Growth Identification and Facilitation", *Development Policy Review*, vol 29, no 3, pp. 298–301.

Pack, H. and K. Saggi (2006) "Is There a Case for Industrial Policy? A Critical Survey", *World Bank Research Observer*, vol 21, no 2, pp. 267–97.

Padayachee, V. (ed.) (2010) *The Political Economy of Africa*, London: Routledge.

Padayachee, V. and R. van Niekerk (2019) *Shadow of Liberation: Contestation and Compromise in the Economic and Social Policy of the African National Congress, 1943–1996*, Johannesburg: Wits University Press.

Pahl, R. (1996) "Comment on Kolankiewicz", *British Journal of Sociology*, vol 47, no 3, pp. 443–46.

Palanovics, N. (2006) "Quo Vadis Japanese ODA? New Developments in Japanese Aid Policies", *Asia Europe Journal*, vol 4, no 3, pp. 365–79.

Palma, G. (2009) "The Revenge of the Market on the Rentiers", *Cambridge Journal of Economics*, vol 33, no 4, pp. 829–69.

Parcel, T. and E. Menaghan (1994) "Early Parental Work, Family Social Capital, and Early Childhood Outcomes", *American Journal of Sociology*, vol 99, no 4, pp. 972–1009.

Park, H. (2007) "Small Business' Place in the South Korean State-Society Relations", *Asian Journal of Political Science*, vol 15, no 2, pp. 195–218.

Patel, M. (2009) "Economic Crisis and Children: an Overview for East Asia and the Pacific", *Global Social Policy*, vol 9 (Supplement), pp. S33–S54.

Pavolini, E. and C. Ranci (2008) "Restructuring the Welfare State: Reforms in Long-Term Care in Western European Countries", *Journal of European Social Policy*, vol 18, no 3, pp. 246–59.

Pelkmans, J. (2006) "European Industrial Policy", in Bianchi and Labory (eds) (2006), pp. 45–78.

Pereira, A. (2008) "Whither the Developmental State? Explaining Singapore's Continued Developmentalism", *Third World Quarterly*, vol 29, no 6, pp 1189–203.

Peres, W. (2011) "Industrial Policies in Latin America", UNU-WIDER, Working Paper, no 2011/48.

Peres, W. and A. Primi (2009) "Theory and Practice of Industrial Policy: Evidence from the Latin American Experience", CEPAL, Santiago de Chile, https://www.cepal.org/en/publications/4582-theory-and-practice-industrial-policy-evidence-latin-american-experience.

Perroux, F. (1950) "Economic Space: Theory and Applications", *Quarterly Journal of Economics*, vol 64, no 1, pp. 89–104.

Pfeifer, M. (2012) "Comparing Unemployment Protection and Social Assistance in 14 European Countries: Four Worlds of Protection for People of Working Age", *International Journal of Social Welfare*, vol 21, no 1, pp. 13–25.

Phelps, N. (2008) "Cluster or Capture? Manufacturing Foreign Direct Investment, External Economies and Agglomeration", *Regional Studies*, vol 42, no 4, pp. 457–73.

Pieterse, J. (1997) "Equity and Growth Revisited: a Supply-Side Approach to Social Development", *European Journal of Development Research*, vol 9, no 1, pp. 128–49.

Pincus, J. and J. Winters (eds) (2002) *Reinventing the World Bank*, London: Cornell University Press.

Piovani, C. and M. Li (2011) "One Hundred Million Jobs for the Chinese Workers! Why China's Current Model of Development Is Unsustainable and How a Progressive Economic Program Can Help the Chinese Workers, the Chinese Economy, and China's Environment", *Review of Radical Political Economics*, vol 43, no 1, pp. 77–94.

Pirie, I. (2005) "The New Korean State", *New Political Economy*, vol 10, no 1 pp. 25–42.

Pirie, I. (2006) "Economic Crisis and the Construction of a Neo-Liberal Regulatory Regime in Korea", *Competition and Change*, vol 10, no 1, pp. 49–71.

Pirie, I. (2008) *The Korean Developmental State: From Dirigisme to Neo-Liberalism*, London: Routledge.

Pirie, I. (2009) "Ha-Joon Chang: a Critique of the Critique", mimeo.

Pirie, I. (2013) "Globalisation and the Demise of the Developmental State", in Fine et al. (eds) (2013), pp. 146–168.

Plummer, J. (2024) "Citizen Engagement: Reflections on the Operationalization of a World Bank Corporate Commitment", in Schmidtke and Vetterlein (eds) (2024), pp. 344–56.

Polak, J. (1998) "The IMF Monetary Model at 40", *Economic Modelling*, vol 15, no 3, pp. 395–410.

Powell, M. and A. Barrientos (2011) "An Audit of the Welfare Modelling Business", *Social Policy and Administration*, vol 45, no 1, pp. 69–84.

Prabhakar, R. (2013) "Asset-Based Welfare: Financialization or Financial Inclusion?", *Critical Social Policy*, vol 33, no 4, pp. 658–78.

Prasad, N. and M. Gerecke (2010) "Social Security Spending in Times of Crisis", *Global Social Policy*, vol 10, no 2, pp. 218–47.

Prince, R. (2012) "Policy Transfer, Consultants and the Geographies of Governance", *Progress in Human Geography*, vol 36, no 2, pp. 188–203.

Putnam, R. (1993a) *Making Democracy Work: Civic Traditions in Modern Italy*, Princeton: Princeton University Press.

Putnam, R. (1993b) "The Prosperous Community: Social Capital and Public Life", *The American Prospect*, vol 13, pp. 35–42.

Putnam, R. (1995) "Bowling Alone: America's Declining Social Capital", *Journal of Democracy*, vol 6, no 1, pp. 65–78.

Putterman, L. (1995) "Social Capital and Development Capacity: the Example of Rural Tanzania", *Development Policy Review*, vol 13, no 1, pp. 5–22.

Putzel, J. (1997) "Accounting for the 'Dark Side' of Social Capital: Reading Robert Putnam on Democracy", *Journal of International Development*, vol 9, no 7, pp. 939–49.

Quijano, M. (2009) "Social Policy for Poor Rural People in Colombia: Reinforcing Traditional Gender Roles and Identities?", *Social Policy and Administration*, vol 43, no 4, pp. 397–408.

Radice, H. (2008) "The Developmental State under Global Neoliberalism", *Third World Quarterly*, vol 29, no 6, pp 1153–174.

Radnitzky, G. and P. Bernholz (eds) (1987) *Economic Imperialism: the Economic Method Applied Outside the Field of Economics*, New York: Paragon House Publishers.

Ramamurti, R. (1992) "Why Are Developing Countries Privatising?", *Journal of International Business Studies*, vol 23, no 2, pp. 225–50.

Ramesh, M. (2009) "Economic Crisis and its Social Impacts: Lessons from the 1997 Asian Economic Crisis", *Global Social Policy*, vol 9 (Supplement), pp. 79–99.

Randall, V. (2007) "Political Parties and Democratic Developmental States" *Development Policy Review*, vol 25, no 5, pp. 633–52.

Rasella D., R. Aquino, C. Santos, R. Paes-Sousa and M. Barreto (2013) "Effect of a Conditional Cash Transfer Programme on Childhood Mortality: a Nationwide Analysis of Brazilian Municipalities", *The Lancet*, vol 382, July 6, pp. 57–64.

Rasella, D. and R. Paes-Sousa (2013) "Combining Conditional Cash Transfers and Primary Health Care to Reduce Childhood Mortality in Brazil", International Policy Centre for Inclusive Growth, UNDP, One Pager, no 242, http://www.ipc-undp.org/pub/IPCOnePager242.pdf.

Ravallion, M. (2008) "Bailing out the World's Poorest", World Bank, Development Research Group, Policy Research Working Paper, no 4763, October.

Reinert, E. (2012) "Neo-classical Economics: a Trail of Economic Destruction since the 1970s", *Real-World Economics Review*, no 60, pp. 2–17, http://www.paecon.net/PAEReview/issue60/Reinert60.pdf.

Reinhart, C. and K. Rogoff (2010) *This Time is Different: Eight Centuries of Financial Folly*, Princeton: Princeton University Press.

Riain, S. (2000) "The Flexible Developmental State: Globalization, Information Technology and the New 'Celtic Tiger'", *Politics and Society*, vol 28, no 2, pp. 157–94.

Riddell, R. (2007) *Does Foreign Aid Really Work?*, New York: Oxford University Press.

Riesco, M. (ed.) (2007) *Latin America: a New Developmental Welfare State Model in the Making?*, Houndmills: Palgrave.

Riesco M. (2009a) "Latin America: a New Developmental Welfare State Model in the Making?", *International Journal of Social Welfare*, vol 18 (Supplement), pp. S22–S36.

Riesco M. (2009b) "The End of Privatized Pensions in Latin America", *Global Social Policy*, vol 9, no 2, pp. 273–80.

Rigg, J., A. Bebbington, K. Gough, D. Bryceson, J. Agergaard, N. Fold and C. Tacoli (2009) "The World Development Report 2009 'Reshapes Economic Geography': Geographical Reflections", *Transactions of the Institute of British Geographers, New Series*, vol 34, no 2, pp. 128–36.

Rigsby, M., M. Rosen, J. Beauvais, J. Cramer, P. Rainey, S. O'Malley, K. Dieckhaus and B. Rounsaville (2000) "Cue-Dose Training with Monetary Reinforcement: Pilot Study of an Antiretroviral Adherence Intervention", *Journal of General Internal Medicine*, vol 15, no 12, pp. 841–7.

Robertson, M. (2014a) "Housing Provision, Finance, and Well-Being in Europe", FES-SUD Working Paper Series, no 14, http://fessud.eu/wp-content/uploads/2013/04/Housing-provision-Finance-and-Well-Being-in-Europe-Working-paper-14.pdf.

Robertson, M. (2014b) "Case Study: Finance and Housing Provision in Britain", FESSUD Working Paper Series, no 51, https://fessud.org/wp-content/uploads/2013/04/Case-Study_-Finance-and-Housing-Provision-in-Britain-working-paper-51.pdf.

Robinson, J. (2009) "Botswana as a Role Model for Country Success", UNU-WIDER, Research Paper, no 2009/40.

Robinson, M. and G. White (eds) (1998) *The Democratic Developmental State: Politics and Institutional Design*, Oxford: Oxford University Press.

Rock, M., J. Murphy, R. Rasiah, P. Seters, S. Managi (2009) "A Hard Slog, not a Leap Frog: Globalization and Sustainability Transitions in Developing Asia", *Technological Forecasting & Social Change*, vol 76, no 2, pp. 241–54.

Rodinelli, D. and M. Iacono (1996) "Strategic Management of Privatization – a Framework for Planning and Implementation", *Public Administration and Development*, vol 16, no 3, pp. 247–63.

Rodriguez, F. (2006) "Growth Empirics When the World Is Not Simple", http://repec.wesleyan.edu/pdf/frrodriguez/2006004_rodriguez.pdf.

Rodrik, D. (2005a) "Rethinking Growth Strategies", https://www.wider.unu.edu/publication/rethinking-growth-strategies-0, reproduced in UNU-WIDER (eds) (2005), pp. 201–23.

Rodrik, D. (2005b) "Why We Learn Nothing from Regressing Economic Growth on Policies", http://www.hks.harvard.edu/fs/drodrik/Research%20papers/policy%20regressions.pdf.

Rodrik, D. (2006) "The Social Cost of Foreign Exchange Reserves", *International Economic Journal*, vol 20, no 3, pp. 253–66.

Rodrik, D. (2007) *One Economics, Many Recipes*, Princeton: Princeton University Press.

Rodrik, D. (2015) *Economics Rules: the Rights and Wrongs of the Dismal Science*, New York: w.w. Norton.

Romer, P. (1986) "Increasing Returns and Long-Run Growth", *Journal of Political Economy*, vol 94, no 5, pp. 1002–37.

Ronald, R. (2013) "Housing Policy in East Asia", in Izuhara (ed.) (2013), pp. 391–415.

Rostow, W. (1957) "The Interrelation of Theory and Economic History", *Journal of Economic History*, vol XVII, no 4, pp. 509–523.

Rostow, W. (1991) *The Stages of Economic Growth: a Non-Communist Manifesto*, Cambridge: Cambridge University Press, third revised edition, first edition of 1960.

Rowthorn, B. and H.-J. Chang (1992) "The Political Economy of Privatisation", *The Economic and Labour Relations Review*, vol 3, no 2, pp. 1–17.

Rubery, J. (2011) "Reconstruction amid Deconstruction: or Why We Need More of the Social in European Social Models", *Work, Employment and Society*, vol 25, no 4, pp. 658–74.

Rubio, M. (1997) "Perverse Social Capital – Some Evidence from Colombia", *Journal of Economic Issues*, vol 31, no 3, pp. 805–16.

Rudyak, M. (2024) "China's Relations with the World Bank: between Great Power and Developing Country", in Schmidtke and Vetterlein (eds) (2024), pp. 154–65.

Runnymede Trust (2005) *Social Capital, Civil Renewal and Ethnic Diversity: Proceedings of a Runnymede Conference*, London: Runnymede Trust.

Saad-Filho, A. (2015) "Social Policy for Mature Neoliberalism: the *Bolsa Família* Programme in Brazil", *Development and Change*, vol 46, no 6, pp. 1227–52.

Sacchi, S., F. Pancaldi and C. Arisi (2011) "The Economic Crisis as a Trigger of Convergence? Short-time Work in Italy, Germany and Austria", *Social Policy and Administration*, vol 45, no 4, pp. 465–87.

Sala-i-Martin, X. (1997) "I Just Ran Two Million Regressions", *American Economic Review*, vol 87, no 2, pp. 178–83.

Sally, R. and R. Sen (2005) "Introductory Overview: Revisiting Trade Policies in Southeast Asia", *ASEAN Economic Bulletin*, vol 22, no 1, pp. 1–2.

Samoff, J. and C. Bidemi (2003) "From Manpower Planning to the Knowledge Era: World Bank Policies on Higher Education in Africa", UNESCO Forum Occasional Paper Series 2, http://unesdoc.unesco.org/images/0013/001347/134782eo.pdf.

Samson, M. (2006) "Presentation to the Third International Conditional Cash Transfers Conference", Istanbul, http://info.worldbank.org/etools/icct06/DOCS /English/Day2/Samson_CCTconferenceJune27EPRIzz.pdf.

Sánchez-Ancochea, D. and L. Mattei (2011) "Bolsa Família, Poverty and Inequality: Political and Economic Effects in the Short and Long Run", *Global Social Policy*, vol 11, no 2/3, pp. 299–318.

Sanders, J. and V. Nee (1996) "Immigrant Self-Employment: the Family as Social Capital and the Value of Human Capital", *American Sociological Review*, vol 61, no 2, pp. 231–49.

Santos, A. (2011) "Behavioural and Experimental Economics: Are They Really Transforming Economics?", *Cambridge Journal of Economics*, vol 35, no 4, pp. 705–28.

Santos, A. and J. Rodrigues (2014) "Neoliberalism in the Laboratory? Experimental Economics on Markets and their Limits", *New Political Economy*, vol 19, no 4, pp. 507–33.

SARDN (2011a) "Southern African Development Community: Reaping the Benefits of Regional Economic Integration", Policy Brief, no 1, http://www.tips.org.za/files /sadrn_policy_brief_1_-_sadc_regional_integration2_1.pdf.

SARDN (2011b) "The Impact of Biofuels on Food Prices in the Southern African Customs Union", Policy Brief, no 2, http://www.tips.org.za/files/sadrn_policy_brief_2_-_bio fuels_and_food_security.pdf.

SARDN (2011c) "The Trade Effects of Regional Economic Integration in the Southern African Development Community", Policy Brief, no 6, http://www.tips.org.za/files /sadrn_policy_brief_6_-_trade_effects_of_regional_integration_in_sadc_v_2.pdf.

SARDN (2011d) "Internationalising Higher Education in Southern Africa with South Africa as the Major Exporter", Policy Brief, no 8, http://www.tips.org.za/files/sadrn _policy_brief_8_-_internationalising_higher_education_with__sa_as_the_major_ exporter_v2.pdf.

SARDN (2011e) "Prospects for Establishing an Education Hub: the Case of Botswana", Policy Brief, no 9, http://www.tips.org.za/files/sadrn_policy_brief_9_-_prospects _for_an_education_hub_botswana_2.pdf.

Sarfaty, G. (2024) "The World Bank and Its Potential for Reform: the Human Rights Perspective", in Schmidtke and Vetterlein (eds) (2024), pp. 383–94.

Saritas, S. (2014), "Review of Pension Provision across the European Union Countries", FESSUD Working Paper Series, no 13, https://fessud.org/wp-content/uploads/2013 /04/REVIEW-OF-THE-PENSION-PROVISION-ACROSS-THE-EUROPEAN-UNION -COUNTRIES_13.pdf.

Saritas, S. (2016) *Financialisation and Turkish Pension Reform*, unpublished Phd, SOAS University of London.

Savage, M. and K. Williams (2008) "Elites: Remembered in Capitalism and Forgotten by Social Sciences", *Sociological Review*, vol 56, no 1, pp. 1–24.

Schmidtke, T. and A. Vetterlein (eds) (2024) *The Elgar Companion to the World Bank*, Cheltenham: Elgar, forthcoming.

Schmitt, C. and P. Starke (2011) "Explaining Convergence of OECD Welfare States: a Conditional Approach", *Journal of European Social Policy*, vol 19, no 5, pp. 120–35.

Schmutzler, A. (1999) "The New Economic Geography", *Journal of Economic Surveys*, vol 13, no 4, pp. 355–79.

Schneider, M., P. Teske and M. Marschall (1997) "Institutional Arrangements and the Creation of Social Capital: the Effects of Public School Choice", *American Political Science Review*, vol 91, no 1, pp. 82–93.

Schonberger, S. (2024) "Quo Vadis? The World Bank's Role in Promoting Environmental Sustainability", in Schmidtke and Vetterlein (eds) (2024), pp. 370–82.

Scott, A. (2009) "Book Review: World Development Report 2009: Reshaping Economic Geography", *Journal of Economic Geography*, vol 9, no 4, pp. 583–86.

Scruggs, L. and J. Allan (2006) "Welfare-State Decommodification in 18 OECD Countries: a Replication and Revision", *Journal of European Social Policy*, vol 16, no 1, pp. 55–72.

Selwyn, B. (2007) "Labour Process and Workers' Bargaining Power in Export Grape Production, North East Brazil", *Journal of Agrarian Change*, vol 7, no 4, pp. 526–53.

Selwyn, B. and D. Leyden (2024) "World Development under Monopoly Capitalism", in Schmidtke and Vetterlein (eds) (2024), pp. 273–84.

Sengupta, A. (2013) "Universal Health Care in India: Making it Public, Making It a Reality", Occasional Paper, no 19, Municipal Services Project (MSP), https://www .municipalservicesproject.org/sites/municipalservicesproject.org/files/publicati ons/Sengupta_Universal_Health_Care_in_India_Making_it_Public_May2013.pdf.

Sent, E.-M. (2004) "Behavioral Economics: How Psychology Made Its (Limited) Way back into Economics", *History of Political Economy*, vol 36, no 4, pp. 735–60.

Sering, L. (2009) "Are Social Cash Transfers to the Poor an Appropriate Way of Fighting Poverty in Developing Countries?", *Global Social Policy*, vol 9, no 2, pp. 246–72.

Seron, C. and K. Ferris (1995) "Negotiating Professionalism: the Gendered Social Capital of Flexible Time", *Work and Occupations*, vol 22, no 1, pp. 22–47.

Shafaeddin, S. (2005) "Towards an Alternative Perspective on Trade and Industrial Policies", *Development and Change*, vol 36, no 6, pp. 1143–62.

Sharkh, M. and I. Gough (2010) "Global Welfare Regimes: a Cluster Analysis", *Global Social Policy*, vol 10, no 1, pp. 27–58.

Shetler, J. (1995) "A Gift for Generations to Come: a Kiroba Popular History from Tanzania and Identity as Social Capital in the 1980s", *International Journal of African Historical Studies*, vol 28, no 1, pp. 69–112.

Shirley, M. (1997) "The Economics and Politics of Government Ownership", *Journal of International Development*, vol 10, no 4, pp. 849–64.

Sindzingre, A. (2007) "Financing the Developmental State: Tax and Revenue Issues" *Development Policy Review*, vol 25, no 5, pp. 615–32.

Singh, A. (2011) "Comparative Advantage, Industrial Policy and the World Bank: back to First Principles", *Policy Studies*, vol 32, no 4, pp. 447–60.

Skidelsky, R. and C. Wigström (eds) (2010) *The Economic Crisis and the State of Economics*, New York: Palgrave Macmillan.

Smith, M., L. Beaulieu, and A. Seraphine (1995) "Social Capital, Place of Residence, and College Attendance", *Rural Sociology*, vol 60, no 3, pp. 363–80.

Snowdon, B. and H. Vane (2005) *Modern Macroeconomics: its Origins, Development and Current State*, Cheltenham: Edward Elgar.

Soares, F. (2009) "Do CCTs Lessen the Impact of the Current Economic Crisis? Yes, but …", International Policy Centre for Inclusive Growth, One Pager, no 96, September, http://www.ipc-undp.org/pub/IPCOnePager96.pdf.

Solow, R. (2006) "Comments on Papers by Saint-Paul, Aghion, and Bhidé", *Capitalism and Society*, vol 1, no 1, Article 3, http://www.bepress.com/cas/vol1/iss1/art3/.

St. Clair, A. (2009) "Conditional Cash Transfers: the Need for an Integrated and Historical Perspective", *Global Social Policy*, vol 9, no 2, pp. 177–79.

Standing, G. (2011) *The Precariat: the New Dangerous Class,* London: Bloomsbury Publishing.

Stern, N. and F. Ferreira (1997) "The World Bank as 'Intellectual Actor'", in Kapur et al. (eds) (1997b), pp. 523–609.

Stern, N., J. Stiglitz and C. Taylor (2022) "The Economics of Immense Risk, Urgent Action and Radical Change: towards New Approaches to the Economics of Climate Change", *Journal of Economic Methodology*, vol 29, no 3, pp. 181–216.

Stiglitz, J. (1997) "An Agenda for Development for the Twenty-First Century", World Bank Ninth Annual Conference on Development Economics, April 30th and May 1st.

Stiglitz, J. (1998a) "More Instruments and Broader Goals: Moving Toward the Post-Washington Consensus", WIDER Annual Lectures, no 2, January 7th, Helsinki.

Stiglitz, J. (1998b) "Sound Finance and Sustainable Development in Asia", Keynote Address to the Asia Development Forum, Manila, March 12th.

Stiglitz, J. (2002) *Globalization and Its Discontents*, New York: w.w. Norton and Co.

Stiglitz, J. (2008) "Turn Left for Sustainable Growth", *Economists' Voice*, vol 5, no 4, pp. 1–3, https://business.columbia.edu/sites/default/files-efs/imce-uploads/Joseph_S tiglitz/2008_Turn_Left_for_Sustainable_Growth.pdf.

Stiglitz, J. (2009) "The Current Economic Crisis and Lessons for Economic Theory", *Eastern Economic Journal*, vol 35, no 3, pp. 281–96.

Stiglitz, J. (2010) *The Stiglitz Report: Reforming the International Monetary and Financial Systems in the Wake of the Global Crisis*, New York: The New Press.

Stiglitz, J. and A. Weiss (1981) "Credit Rationing in Markets with Imperfect Information", *American Economic Review*, vol 71, no 3, pp. 393–410.

Stone, D. (1995) "Commentary: the Durability of Social Capital", *Journal of Health Politics, Policy and Law*, vol 20, no 3, pp. 689–94.

Stone, D. and C. Wright (2007) "Introduction", in Stone and Wright (eds) (2007), pp. 1–23.

Stone, D. and C. Wright (eds) (2007) *The World Bank and Governance. A Decade of Reform and Reaction*, Oxford: Routledge.

Stone, R. (2024) "Rational Choice: Actors, Preferences and Power", in Schmidtke and Vetterlein (eds) (2024), pp. 74–84.

Stubbs, R. (2009) "What Ever Happened to the East Asian Developmental State? The Unfolding Debate", *Pacific Review*, vol 22, no 1, pp. 1–22.

Stuckler, D. and S. Basu (2013) *The Body Economic: Why Austerity Kills*, Philadelphia: Basic Books.

Stuckler, D., S. Basu and M. McKee (2011) "Global Health Philanthropy and Institutional Relationships: How Should Conflicts of Interest Be Addressed?" *PLoS Medicine*, vol 8, no 4, pp. 1–10, http://www.plosmedicine.org/article/info%3Adoi%2F10 .1371%2Fjournal.pmed.1001020.

Sugden, R. (2009) "On Nudging. A Review of *Nudge: Improving Decisions about Health, Wealth and Happiness* by Richard H. Thaler and Cass R. Sunstein", *International Journal of the Economics of Business*, vol 16, no 3, pp. 365–73.

Sunstein, C. (2014) *Why Nudge? The Politics of Libertarian Paternalism*, New Haven, CT: Yale University Press.

Suryahadi, A., V. Febriany and A. Yumna (2014) "Expanding Social Security in Indonesia: Processes and Challenges", The SMERU Research Institute, Towards Universal Social Security in Emerging Economies: Process, Institutions and Actors, UNRISD Background Paper.

Swedberg, R. (1986) "The Doctrine of Economic Neutrality of the IMF and the World Bank", *Journal of Peace Research*, vol 23, no 4, pp. 377–90.

Swedberg, R. (ed.) (1996) *Economic Sociology*, Cheltenham: Edward Elgar.

Swyngedouw, E. (2009) "The Antinomies of the Postpolitical City: in Search of a Democratic Politics of Environmental Production", *International Journal of Urban and Regional Research*, vol 33, no 3, pp. 601–21.

Swyngedouw, E. (2010a) "Apocalypse Forever? Post-Political Populism and the Specter of Climate Change", paper published in *Theory, Culture and Society*, vol 27, no 2–3, 2010, pp. 213–32.

Swyngedouw, E. (2010b) "The Communist Hypothesis and Revolutionary Capitalisms: Exploring the Idea of Communist Geographies for the Twenty-First Century", *Antipode*, vol 41, Supplement 1, pp. 298–319.

Tarp, F. (2006) "Aid and Development", *Swedish Economic Policy Review*, vol 13, no 2, pp. 9–61.

Taylor-Gooby, P. (2012) "Root and Branch Restructuring to Achieve Major Cuts: the Social Policy Programme of the 2010 UK Coalition Government", *Social Policy and Administration*, vol 46, no 1, pp. 61–82.

Teachman, J., K. Paasch and K. Carver (1996) "Social Capital and Dropping out of School Early", *Journal of Marriage and the Family*, vol 58, no 3, pp. 773–83.

Teitelbaum, E. (2007) "Can a Developing Democracy Benefit from Labour Repression? Evidence from Sri Lanka", *Journal of Development Studies*, vol 43, no 4, pp. 830–55.

Thaler, R. and C. Sunstein (2003) "Libertarian Paternalism", *American Economic Review*, vol 93, no 2, pp. 175–9.

Thaler, R. and C. Sunstein (2008) *Nudge: Improving Decisions about Health, Wealth and Happiness*, New Haven, CT, and London: Yale University Press.

Thun, E. (2006) *Changing Lanes in China: Foreign Direct Investment, Local Governments, and Auto Sector Development*, Cambridge: Cambridge University Press.

Thurbon, E. and L. Weiss (2006) "Investing in Openness: the Evolution of FDI Strategy in South Korea and Taiwan", *New Political Economy*, vol 11, no 1, pp. 1–22.

Tommasi, M. and K. Ierulli (eds) (1995) *The New Economics of Human Behaviour*. Cambridge: Cambridge University Press.

Toussaint, E. (2023) *The World Bank: A Critical History*, London: Pluto.

Treyvish, A. (2008) "The Downfall of the Soviet Union: a Spatial Explanation", Background Note to the 2009 World Development Report, available at http://sitere sources.worldbank.org/INTWDR2009/Resources/4231006-1204741572978/Treyv ish.pdf.

Triantafillou, P. (2011) "The OECD's Thinking on the Governing of Unemployment", *Policy and Politics*, vol 39, no 4, pp. 567–82.

Tridico, P. (2012) "Financial Crisis and Global Imbalances: Its Labour Market Origins and the Aftermath", *Cambridge Journal of Economics*, vol 36, no 1, pp. 17–42.

Tunberger, P. and W. Sigle-Rushton (2011) "Continuity and Change in Swedish Family Policy Reforms", *Journal of European Social Policy*, vol 21, no 3, pp. 225–37.

Tversky, A. and D. Kahneman (1974) "Judgment and Uncertainty: Heuristics and Biases", *Science*, vol 185, no 4157, pp. 1124–31.

Tversky, A. and D. Kahneman (1981) "The Framing of Decision and the Psychology of Choice", *Science*, vol 211, no 4481, pp. 453–8.

UNRISD (2014) "New Social Policy for the 21st Century", New Directions in Social Policy Background Paper, UNRISD.

UNU-WIDER (eds) (2005) *WIDER Perspectives on Global Development*, London: Palgrave-Macmillan.

Utting, P., S. Razavi and R. Buchholz (eds) (2012) *Global Crisis and Transformative Social Change*, London: Palgrave MacMillan.

Valenzuela, A. and S. Dornbusch (1994) "Familism and Social Capital in the Academic Achievement of Mexican Origin and Anglo Adolescents", *Social Science Quarterly*, vol 75, no 1, pp. 18–36.

Välilä, T. (2008) "'No Policy Is an Island': on the Interaction between Industrial and Other Policies", *Policy Studies*, vol 29, no 1, pp. 101–18.

van der Hoeven, R. (2008) "Reflections – Alice Amsden", *Development and Change*, vol 39, no 6, pp. 1091–1099.

van Dijk, M. (2013) "The Social Costs of Financial Crises", Rotterdam School of Management, Erasmus University, June, http://papers.ssrn.com/sol3/papers.cfm ?abstract_id=2278526.

van Hooren, F. and U. Becker (2012) "One Welfare State, Two Care Regimes: Understanding Developments in Child and Elderly Care Policies in the Netherlands", *Social Policy and Administration*, vol 46, no 1, pp. 83–107.

van Kersbergen, K. (2013) "What Are the Welfare State Typologies and How Are They Useful, If at All?", in Greve (ed.) (2013), pp. 139–47.

van Oorschot, W. and B. Meuleman (2012) "Welfarism and the Multidimensionality of Welfare state legitimacy: Evidence from The Netherlands, 2006", *International Journal of Social Welfare*, vol 21, no 1, pp. 79–93.

Van Waeyenberge, E. (2009) "Selectivity at Work: Country Policy and Institutional Assessments at the World Bank", *European Journal of Development Research*, vol 21, no 5, pp. 792–810.

Van Waeyenberge, E. and B. Fine (2011) "A Knowledge Bank?", in Bayliss et al. (eds) (2011), pp. 26–45.

Van Waeyenberge, E., B. Fine and K. Bayliss (2011) "The World Bank, Neoliberalism and Development Research", in Bayliss et al. (eds) (2011), pp. 3–25.

Vetterlein, A. (2024) "Responsibility Avoidance in the World Bank's Approach to End Poverty", in Schmidtke and Vetterlein (eds) (2024), pp. 285–96.

Vetterlein, A. and S. Park (2024) "Constructivism, Norms, and the World Bank", in Schmidtke and Vetterlein (eds) (2024), pp. 96–106.

Vickers, J. and G. Yarrow (1988) *Privatisation: an Economic Analysis*, Cambridge: The MIT Press.

Vis, B., K. van Kersbergen and T. Hylands (2011) "To What Extent Did the Financial Crisis Intensify the Pressure to Reform the Welfare State?", *Social Policy and Administration*, vol 45, no 4, pp. 338–53.

Vogel, S. (1996) *Freer Markets; More Rules: Regulatory Reform in Advanced Industrial Countries*, Ithaca: Cornell University Press.

Vromen, J. (2009) "The Booming Economics-Made-Fun Genre: More than Having Fun, but Less than Economics Imperialism", *Erasmus Journal for Philosophy and Economics*, vol 2, no 1, pp. 70–99.

Wade, R. (1990) *Governing the Market: Economic Theory and the Role of Government in Taiwan's Industrialization*, Princeton: Princeton University Press.

Wade, R. (1996) "Japan, the World Bank, and the Art of Paradigm Maintenance: *The East Asian Miracle* in Political Perspective", *New Left Review*, no 217, pp. 3–37.

Wade, R. (2002) "US Hegemony and the World Bank: the Fight over People and Ideas", *Review of International Political Economy*, vol 9, no 2, pp. 201–29.

Wade, R. (2010) "After the Crisis: Industrial Policy and the Developmental State in Low-Income Countries", *Global Policy*, vol 1, no 2, pp. 150–61.

Wade, R. (2011) "Why Justin Lin's Door-Opening Argument Matters for Development Economics: a Response to 'Six Steps for Strategic Government Intervention'", *Global Policy*, vol 2, no 1, pp. 115–16.

Wade, R. (2012) "Return of Industrial Policy?", *International Review of Applied Economics*, vol 26, no 2, pp. 223–39.

Walker, A. and C. Wong (2013) "Social Protection, Governance and the Dynamics of Inclusion and Exclusion in East Asia", in Izuhara (ed.) (2013), pp. 226–44.

Walker, G., B. Kogut and W. Shan (1997) "Social Capital, Structural Holes and the Formation of an Industry Network", *Organization Science*, vol 8, no 2, pp. 109–25.

Weaver, C. (2024) "The Hypocrisy of the World Bank", in Schmidtke and Vetterlein (eds) (2024), pp. 107–117.

Weiss, J. (2011) "Industrial Policy in the Twenty-First Century", UNU-WIDER, Working Paper, no 2011/55.

Weiss, L. (1999) "State Power and the Asian Crisis", *New Political Economy*, vol 4, no 3, pp. 317–42.

Wendt, C. (2009) "Mapping European Healthcare Systems: a Comparative Analysis of Financing, Service Provision and Access to Healthcare", *Journal of European Social Policy*, vol 19, no 5, pp. 432–45.

White, G. (1998) "Constructing a Democratic Developmental State", in Robinson and White (eds) (1998), pp. 17–51.

White, M. and G. Kaufman (1997) "Language Usage, Social Capital, and School Completion among Immigrants and Native-Born Ethnic Groups", *Social Science Quarterly*, vol 32, no 1, pp. 3–30.

Whittaker, D., T. Zhu, T. Sturgeon, M. Tsai, and T. Okita (2008) "Compressed Development", MIT IPC Working Paper, no 08-005, http://web.mit.edu/ipc/publi cations/pdf/08-005.pdf.

Wiegratz, J., P. Behuria, C. Laskaridis, L. Pheko, B. Radley and S. Stevano (2023) "Common Challenges for All? A Critical Engagement with the Emerging Vision for Post-pandemic Development Studies", *Development and Change*, https://doi.org/10 .1111/dech.12785, forthcoming.

Willemse, N. and P. de Beer (2012) "Three Worlds of Educational Welfare States? A Comparative Study of Higher Education Systems Across Welfare States", *Journal of European Social Policy*, vol 22, no 2, pp. 105–17.

Wilson, P. (1997) "Building Social Capital: a Learning Agenda for the Twenty-First Century", *Urban Studies*, vol 34, no 5–6, pp. 745–60.

Wolfensohn, J. (1996) "The World Bank as a Global Information Clearinghouse", Presented at the Annual World Bank Conference on Development Economics. Washington, DC: World Bank.

Wong, L. (2013) "From Apartheid to Semi-Citizenship: Chinese Migrant Workers and their Challenges to Social Policy", in Izuhara (ed.) (2013), pp. 416–33.

Woolcock, M. (1998) "Social Capital and Economic Development: toward a Theoretical Synthesis and Policy Framework", *Theory and Society*, vol 27, no 2, pp. 151–208.

World Bank (1993) *The East Asian Miracle: Economic Growth and Public Policy, a World Bank Policy Research Report*, Oxford: Oxford University Press.

World Bank (1995) *Bureaucrats in Business: the Economics and Politics of Government Ownership*, Oxford: Oxford University Press.

World Bank (1996) *From Plan to Market*, World Development Report, Washington DC: World Bank.

World Bank (1997a) *The State in a Changing World*, World Development Report, Washington DC: World Bank.

World Bank (1997b) "Social Capital: the Missing Link?", *Monitoring Environmental Progress – Expanding the Measure of Wealth*, Environment Department, Washington DC: World Bank, draft.

World Bank (1998) *World Development Report 1998/9: Knowledge for Development*, New York: Oxford University Press for the World Bank.

World Bank (2008) *Reshaping Economic Geography, World Development Report 2009*, Oxford: Oxford University Press, *available at* https://documents1.worldb ank.org/curated/en/730971468139804495/pdf/437380REVISED01BLIC109780821 3760720.pdf.

World Bank (2009a) *Conditional Cash Transfers: Reducing Present and Future Poverty*, Washington: World Bank.

World Bank (2009b) *Development and Climate Change, World Development Report 2010*, Oxford: Oxford University Press, *available at* https://documents1.worldbank.org /curated/en/201001468159913657/pdf/530770WDR02010101OfficialoUseoOnly1.pdf.

World Bank (2010) "Transforming the Bank's Knowledge Agenda: a Framework for Action", Knowledge Strategy Group, Washington, DC.

World Bank (2011) *The State of World Bank Knowledge Services. Knowledge for Development 2011*, Washington, DC: World Bank.

World Bank (2012a) "Research at Work. Assessing the Influence of the World Bank", Research Report, Washington, DC: World Bank, Development Economics Vice-Presidency.

World Bank (2012b) *Light Manufacturing in Africa. Targeted Policies to Enhance Private Investment and Create Jobs*, Washington, DC: World Bank.

World Bank (2015) *World Development Report 2015: Mind, Society and Behaviour*, Washington, DC: World Bank.

World Bank Group (2014) *Knowledge for Change. Annual Report 2014*, Washington, DC: World Bank Group.

Xia, M. (2008) *The People's Congresses and Governance in China: toward a Network Mode of Governance*, London: Routledge.

Yarrow, G. and P. Jasinski (eds) (1996) *Privatization: Critical Perspectives on the World Economy*, four volumes, London: Routledge.

Yazid, M. (2007) *Hegemonic Powers, Radical Politics and Developmental State: the Case of Indonesia-Malaysia Political Relations during the Cold War*, Kota Kinabalu: Penerbit Universiti Malaysia Sabah.

Ye, I. (ed.) (2017) *Towards Universal Health Care in Emerging Economies: Opportunities and Challenges*, London: Palgrave MacMillan.

Yerkes, M. and R. van der Veen (2011) "Crisis and Welfare State Change in the Netherlands", *Social Policy and Administration*, vol 45, no 4, pp. 430–44.

Yeung, H. (2009) "Regional Development and the Competitive Dynamics of Global Production Networks: an East Asian Perspective", *Regional Studies*, vol 43, no 3, pp. 325–51.

Yivayanond, P. and P. Hanvoravongchai (2013) "The Impacts of Universalization: a Case Study on Thailand Social Protection and Universal Health Coverage", Towards Universal Social Security in Emerging Economies: Process, Institutions and Actors, UNRISD Background Paper.

Young, A. (1994) "Lessons from the East Asian NICs: a Contrarian Review", *European Economic Review*, vol 38, no 3–4, pp. 964–73.

Young, A. (1995) "The Tyranny of Numbers: Confronting the Statistical Realities of the East Asian Growth Experience", *Quarterly Journal of Economics*, vol 110, no 3, pp. 641–80.

Yusuf, S. (2009) *Development Economics through the Decades: a Critical Look at Thirty Years of the World Development Report*, with commentaries by A. Deaton, K. Derviş, W. Easterly, T. Ito and J. Stiglitz, Washington: The World Bank.

Zaccaria, G. (2024) "Let's Be Friends not Foes: an Assessment of the Strategic Co-evolution of the World Bank and the AIIB in the Face of Institutional Overlap", in Schmidtke and Vetterlein (eds) (2024), pp. 166–77.

Zakrevskaya, O. and S. Mastracci (2013) "The Job Deficit: Differential Effects of the Great Recession by Household Type, Evidence from a Longitudinal Survey", *Challenge*, vol 56, no 6, pp. 87–114.

Zebregs, H. (2004) *Intraregional Trade in Emerging Asia*, Washington, DC: IMF.

Zhou, M. and C. Bankston (1994) "Social Capital and the Adaptation of the Second Generation: the Case of Vietnamese Youth in New Orleans", *International Migration Review*, vol 28, no 4, pp. 821–45.

Zhu, A. and D. Kotz (2011) "The Dependence of China's Economic Growth on Exports and Investment", *Review of Radical Political Economics*, vol 43, no 1, pp. 9–32.

Index